# Quantitative Approaches in Business Studies

**THIRD EDITION**

## Clare Morris

MA (Oxon), MSc, PhD (Bristol)
*Warwick Business School, University of Warwick*

PITMAN
PUBLISHING

Pitman Publishing
128 Long Acre, London WC2E 9AN

A Division of Longman Group UK Ltd

Lotus and Lotus 1-2-3 are registered trademarks in the
United Kingdom and other countries of Lotus Development
Corporation.

First published in Great Britain 1983
Second edition 1989
Third edition 1993

**British Library Cataloguing in Publication Data**
A CIP catalogue record for this book is available from the
British Library.

ISBN 0 273 60116 4

Printed in England by Clays Ltd, St Ives plc

# CONTENTS

# PREFACE TO THE THIRD EDITION

The first edition of this book was used on a wide range of undergraduate, postgraduate and post-experience courses and grew out of my experience in teaching on such courses. The aim of that edition, which remains unchanged, was to recognise that most students on such courses are not mathematicians, never will be mathematicians, and have no wish to be mathematicians. At the same time, they undoubtedly have other skills – in problem-solving, communication, and business operations – which must be exploited by anyone attempting to interest them in a quantitative approach to business problems.

Accordingly, this book has a high proportion of words, and a correspondingly low proportion of numbers, mathematical symbolism, and jargon. Few proofs of results are given; instead, the effectiveness of the methods may be judged by whether they give sensible and useful solutions to practical problems. By adopting a problem-driven approach, I hope to convince students that quantitative methods, while not always easy to get to grips with, really do have something irreplaceable to offer as a tool of management.

The range of topics covered is probably larger than would be included in any single HND or first-year degree course, particularly as far as Part Four is concerned. The topics selected for any individual course will naturally reflect the interests of the lecturer and the specialist needs of the students involved. I have therefore tried to make the chapters of that Part as independent as possible of each other. Where there is a dependence on preceding material, the fact is indicated in the list of prerequisites at the start of the chapter. Further details about possible topic sequences will be found in the section, How this book is organised, p. xi.

No major changes of content have been made for this edition; the main alteration has been the incorporation of references to MINITAB and LOTUS 1-2-3 throughout the text, in conjunction with an optional diskette containing data sets and ready-written worksheets. This should enable users of MINITAB, LOTUS, and indeed of other software, to make use of it to enhance their reading of the book. However, it remains perfectly possible to use the book quite independently of any particular software; for this reason, extended descriptions of software procedures have mainly been confined to new sections at the ends of chapters. There is also a new Chapter 2 which briefly describes the software referred to, and the use of the material on the diskette. Material associated with the use of computer software is distinguished by the label **C** so that readers who wish to ignore it may conveniently do so.

Once again I am very greatly indebted to the many readers of the book, both students and colleagues, who have taken the trouble to inform me of errors and confusions they have encountered. Please continue to let me know of any which remain.

I am grateful to the Literary Executor of the late Sir Ronald A. Fisher, FRS, to Dr Frank Yates, FRS, and the Longman Group Ltd, London, for permission to reprint Tables IV and VII from their book *Statistical Tables for Biological, Agricultural and Medical Research* (6th edition, 1974). I would also like to thank Macmillan, London and Basingstoke, for permission to use part of Tables 1 and 2, and Tables 3 and 7, from *Statistical Tables* by J. Murdoch and J. A. Barnes; the Biometrika Trustees for permission to use material from Table 8 of *Biometrika Tables for Statisticians*, vol. I (3rd edition,

1966), and to the Controller of Her Majesty's Stationery Office for permission to reproduce Fig. 3.1 from the *Monthly Digest of Statistics*.

I would like to thank Minitab, Inc., 3081 Enterprise Drive, State College, PA 16081, USA (Telephone 814/238–3280, Telex 881612) for their cooperation in supplying material relating to their Statistical Software.

Thanks go to Lotus, Lotus Development Corporation, Lotus Park, The Causeway, Staines, Middlesex TW18 3AG, for their permission to make reference to LOTUS 1-2-3 in this book and to use their sample worksheets on the disk that accompanies this book.

I am also grateful to The University of the West of England at Bristol and Avon Education Committee for permission to include among the Practical Exercises some which were originally set by me as assignments or examination questions on Bristol Polytechnic courses.

Clare Morris
August 1992

A *Lecturer's Guide* is available to lecturers adopting this textbook.

# NOTE TO THE READER

Although I hope that you're going to find this book fairly readable, it would be silly to pretend that you can read it – or any other textbook on a numerical subject – in quite the same way as you would read, say, a detective story, or even a textbook in a more 'wordy' subject such as law or sociology. Since I naturally want you to benefit as much as possible from reading this book, and since it may be some time since you last studied a numerical subject, you may find the following points helpful.

At the start of each chapter you will find a list of the prerequisites for reading that chapter – the things which you need to understand in order to follow the material contained in the chapter. If you are doubtful about any of these, go back to the section in which the topic was covered (you'll find a reference given) and check your understanding of that topic. *Don't* just carry on into the chapter hoping for the best – that's the way to get confused and demoralised! To a large extent mathematics and statistics are cumulative subjects, in which one topic builds on another, so it's important to get each stage clear before going on to the next.

You will also find at the start of the chapters a list of the things which you should be able to do by the end of the chapter; when you've read the chapter, and gone through some of the practical work at the end – particularly the more straightforward problems – then waited a few days for the material to fall into place, you can use this list to check that you've grasped the main points of the chapter. You may also find that these lists are useful when you come to revise for examinations, in reminding you of the major areas within each topic.

Always have a pencil and paper to hand when you are reading the book, so that you can follow the workings of problems for yourself, or perhaps work out in more detail steps of a calculation which I have abbreviated. And don't worry too much if you feel you haven't grasped every single idea in a section immediately – most people find that numerical ideas may take two or three readings, plus some work on practical examples, before they make complete sense.

Finally, and most importantly, remember that all the skills which you bring to bear in other areas of your work – your ability to communicate effectively, your knowledge of business, your problem-solving skills, and above all your plain common sense – can be used in the numerical context too. Is this a sensible result? Is it about the size of answer which I would have expected to get? Is it realistic in terms of the original problem we set out to solve? – these are the kinds of questions you should constantly be asking yourself as you work through the book, so that by the end numbers, and the ability to handle them effectively, will be just another of your everyday skills.

## How this book is organised

Although most of the topics covered in this book appear in many courses on Quantitative Methods for business and management, you may find that your course does not include all of them. Or perhaps you are reading the book for interest only, and would like to be able to skip some material without getting lost.

For your guidance, here is an indication of how the book fits together, and of possible routes through it. You will find more detailed information about the prerequisites for understanding each chapter at the start of the chapter. The order in which topics are covered is to some extent a matter of taste; I have tried to provide a logical structure by subdividing the book into four parts, but there are many other possible and equally logical orders which you could follow.

Chapter 1 is necessary only if you are not very confident of your basic mathematical skills; try the test at the start to find out if you have the level of ability needed for later work.

Chapter 2 is necessary for those of you who will be using either MINITAB or LOTUS software as an adjunct to your work with this book. Even if you will not be doing so, you may still wish to skim through this chapter to find out what the software has to offer.

Chapters 3–6 should be read sequentially, and cover the essentials of what is called Descriptive Statistics.

Chapter 7 on Index Numbers could be omitted without affecting later work.

Chapters 8–11 are also sequential; they cover probability and the problems of drawing conclusions from samples, and could be left out if you are only interested in the descriptive aspects of the subject.

Chapters 12 and 13 are chiefly devoted to correlation and regression, very important topics which are widely used in many business problems. They do not require you to have read Chapters 8–11.

Chapter 14 covers the topic of forecasting, again a very important area of interest for business applications. This chapter does not depend on previous work, and could be read much earlier in the sequence if you wish.

Chapters 15–19 are each devoted to a separate topic in Operational Research, and each is pretty well free-standing, except that Chapter 19 needs some of the material on distributions covered in Chapters 6 and 9.

# PART 1

# Numbers – how we handle them

This Part covers the essential tools which you will need to use in order to get the most out of your reading of the rest of the book. Chapter 1 summarises the mathematical methods required, with material to help you revise and improve your understanding of these methods if necessary, and exercises to help you discover if you have done so satisfactorily. Chapter 2 introduces the optional diskette which accompanies this book, and the two software packages – MINITAB and LOTUS – with which the diskette may be used.

# CHAPTER 1

# Tools of the trade: basic numeracy skills

## Objectives

Before starting work on this chapter, try the short test of basic mathematical skills in this section; you will find the answers are given in Appendix 2 and according to which questions you find difficult, you will be directed to the appropriate section of this chapter. This will save you time and prevent your having to read through a lot of things which in fact you can already cope with. If, however, you get more than half of the test questions wrong I would advise you to read the entire chapter.

By the end of your work on this chapter you should be able to:

(a) carry out the four operations of basic arithmetic (addition, subtraction, multiplication and division) with positive and negative integers, fractions and decimals;
(b) round off the results of your calculations to a given number of decimal places or significant figures;
(c) perform calculations involving percentages;
(d) handle expressions involving powers and roots of a variable;
(e) remove brackets from algebraic expressions;
(f) construct a linear equation or inequality from a verbal problem;
(g) solve linear equations;
(h) solve a pair of simultaneous equations;
(i) plot the graphs of linear equations or inequalities;
(j) make efficient use of your calculator.

## Test

**1** $-3 + 4 =$    **2** $-5 \div 2 =$    **3** $\dfrac{3}{8} + \dfrac{4}{5} =$    **4** $\dfrac{7}{8} \times \dfrac{3}{5} =$

**5** $2 \div \frac{1}{2} =$    **6** $0.05 \times 2.5 =$    **7** $8 \div 0.2 =$

**8** Convert 5/12 to a decimal.

**9** Express 0.28 as a fraction.

**10** What is 67.469 to 3 significant figures?

**11** 16% of 8 =    **12** 18 as a percentage of 64 =

**13** The price of an item including the dealer's 20% mark-up is £36. What did it cost before the mark-up?

**14** $x^2 \times x^4 =$ **15** $\sqrt{x^{16}} =$

**16** $2(3a + b) - (a - 2b) =$

**17** If it costs £6 to drive $k$ miles then what is the cost of driving 4 miles?

**18** Items priced at $m$ pence per dozen are repacked in boxes of 100. What will the cost of such a box be, in pounds?

**19** There are $f$ female workers and $m$ male workers in a factory. Write down an algebraic expression to show that the total work-force must be less than 150.

**20** $3x - 5 = 10; x =$ **21** $\dfrac{4}{y} = \dfrac{7}{8}; y =$

**22** $\begin{cases} 3p + 2q = 9 \\ 4p - 6q = 25 \end{cases}$      Find $p$ and $q$.

**23** Where does the graph of $s = 3t + 5$ cross the $t$-axis?

**24** Which of these could be the graph of $y = x^2 + 3x - 4$:

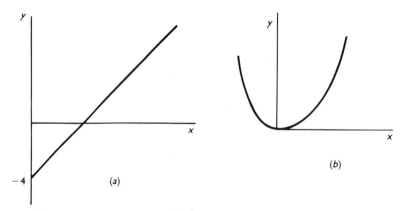

(a)

(b)

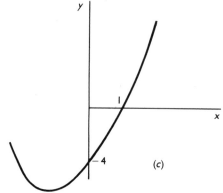

(c)

**25** On which side of the line in the following diagram will the inequality $x > 2y$ be satisfied?

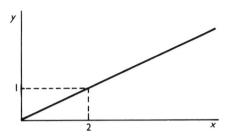

## ALMOST EVERYBODY'S PROBLEM

If you are reading this book then you are almost certainly not a mathematician. You have probably chosen to do a course in business studies, management or accounting, only to discover that among the obviously relevant and useful subjects, like economics and law, you are expected to study mathematics (possibly disguised under the title of statistics, but that doesn't fool you).

To this news, if you are like ninety-nine per cent of students in my experience, your reaction was close to horror. It is quite likely several years since you last studied mathematics, and your recollections of those days may not be very pleasant. But in fact your apprehension is groundless. What you will be studying in this book is not mathematics for its own sake, however appealing that may be to some of us, but *useful* mathematics – the sort of mathematics which can lead quickly and effectively to the solution of practical, business-oriented problems.

However, it would be misleading to pretend that you aren't going to need to dredge up a little of what you learned at school, and this first chapter is designed to help you do just that. There is probably hardly anything which will be completely new to you; there will be some things which you once knew but have forgotten, others which you've heard about before but which may not have made much sense the first time around. You will find plenty of exercises to practise on, since practice is essential in achieving facility in the basic techniques we'll be calling on later in the book.

And, in case you suspect that some topics are included just because they are good for you and can't conceivably have any relevance to business, you'll find a reference at the beginning of each section to the points at which the material of that section will be needed in later chapters.

## NUMBERS AND HOW WE COMBINE THEM

This is fundamental to all later work.

It's often helpful to think of all numbers as strung out in a straight line as follows:

In the middle we have zero, to the right are the *positive* whole numbers $+ 1, + 2 \ldots$ (we don't usually bother to write the + sign) and to the left are the *negative* whole numbers $-1, -2 \ldots$ The '...' here indicates that the numbers can be continued without limit in either direction. The jargon name for these whole numbers is *integers*.

In between the integers, positive and negative, we can think of the entire line as being filled up with the remaining non-integer numbers – fractions and/or decimals – which we will be returning to later.

For most people, adding up positive integers is no problem; the difficulties start to appear with the minus signs. This is where the idea of the number line can be quite helpful. Consider the expression $42 - 36 + 27$. Should we say '36 + 27' first, and then take the answer away from 42, or should we take '42 – 36' and then add on the 27?

In fact, with + and – signs we are safe in performing the operations from left to right, unless there are brackets telling us otherwise (of which more later). Looking at it another way, saying 'subtract 36' is exactly the same as saying 'add the negative number – 36', so the whole expression can be thought of as '42 plus – 36 plus 27'. In other words, subtraction means adding negative numbers. So on the number line, adding corresponds to moving to the right, subtraction to moving to the left.

Taking a simpler case, $4 - 9 + 2$ can be interpreted as: start at 4 on the line, move 9 steps to the left (which brings us to $-5$) and then 2 to the right, ending up at $-3$. Of course, after a while you won't need to use the line explicitly, but this is the basis of 'rules' you may have learned, such as 'in subtraction put the sign of the larger to the difference'.

Another example:

$$-6 - 7 + 4 = -13 + 4 = -9.$$

When it comes to multiplication and division, there are a few different ways of writing things which you should be aware of. $2 \times 6$ is sometimes written as 2.6 (I would not recommend this because of the obvious possibility of confusion with the decimal point), and $4 \div 2$, 4/2 and $\frac{4}{2}$ all mean the same thing.

As far as multiplying or dividing negative numbers goes, this is one of the few cases where I would advise you to remember some rules (they can be proved, but in a rather long-winded way):

**Two *like* signs (two pluses or two minuses) multiplied together or divided give a positive answer.**

**Two *unlike* signs (one plus and one minus) multiplied together or divided give a negative answer.**

For example:

$$(-2) \times (-4) = 8; \qquad 12 \div (-6) = -2;$$
$$-8/-2 = 4.$$

In division, if the result is not an integer – that is, if the number being divided is not an even multiple of the *divisor* (the dividing number) – then the remainder can be expressed either as a fraction or a decimal. To express it as a fraction, simply put the remainder over the divisor. For example, $20/7 = 2$ with remainder 6, or $2\frac{6}{7}$. We will find out how to turn this into a decimal later.

One final point on the four basic rules of arithmetic: there is a standard convention about the priority which operates if you have + and – signs mixed up with $\times$ and $\div$. The rule is that the multiplications and divisions are done first, unless there are brackets indicating otherwise. For instance, $2 \times 6 + 5 = 12 + 5 = 17$, **not** $2 \times 11 = 22$. If we wanted this, we would have to put $2 \times (6 + 5)$, to show that the addition is to be done first.

There is, however, no difference in meaning between $\frac{-1}{2}$, $\frac{1}{-2}$ and $-\frac{1}{2}$; we usually prefer to attach the minus sign to the front of the expression, as in the last of the three expressions, but it really doesn't matter. It's important to remember these rules about the order of operations, since they are implicit in the way many computer packages work.

## Exercise 1

| | | | |
|---|---|---|---|
| **1** | $-5 - 4 - 7$ | **7** | $6 \times (-2)$ |
| **2** | $6 + 4 - 10$ | **8** | $18 \div (-3)$ |
| **3** | $2 + 2 - 2$ | **9** | $(-4) \times (-6)$ |
| **4** | $-11 + 18 + 25$ | **10** | $27/-3$ |
| **5** | $16 - 9 + 7$ | **11** | $\dfrac{-16}{-8}$ |
| **6** | $-8 + 3 + 2$ | **12** | $3 \times 7 + 4$ |

## OPERATIONS WITH FRACTIONS

You will need to be able to handle addition, subtraction and multiplication of fractions when we come to discuss probability in Chapter 8. Although it *is* possible since the advent of electronic calculators to turn all your fractions to decimals and use the calculator to work out the arithmetic, doing so would waste a great deal of time, and in many cases the results are easier to interpret when expressed in fraction rather than decimal form.

There are actually three ways of writing fractions – as decimals, percentages or 'ordinary' fractions such as $\frac{1}{2}$ or $\frac{3}{4}$ – but we will concentrate in this section on the last of three ways, leaving the first two to later sections. For addition and subtraction, the magic words are 'common denominator'. Actually there is nothing magic about it; the point is that trying to add sixths and sevenths is like trying to add apples and bananas – they are quite different things; we must express them in the same terms before we can do anything with them.

For example, to add $\frac{5}{6}$ and $\frac{2}{7}$ we must write them both with the same bottom line or *denominator* – in this case both can be written in terms of forty-seconds as:

$$\frac{35}{42} + \frac{12}{42} = \frac{47}{42}$$

(or $1\frac{5}{42}$, but we do not generally use such 'mixed' fractions).

It is easy to see why we chose 42 here – it is $6 \times 7$. Sometimes a smaller number will do, but if you find it difficult to spot this, multiplying the denominators of the fractions always works.

Another example:

$$\frac{4}{5} - \frac{1}{4} = \frac{16}{20} - \frac{5}{20} = \frac{16 - 5}{20} = \frac{11}{20}.$$

Cancellation of fractions sometimes causes confusion but to *cancel* a fraction simply means to divide the top and bottom by the same figure; for example: $4/8 = 1/2$, $12/16 = 3/4$, etc. It is generally preferable to express a fraction in its lowest terms, that is, to cancel it as far as possible. Notice that, as what we are really doing here is saying $12/16 = (3 \times 4)/(4 \times 4) = 3/4$, it is *not* permissible to say $(4 + 1)/2 = (2 + 1)/1 = 3/1 = 3$, because we have not divided the *whole* of the top by 2, but only part of it. If you are tempted to perform a cancellation like this where plus and minus signs are involved, either leave well alone, or put in some simple numbers to see whether the operation is really valid. In the example above, $(4 + 1)/2 = 2\frac{1}{2}$, whereas the 'cancelled' expression = 3, so clearly this doesn't work.

Multiplication is the easiest of all fraction operations – multiply the tops or *numerators* and the denominators of the fractions separately.

Examples:

$$\frac{1}{5} \times \frac{5}{7} = \frac{1 \times 5}{5 \times 7} = \frac{5}{35}; \frac{2}{3} \times \frac{8}{9} = \frac{16}{27}, \text{ etc.}$$

Of course, in the first case here we could cancel by 5, to reduce the fraction to $\frac{1}{7}$.

For division, the rule is *turn the divisor upside down and multiply by this number*. Example:

$$\frac{5/6}{2/3} = \frac{5}{6} \div \frac{2}{3} = \frac{5}{6} \times \frac{3}{2} = \frac{15}{12} = \frac{5}{4},$$

cancelling by 3. We could have cancelled at an earlier stage but if you are doubtful about cancellation it's safer to leave it until the end, when you have only one fraction to deal with.

Another example:

$$\frac{3}{16} \div \frac{7}{8} = \frac{3}{16} \times \frac{8}{7} = \frac{24}{112} = \frac{3}{14},$$

cancelling by 8.

A phrase you may have heard in the past is '*of* means *multiply*'. This simply means that to get a certain fraction *of* a number, you multiply the number by that fraction. For example, two-thirds of $12 = \frac{2}{3} \times 12 = \frac{2}{3} \times \frac{12}{1} = \frac{24}{3} = 8$. Notice too that a whole number can always be written as a fraction with 1 as the denominator, as we have done with the 12 here.

Finally, if you have to deal with negative fractions, exactly the same rules apply as for operating with negative integers.

Now try the following exercise.

## Exercise 2

**1** $\frac{1}{6} \times \frac{7}{8}$

**2** $\frac{1}{4} - \frac{1}{3}$

**3** $\frac{1}{11} + \frac{1}{22}$

**4** $-\frac{1}{2} + \frac{3}{4} - \frac{1}{8}$

**5** $\frac{2}{7} \times 9$

**6** $\frac{2}{5} \div \frac{4}{7}$

**7** $10 \div \frac{1}{2}$

**8** $\frac{3}{4} \times \frac{1}{4} \div \frac{4}{5}$

**9** $(\frac{3}{8} - \frac{3}{4}) \div \frac{4}{3}$

**10** $(\frac{1}{9} + \frac{5}{6}) \times \frac{3}{17}$

## DECIMALS: A SPECIAL KIND OF FRACTION

Now that pocket calculators are an everyday matter, nearly all the calculations you perform will be done in terms of decimals, but you can't abdicate all responsibility for the accuracy of your calculations to the calculator because it is fatally easy to press a wrong key in the course of entering the figures. So a familiarity with the rules for handling decimal points – in order that you can check that the answer is roughly what it should be – is, if anything, even more necessary now.

Sometimes one hears the expression 'decimal fractions' still used, and the phrase gives the clue to what decimals really are – a system of fractions based on multiples of ten. When we write 0.75, for example, this is a shorthand for 'seven tenths and five hundredths' – the seven, one place to the right of the decimal point, represents tenths, the five, two places to the right, represents hundredths, and so on. But it would be tedious to have to convert back to fractions every time we wanted to operate with decimals, so there are a few simple rules to enable us to use them directly.

Addition and subtraction work much as for integers, as long as you remember to keep the decimal points lined up – that is, add tenths to tenths, hundredths to hundredths, etc. For instance, to add 2.15 and 3.4 we think of the 3.4 as 3.40, then add the 5 to the 0, the 1 to the 4 and the 2 to the 3, to get 5.55.

In multiplication, the number of decimal places in the answer is the total of the number of places in the figures being multiplied. For example:

$$3.2 \times 0.5 \times 0.2 = 1.60 \times 0.2 = 0.320$$

(notice that the final zero must be included in the count of places).

Multiplication by 10, 100, etc., is particularly easy because the decimal system is based on tens. To multiply by 10, 100, etc., move the decimal point one, two, etc., places to the right.

You may say, 'But suppose there isn't a point?' However, you can always think of a whole number like 54 as being 54.0, so the point is there implicitly. Thus $54 \times 100 = 5,400$, $3.9 \times 10 = 39$, and so on.

Division is a bit more complicated. What we do is to get rid of decimals in the denominator altogether by shifting the point the same number of places to the right in numerator and denominator – in other words, multiplying top and bottom by 10, 100 or whatever. We can do this because multiplying the top and bottom of a fraction simultaneously by the same figure makes no difference to its value. Once we have got rid of the decimals in the denominator in this way, we are back to division by an integer, and all we have to do is keep the point in the answer in the correct place:

$$3.2/0.2 = 32/2 \text{ (multiplying top and bottom by 10)} = 16$$
$$3.2/0.02 = 320/2 \text{ (multiplying by 100)} = 160$$
$$0.32/0.2 = 3.2/2 = 1.6, \text{ and so on.}$$

To divide by 10, 100, etc., we move the point (or implied point) one, two, etc., places to the left, e.g. $4.3/100 = 0.043$.

Frequently we have to turn fractions into decimals, or vice-versa. To turn a fraction into a decimal, divide the denominator into the numerator according to the usual process of division, as in $4/5 = 0.8$, $5/16 = 0.3125$, etc. Sometimes the process doesn't stop, but repeats itself after a certain number of decimal places. For example, $1/3 = 0.333 \ldots$, $6/7 = 0.8571428571428 \ldots$ This is called a *recurring* decimal. There *are* numbers – $\pi$ is one you may have come across – which are decimals which neither repeat nor stop – they just carry on for ever with no discernible pattern!

You should remember the decimal equivalents of a few commonly-used fractions: $0.5 = \frac{1}{2}$, $0.25 = \frac{1}{4}$, and so on.

The process the other way round – to write a given decimal as a fraction – is easy. If we want to turn 0.18 into a fraction, we have only to recall that this means 'one tenth and eight hundredths', that is, eighteen hundredths or 18/100. If you wish you can cancel this to 9/50.

## SIGNIFICANT FIGURES AND ROUNDING

Throughout all your calculations you will need to be able to round off answers to a certain number of decimal places or significant figures. Although your calculator probably spits out up to eight decimal places, it may not be sensible to quote them all – if, for instance, you are working in pounds and pence, there is no point in quoting an answer of £45.873438. Indeed, the last few digits may not even be worth believing. There is no 'right' number of figures to quote in a given situation; you have to develop a feeling based on such things as the figures which went into the calculation, what you want to use the answer for, and so on. We will mention this at appropriate points in later chapters, but at the moment we will simply discuss the mechanics of rounding.

If we want to round a number to a given number of decimal places, the rule most commonly applied is that 5 and upwards are rounded up, everything below 5, down. So 3.675 to two decimal places is 3.68, 0.0689 to three places is 0.069, and so forth. This system does lead to slight bias in that rather more figures are rounded up than down (those ending in 5, 6, 7, 8 and 9 go up as against only 1, 2, 3 and 4 going down), but this is only important in situations where there are a lot of figures ending in 5s to be rounded. So although alternative methods have been devised to get round this problem we will stick to the common rule.

An alternative way to specify the accuracy required of a number is to require a certain number of significant figures. A figure is significant if it carries information; in this sense the zeros on the end of 15,000 or immediately after the decimal point in 0.0035 are not significant, but the zero in 7,053 is. Thus 34,722 to three significant figures is 34,700; 0.00256 to two significant figures is 0.0026, 7,045 to three significant figures is 7,050, and so on.

## Exercise 3

1 Express 4/9 as a decimal to three places.

2 0.63/0.009    3 0.045 × 320    4 7.2/0.06

5 What is 16,527 to two significant figures?

6 Express 0.85 as a fraction.

7 3.5 × 1.2    8 0.005/0.05    9 400 × 0.0025

## PERCENTAGES

A percentage is really only a fraction in which the denominator is always 100, so that we do not bother to write it − or rather, the writing of '/100' has degenerated into the % sign. The term per cent on its own means nothing, unless we specify per cent *of what*. For example, the statement 'prices are ten per cent lower during the sale' is meaningless unless we say 'lower than list price' or 'lower than last week's price' or whatever.

The idea of expressing fractions as percentages is that for most people it's a good deal easier to visualise an amount like 70 per cent, i.e. 70/100, than something like 13/17. So it has become conventional to use 100 as a sort of standard denominator.

To find a given percentage of a quantity, multiply the quantity by the percentage figure over 100. For example:

$$16\% \text{ of } 40 = \frac{16}{100} \times 40 = \frac{640}{100} = 6.4.$$

All that we are doing here is recalling that 16 per cent means 16/100, and finding sixteen hundredths of 40.

To express one quantity as a percentage of another, put the first over the second and multiply by 100. For example:

$$£6 \text{ as a percentage of } £8: \frac{6}{8} \times 100 = \frac{600}{8} = 75\%.$$

Again, you should remember a few common percentages as fractions and vice versa, such as $50\% = \frac{1}{2}$, $25\% = \frac{1}{4}$, and so on.

To convert decimals into percentages, or the other way round, is a matter of moving the point. For instance, 0.08 as a percentage is 8 per cent (multiply by 100, i.e. move the point two places right) and 68 per cent as a decimal is 0.68 (move point two places left).

In dealing with practical problems involving percentages, be very careful to ask, 'Percentage of what?' As an illustration, suppose that we are told that a bill which includes 15 per cent VAT comes to £16. What was it before the VAT was added? The 15 per cent here is *not* 15 per cent of £16; it's 15 per cent of what the bill was *before* the VAT was added − the thing we're trying to find. If we call this amount *x*, what we can say is that $x + 15$ per cent of *x* comes to £16, or in symbolic terms:

$$x + \frac{15x}{100} = £16.$$

So $\frac{115x}{100} = £16$

whence $x = £16 \times \frac{100}{115} = £13.91.$

## Exercise 4

1  What is 8 per cent of 40?

2  Express 17 per cent as a decimal.

3  Express 45 as a percentage of 108.

4  A price of £12.50 is increased by 20 per cent. What is the new price?

5 An item now priced at £12 carries a label 'Original price reduced by 25%'. What was the original price?

## LETTERS FOR NUMBERS

As far as most people are concerned, I suppose of all the branches of mathematics they have studied at school, algebra seems the most rarefied and abstract. Certainly the higher reaches of algebra *can* be very abstract, but the kind of algebra we need to use is about as practical as it could be. The main purpose of using letters to represent numbers or quantities – which is what our kind of algebra is about – is that it enables us to express practical truths about the real world neatly, succinctly, and in more general terms than we could if we insisted on sticking to definite numbers all the time.

To take a specific example: if you want to explain to someone how to find the area of a rectangle 4 cm by 3 cm, you can tell them to multiply 4 by 3. But if you call the length of the rectangle $l$ and its width $w$, then you can say that the area is $l \times w$ – this will be true for *any* values of $l$ and $w$. Again, consider the rule we've just encountered for expressing one quantity as a percentage of another: 'Put the first quantity on top of the second and multiply by 100'. What a mouthful! But if the first number is denoted by $x$ and the second by $y$, then the rule boils down to $\frac{x}{y} \times 100$ – and once again, it holds good for whatever values of $x$ and $y$ we want to use.

This is the great strength in using letters to represent numbers – we are then able to write down rules, expressions and so on which are completely general, so that to find the answer in a particular case, all we need to do is substitute our particular values of $x$ and $y$ or whatever into the appropriate algebraic expression.

You will be coming across this application of algebra – the use of formulae to express rules – over and over in later chapters. But there are also some specific techniques which will be needed; we will begin with powers and roots, which will be referred to particularly in Chapter 15 on compound interest.

## POWERS AND ROOTS

We write $x^2$ as a shorthand for $x \times x$, $x^3$ to mean $x \times x \times x$, and in general $x^n$ to mean $x$ multiplied by itself $n$ times. If we wish to multiply two such numbers together, say $x^m \times x^n$, where $n$ and $m$ are whole numbers, we will have:

$$\underbrace{(x \times x \times x \ldots \times x)}_{m \text{ times}} \times \underbrace{(x \times x \times x \ldots \times x)}_{n \text{ times}}$$

that is, $x$ multiplied by itself $m + n$ times altogether, which can be written as $x^{m+n}$. So we have the first rule for operating with indices (indices is the plural of index, which means the $n$ in $x^n$):

In multiplication, *add* the indices.

We can develop the rule for division in the same way. If we have $x^3/x^2$, we can cancel to get $x^1$ (this is, of course, the same as $x$, since we don't usually bother writing the 1).

Similarly, if we have $x^m/x^n$, with $m > n$, cancelling gives $x^{m-n}$, suggesting the division rule:

In division, *subtract* the indices.

This in turn gives a meaning to a negative power of $x$. Consider $x^2/x^3$; by cancellation this becomes $1/x$, but by the division rule we've just derived it must also be equal to $x^{2-3} = x^{-1}$. So to be consistent we have to interpret $x^{-1}$ as meaning $1/x$, and more generally $x^{-n}$ as meaning $1/x^n$. We can also use the division rule to give $x^0$ a definition. Of course, $x^2/x^2$ is just 1, but it's also, by the division rule, $x^{2-2} = x^0$. Thus $x^0$ has to be equal to 1; and, there being nothing special about $x$, we can say:

Anything to the power 0 is 1.

Finally, what about fractional powers, such as $x^{\frac{1}{2}}$? By the multiplication rule, $x^{\frac{1}{2}} \times x^{\frac{1}{2}}$ $= x^{\frac{1}{2}+\frac{1}{2}} = x^1$; in other words, $x^{\frac{1}{2}}$ is the thing which, when multiplied by itself, gives $x$. This is what we call the *square root* of $x$; so $x^{\frac{1}{2}}$ means $\sqrt{x}$. Similarly. $x^{\frac{1}{3}}$ means $\sqrt[3]{x}$, the cube root of $x$, and in general:

$$x^{1/n} = \sqrt[n]{x}, \text{ the } n\text{th root of } x$$

(that is, the number which, multiplied by itself $n$ times, gives $x$).

To see how all these rules work in combination, we will simplify the following:

$$\frac{y^4 \times y^2}{\sqrt{y^3}} = \frac{y^{4+2}}{y^{3/2}} = \frac{y^6}{y^{3/2}} = y^{6-3/2} = y^{9/2}.$$

If you find these complicated powers a bit difficult to get hold of, try putting in numbers rather than letters. For example:

$$4^{\frac{1}{2}} = \sqrt{4} = 2, \qquad 2^{-2} = \tfrac{1}{4} \text{ or } 0.25,$$

and so on. (Strictly $\sqrt{4} = \pm 2$, since $(-2)^2 = 4$.)

## Exercise 5

Simplify:

1 $y^4 \div y^2$      4 $p^2 \times pq \times q^2$      7 $y^2 \times y^{-2}$

2 $1/\sqrt[3]{x}$      5 $1/n^3$      8 $3x^2/9x$

3 $x^3/x$      6 $a \times \dfrac{b}{a^2}$      9 $\dfrac{x^2 \times x^4}{\sqrt{x}}$

*Note*: when we write two symbols next to each other with no sign between, as in question 4 above, they are interpreted as being multiplied.

## THE USE OF BRACKETS

In several of the formulae we shall be encountering in later chapters, particularly Chapter 15, you will find brackets used to clarify the order in which operations are to be carried out. The basic rule for dealing with these is that operations in brackets are done first.

Suppose we want to find the value of $4(6y + 3)$ when $y$ is 9. We must work out the $6y + 3$ first, which comes to $6 \times 9 + 3 = 54 + 3 = 57$ (remember that $\times$ comes before $+$ )

and then multiply this by 4 to get 228. So the 4 multiplies *everything* inside the bracket, and this applies also when we have a letter rather than a number outside. For example:

$$2p(3p - 8) = 2p \times 3p - 2p \times 8 = 6p^2 - 16p.$$

Be careful if there's a − sign outside the brackets: remember the rules for multiplying by a negative number; for example:

$$-2x(x - 1) = -2x^2 + 2x.$$

Even if there is no number or other expression in front of a bracket, just a minus sign, the same applies:

$$8x - (x - 1) \text{ means}$$

$$8x - 1(x - 1) = 8x - x + 1 = 7x + 1.$$

It is important to realise that if we write $6x^2$ what we mean is 'square $x$ first and then multiply by 6', whereas $(6x)^2$ means multiply $x$ by 6 and then square the result'. In later statistical work we will encounter a case where this distinction is very important. Also note that $xy$ and $yx$ mean the same thing.

Where there are two bracketed expressions to be multiplied together, a useful mnemonic to help you ensure that you have included all the terms is FOIL, standing for First, Outer, Inner and Last:

$$(x - 2)(x + 3) = x^2 + 3x - 2x - 6 = x^2 + x - 6.$$

$$\text{First} \quad \text{Outer} \quad \text{Inner} \quad \text{Last}$$

With more than two bracketed expressions, it is easiest to multiply out two at a time:

$$(x + 2)(2x - )(x + 3) = (2x^2 + 3x - 2)(x + 3)$$

$$= 2x^3 + 9x^2 + 7x - 6.$$

Finally, if you encounter brackets within brackets, remove the inner ones first:

$$4(x + 3[x - 2]) = 4(x + 3x - 6)$$

$$= 4(4x - 6)$$

$$= 16x - 24.$$

## Exercise 6

Simplify:

**1** $3x(2x - 6)$      **2** $(a - 1)(a + 2)$      **3** $x(3y + z)$

**4** Find $8x^2$ and $(8x)^2$ when $x = 2$.

**5** Evaluate $3pq(q - p)$ when $p = 5$ and $q = \frac{1}{2}$.

**6** $(x + y)(x - y)(2x - 1)$.

## SOLVING EQUATIONS

Throughout the rest of this book, particularly in Chapter 13 where we discuss regression, Chapter 16 on inventory problems and to a lesser extent Chapters 10 and 11, you will come across equations which have to be solved, or algebraic expressions which have to be manipulated – two very similar processes in practice.

We speak of *solving* an equation when we express an unknown quantity in terms either of other quantities or of numbers. We can only solve a single equation for *one* unknown quantity; if there is more than one, then more than one equation will be required. In this section, we will concentrate on a single equation involving a single unknown, and in fact we will deal only with *linear* equations – those which don't involve any powers of $x$ higher than the first. You may have grappled with quadratic equations – those including $x^2$ terms – at school, but as we don't need those anywhere in later chapters we will not discuss them.

Our aim in solving an equation, then, is to isolate $x$ – or whatever the unknown quantity may be called – on one side of the equals sign (usually the left, but there's no reason why it must be); we can work towards this end by all the legitimate processes of algebra – adding and subtracting things, multiplying or dividing by things – as long as we do the same to both sides of the equation at every stage. This is the only real rule in solving equations; other rules you may have learnt, such as 'change side, change sign', or 'cross multiplication', are really only special cases of this general rule.

Suppose we have the equation $3x + 2 = 9$. We want to isolate $x$ on the left-hand side. As a first step towards this, let us get rid of the $+2$ by taking 2 away from each side:

$$3x + 2 - 2 = 9 - 2$$

i.e. $3x = 7$, since $+2 - 2 = 0$.

Now get rid of the 3 from the left-hand side by dividing by 3:

$$\frac{3x}{3} = \frac{7}{3}$$

i.e. $x = \frac{7}{3}$ or $2\frac{1}{3}$.

Let us work through another example:

$$\frac{4}{y} = \frac{7}{2}.$$

The $y$ here is on the bottom of a fraction, which we certainly don't want. Get rid of it from the bottom by multiplying through by $y$:

$$\frac{4}{y} \times y = \frac{7}{2} \times y, \text{ or } 4 = \frac{7y}{2}.$$

If you find it hard to remember that $\frac{7}{2} \times y$ is the same thing as $\frac{7y}{2}$, note that $y$ can can always be thought of as $\frac{y}{1}$. Now multiply each side by 2, obtaining $8 = 7y$. Finally, divide both sides by 7 to get $y = 8/7$.

The same sorts of processes apply if we are trying to transform a formula rather than solve an equation. For example, given the equation $A = l \times b$ for the area of a rectangle, we can get $b$ in terms of the other two variables by dividing both sides by $l$, to give $b = A/l$.

Let us take a more complicated case; the formula $1/u + 1/v = 1/f$ relates the distances of object and image in a lens of a certain focal length. Suppose we want to find $v$ in terms of $u$ and $f$. First, subtract $1/u$ from each side: $1/v = 1/f - 1/u = \dfrac{u - f}{uf}$, putting the right-hand side over a common denominator. Now invert both sides to get $v = \dfrac{uf}{u - f}$. We have contracted some of the steps here, as you will be able to do when you are familiar with the processes; but if in any doubt, ask yourself, 'What am I doing to *this* side of the equation? Have I done it to the *other* side too?'

A final example before you try to solve some equations yourself: if $y + z^2 = x$, find $z$ in terms of $y$ and $x$:

$$z^2 = x - y, \text{ and so } z = \pm \sqrt{x - y}$$

## Exercise 7

Solve the following equations. (Some of them look as if they might be quadratics – but they aren't!)

1  $x + 2 = -3$

2  $2 + x = 3 - x$

3  $6x^2 = 54$

4  $2x + 3 = 5$

5  If $v = u + ft$, find $f$.

6  $x^2 - 2 = x^2 + 4x + 8$

7  If $P = R - (F + nV)$, find $V$.

8  If $(a + b)^2 = 16c$, find $a$.

9  If $\sqrt[3]{x^2 y} = 3z$, find $y$.

## EQUATIONS FROM PROBLEMS

When one is concerned, as we are, not so much with handling algebraic expressions for their own sake as with using them in the course of solving practical problems, the major difficulty may well be, not solving the equation, but extracting it from the 'wordy' problem in the first place. The line of approach can best be demonstrated by an example, since this is not an area where cut-and-dried 'rules' can be laid down.

Suppose we are told that a return bus ticket for a certain trip costs half as much again as a single one, and that when a passenger books three return and two single tickets he pays £3.25. How much does each type of ticket cost?

The first step is always to give the unknown quantity a name. Here we appear to have two unknown quantities – the price of a single ticket and that of a return – but they are related in such a way that if we call the price of a single ticket £$x$, then a return costs $1.5 \times £x$. Thus the statement of the problem can be reduced to

$$3 \times 1.5 \times x + 2 \times x = 3.25$$

whence

$$4.5x + 2x = 6.5x = 3.25$$

so that $x = 0.50$.

A single ticket costs 50p, therefore, and a return 75p.

This was, of course, a very easy example. In more complicated cases, it can help to get to the general expression via particular figures. For example, if we are told that a firm orders items in boxes of $x$ at a time, and asked how many boxes will be needed to supply 500 items, we can get an idea of how to proceed by saying: 'Suppose they came in boxes of 50 at a time; how many would then be needed to supply 500 items?' The answer is clearly 10. What have we done to get this? Obviously, divided the 50 into the 500. So more generally, if the boxes contain $x$ items, we will divide $x$ into 500 to find that they need $500/x$ boxes.

## SOME UNFAMILIAR SYMBOLS

Many of the problems we will be concerned with, especially in Chapter 17, are expressible not as equations but as inequalities: the number of workers needed to operate a production line is at least eight, we cannot spend more than £500 on this new machine, and so on.

Just as we use = to represent the fact that two quantities are equal, so we have symbols to represent these inequalities: $a \leqslant b$ means '$a$ is less than or equal to $b$'. So we might say $x \leqslant 100$ to express the fact that a sum of money, $x$ pence, is never greater than £1. Or, if $y$ denotes the number of students out of a class of 20 who pass an exam, we could say $y \leqslant 20$, because obviously 20 is the maximum number who can pass.

In a similar way, $p \geqslant q$ means '$p$ is greater than or equal to $q$'. If I am manufacturing $p$ items in a week and already have advance orders for 16, I might say $p \geqslant 16$ to express the fact that I must make at least 16 items.

If you find it confusing to recall which symbol is which, notice that the bigger end of the symbol points to the bigger quantity.

There are also two other symbols, related to these but not quite so widely used, < and > . These mean 'less than (or greater than) but not equal to'. So if you've only got enough raw material to make 20 items, you could write 'number of items < 21'.

### Exercise 8

1  The cost of a journey is reckoned to be 50p plus 5p per mile. Write down an expression for the cost of travelling $m$ miles.

2  I am buying handkerchiefs and socks for my family's Christmas presents – a box of handkerchiefs costs £1.50 and a pair of socks £1.25. I don't want to spend more than £12 altogether. If I buy $h$ boxes of handkerchiefs and $s$ pairs of socks, write down an expression representing my financial limitation.

3  A spoon costs twice as much as a fork, and six forks and ten spoons cost £20.80. How much does a spoon cost?

4  Balloons can be bought in packets of 12 for 25p, or separately for 3p each. Write down an expression for the cost of buying $y$ balloons ($12 \leqslant y \leqslant 23$).

## SIMULTANEOUS EQUATIONS

You will need to be able to solve simultaneous equations – a pair of linear equations with two unknowns – to cope with material in Chapter 17. The equations are called simultaneous because we have to consider them both at once if we are to be able to solve them.

The method of solution is best illustrated by an example:

$$2x + y = 4$$

$$3x - 2y = 7.$$

Our aim is to get the same number either of $x$s or of $y$s in the two equations, so that we can get rid of one variable by either adding or subtracting the equations, to give a single equation in one variable which we already know how to solve. To achieve this end, we may operate on either or both of the equations according to the rules of algebra, as long as we remember the cardinal rule that we must perform an operation *throughout* an equation – that is, to both sides.

Here, if we multiply the top equation by 2 and leave the bottom one alone, we get:

$$4x + 2y = 8$$

$$3x - 2y = 7$$

which, added, give:

$$7x = 15, \text{ since } + 2y - 2y = 0.$$

Thus $x = 15/7$, and we can now substitute this value in either of the *original* two equations to find $y$. Choosing the original first equation, because it's slightly simpler:

$$2 \times 15/7 + y = 4$$

$$\text{i.e. } 30/7 + y = 4$$

$$\text{i.e} \qquad y = 4 - 30/7$$

$$= -2/7.$$

This basic method *nearly* always works. The only cases where it may go wrong are where the equations are either:

(a)  *inconsistent*, that is, they just can't both be true at once (for example, $x + y = 9$ and $x + y = 7$);

(b)  really the *same* equation, such as $2x - y = 4$ and $x = 2 + \frac{1}{2}y$.

It's a good idea to check your answer by putting the $x$ and $y$ values you've found back into the equation you *didn't* use to find the second variable and making sure that they satisfy it. In the above case, $3 \times 15/7 - 2 \times (-2/7) = 45/7 + 4/7 = 49/7 = 7$, so that the second equation *is* satisfied.

## Exercise 9

Solve, where possible, the following pairs of equations:

**1**  $2x + y = 3$; $x - y = 6$.

**2**  $7x + 2y = 11$; $4x + 3y = 10$.

**3**  $x - y = 4$; $2x = 2y + 8$.

**4**  $2x + y = 1$; $2x - 3y = 9$.

**5**  $x + y = 3$; $x - 2y = 3$.

## STRAIGHT LINE GRAPHS

In Chapters 13, 16 and 17, there will be quite a lot of graphical work, so it is important that you should be able to plot or sketch simple graphs without too much trouble.

The idea behind almost all graphs is to show pictorially the relationship between two quantities, often called $x$ and $y$, though it's a good idea not to get too attached to this notation. Graphs which result in straight lines are going to be particularly important to us, since a straight line is the only form one can be quite definite about; plotting it accurately is simply a matter of using a ruler, whereas plotting any kind of curve involves some degree of skill and judgement (or the use of a computer package, as we will see in the next chapter). Moreover, to plot a straight line graph we need know only two points on the line (three if we want an extra point for checking purposes), whereas to obtain a reasonably accurate curve, a whole set of points is needed.

It is therefore useful, and saves wasting time, if you are able to recognise when an equation will result in a straight line graph. Consider the case of a manufacturer who, in producing some commodity, has fixed costs of £300 plus a variable cost of £2 per item. We will call the number of items being made $n$, and will construct a graph to show the relationship between the number of items made and the total cost of making them.

If no items at all are made, there will still be the fixed costs of £300 to pay, so when $n = 0$, cost = £300. The total cost will then increase by £2 for every extra item which is made; so 10 items will cost £320, 20 items will cost £340, and so on. It is clear that the graph representing the relationship will climb at a steady rate – that is, it will be a straight line. The graph is shown in Fig. 1.1 and illustrates a number of general points about graph-plotting.

First, we have chosen to put the number of items being made on the horizontal axis, and the costs on the vertical axis. This is in accordance with the convention that the *independent* quantity goes horizontally and the dependent one vertically; in this case cost depends on the numbers of items being made. Of course it is not always totally clear which *is* the dependent quantity, so in some cases there may be scope for alternative ways of plotting. However, it's fairly safe to say that amounts of money – costs, profits, revenues and so on – are nearly always plotted on the vertical axis.

The second thing to notice is the choice of scales. The question of the *range* of $n$-values we choose to plot is one to which we will return later, but for now you should notice that the $n$-scale goes up in steps of 10, and the Cost-scale steps of £20. When you are using graph-paper which is divided into multiples of ten squares, it is asking for trouble to choose a scale which goes in multiples of seven, or three, or some other amount not easily related to ten; you are very likely to go wrong in trying to estimate intermediate values by eye. It is much safer, therefore, to use steps of 5, 10 and so on which are easily related to the sub-divisions on your graph paper.

I hope it is hardly necessary to point out that the scales on both axes increase by *equal* steps; it would be quite wrong, and could result in some very funny-shaped graphs, if we started off with one large division on the scale representing ten items, and then suddenly changed half-way along the axis to one division representing twenty.

If we now look at the graph line itself, we see that it commences when no items are being made at a cost of £300, as already calculated, and then climbs by £20 for every ten items made. We can relate these facts to the equation representing the line, as follows. The total cost, £$C$ say, is given by the fixed cost of £300 plus £2 per item made – that will be £$2n$ for $n$ items. Thus $C = 300 + 2n$ is the equation of the cost line. Now, comparing this with the graph, you can see that the 300 – the 'fixed' part which does

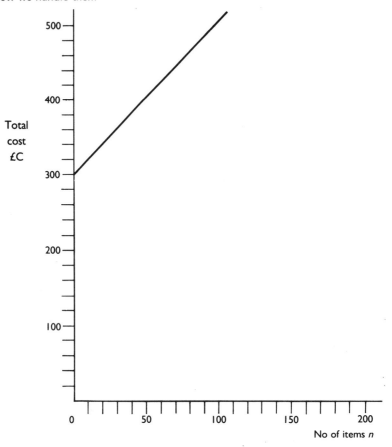

**Fig. 1.1** Plotting a graph

not change with $n$ – is represented by the point where the graph crosses the vertical axis (the technical name for this is the *intercept*). As for the £2 per item, that gives us the *slope* of the line – the amount by which $C$ increases for each increase of one unit in $n$. We could find this slope by taking any convenient increase in $n$, and dividing it into the corresponding increase in $C$.

In fact, *any* straight line equation will have the form $y = a + bx$, where $a$ and $b$ are some numbers, and $x$ and $y$ are the variable quantities. Comparing this general equation with the cost equation just discussed, which had values of 300 for $a$ and 2 for $b$, you can see that $a$ is going to tell us where the graph crosses the vertical axis (assuming that the horizontal scale starts from zero) and $b$ tells us the slope. By giving $a$ and $b$ different values, we can obtain all possible straight lines.

For example, equations in which $a$ is zero will pass through the origin of the graph; particular cases would be $y = 2x$ and $C = \frac{1}{2}n$. If we wish to have a line which slopes *downhill* from left to right, then we must give the slope a negative value, expressing the fact that as $x$ increases, $y$ gets smaller. So, for instance, the graph of $y = 20 - 2x$ is as shown in Fig. 1.2.

It is easy to see why equations involving powers of $x$ higher than 1 cannot result in straight lines. If we had $y = x^2$, then as $x$ increases from 1 to 2, $y$ will increase from 1 to 4 – an increase of 3. But as $x$ goes from 2 to 3, the corresponding $y$-increase is from

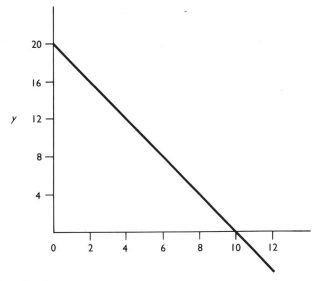

**Fig. 1.2** Graph of $y = 20 - 2x$

4 to 9, a change of 5 units. In fact the bigger $x$ gets, the faster $y$ increases, so we no longer have the steady rate of increase which would produce a straight line.

Having said this, however, I should warn you that sometimes straight-line equations may arise in a form which doesn't immediately look like $y = a + bx$. For example, $x/y = 6$ looks as if it involves a $y$ on the bottom of a fraction – a $y^{-1}$, in fact – but a bit of algebraic juggling turns the equation into $x = 6y$, or $y = \frac{1}{6}x$, the equation of a line through the origin with a slope of $\frac{1}{6}$. So you must be prepared for such possibilities.

Having recognised an equation as giving a straight line, how should you go about plotting it? It is safest to find three points on the line, two for plotting and one for checking. Take $y = 20 - 2x$, and suppose we want to plot it for values of $x$ from 0 to 10. We could use $x = 0$, 1, and 2 as our three points, but it is much safer to use values as far apart as possible, since this will minimise the effect of any errors in plotting, as is shown by Fig. 1.3. So we choose $x = 0$, which gives $y = 20$; $x = 5$, giving $y = 10$; and $x = 10$, for which $y = 0$. We plot points at 0 on the horizontal scale and 20 on the vertical; and at 10 on the horizontal and 0 on the vertical; join them together and then verify that the third point, $x = 5$ and $y = 10$, does indeed lie on the line we have plotted.

## OTHER TYPES OF GRAPH

If for some reason you have to plot a graph which you recognise will *not* give a straight line, the process is not dissimilar, but you need to use a lot more points in order to be able to draw a smooth curve through them. In this case it is easier to set out the calculation of points as a table. To plot $y = x^2 + 3x$, for example, I would recommend a layout as follows:

| $x$ | 0 | 1 | 2 | 3 | 4 ... |
|---|---|---|---|---|---|
| $x^2$ | 0 | 1 | 4 | 9 | 16 ... |
| $+ 3x$ | 0 | 3 | 6 | 9 | 12 ... |
| $y$ | 0 | 4 | 10 | 18 | 28 ... |

(a)

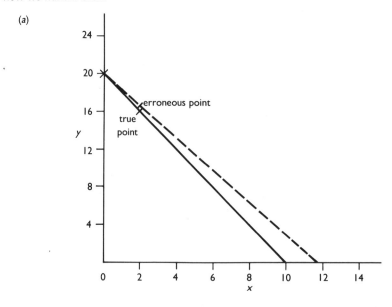

(b)

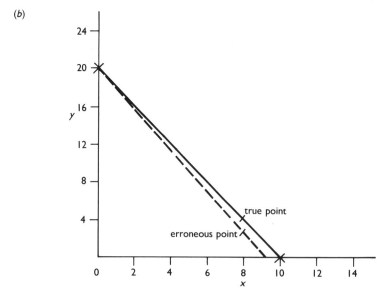

**Fig. 1.3** The need to use points as far apart as possible when plotting straight-line graphs. (a) Small error in plotting gives large errors as x increases. (b) Small error in plotting gives only small errors throughout

Points would then be plotted at $x = 0$ and $y = 0$, $x = 1$ and $y = 4$, etc., and as smooth a curve as possible drawn through them. If you find it very difficult to get your curve to go through one particular point, go back to check your calculation – it might be in the wrong place!

Before we end this section, we will take a brief look at how inequalities, introduced on page 18, can be shown graphically. Taking a very easy case first, consider $y \geqslant 6$. We want to identify the region of the graph in which the value of $y$ is equal to, or bigger than, 6, regardless of what's happening to $x$. It is not hard to see that that will be true everywhere on and above the horizontal line through $y = 6$. We generally choose to indicate this on the graph by shading the side of the line where the inequality is *not* satisfied, as shown in Fig. 1.4.

A more complicated case would be $3x + 5y \leqslant 15$. We begin by plotting the line $3x + 5y = 15$; the easiest way to do that is to note that $x$ is 5 when $y$ is zero, and $y$ is 3 when $x$ is zero. Then we must decide on which side of this line the inequality is satisfied. Take some simple point below the line, such as the origin. Here $3x + 5y$ is zero, which is certainly less than or equal to 15, so the side of the line including the origin satisfies the inequality but points above the line don't (*see* Fig. 1.5).

We have been concentrating throughout this section on what's called the *positive quadrant* – the region of graphs in which both $x$ and $y$ are positive. In many of the practical applications we're concerned with, that will be the region of interest, because real variables such as costs, quantity produced, numbers of employees and so on can't be negative. Nevertheless, you should not forget that there *are* cases where we might need to extend our graphs to cover negative regions; an example would be the profit graph of a firm making a loss – that is to say, a negative profit.

This has been a rather long section, but the plotting of graphs is fundamental to many topics later in the book. Try the following exercise to make sure you have understood the section.

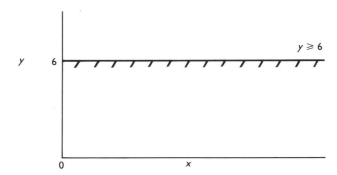

**Fig. 1.4** Graphing a simple inequality

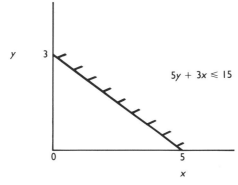

**Fig. 1.5** Graphing a more complicated inequality

**Exercise 10**

1 Which of the following equations would give straight line graphs:
(a) $y = 2x - 17$; (b) $xy = 4$; (c) $p = 6q + 44$; (d) $2/x = 5/y$?

2 Find the slope of the graphs in 1 above which give straight lines.

3 Plot the graph of $R = 200n - 8n^2$ for values of $n$ between 0 and 30.

4 Show on the same graph the regions satisfying $x \geqslant 4$ and $3x + 2y \geqslant 12$.

## MAKING USE OF GRAPHS

In the previous section we discussed plotting graphs and inequalities without reference to what practical situation they might represent. We will now take a brief look at the applications to which they may be put.

One of the most important of these is in the solution of equations. For instance, if we have the graph of $y = 2x + 3$ (a straight line) then the point where this crosses the $x$-axis – that is, where $y = 0$ – gives the solution of the equation $0 = 2x + 3$, or, as we would more usually express it, $2x + 3 = 0$. This is a very simple equation which could easily be solved without the use of a graph, but the same method works for the more complex equations, such as quadratics, which give rise to curves.

To find the solution of the quadratic $x^2 + 2x - 15 = 0$, as an example, we would plot the graph $y = x^2 + 2x - 15$ as explained on pp. 21–2, and then look for the points at which the curve crosses the $x$-axis (where $y = 0$). These turn out to be $x = 3$ and $x = -5$, which are exactly the values satisfying the quadratic, as you can check for yourself.

Perhaps even more important is the use of graphs to solve two equations simultaneously. The points at which two equations are simultaneously satisfied are the points at which their graphs cross, as you can verify by plotting the graphs of one of the pairs of simultaneous equations you solved in Exercise 9. This gives us a method for solving two simultaneous equations even when one of them is not linear and the methods of the section on simultaneous equations (pp. 17–18) won't work.

## A BUSINESS APPLICATION

All these points are best illustrated by taking a look at one of the major applications of graphical methods in business – the *break-even graph*. The idea behind this is simple: a firm is said to break even when costs are just balanced by revenues. The break-even point is, in fact, the point at which they begin to make a profit.

Suppose that we return to the item whose production costs were discussed on pp. 19–21, giving rise to the straight-line cost equation $C = 300 + 2n$ where $n$ was the number produced. We will now imagine that the demand for the product is related to the price being charged for it by the equation $n = 600 - 50p$, where $n$ is the number sold at a price $p$ pounds. This means that if a price of £2 is charged, 500 items will be sold; at £3 each, the number sold will be 450, and so on.

We can manipulate this expression to give price in terms of number sold, using the processes discussed on p. 15, to get $p = (600 - n)/50$, or $p = 12 - 0.02n$. This is the price at which $n$ items could he sold, so the revenue generated by the sale of these $n$ items will be price × quantity. The revenue equation is thus $R = n(12 - 0.02n)$, or $R = 12n - 0.02n^2$. Notice here how we use meaningful notation – $R$ for revenue, $n$ for number – rather than $x$ and $y$.

To find the output at which the firm will break even, then, all we need do is plot, on the same pair of axes, the revenue and cost graphs. A point which often causes problems in cases of this kind, though, is what sort of range of values of $n$ we should be looking at. Should we draw up tables of values for $C$ and $R$ with $n = 1, 2, 3 \ldots$, or with $n = 1,000$, $2,000, 3,000 \ldots$? Well, it's pretty clear that since we are talking about a commodity where the fixed costs of production are £300, while prices, as we have just seen, are of the order of a few pounds, we are going to have to sell a fair number before we even cover the fixed costs, let alone start making a profit.

So we try a couple of values of $n$ of the order of several hundreds, to get a better idea what sort of range we should be considering. If $n = 500$ then the costs are $300 + 2 \times 500 = £1,300$, while the revenue generated is $12 \times 500 - 0.02 \times 500 \times 500 = £1,000$, so a loss is being made. If $n = 300$, then in a similar way the costs are £900 and the revenue £1,800 (you should check these calculations), so a profit of £900 is made. Thus the change from profit to loss comes somewhere between $n = 300$ and $n = 500$.

Knowing this, we choose to set up a table as follows:

| $n$ | 50 | 100 | 150 | 200 | 250 | 300 | 350 | 400 | 450 | 500 |
|---|---|---|---|---|---|---|---|---|---|---|
| $C(£)$ | 400 | 500 | 600 | 700 | 800 | 900 | 1,000 | 1,100 | 1,200 | 1,300 |
| $12n$ | 600 | 1,200 | 1,800 | 2,400 | 3,000 | 3,600 | 4,200 | 4,800 | 5,400 | 6,000 |
| $0.02n^2$ | 50 | 200 | 450 | 800 | 1,250 | 1,800 | 2,450 | 3,200 | 4,050 | 5,000 |
| $R(£)$ | 550 | 1,000 | 1,350 | 1,600 | 1,750 | 1,800 | 1,750 | 1,600 | 1,350 | 1,000 |

It is clear from the table that the firm begins to make a profit at some output below 50 items; there is already a profit at $n = 50$, but we know there must be a loss at $n = 0$, where there is no revenue to offset costs of £300. A profit ceases to be made between 450 and 500 items. To determine the values more exactly, the two curves, one for revenue and one for costs, are plotted as shown in Fig. 1.6, from which the approximate break-even points can be read off as $n = 32$ and $n = 468$. Strictly speaking only the first of these is called a break-even, though of course it's as important to know where you stop making a profit as where you start to make one!

## Exercise 11

1 A firm has fixed costs of £500 and a variable cost of 50p per item. It sells its product at a price of 80p per item, regardless of the number sold. Draw a graph to find at what output the firm breaks even.

2 Draw a suitable graph to determine the solution of the equation $x^2 - 6x + 5 = 0$.

3 A firm has the choice of two machines; machine A will give a fixed cost of £20 plus £1 for every 100 items produced; machine B has no fixed costs, but will incur variable costs at a rate of £1 multiplied by the square of the number of hundreds of items produced. At what output does machine A become cheaper than machine B?

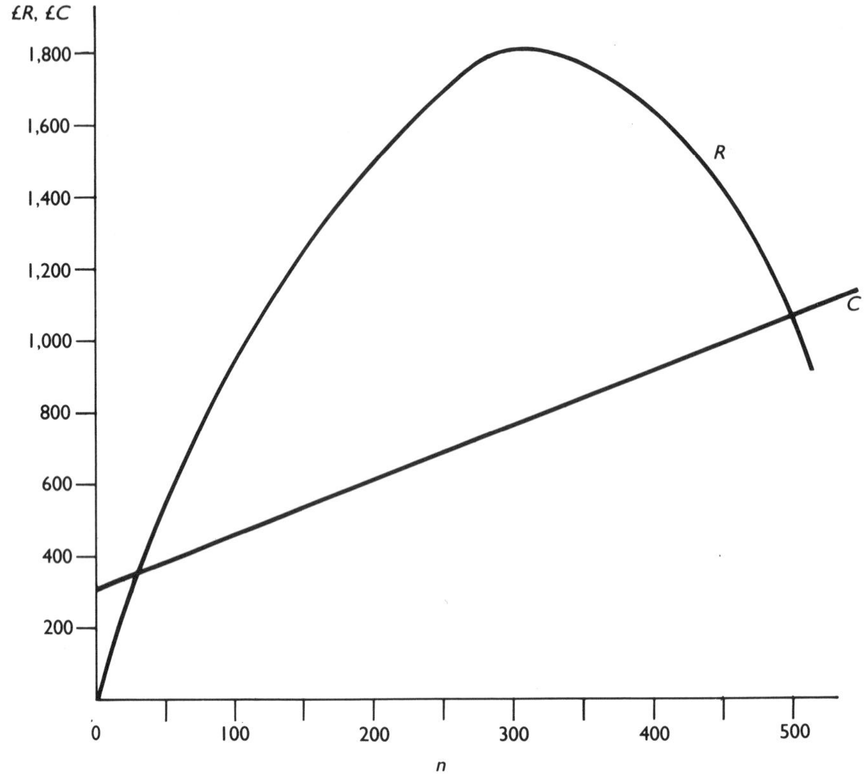

**Fig. 1.6** Break-even graph

## A WORD ABOUT CALCULATORS

Although it is important that you should be happy with the basic mathematical skills described in this chapter, it would be silly to ignore the fact that the great majority of calculations are now carried out either by electronic calculator or computer. The topic of computer packages for carrying out statistical calculations will be discussed in the next chapter; here I mention a few points concerned with getting the most out of your calculator.

I will not constantly mention the fact that you should be using a calculator for your computations – that goes without saying. What I will do is point out particular processes which can be speeded up by making efficient use of things like the constant key or the memory on your calculator. It would be impossible actually to tell you what key-sequences to use, since there are so many different models of calculator on the market, and each has its own quirks of operation. It is up to you to read the literature which came with your calculator when you bought it, and make sure you exploit to the full all those buttons you have paid for.

If you are about to buy a calculator before embarking on your course, the minimum you need is a machine with the four basic functions ( + , – , × , ÷ ) plus a memory – preferably one with both M + and M − facilities – and a square root. Many of you will already have scientific calculators, which can compute means, standard deviations and so on automatically — that is, without requiring the user to understand the details of the calculation. You should certainly know how to use these facilities, and they come in very handy for checking answers, but many examinations, particularly those set by external bodies such as the accountancy institutes, will not permit you to quote the results from such a machine in isolation. They preface exam papers by a statement such as 'All workings must be shown to obtain full credit'. Be careful, therefore, not to become too dependent on your calculator if you are doing a course of this kind.

Below is a set of exercises to make sure you are comfortable with your calculator and get the best out of it. If you get stuck on any of them, go back to the instruction manual!

## Exercise 12

You should be able to perform all these calculations on a four-function, single memory calculator with per cent key and square root, *without* having to write down any intermediate steps.

**1** $17 \times 82$      **2** $83 + 66 + 947$

**3** $54 - 76 + 12$      **4** $95 \div 8.3$

**5** $0.002 \times 10304$      **6** $12 \times 8 + 13 \times 11$

**7** $11/7 + 5/3 + 9/13$      **8** $16 \times 16 + 17 \times 17 + 18 \times 18$

**9** $14 \div \sqrt{2}$      **10** $\sqrt{8} \times 4$

**11** Find the total cost of 3 loaves at 58p each, 2lb of cheese at £1.60 per lb, and 6 lettuces at 65p each.

**12** There are 2.54 cm in one inch. Convert the following set of lengths to inches: 8 cm, 27 cm, 33 cm, 49 cm, 72 cm.

**13** An examination is marked out of 80. What is the percentage mark of a student who gets 66 out of 80?

**14** In the same exam, five students gain 23, 37, 44, 59, 73 out of 80. Convert all these marks to percentages (nearest whole per cent).

**15** What is 33 per cent of £900?

**16** Find the cost inclusive of $17\frac{1}{2}$ per cent VAT of an item which without VAT costs £17.

**17** $\sqrt{\dfrac{8 \times 13 + 5 \times 17}{86}}$      **18** $\dfrac{11 + 17.3}{2.8 \times 4.3 + 3.6 \times 9}$

**19** $1.1 + 1.1^2 + 1.1^3 + 1.1^4$

For calculators with an M− key:

**20** $2.3 \times 6 - 1.9 \times 4$      **21** $\sqrt{\dfrac{263}{7} - 4.9^2}$

**22** $\dfrac{16}{8 \times 18.2 - 4 \times 13.7}$      **23** $2 \times 3 + 4 \times 5 - 6 \times 7$

**24** A shopkeeper pays his wholesaler for a dozen items at £1.72 each, 40 at £8.84 each, and 200 at 63p each, and receives a refund for 60 items costing 52p each which he returns. How much does he pay when 8 per cent cash discount has been deducted?

## Conclusion

If you have worked carefully through the material of this chapter plus the exercises, and not had too much difficulty, you should be well equipped to tackle the rest of the book. However, if you feel your difficulties need a more thorough revision of basic maths, references (1)–(3) in the Suggestions for Further Reading in Appendix 1 should help.

## CHAPTER 2

# Computational aids: LOTUS 1-2-3 and MINITAB

## INTRODUCTION

This chapter is designed for those of you who have access to one or both of the computer packages, LOTUS 1-2-3 and MINITAB, and who wish to make use of them to enhance your reading of this book, possibly in conjunction with the optional diskette. It is not intended to teach you in detail how to use these packages – if you need more detailed information of that kind, you should look at references (15) or (16) in the Suggestions for Further Reading in Appendix 1. I will assume that if you wish, for example, to use LOTUS in your learning of statistics, you will already have familiarised yourself with the basics of using the package. I will, however, give a brief discussion of the use of packages as an aid to statistics, and contrast the strengths and weaknesses of MINITAB and LOTUS with regard to statistical computation. I will also introduce you to the three major datasets provided on the diskette, which will be used throughout the rest of the book to give you practice in carrying out the various statistical procedures.

It is worth noting that all my examples use MINITAB version 7.1 and LOTUS version 2.3, so if you are using a different version, you may notice slight differences in format.

## SOFTWARE FOR STATISTICS

There are many large and powerful packages available which are specifically designed for carrying out statistical computations; you may come across some of the better-known of these, such as SPSS (Statistical Package for the Social Sciences), GLIM (Generalised Linear Interactive Modelling), or SAS (Statistical Analysis Software). In carrying out advanced statistical work, it is essential to use a package of this kind, but the drawback is that it generally takes quite a lot of time and effort to learn how to actually use the package, and if you only wish to carry out simple computations, this may be rather a sledgehammer to crack a nut.

One alternative is not to use a special statistical package at all, but to use something with which most people are more familiar – a spreadsheet. The one I will use for illustrations is LOTUS 1-2-3, but all spreadsheets have many features in common. The advantage of this option – apart from its familiarity – is that formulae for carrying out common operations (like working out a moving average – *see* Chapter 14) can be stored in a worksheet and reused in conjunction with different sets of data. If you are using the optional diskette with this book, then you will be exploiting that feature – you will find that the diskette contains ready-written worksheets, referred to at relevant points in the book, which you can make use of for carrying out necessary calculations.

The drawback of a spreadsheet is quite simply the fact that it was not designed mainly for statistical use, and so in some applications (for instance regression analysis – see

Chapter 13) information is not necessarily provided in the format which a statistician would prefer. And there are certain operations, as we will see, in which a lot more work is involved in using a spreadsheet than if we used a dedicated statistical package.

On the other hand, a spreadsheet will prove useful in some of the later chapters of the book where we are discussing not statistics but other quantitative techniques from the field of Operational Research – and in those areas a specifically statistical package would be of much less use. So if you are already accustomed to using a spreadsheet, then you are probably best advised to stick with it for your work with this book.

If, on the other hand, you wish to use a dedicated statistical package, then MINITAB has the advantages of being widely available in educational establishments, very friendly and easy to get started with, and carrying out most of the statistical calculations we will need to undertake. Its main drawback, for anyone who has been used to using a menu-driven system like LOTUS, is that it is command-driven – it requires you actually to type in instructions, rather than simply select them from a list, so there is a bit more work to do.* Once you get used to this, however, it becomes very simple to instruct the computer to do what you wish, since the commands look much like English sentences.

So the choice is yours; reference will be made to both MINITAB and LOTUS at appropriate points in the text, though you can manage perfectly well without using either (with rather more computational effort!). In any case, whether you use a calculator or a computer, the major objective is not 'getting the answer', but thinking about what it means once you've got it.

## THE DATASETS AND WORKSHEETS

The diskette contains four large sets of data to which we will be referring in examples throughout the book. These are stored in three formats: as MINITAB worksheets (denoted by a filename with an extension .MTW), as LOTUS worksheets (denoted by .WK1), and as ASCII files (denoted by .DAT) in case you wish to use them in conjunction with other software. The data sets are as follows:

(a) STUD.MTW/STUD.WK1/STUD.DAT contains information about a large class of students on a postgraduate management course. There are four columns of data: the first gives the student's age; the second, his/her nationality (coded 1 = British, 2 = other); the third, gender (0 = female, 1 = male); and the fourth, the subject area of the student's first degree (1 = business/economics, 2 = engineering, 3 = science, 4 = arts).

(b) MACH.MTW/MACH.WK1/MACH.DAT contains details of weights of packets of tea (nominal weight 250 gm) filled by three automatic machines. Column 1 gives the actual weight, while column 2 gives a code indicating whether the packet was filled by machine 1, 2 or 3.

(c) QUAL.MTW/QUAL.WK1/QUAL.DAT gives the results of a survey of branches of a large retail chain. Column 1 contains the gross takings of the branch for the past month, column 2 contains the number of square metres of floorspace in the branch, column 3 indicates whether the branch is in a shopping precinct (1) or on a street (2), and column 4 shows number of sales staff employed at the branch.

---

* The recently-launched version 8 is now menu-driven.

(d)  EMP.MTW/EMP.WK1/EMP.DAT contains details of the workforce of an organisation. There are three columns of data: the first gives the status of the employee (0 = full-time, 1 = part-time); the second, the gender (0 = male, 1 = female); and the third, the employee's age last birthday.

In practice large sets of data may well contain missing and/or erroneous values, and part of the job of the person analysing the data is to identify these and decide what to do about them. However, for simplicity there are no missing values in the four datasets described above, and no erroneous entries (at least, not deliberate ones!).

In addition to these data sets, you will find on the diskette the ready-written LOTUS worksheets referred to above, for carrying out the quantitative operations about which you will be reading in later chapters. These will be described as we come to them.

# PART 2

# Numbers – a means of communication

In this section we shall discuss why we need to be able to communicate numerically as well as verbally. We will examine some of the ways in which we can best gather numerical information and convey it to other people, and in which we can make the most of numerical information which other people are trying to convey to us.

## CHAPTER 3

# Obtaining the figures: sampling methods

## Objectives

There are no prerequisites for understanding this chapter. By the end of your work on this chapter you should be able to:

(a) recognise qualitative and quantitative, discrete and continuous scales of measurement, and decide which type would be suitable in a given case;
(b) explain the difference between primary and secondary data, and decide in practical cases which type could most appropriately be used;
(c) define the major methods of selecting a sample from a population, and comment on their advantages and disadvantages;
(d) design a simple questionnaire, and make constructive criticisms of those designed by other people;
(e) name some of the more important sources of published statistical data.

## THE MANAGING DIRECTOR'S PROBLEM

A business concern of any kind, even the smallest, today depends to a very great extent on having ready access to large amounts of information, ranging from details of the potential market for its goods or services to estimates of next year's labour requirements, from the attendance record of each employee to the numbers of breakdowns per week for each piece of equipment it owns. The more accurate and complete this information is, the more effective, all other things being equal, the operation of the business can be.

The key words here, however, are 'accurate' and 'complete'. Information which is vague or imprecise, or which is reliable as far as it goes but contains serious gaps or omissions, is actually worse than useless, since it may mislead management into making decisions which turn out, in the light of further evidence, to be positively contrary to the well-being of the organisation.

In this preliminary chapter, then, we are going to investigate how this accuracy and completeness can be achieved – in other words, how can we devise ways of pinning down information as precisely as possible, and how can we collect adequate amounts of information as the need arises?

## MULTIFARIOUS MEASUREMENTS

At first sight it would appear that many of the facts about a business are simply not measurable in the ordinary sense in which we use that term. How, for example, could we 'measure' in any straightforward numerical way the efficiency with which a worker performs his job, or the reaction of a consumer to a new variety of chocolate biscuit? And yet numerical measurements are what, ideally, we are after; mere verbal information can never convey the same accuracy. To take a rather trivial example: if you were looking at the profitability of various companies with a view to purchasing shares in one of them, I doubt whether you would be very satisfied to be told, 'Oh, we made a nice little profit last year', or, 'Well, last year's performance *was* a bit disappointing'! Only the actual *figures* for profit, dividends declared and so on can convey the facts you want in an unequivocal way. And the same applies, in a less obvious fashion, to almost any kind of information you can think of.

Of course, there *are* variations in the *way* in which different kinds of information can be quantified – that's to say, rendered into numerical terms. In fact, we might define a sort of hierarchy of measurements, in ascending order of precision.

## Descriptive classes

First of all we have information which is purely qualitative or descriptive, so that about the best we can do is to classify it into groups or classes according to the characteristics we are interested in, and then count the number of items in each class. For instance, a biscuit manufacturer might classify the various lines he produces into 'plain', 'chocolate-covered' and 'cream-filled', and then count how many lines fall into each category. Naturally it's important to make sure that as far as possible the categories are unambiguous and don't overlap, otherwise questions arise as to which category an individual item belongs to – for example, into which group should our biscuit manufacturer place lines which are both chocolate-covered and cream-filled? Such problems apart, however, even such an apparently crude system of 'measurement' can convey a good deal of useful information such as which category has the most members, whether items are evenly spread overall the categories, and so on.

## Ordered classes

Our second 'level of measurement' is the situation in which, as before, items can be grouped into classes according to some characteristic, but this time there is an *order* among the classes. One obvious example is the way in which most degree courses classify their results – into first, upper and lower second, third, pass and fail. The ordering here is clear, but no one would claim that all students within each class are in any sense identical in their performance. The same sort of system would apply to the social-class groupings employed by sociologists, whereby people are classified as A, B1, B2, and so on; again there's a clear order *between* the classes, but no necessary equivalence of individuals *within* classes.

## Rankings

One step more precise again is what we might call a *ranking* of items; you are probably familiar with this from the idea of 'places' – first, second, third and so on – in class or subject, employed at school. This differs from the previous case in that each individual item is given a definite position in the ranking, which may or may not be the same as that for any other item. In the case of 'places' at school, of course, the rankings are usually derived from the actual marks obtained by pupils, but the system is particularly useful in situations where proper numerical measurements such as marks are difficult or impossible to obtain.

Consider, for example, the position of a foreman required, when promotion is under consideration, to report on the efficiency of the workers in his charge. A whole conglomeration of separate measurements might be needed for this purpose – how fast does the worker perform his task, how good is the finished quality of the goods he produces, how often has he been absent during the past month, and so on. But simply ask the foreman to *rank* the workers according to their efficiency, and he probably won't have too much trouble deciding who is the best, who comes second, and so on down to the absolutely useless! So the multitude of measurements needed can be reduced to the set of rankings 1, 2, 3 . . . . For this reason, rankings are immensely useful, particularly in situations which would have too many dimensions to measure individually; another example might be provided by the market researcher who wants to assess the consumer reaction to a new range of products: 'Which of these do you like most? least? . . .'.

Moreover, the set of 'measurements' with which we end up when we have ranked items is of a particularly simple kind – it's just the set of whole numbers 1, 2, 3 . . . . So, even in cases where it's perfectly possible to get a genuine numerical measurement, we often resort to rankings in order to simplify further calculations. After all, it's a good deal easier to say 'Northern Sales Region was third in terms of turnover last year' than 'The turnover last year in Northern Sales Region was £247,346.10'! Inevitably, we have lost detail in making the transition from one statement to the other – in this case, the detail being precisely what the turnover was – but in many cases that's a penalty we're prepared to pay in the interests of simplicity and clarity.

## Measurements

Finally, at the top of our hierarchy of scales of measurement, we come to what is probably understood by 'measurement' in the colloquial sense – quantities which can be assigned a definite, unique position on a numerical scale. The examples which could be given are endless – weights of bags of sugar, densities of samples of metal, ages of customers in a store – you can continue the list for yourself. Quantities such as these, which can be measured numerically and which have different values for different people or items, are often referred to as *variables*, because their value varies from one item to another.

Within this final category, there is one more important sub-division of which you need to be aware. When official statistics are being held up to ridicule, one figure which is commonly cited to demonstrate the silliness of the whole business is that 'the average British family has 2.3 children' or whatever. Whoever saw 0.3 of a child – what peculiar ideas these statisticians have! Now although of course this is a caricature (for reasons which I hope you can see!) there is a valid point being made – namely, that numbers of children in families are always *integers* – that is, whole numbers. In exactly the same way, numbers of rooms in houses, number of employees, or production of motor-cars in a factory will always take only integer values.

Variables of this kind are called *discrete* (note the spelling!) variables; they can take on only certain definite and separate values. These values are nearly always integers, but not invariably so; one often-cited example of a discrete variable which takes non-integer values is British shoe-sizes.

The other type of variable, which can take on absolutely any value (perhaps restricted to a certain limited range) as long as we can measure it accurately enough, is called a *continuous* variable. Things like height and weight would come into this category; we don't expect to find people with heights much above 7 feet or below 3 feet, but within this range, given a sufficiently accurate tape-measure, we could encounter any height – there is no rule, as yet, which says that people *must* have heights in tidy multiples of 1 inch!

Like many definitions within statistics, the ideas of 'discrete' and 'continuous' variables are not watertight – to some extent they depend on how we decide to measure things – and there is a kind of grey area where we might treat a variable as either. Wages, for instance, are strictly discrete, since one's pay must be a whole number of pence; however, for practical purposes we might regard wages as measured on a continuous scale since the discrete steps are so very tiny compared with the actual amounts being considered.

By now you may well be thinking that this discussion of different types of measurement is all very well, but somewhat philosophical. However, it *is* also very practical, for two reasons. Firstly, you may well be in a position at some time in your career of having to devise a way of measuring some hitherto unquantified variable – such as the nuttiness of different recipes of chocolate bar – in which case a knowledge of different possibilities will be very useful. Secondly, when we discuss in Chapters 5 and 6 methods for presenting and summarising information, we will find that the means at our disposal depend very much on the type of information concerned, whether it is quantitative or qualitative, discrete or continuous, and so on.

## WHENCE INFORMATION?

Now that we have some idea of the kinds of information we are going to be discussing, we can address ourselves to the problem of getting hold of it. In some respects this is rather a chicken-and-egg question – how you collect the information depends on what you want to do with it. For this reason, you will find that many elementary statistics textbooks defer a discussion of how information is obtained until after they have talked about the techniques available for analysing it. Although there are good arguments in favour of this approach it *is* a little like cooking the dinner before you've bought the ingredients; so, at the expense of a bit of cross-referencing later on, we will adopt the alternative course.

Two definitions before we continue will enable us to use more compact terminology than we have done so far. We have been talking about 'measurements', or even more vaguely 'information', but from now on we will refer simply to 'data' – the set of facts, figures or whatever, with which we are concerned in a particular problem. It will also be useful to talk about the 'population' – the statistician's term, not just for a collection of people, but for *any* collection of items about which we have, or wish to obtain, data. Thus we could refer to the population of sheep in the county of Powys, the population of bags of sugar filled by a machine, and so on.

Getting hold of data is rather like doing one's maths homework at school: there are basically three ways to go about obtaining the answers. One can find them oneself, 'borrow' them from someone else, or hope to find them in the textbook. Data which one finds for oneself is called *primary* data; anything else, whether obtained from published sources or directly, perhaps from a colleague in your firm, is *secondary*. There are arguments for and against both types, knowledge of which will enable you to make an informed choice in a practical situation.

It is certainly true that the only data you can be sure of having tailor-made to your requirements is that which you collect yourself. It is also likely to be much more up-to-date than anything from a published source; the most rapidly-published of the government's statistical periodicals, for example, tends to be about six weeks out of date.

On the other hand, large organisations, particularly the government, are able to obtain access to information which you, as a private individual or a representative of your firm are unlikely to discover. The government actually imposes a statutory requirement on organisations to provide certain details about wages, hours worked and so on, thus ensuring a completeness of coverage which you could not possibly obtain; it also has at its disposal large resources of money and manpower entirely devoted to the collection and processing of statistical data. Thus a figure such as the Retail Price Index, for example, possesses a generality, in terms of the number of prices which go into its calculation, coverage of prices over the whole country, and consideration of price variations between different types of retail outlet, which no individual could hope to emulate.

Other large organisations, too, can obtain data not available to the casual enquirer. A trade organisation such as the Federation of Motor Manufacturers and Traders may ask all its members to supply returns concerning their turnover, profits, and other matters which they will be willing to supply, secure in the knowledge that the information will be used for the benefit of their entire industry – and that if it *is* published, it will appear in the anonymity of a large collection of data referring to many member firms. The reaction if one individual firm were to ask its nearest rival to provide such details can be imagined!

Then there are questions of time and cost to be considered. Data collection can be an expensive business – why go to the trouble of 'doing-it-yourself' when a trip to the nearest library subscribing to the government's *Monthly Digest of Statistics*, or a telephone call to Bloggs in the accounts department, could produce the same results? Ultimately, like many such questions we will encounter later in the book, the 'primary or secondary' problem resolves itself into a matter of compromise: are we prepared to settle for secondary data which may not be *exactly* what we were looking for, but which is available here, now, and quite cheaply; or is the accuracy of the data such an important feature that we are prepared to pay for it in terms of time, money and effort?

## COLLECT-IT-YOURSELF

### Who shall we ask?

Assuming that we have decided to try to obtain our data first hand, the immediate problem we face is to define the population we are interested in. This sounds pretty obvious, but it's vital that we are very precise about this definition particularly if we are going to rely on outside help, such as part-time market research interviewers, to do some of the data collection. It's no use telling your interviewers to question 'housewives'; does this mean people who are solely occupied in keeping house, or do you want to include those who have outside jobs? And does *housewives* include single parents who are at home taking care of children? If you intended the term to be interpreted in one way, and your interviewers interpret it differently, your results may be invalid and even downright misleading.

Even when we have managed to specify the population in a sufficiently detailed way, we almost certainly won't be able to collect information from absolutely every member of that population. Even the government, in the ten-year census the completion of which is a statutory requirement, cannot obtain data which is totally complete; there will always be those who for reasons of their own do not wish to give the government details of their present address! More important, in most practical cases, are considerations of time and money. Manufacturers carrying out nationwide market research surveys would have colossal bills were they to attempt total coverage of their target population, and the mass of results would probably take months to analyse. When the question at issue is, say, the reaction of schoolchildren to a new curry-flavoured potato crisp, it clearly just isn't worthwhile going to such lengths to carry out a census (the term, incidentally, applies not only to the ten-yearly census but to any data-collection operation which covers an entire population).

So, in most cases, we have to be content with taking a *sample* from the population, and hoping that the results we get from our sample won't be too far from those which would apply to the rest of the population. Actually, it isn't only a question of hoping – if we select our sample in the right way we can be quite precise about how reliable the results we get will be. But what is the right way? And what are our criteria for 'rightness' in this context?

## What sort of sample?

### A simple random sample

Most people would, I think, agree that a well-selected sample should represent the population from which it is taken fairly – that is, it should not be *biased* towards any particular part of the population. We might go further and demand that to be completely fair, every member of the population should have *exactly* the same chance of being included in our sample. If we make this demand, we are asking for a *simple random sample*, and it's not hard to see how we might achieve such a sample, certainly from a fairly small population. We could put all the names or identifying numbers of the members of the population on to identical pieces of paper, put them in a hat, shake it well, and pull out as many as we need for our sample.

If we have a large population, however, we would need a very big hat to carry out this process; but actually with the aid of a table of *random numbers* like those in Appendix 3 we can *simulate* the pulling-out-of-the-hat procedure quite simply even for large populations – especially if we also happen to have a computer handy. All we need to do is assign a number to every member of our chosen population (and this is often already done – workers have works numbers or National Insurance numbers, bank accounts have account numbers, and so on). Then we read off numbers from the table – in three-digit sets if the numbers assigned to our population have three digits – and our sample consists of the members of the population with the corresponding numbers. You'll be encountering the term 'simulate' again, and learning more about random numbers, in Chapter 19. For now, we can see how the process works by looking at a simple example.

Suppose we want to choose three out of eight workers in a production team to receive special experimental training, and in order for the experiment to work the choice has to be random. Then, if we are too idle to write the eight names on bits of paper and put them in a hat, we give each of them a number: 1 Adams, 2 Brown, 3 Carter, 4 Davies, 5 Evans, 6 Finch, 7 Goss, 8 Hall. Then we look at row 16 say, of the Appendix 3 table, and find the first three numbers within the range 1 to 8 are 5, 6 and 1 (we ignore the 9s because they are outside the range of interest). So our sample will consist of Messrs Evans, Finch and Adams.

A computer can generate the random numbers for us, and even, if the details of the population are stored within it, print out for us a list of the members of the sample. This is exactly what ERNIE does when choosing premium bond winners – in fact he is really just a glorified electronic hat. Some scientific calculators, too, include a random number key, and there is an @RAND function available in LOTUS.

### A stratified sample

This all seems very satisfactory, and certainly fits in with our intuitive ideas of what constitutes a 'fair' sample. But there are at least two very valid criticisms to be levelled at the method. First, it requires that we have a 'list' of all the members of our population – the technical name for such a list is a *sampling frame*. In many cases this isn't too serious a problem; market research enquirers often use the electoral roll, and organisations like the AA and the Consumers Association generate income by selling lists of their members to commercial firms. Bias may creep into your sample, though, if you use as your sampling frame something like the telephone directory; ownership of a telephone is quite strongly linked to social class/income bracket. However, the defect *can* usually be got around, and in any case also applies to many other methods of sampling.

More serious is the problem that you may actually get a perfectly respectable simple random sample which is nevertheless very *un*representative of its *parent* population. For instance, if you took a simple random sample of twenty workers from a firm with a work force of 200 part-time and 800 full-time staff, all the names which came out of your hat *might* be those of part-time workers – in which case, if your enquiry was concerned with the adequacy of canteen facilities in the firm, you might get very odd results because all the part-timers go home before lunch. To overcome this drawback, an alternative type of sample called a *stratified sample* has been devised.

The origin of the word is the Latin 'stratum' meaning a layer, and the sample is designed to give fair representation to the various 'layers' or sub-groups within a population. In the example above, for instance, we could insist that our sample of 20 workers must contain 4 part-timers and 16 full-timers, so as to reflect accurately the proportions of the two groups in the whole workforce. Within each group, the 4 and the 16 would be chosen randomly as already described. This way the sort of anomaly described above just can't arise.

### A multi-stage sample

But with any kind of random selection, simple or stratified, further difficulties may become apparent when we look at the names which emerge from our 'hat'. If the first is P Smith of Dover, the second H Macdonald of Inverness and the third J Williams of Aberystwyth, it is clearly going to be a slow and expensive business for someone to rush about the country interviewing them. Ruling out for the moment the possibility of a postal questionnaire, which we will consider later in the chapter, we could surmount this difficulty by adopting *multi-stage sampling* instead. With this method, the country is first of all divided up into a small number of large areas – the Independent Television Regions are popular ones for use in market research surveys – and two or three of these are chosen at random in the usual way. Then within the selected areas, we subdivide into, perhaps, parliamentary constituencies or local authority regions, and choose a few of *these* at random. So the process continues, working through to streets and finally to individuals, the advantage of the method being that those selected at the last stage will be concentrated geographically into a few areas, thus cutting down greatly on the amount of travelling required of interviewers.

### A quota sample

Where a great deal of accuracy isn't required in the final results, the demand for random sampling is often abandoned altogether in favour of an easier-to-implement alternative known as *quota sampling*. If you have ever been stopped in the street by a person – usually female – with a clipboard, and asked to give your views on a new sort of chocolate or last night's TV programmes, you were probably part of a *quota* which the interviewer had been told to fill: 20 white-collar males between the ages of 30 and 65, 15 unemployed housewives aged 18–30, and so on. The advantage of this method to the interviewer is that, while the correct proportions of different subgroups in the population are preserved, she can choose *anyone* who satisfies the criteria of a particular subgroup as her victim. Perhaps this is the place for a note on the confusion caused by the colloquial understanding of 'random' as 'haphazard'; one hears statements like 'We interviewed a sample of 10 people randomly in the street as they came along'. Now this may be haphazard, but it certainly isn't random in the statistical sense of everyone having the same chance of selection; people who just happened not to be passing when the survey was being carried out had no chance at all of selection. In the same way, a quota sample is non-random because, if you are an Irish bus-conductor who happens to pass the interviewer when she has already filled her quota of Irish bus-conductors, then your chance of selection is nil.

The method is also subject to interviewer abuse, in that an interviewer who is tired of standing in the rain trying to fill her quota of former train-drivers aged over 90 may well get fed up, fill in the details of the next person to pass in the relevant box and go home! However, reputable research agencies carry out checks designed to eliminate 'fiddling' of this kind by interviewers, though there *is* an authenticated case of a single interviewer filling in all 500 forms in his quota himself – all with different, imaginary details, of course!

### A systematic sample

Yet another kind of non-random sample, perhaps the simplest of all, is the *systematic sample*, whereby, if we want a sample which is 10 per cent of the population, we go through our sampling frame selecting, say, every tenth person beginning with person number 7. Again, this isn't random since persons 11, 12 ... 16, and all the other 'in-between' ones have no chance of selection; but it is almost as satisfactory in many cases. The only situation where such a sample *might* introduce bias is where your pattern of sampling picks up some underlying pattern in the population; for example, if you choose to examine every twentieth screw produced by a machine in order to check the quality of production, and the machine has developed a vibration which causes it to hiccup every twenty screws, then you could well gain the impression, should you happen to coincide with the hiccups, that the entire production is faulty, whereas in fact the other nineteen (95 per cent of the output) are perfectly satisfactory. However, in most situations this is not likely to arise; there is no reason to suppose, for instance, that if you choose to question every tenth worker emerging from a factory gate about his political views, they will carefully line up inside so that every tenth person has views either of the darkest blue or the brightest red, simply in order to invalidate your sample!

## Deductions from samples

Whichever sampling method you choose to use, one thing is certain: data obtained from a sample won't give you totally accurate information about a population in the way that a complete census would. This is simply common sense: just because a sample pack of 'Mixed Nuts' contains 20 per cent almonds, no one would expect the entire population to contain exactly the same proportion.

However, for certain kinds of sample – namely, those whose selection includes a random element – what we can do is make definite quantitative statements about how much the sample could be in error, relative to the entire population. We will see how to do this in Chapter 10. At present it is sufficient to note that for this reason, such samples (they include simple random, stratified and multi-stage samples) are to be preferred to those (such as quota samples) in whose selection no random element is allowed to operate.

## How shall we ask them?

There is a saying 'If you want a job doing, do it yourself'. We might modify that to 'If you want data collecting, collect it yourself'. The only way in which we can be sure that we are getting the facts we want, all the facts we want and nothing but the facts we want is to gather them by personal observation. This of course, is what 'pure' scientists are doing all the time; there is no point in asking a mouse to rate its chances of finding a piece of cheese in the middle of a maze on a scale from one to ten – you just have to let it try, and watch what happens.

In the same way, the only way we can determine with certainty how many slices of bread a family consumes per day is to watch them doing it; if we rely on asking for the information, they may well make a guess because they don't really know, or deliberately misinform us because they feel they eat too much and don't like to admit it, or say 'Well, it depends whether Aunty Mary comes round for supper' ... and so on. Unfortunately – or perhaps fortunately – people aren't laboratory animals, and our chances of stationing an observer in every household in our sample are very small indeed; so in spite of the drawbacks, we nearly always have to rely, in market research and similar enquiries, on asking for information.

Nevertheless, a well-designed questionnaire rather than a haphazard series of questions can make a great deal of difference to the accuracy of the data we collect, as well as simplifying the task of analysing responses. The whole area of questionnaire design, like that of sampling, is one which has received a lot of attention from agencies concerned with market research, and also from psychologists and sociologists who often have to rely on such methods to gather their data. Questions such as the effects of different-coloured paper and printing on the rate of response to questionnaires, for example, have been investigated in detail. We, however, will confine ourselves to a few of the more important points to be borne in mind when designing a questionnaire. Most of these are common-sense, maybe even obvious, though putting them into practice may not be quite so obvious!

First and foremost, keep your questions, and the questionnaire as a whole, as brief as is consistent with getting the facts you want. No one wants to spend hours answering a string of questions, particularly if you are asking them on a crowded rush-hour station platform or in a wet city street. They will, however, probably feel a good deal more co-operative about answering if they can see some kind of logical sequence to your enquiries – so don't just arrange them in any old order as they occur to you. And start with the simple ones, leaving any which are either complex or a bit 'sensitive' to the end.

Of course, common-sense suggests that there *are* questions to which one can hardly hope to get one hundred per cent honest replies. If you ask 'How often do you take a bath?', someone who does so every six months is not likely to say so, such behaviour being generally considered undesirable! Still, a glance through the pages of the Kinsey report will show that there is *hardly* anything about people's lives you cannot find out from them, if you go about it in the right way.

It is almost always preferable, from the point of view of a data analyst, to provide codified responses for respondents to select rather than to give them a completely open question. You will undoubtedly be familiar with this in application forms for colleges or jobs; a question such as 'State highest level of educational attainment' will usually be provided with a choice of possible replies: 'GCSE/A-level/degree/other (specify). Notice that last item; we don't want to *force* our respondents into a strait-jacket by providing them with too limited a range of replies, so we allow for possibilities we may not have anticipated by including a 'catch-all' category at the end. The adequacy of our choice of responses, as well as the general comprehensibility of our questions, can often be assessed by carrying out a *pilot survey* before administering the questionnaire to the whole of our sample; in the light of the results of the pilot, we may want to modify our questions before the larger-scale enquiry. Naturally, we must use as our pilot group a sample of similar composition to the larger sample; if we are carrying out research on the market for 'comfort shoes' of the kind featured in small ads in the Sunday newspapers, it is no good taking as our pilot group the dozen seventeen-year-old typists in the office pool.

Other fairly self-evident requirements in a good questionnaire are that it shall be unambiguous, couched in language which the intended respondent will be able to understand, and not lead him/her towards a particular answer. Clearly 'Are you in favour of the exploitation of workers by the Boss-Class?' is a loaded question whichever way you look at it; but there are more subtle ways in which bias may creep in. A well-meaning interviewer, hoping to clarify a question to an uncomprehending respondent, may rephrase it in language which is less non-committal than the original; and I well remember when I was questioned one Christmas as part of a survey on chocolate products aimed at the Christmas-stocking market. One question required the choice of the most attractive wrapping out of a set of half a dozen. I duly considered and made my selection, to be met with a pitying look and an exclamation of 'Oh' in dubious tones from the interviewer, who clearly thought I had no taste whatsoever! A person less pig-headed than myself might well have decided to select a different option at that point, rendering the result fairly useless to the chocolate manufacturer.

Which brings us to the question of how our survey should be administered. Human beings *are* fallible; maybe we should rely on sending our questionnaires through the post. On the other hand, how many postal surveys would *you* bother replying to – even if a stamped return envelope *were* provided? It is fatally easy for questionnaires to be dropped in the bin; a response rate of 15 per cent is considered to be good in many political surveys. And not only does this mean you must send out about 10,000 surveys if you wish to get 1,500 replies – the results may actually be biased by the non-responses. Human nature being what it is, if you send out a questionnaire to people who purchased your refrigerators two years ago, asking them whether they are satisfied with performance so far, those who are not will seize the opportunity of telling you exactly why not, while those who are, probably won't bother to reply. As a result, you end up with the impression that the country is filled with your ex-customers with mouldy fish-fingers in the freezing compartment and pools of water on the kitchen floor!

You *can* try to counteract this effect by sending interviewers to follow up non-respondents, and find out *why* they did not respond – but then you might perhaps have done better to send them to ask the questions in the first place. Equally, if you include a free gift – perhaps a sample of your product – as an incentive to reply, some of the polite members of your sample may be inhibited by feelings of gratitude from responding honestly to your questions.

So, in very many cases, administration of the questionnaire by personal interview is the method chosen. There are many advantages to this system, as well as drawbacks some of which have already been mentioned. An interviewer who has been sitting in someone's living room for half an hour has made a sort of relationship with the respondent which may perhaps permit them to obtain responses to questions which, if asked the moment the front door opened, would have earned them a black eye! More seriously, the accuracy of answers can be checked – not just 'Do you eat Weety Smashers for breakfast?' but 'Can you show me the packet?' An interviewer can use pictures of the product concerned, or copies of advertisements, to jog the respondents' memories in a controlled way; and, very importantly for computerised analysis of the responses, can be trained to enter the replies in a codified fashion on the response-sheet so that it can be read directly by the computer.

There are many other points which could be mentioned in this context, but it is an area where even a little practical experience is worth a thousand words. At the end of the chapter, therefore, you will find some suggested topics on which you might like to design and carry out your own survey – an opportunity for you to indulge your curiosity on a perfectly legitimate pretext! And if you would like to do some more reading on this topic, reference (12) in Suggestions for Further Reading in Appendix 1 is a classic text which is full of useful ideas.

## WHERE TO FIND SECOND-HAND STATISTICS

If on reflection you have decided that the data you need should already have been collected by someone, how do you decide where to begin looking? A visit to a well-stocked library of commerce will show that there is a vast and baffling – to the layman – array of statistical information churned out by central government, local authorities, trades federations and so on. I certainly do not intend to provide lists of such publications – a task which would be (*a*) boring, and (*b*) pretty pointless. Rather I will mention just a few of the most important sources, and then give ideas as to how you might go about finding others.

Most official government statistics are collected and published via the Government Statistical Service. They publish the *Monthly Digest of Statistics*, which as its name suggests is a compilation of statistics on all sorts of topics, ranging from wages to weather, from road accidents to retail prices, appearing once a month. This is always a good place to begin looking for statistical information on fairly broad issues, as are the various *Abstracts* made from the *Monthly Digest* at the end of the year or less frequently. These include the *Annual Abstract*, a general collection, and the more specialised *Economic Trends and Social Trends*, which often contain articles and more appealing graphical or diagrammatic presentations of information as well as tables of data relating to their specialised areas.

If these major publications fail to produce the data you need, probably the best course of action is to consult the *Guide to Official Statistics* also produced by the Government Statistical Service. This has an exhaustive index in which taking a topic at random, the entry under 'margarine' contains references to *Business Monitors* PQ229.1 and 2, the *Monthly Digest, Annual Abstract, Scottish Abstract, Statistical Information Notice*, and the *Census of Production* reports.

## 8.8 Sales by the gas and public electricity supply systems

| | Gas: million therms | | | | | | Electricity: TWh | | | | |
|---|---|---|---|---|---|---|---|---|---|---|---|
| | Power stations[1] | Iron and steel industry[2] | Other industries | Domestic | Other[3] | Total | Industrial | Commercial[4] | Domestic | Other[5] | Total |
| | BHIB | BHIC | BHID | BHIE | BHIF | BHIA | FTAE | FTAF | FTAG | FTAH | FTAI |
| 1984 | 177 | 462 | 5 307 | 8 931 | 2 424 | 17 302 | 83.85† | 53.32† | 84.04† | 8.15† | 229.36† |
| 1985 | 197 | 465 | 5 369 | 9 682 | 2 679 | 18 390 | 86.28 | 57.78 | 88.30 | 8.21 | 240.58 |
| 1986 | 75 | 420 | 4 854 | 10 242 | 2 908 | 18 499 | 86.97 | 61.44 | 91.83 | 7.86 | 248.09 |
| 1987 | 79 | 472 | 5 336 | 10 501 | 2 990 | 19 373 | 90.77 | 64.18 | 93.25 | 7.98 | 256.19 |
| 1988 | 83 | 449 | 4 856 | 10 255 | 2 996 | 18 637 | 94.13 | 67.31 | 92.36 | 7.99 | 261.79 |
| 1989 | 82 | 472† | 4 964 | 9 914 | 2 919 | 18 350 | 93.74 | 73.40 | 92.27 | 7.93 | 267.34 |
| 1986 Q3 | 18 | 84 | 929 | 1 026 | 348 | 2 405 | 20.24† | 13.45† | 16.97† | 1.82† | 52.48† |
| Q4 | 21 | 115 | 1 399 | 2 833 | 783 | 5 151 | 22.02 | 15.95 | 25.09 | 2.23 | 65.29 |
| 1987 Q1 | 19 | 128 | 1 636 | 4 588 | 1 237 | 7 608 | 23.67 | 18.25 | 30.18 | 2.15 | 74.25 |
| Q2 | 20 | 111 | 1 194 | 1 745 | 566 | 3 635 | 21.90 | 14.62 | 19.46 | 1.72 | 57.70 |
| Q3 | 19 | 95 | 1 054 | 971 | 310 | 2 449 | 21.40 | 14.12 | 17.02 | 1.81 | 54.35 |
| Q4 | 21 | 138 | 1 452 | 3 197 | 877 | 5 681 | 23.80 | 17.19 | 26.60 | 2.30 | 69.89 |
| 1988 Q1 | 21 | 138 | 1 524 | 4 096 | 1 166 | 6 945 | 24.66 | 18.68 | 28.58 | 2.10 | 74.03 |
| Q2 | 20 | 109 | 1 127 | 1 810 | 590 | 3 655 | 23.10 | 15.44 | 19.69 | 1.74 | 59.98 |
| Q3 | 20 | 89 | 929 | 1 128 | 349 | 2 514 | 22.16 | 15.20 | 17.80 | 1.84 | 57.00 |
| Q4 | 22 | 113 | 1 276 | 3 221 | 891 | 5 523 | 24.21 | 17.98 | 26.28 | 2.31 | 70.79 |
| 1989 Q1 | 22 | 124 | 1 371 | 3 766 | 1 072 | 6 355 | 24.15 | 19.94 | 28.04 | 2.11 | 74.24 |
| Q2 | 20 | 120 | 1 216 | 1 881 | 606 | 3 844 | 23.45 | 17.43 | 20.19 | 1.75 | 62.83 |
| Q3 | 19 | 98 | 960 | 962 | 308 | 2 346 | 22.48 | 16.66 | 17.20 | 1.85 | 58.20 |
| Q4 | 21 | 130 | 1 417 | 3 305 | 933 | 5 805 | 23.65 | 19.37 | 26.84 | 2.22 | 72.08 |
| 1990 Q1 | 22 | 132 | 1 555 | 3 742 | 1 106 | 6 558 | 24.45 | 20.48 | 28.28 | 2.13 | 75.33 |
| Q2 | 22† | 116† | 1 122† | 1 827† | 580 | 3 666† | 23.78 | 17.16 | 20.66 | 1.58 | 63.18 |
| Q3 | 21 | 94 | 973 | 1 098 | 340† | 2 525 | . | . | . | . | . |

1 Public supply and transport power stations.
2 Prior to 1984, as reported by the Iron and Steel Statistics Bureau. From 1984, as reported by British Gas plc.
3 Public administration, commerce and agriculture.
4 Commercial premises, transport and other service sector consumers.
5 Agriculture, public lighting and combined domestic/commercial premises.

Source: Department of Energy

**Fig. 3.1** (Reproduced by permission of the Controller of HMSO)

If the information you require is of an international character, the *Statistical Yearbook* produced by the United Nations may be of help; while for detailed information about particular industries, publications of the trade federation or association concerned might be useful – though these are often available to the general public only at great expense.

Whatever the source in which you eventually track down the published data you are seeking, there are some general points to be borne in mind when consulting it. Do make sure that you read any explanatory notes which accompany the publication – with the *Monthly Digest*, for example, there is a once-yearly booklet explaining terminology used in that year's *Digests*. *Do* read all footnotes to tables – they will draw your attention to factors which may have distorted the figures in the tables, such as industrial action by civil servants which may have resulted in some data being unavailable, changes in definitions of the quantities in the table which may produce sudden discontinuities in the data, and so on. To give you some idea of the sort of thing we are talking about, you'll find in Fig. 3.1 a typical table taken from an issue of the *Monthly Digest*.

You can also see in Fig. 3.1 that the figures are given in units of millions of therms (gas) and TWh (Terawatt-hours-electricity) to avoid cluttering up the table with a great many large figures. Again, failure to notice this might give a very misleading impression – though few readers, I hope, would follow the example of one student who, writing about unemployment statistics, missed the '1,000s' note at the top of the table and wrote throughout of the dreadful soaring figures of over 2,000 unemployed. No doubt the government wishes it could lose a factor of 1,000 unemployed as easily!

## A WORD OF WARNING

You should now have a fair idea of the various ways in which we may go about obtaining numerical information, but there is one principle which should be borne in mind when doing so, by whatever means. Simplicity should be the keynote; collect no more data than you actually need for the enquiry on hand. There is a great temptation, particularly when designing an investigation yourself, to collect data which *might* come in useful, or even to ask questions from force of habit. For instance, many questionnaires include a question as to the sex of the respondent. But unless this is really relevant to the topic of the enquiry – unless you suspect that males and females may differ in their responses in some manner pertinent to the enquiry – the question is pointless. Not only is it a waste of time to collect redundant data; when we concern ourselves in the next few chapters with the presentation and summarisation of data, we will find that presenting even relatively small amounts of data is quite time-consuming. Certainly we do not want to have to spend time and effort dealing with information which is never going to be used.

### Practical exercises

1  What kind of sample do you think might best be used in each of the following enquiries?

   (a) You want to select a 10 per cent sample of all people collecting their social security payments on a certain day, to take part in an investigation of the effects of unemployment.

   (b) You want to select a sample of 200 employees, covering all grades, both manual and non-manual, from the workforce of a large factory employing 1,500 people.

The object of your survey is to determine respondents' reactions to a proposal to re-site the factory in new premises some miles from its old site.

(c) You want to determine by examining a sample of customers at a large supermarket what proportion of them are male.

(d) You want to take a sample of receipted accounts from records stored on your firm's computer, with a view to analysing the occurrence of errors.

**2** Which of the following do you think are discrete and which continuous variables?

(a) The weights of bags of fruit-drops (nominally 100 g and 200 g bags) filled by an automatic machine.

(b) The numbers of sweets in these bags.

(c) The stock-levels of a retail shoe dealer.

(d) The stocks of grain held by a wholesale animal-feed merchant.

**3** Criticise, and if necessary suggest improved versions of, the following questions taken from a (hypothetical) survey carried out by the town council of a popular holiday resort among its residents.

(a) 'Don't you mind all the litter and mess that summer visitors create?'

(b) 'How would you describe your social class?'

(c) 'Does the council provide adequate facilities for visitors, and if not, what further facilities do you think are needed?'

(d) 'Do you think you would use a town swimming-pool if one were built?'

**4** Suggest ways in which the following might be measured.

(a) The efficacy of a new training programme for recruits to a company.

(b) The market potential of a new kind of biscuit.

(c) The 'favourability' of workers towards a new kind of protective clothing for use in a factory.

(d) The over-all level of academic achievement of applicants for an advertised post.

**5** Use government and other statistical publications to try to find the answers to the following and suggest how the information you have found might be of use to a business.

(a) How many cars were exported to the UK from Japan last year? How many cars were imported from Japan to the UK? Why do you think there is a difference between the two figures?

(b) What region of Britain has the highest percentage of homes with central heating?

(c) What was the average consumption per head in Britain last year of (i) potatoes, (ii) bread, (iii) cakes and biscuits?

(d) How many butchers' shops were there in England last year, and what was their turnover?

(e) How many first-class letters were posted in the British inland mail system last year?

## Case study

Note: All the case study problems at the ends of subsequent chapters refer to the same situation, as follows:

A friend of yours, Jane Adams, has just received a small legacy from a distant relative in Australia. She decides, rather than frittering the money away or investing it in someone else's business, to set up a small company of her own. We will follow the progress of the company as she develops it. From time to time, as the company grows and prospers, she will ask your advice on statistical problems which have arisen. The help you give in solving these problems forms the basis of the case study questions.

## Case study problem

Dear X

I told you in my last letter about the windfall I had from dear old Uncle William. Well, I've decided to show a little enterprise and set up on my own account – you know I have never been very happy at Arkwright's Mills. As I so much enjoy cooking, I think a catering business would be very suitable; I could begin by running it from home, dealing with functions such as tennis club dinners and wedding receptions.

However, all the literature I read on setting up your own business emphasises the need for good market research, so l wonder if you could help me to carry out a small survey. I would like to find out from members of the general public whether, when they attend a function such as a wedding reception, they prefer a stand-up buffet, a sit-down meal, or something in between, also what they feel they would be prepared to pay for this kind of catering, whether they like to go to a hotel or hall or have it at home, and any other information you think might be useful.

I realise this is rather vague, but I am at a very early stage of planning as yet, and will greatly appreciate any help you can give me.

Many thanks, and I hope to hear from you soon,

Jane Adams

## Case study questions

1  Discuss the design of a sample to be used for this survey, paying attention to the sampling frame you would use (if any) and the problems you might expect to encounter.

2  Draft the questionnaire you would use for the survey (aim for 6–10 questions), in the format in which it would be used if analysis were to be carried out using a computer.

3  Carry out a pilot survey on 25–40 people using your questionnaire.

4  Show, using the results of your pilot survey as illustrations, how you would present the findings of the larger-scale survey.

5  Discuss any problems which have come to light in carrying out the pilot survey, and indicate the changes you would want to make if the larger-scale study were to be undertaken.

## CHAPTER 4

# Making sense of the figures: data interpretation

## Objectives

There are no prerequisites for understanding this chapter. By the end of your work on this chapter you should be able to:

(a) examine a set of numerical data and extract from it the major features, without resorting to long calculations;
(b) carry out rough 'check' calculations to verify the accuracy of operations performed by a calculator or computer.

## THE FACTORY MANAGER'S PROBLEM

The factory manager of Universal Biscuits Ltd has been handed the figures for the outputs of two production lines making the same type of biscuits, just as he is leaving the office to catch a train to a management conference. He is now looking at the figures while on the train, with no calculator or paper on which to perform arithmetic; he wishes to check the figures and discover their main features so that he can present them in his talk at the conference. What sort of things should he be looking for?

Clearly he has to take the overall reliability of the figures on trust, although he may have a good idea as to roughly how big they should be. But there are several lines of thought which he might follow, without the need for heavy arithmetic, to help him grasp the salient points about the data.

## ERRORS AND EXPLANATIONS

The figures which the factory manager is examining can be seen in Fig 4.1. If he looks at the output figures first (Fig. 4.1(a)), probably the most obvious feature to catch his eye will be the total absence of an entry for Tuesday, 15th April. Is this merely an oversight on the part of whoever compiled the figures? Maybe on reflection he recalls that there was a serious machine breakdown on Line A that day, so the blank entry really should be a zero output.

Continuing his inspection of Line A's record, he reaches the total at the bottom of the column. It's a pretty big number – but then, we're adding up a lot of figures. Nevertheless, it doesn't look quite right. Very roughly, there are 21 figures which are round about the 2,000 mark – that will be rather an underestimate because more of them are over 2,000 than under. Then there are the Saturday figures, four of them each around 800; so we might expect the total to be somewhere in the region of $21 \times 2,000 + 4 \times 800$ which works out to 45,200. The actual total shown is 499,200; although we expected our

| Date | Line A | Line B | Total |
|------|--------|--------|-------|
| T 1st | 2,147 | 1,420 | 3,567 |
| W 2nd | 2,329 | 1,450 | 3,774 |
| T 3rd | 2,843 | 1,610 | 4,452 |
| F 4th | 1,712 | 1,320 | 3,030 |
| S 5th | 819 | 600 | 1,419 |
| | | | |
| M 7th | 2,049 | 1,220 | 3,269 |
| T 8th | 2,163 | 1,480 | 3,641 |
| W 9th | 2,496 | 1,490 | 3,986 |
| T 10th | 2,730 | 1,570 | 4,298 |
| F 11th | 1,615 | 1,370 | 2,984 |
| S 12th | 842 | 630 | 1,468 |
| | | | |
| M 14th | 1,923 | 1,230 | 3,153 |
| T 15th | | 1,450 | 1,448 |
| W 16th | 2,318 | 1,470 | 3,788 |
| T 17th | 2,811 | 1,600 | 4,411 |
| F 18th | 1,844 | 1,350 | 3,193 |
| S 19th | 803 | 630 | 1,430 |
| | | | |
| M 21st | 2,007 | 1,190 | 3,197 |
| T 22nd | 2,152 | 1,430 | 3,582 |
| W 23rd | 2,372 | 1,460 | 3,828 |
| T 24th | 2,821 | 1,610 | 4,425 |
| F 25th | 1,745 | 1,690 | 3,430 |
| S 26th | 793 | 710 | 1,502 |
| | | | |
| M 28th | 1,969 | 1,560 | 3,529 |
| T 29th | 2,206 | 1,430 | 3,636 |
| W 30th | 2,411 | 1,880 | 4,290 |
| Total | 499,200 | 34,580 | 85,229 |

**Fig. 4.1(a)** The factory manager's problem – output figures

rough check figures to be somewhat of an underestimate, it's unlikely that they would be under by 454,000! What has happened is that an extra zero has been added to the total by mistake.

Next he glances down Line B's figures, and notices something rather odd about them: they all end in zeros, whereas Line A's showed no such feature. This is hardly a coincidence; the Line B figures have probably been rounded off to the nearest ten, while the Line A data is given to the nearest unit. This immediately makes him suspicious about the 'totals' column, which is the sum of the Line A and Line B figures. If Line B's data is only accurate to the nearest ten, then of course the total can't be accurate to the unit, and so it might have been more sensible to quote that rounded to the nearest ten as well.

However, there's another worrying thing about the totals, even allowing for the rounding-off of Line B's figures. Some of the totals simply aren't right – the one for 2nd April, for instance, should be 3,779, not 3,774. Is this just an error in arithmetic? As he inspects other totals further on in the month which also seem to be wrong, he notices that they are all *less* than they should be – none is too *big* – and at once he realises what is going on. The separate figures for Line A and Line B include *all* packets produced, some of which will in fact be rejected as sub-standard. The totals, however, only include the

| Weight to | Number of packets sampled | |
|:---:|:---:|:---:|
| nearest gram | Line A | Line B |
| 215 | 8 | 6 |
| 216 | 2 | 7 |
| 217 | 2 | 7 |
| 218 | 1 | 5 |
| 219 | 0 | 6 |
| 220 | 12 | 9 |
| 221 | 15 | 11 |
| 222 | 16 | 10 |
| 223 | 11 | 13 |
| 224 | 14 | 12 |
| 225 | 27 | 15 |
| 226 | 13 | 14 |
| 227 | 11 | 15 |
| 228 | 11 | 17 |
| 229 | 12 | 13 |
| 230 | 19 | 11 |
| 231 | 8 | 10 |
| 232 | 5 | 12 |
| 233 | 1 | 9 |
| 234 | 0 | 4 |
| 235 | 7 | 0 |
| 236 | 0 | 0 |
| 237 | 1 | 0 |

**Fig. 4.1(b)** The factory manager's problem – quality inspector's reports

packets actually sent out, so that means that on 2nd April there must have been about five rejects – we can't say *exactly* five, because of the rounding-off of Line B's figures.

The factory manager has no intention of checking the addition of this column, but his experience with the Line A total has made him suspicious, although this one certainly looks about the right size. Anyway, there's an easy check he can carry out. If two odd numbers are added together, the total is even; the same is true for two even numbers, but an odd and an even add to an odd figure. So he casts his eye down the Line B column looking at the next-to-last digits because, of course, all the last ones are zero. He ignores the even digits, and just examines the odd ones (can you see why?). There are seventeen of them, so the total should be odd – but it isn't! Oh dear, not *another* error! (Actually this one isn't so serious; if you check the addition you'll find that the total ought to be 34,850 but it has been recorded as 34,580. Transposition of digits like this is a very common error.)

By now, our manager is reasonably happy about the general correctness of the data, so he turns his attention to the information conveyed by it. One feature which is not surprising to him is the low production on Saturdays for both lines – the factory only operates on Saturday morning, shutting down at noon, so the output for Saturdays, as it is the product of only three hours' work instead of eight, is rather less than half that of the other days.

More disturbing is the peak of production at mid-week, a feature common to both lines. There is no good reason that he knows of for this; it is probably due to absenteeism or declining attention to work towards the end of the week, and that 'after the weekend' feeling, or further absenteeism, on Mondays. This is something he might well decide to look into.

Turning to a comparison of Lines A and B, he is struck by the sudden jump in B's production in the last five days of the month; before that, B was well behind A, but from 25th April the gap narrows noticeably. Then he recalls that that was when the conveyor belt on Line B was overhauled; it is an older machine than A's, so it's not surprising that the production figures should, overall, be lower, but clearly having it overhauled was a good thing and has improved B's output quite a bit.

Finally he examines the quality inspector's reports on the output of the two lines (*see* Fig. 4.1(*b*)). The inspector on A is a new man, and the production manager isn't at all surprised when he sees that the weight distribution he records shows a very small number of underweight packets – and a peculiar gap just below the 'passable' weight of 220 grams! Of course, the new inspector is not *deliberately* 'fiddling' his records; but subconsciously he wants to pass as many packs as possible, so if there is one which is just a tiny bit underweight, he will slightly misread the scale and record it as over. In fact, he seems to be having trouble reading the scale altogether – can the large numbers of packets at 225, 230 and 235 grams really reflect the true position? More likely they just reflect the fact that those divisions on the scales are bigger and easier to read than the in-between ones.

The factory manager makes a mental note to have a word with the new inspector, and settles down to try to finish the *Telegraph* crossword before he reaches his destination . . . .

## WHAT NEXT?

Hopefully the factory manager's tale will have given you some idea of the kind of things you can deduce from numerical data without any elaborate calculations. But no one could pretend that this is the whole story; he still has a great many figures, which would be hard to convey verbally – he can hardly read out the whole lot to his colleagues at the conference, unless he wants to send them to sleep! Now a few appealing diagrams would be a different matter . . . .

### Practical exercises

No formal suggestions for this chapter – developing your 'feel' for numbers is something you can be doing all the time. Try getting hold of several sets of interconnected data from the *Monthly Digest*, such as figures for school population, government expenditure on education, and amount spent on new school buildings. Then see if you can spot patterns running through all the data, or apparent discrepancies which you can explain. Question the accuracy of numerical data you see in newspapers, and apply the rough checks we've looked at to test it. And, of course, apply the same thinking to your own calculations!

## CHAPTER 5

# Presenting the figures: tables and diagrams

## Objectives

Before starting work on this chapter, make sure you are happy with the following topics:

(a) calculation of percentages (see Chapter 1, pp. 11–12);
(b) plotting points on graphs (see Chapter 1, pp. 19–24)

By the end of your work on this chapter you should be able to:

(a) construct one-, two- and three-way tabulations of data, and include derived statistics as appropriate;
(b) make an informed choice of method of diagrammatic presentation for a given set of data, and draw the chosen diagram (pictogram, bar chart, pie chart, statistical map);
(c) plot simple numerical graphs;
(d) construct grouped or ungrouped frequency tables from raw numerical data and display the data by means of a histogram or ogive;
(e) critically interpret other people's tabular and diagrammatic presentations of data;
(f) ◪ use the resources of a suitable software package to produce graphical displays.

## THE MANAGEMENT TRAINEE'S PROBLEM

Charles Andrews has been working for about six months as a management trainee with Weatherguard Ltd, a medium-sized firm which manufactures weatherproof outerwear for the specialist outdoor activities market. Recently the firm has been trying to increase its sales by diversifying from the sports shops and camping centres, which have hitherto formed its major outlets, into department stores and other more general clothing retail stores. The first major task which Charles has been given is to write a detailed report on the success of this diversification.

He *thought* he had done a pretty good job on the report; he spent a lot of time getting hold of really detailed facts and figures, often collecting the information himself rather than asking other people within the firm, just to be on the safe side. It was therefore a nasty shock when, two days after the report had gone in to the managing director of Weatherguard, he received a summons to the great man's office . . . .

We will pass over some of the more painful sections of the ensuing interview but the conversation went something like this:

*Managing director* (*waving copy of report*): So you were responsible for this, were you?
*Charles* (*blushing modestly*): Er, yes.
*MD*: Hm ... and what the *** sense do you expect *me* to make of it, eh?

*C* (*sensing that all is not well*): Er, well, you know . . . .

*MD*: *I* know that I'm a very busy man, and that I haven't got time to waste plodding through all these damned figures. Look at 'em – pages and pages of the stuff – I though I was paying *you* to go through them all and give *me* the important facts. Just look at this here: 'While sales of female-sized anoraks in the North-western sales division hardly increased at all over last year's total of 3,500 items, the situation was much brighter in the Scottish division with 4,300 items sold compared with last year's disappointing figure of 2,700 . . . .' – and so it goes on. Disappointing! – I'll tell you who's disappointing – *you*! Now, what I want, by next Friday mind, is something half the size of this tome, with the figures put together so that I can get hold of them in five minutes. I don't know *what* you thought you were doing – look, what kind of sense does *this* make . . . .

Poor Charles! He has failed to grasp the basic fact that, mathematical professionals apart, the great majority of people are at best bored by numbers, and at worst frightened of them. Even those who, like the managing director, have to deal with a good deal of information in numerical form find it easier to digest if it has been preprocessed in some way. What we will do, therefore, in the remainder of this chapter is examine some of the figures from Charles' report and discuss the ways in which they might have been more effectively presented.

## THE NARRATIVE APPROACH

The bit of Charles' report which is reproduced in the managing director's speech above suggests that he has made use largely of the so-called *narrative method* of presenting his data – that is, he has embedded the figures in sentences of English prose. This can, of course, be very effective in certain situations; you need look no further than the financial pages of your daily newspaper to find articles in which, for example, the annual report and accounts of some major public company are summarised, including the salient figures, in a couple of well-designed paragraphs.

But the point about such articles is that they are generally concerned to present only a few key figures, not a mass of numerical information. The effectiveness of such a method of presentation diminishes very sharply as the amount of data increases, and if the recipient of the information wants, not only to get a general 'feel' for the figures, but actually to use them – perhaps to try and relate the behaviour of one set of figures to that of another, or to look for patterns in the values of a quantity – he or she will probably have to do quite a lot of sorting out to assemble the data required, which may be widely scattered throughout the article, interspersed with many other figures which are totally irrelevant as far as one particular user is concerned.

This is not to condemn the narrative approach altogether, nor to suggest that all reports on numerical data should consist entirely of columns of figures unmixed with any word of English. That would be even harder to swallow than the opposite extreme! It is *always* a good idea to include a few sentences of verbal explanation of any method of data presentation you choose to use – be it a graph, table, or whatever – in order to point out, for the benefit of your readers, what you consider to be the important features of the data; that way, even if they never bother to look at the data at all, you can at least feel assured that the major points have been got across. But you will increase the likelihood that they *will* look at the figures properly if, rather than leaving them to a do-it-yourself job, you present your data in the form of a well-arranged *table*.

## THE DOS AND DON'TS OF EFFECTIVE TABULATION

The major principle to bear in mind when designing a table – or, for that matter, any of the other forms of data presentation which we will be looking at later – is that your objective is *simplification* of the task of grasping the information contained therein. If it takes a reader twenty minutes to work out just what the figures in column 6(b) are supposed to mean, then your presentation, however ingenious, has failed, and you might as well have given them the raw data and told them to get on with it! Of course, the person who has designed a table isn't always the best one to judge whether it's clear or not – naturally it will be clear to *him*! So it is a good idea, if you have really complicated information to get across, to find a guinea-pig who will look at your proposed table and tell you if it is transparently clear.

Nevertheless, there are several general points which can be made about good table construction; we will illustrate them by using some of the data from the Weatherguard Ltd report mentioned in the previous section, the narrative approach. For the present, we will concentrate primarily on tabulation of qualitative data, leaving a discussion of quantitative data until later (in the section 'Tabulating quantitative data', p. 66).

The relevant section of the report originally read as follows:

'Although in 1986 much the larger part of our profits was generated by the heavy-duty "Hailguard" range, which contributed £70,000 to a total profit before tax of £90,000, the policy of diversifying our retail outlets has altered this situation. In 1987 profits from "Hailguard" sales had increased to £82,000, but those from our lighter "Rainguard" range had gone up from £20,000 to £46,000 over the same period. By 1988 this trend was even more pronounced, with "Rainguard" sales accounting for £68,000 out of a total profit of £161,000.'

Relatively simple though the data in this paragraph is, it does illustrate some of the defects of a narrative presentation. In particular, the figures are not given for each year in the same order, and in fact for two of the years you would need to calculate the sales of one type of product by subtracting the figure given for the other from the total, since only one is given explicitly.

We might start by drawing up the simplest possible type of table to show just the *total* profit for each year. This will be a one-way table, since we have profits classified according to just one criterion – the year in which they occurred. Our first attempt might look something like this:

| | |
|---|---|
| 1986 | 90,000 |
| 1987 | 128,000 |
| 1988 | 161,000 |

All the facts we wish to convey are there, but as a table this has several defects. It would be good to know what the figures in the two columns represent – it's pretty clear that the first lot are dates, but you would have to refer to the text to find out that the second column shows profits – and searching about for that information won't put your readers in a good mood! So why not include a self-explanatory *heading* to each column? And while we're at it, a *title* for the whole table wouldn't be a bad idea. That would give us the following:

**Total profits of 'Weatherguard' for the last three years**

| Year | Profit |
|------|--------|
| 1986 | 90,000 |
| 1987 | 128,000 |
| 1988 | 161,000 |

This is certainly an improvement; the italic typeface of the headings helps to clarify the fact that they aren't part of the data, and the title tells us exactly what's in the table. However, one defect of the first attempt hasn't yet been corrected. If you look at the profit figures, your eye almost certainly scans down the first digit or two of each entry in the column, and receives the impression that profits have declined drastically! True, this impression shouldn't last very long, because a second glance would show that there is an extra 0 on the end of the second and third year's figures. Nevertheless, it's another minor irritation which can easily be eliminated by making sure that the *right*-hand ends of all figures are lined up. It would, of course, be even more annoying if you wanted to add the figures up, because digits to be added would not be under each other, and you might easily make a mistake. (If you are constructing your table using a spreadsheet such as LOTUS 1-2-3, this aligning will be done automatically.)

The table is also rather cluttered up with zeros. Since *all* the profits are expressed as a round number of thousands of pounds, why not knock off the zeros and indicate in the column heading that the units are thousands of pounds. At least, we're *assuming* the profits are in pounds, and not dollars or yen — the table as it stands doesn't actually indicate this. So let's include *that* in the column heading, too. The result of all these changes will be:

**Total profits of 'Weatherguard'**
**for the last three years**

| Year | Profit (£000s) |
|------|----------------|
| 1986 | 90  |
| 1987 | 128 |
| 1988 | 161 |

This is much better, but there are still one or two things we could do to improve it, particularly if it were to be given to someone with no further explanation as a summary of 'Weatherguard's' performance. The skeptical recipient might well respond 'Who says so?' In other words where did this data come from? Even a more kindly-disposed recipient might need to know the *source* of the data, so that if necessary he could go back to that source to get further details which he might need, but which aren't given in the table as it stands. For this reason, every table should include a statement of the source from which it derives its figures, even if it's only of the form 'Company records' or 'Personal observation'.

The final change is to add the words 'Before tax' to the title, to make it absolutely unambiguous. So the ultimate version of the table is reached:

**Table I.   Total before-tax profits of 'Weatherguard'**
**for the last three years**

| Year | Profit (£000s) |
|------|----------------|
| 1986 | 90  |
| 1987 | 128 |
| 1988 | 161 |

(*Source*: Company annual reports.)

## MORE COMPLICATED TABLES

We made rather a meal out of drawing up the very simple table in the previous section, but all the points made apply, if anything with greater force, in constructing more complex tabulations. For instance, if we wished to include the breakdown into the two ranges 'Hailguard' and 'Rainguard' in the table, then we would require a two-way construction, because we have two classifications of the data – by years, and also by range. We *could*, it is true, show just the 'Hailguard' profits and the total, but this would be undesirable for two reasons – first the obvious one, that anyone who wants to know about the profits on 'Rainguard' will have to do a subtraction sum, which is annoying and might lead to errors; and second, because as far as possible it's preferable to have *non-overlapping* categories. For example, a table of births which shows four columns, headed 'Male', 'Female', 'Illegitimate', and 'Total, is confusing because, of course, the 'Total' column *isn't* the total of the other three – the babies who are counted as 'Illegitimate' also appear in either the 'Male' or 'Female' column. (This is an example which actually appears in one of the government's statistical publications!)

The best way, then, of giving the information as to the two ranges is to have the years, as before, as one set of 'headings' and the two types of product as the other. Which we put horizontally, and which vertically, is to a large extent a matter of choice, though it usually looks better to have more rows than columns in a table. There is also the point that we find it more convenient to scan a column of figures than a row mainly because we can then take in just the important first few digits (which will all be lined up under each other) more easily – so any figures which are likely to need comparing should ideally go in columns. The need to have figures which are to be totalled also underneath rather than beside each other isn't so great now that the addition will probably be done with a calculator, but could still be borne in mind.

All this having been said, we have one possible tabulation for the more detailed profits data:

**Before-tax profit breakdown of 'Weatherguard' for the past three years**

| Year | Hailguard | Rainguard |
|------|-----------|-----------|
| 1986 | 70 | 20 |
| 1987 | 82 | 46 |
| 1988 | 93 | 68 |

All figures in £000s. (*Source*: Company annual reports.)

You'll notice that we have adopted the alternative policy here of indicating the units of the data in a footnote to the table, rather than having to repeat the statement in each column heading. Now that things are getting more complicated, use has also been made of ruled lines to distinguish between row and column headings and actual data. The table is quite useful as it stands, but although we can see at a glance that both ranges are generating increasing amounts of profit, and maybe even that the balance between the two ranges is altering in favour of 'Rainguard' as time goes on, a few so-called *derived* statistics – that is, figures calculated from the original data to assist the reader – would make things much clearer.

First, we could put in a 'Total' column – clearly distinguished, of course, from the other two – but even that isn't a great deal of help on its own. So the 'Rainguard' profits went up from 20 out of 90 to 68 out of 161 over the three years – what does that tell us?

To most people, those fractions don't convey very much, because both their numerators and denominators are different. If they were expressed as percentages, however, it would be a different matter; we could then see how the shares of the profits accounted for by the two ranges of product have altered over the three-year period, without being distracted by the fact that the overall profits have also increased.

So we will add to our table the percentage figures, putting them in brackets to separate them from the actual profits. The table now looks like this:

**Table II. Before-tax profit breakdown of 'Weatherguard' for the past three years**

| Year | Hailguard | | Rainguard | | Total |
|------|-----------|------|-----------|------|-------|
| 1986 | 70 | (78) | 20 | (22) | 90 |
| 1987 | 82 | (64) | 46 | (36) | 128 |
| 1988 | 93 | (58) | 68 | (42) | 161 |

All figures in £000s. Bracketed figures are % of year's total.
(*Source*: Company annual reports.)

We could, of course, have indicated the percentage figures by a subsidiary heading rather than by a footnote; naturally, too, the percentages for each year total to 100 per cent, which could provide a useful check particularly in a situation where there might be more categories.

When we want to go one stage further again and tabulate data which is classified in three ways, we encounter the problem of drawing up our tables on a two-dimensional sheet of paper – there is no way in which we can use a separate direction for each classification. This means that inevitably we will have to repeat one of our sets of headings. This will become clear if we continue using the data above, but now imagine that we also have the figures broken down into profits on male and female garments. Then we might produce the tabulation shown below:

**Table III. Before-tax profit breakdown of 'Weatherguard' for the past three years**

| Year | Hailguard | | Rainguard | | Total | | Over-all total |
|------|-----|-----|-----|-----|-----|-----|----------------|
| | M | F | M | F | M | F | |
| 1986 | 40 | 30 | 14 | 5 | 55 | 35 | 90 |
| 1987 | 45 | 37 | 34 | 12 | 79 | 49 | 128 |
| 1988 | 53 | 40 | 46 | 22 | 99 | 62 | 161 |

All figures in £000s.
(*Source*: Company annual reports.)

You can see that we have had to repeat the male/female column headings. Of course, this isn't the only way of setting out the table – there are actually six different arrangements of this data, and which you choose depends very much on what you want to get out of the table. As arranged here, the table makes comparisons between the male and female figures for each product range easy, but we no longer have the overall total profits for each product range separately. If that were the major point of interest, then we might select one of the alternative ways of drawing up the table. We have also omitted the percentage figures, in the interests of clarity. We *could* have included them – and, for that matter, more subsidiary totals – but only at the expense of further complicating the table. In general, if you do want to fit in a lot of information of this kind, and certainly if you want to include more than three classifications of the data, it is better to draw up two or three smaller tables rather than try to cram everything on to one.

The construction of good tables is made much easier these days by the availability of computer packages, which can be used to try out several formats of a table very quickly. You should get into the habit of using the computer packages to which you have access in this way; too often students don't want to use a package unless they know exactly what they are going to do with it, whereas the great strength of computing power is in its ability to perform 'try-it-and-see' exercises without taking up time and effort.

Moreover, in a business context you might well wish to keep the format of a table fixed over a period of time, while constantly updating the figures within it. Again, this is precisely what a spreadsheet enables you to do; the skeleton of the table can be stored and the figures in it revised as the need arises. You will find more details about using LOTUS and MINITAB for tabulation in the section, 'Tables and diagrams with MINITAB and LOTUS', p. 79.

If you want to look at further examples of excellent tabulation techniques (as well as some examples of highly ingenious but totally impenetrable data presentations!) you cannot do better than to dip into the publications of the Government Statistical Service, particularly the summary publications such as *Social Trends* and *Economic Trends*. You will also notice that in these volumes, considerable use is made of charts, diagrams and so on to present the data of the tables in even more easily assimilated form.

## EASILY DIGESTED DIAGRAMS

Having gone to the trouble of presenting your data in the form of a well-designed table, you may feel that you have done your duty by your reader, and that if he *still* won't take note of the figures, then that's just his own silly fault. But to many people, even the best-organised table still consists of a mass of figures, which as far as they are concerned is an incentive to turn the page as quickly as possible. A picture of some sort, however, is a different matter, especially if it makes use of colour or striking images to attract the eye. It is this fact which advertisers are exploiting all the time, and it is this fact which you, too, must learn to exploit in devising effective presentations for your numerical data.

### The pictogram

You will almost certainly be familiar with at least the first two types of statistical diagram we are going to look at. The first, called the *pictogram*, is widely used in the press since it combines eye-catching quality with being easy to understand. You will find in Fig. 5.1 a pictogram representing the data about 'Weatherguard' shown in Table I. As you can see, the idea is simply that we represent every £10,000 of profit by one little drawing of an anorak – chosen because the image represents one of the firm's products. Then the growth in profits over the three years is shown quite graphically, and we can even get some idea of the actual size of the profits in each year.

It won't however, be a very accurate idea – just what does an anorak with one sleeve removed, as shown for 1980, represent? Clearly it will be something over £5,000, but to find out the exact figure we would have to return to the original source of the data, which should therefore always be stated. This inability to convey accurate figures limits the usefulness of pictograms to cases where you want to convey a general impression of a set

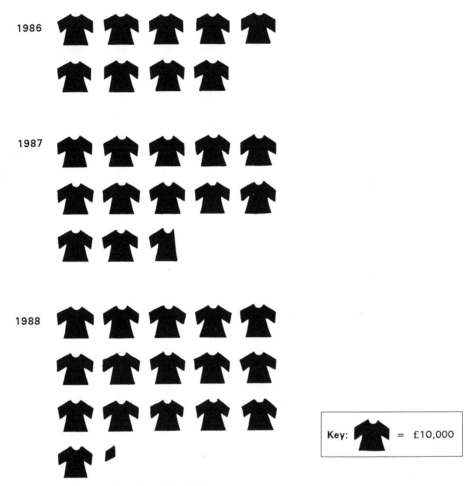

**Fig. 5.1** Pictogram showing data of Table I

of figures – preferably with not too many categories of classification – without worrying too much about the details.

There is another possible drawback to the use of pictograms which you should be aware of, although I hope you won't try to exploit it! That is that, like many forms of data presentation, they *can* be used to give a misleading impression of a set of data. For instance, suppose that 'Weatherguard' have increased their sales of ladies' overtrousers from 3,000 to 6,000 pairs during the period 1986–88. They *might* try to show this growth by drawing two pairs of trousers, the second twice as long as the first. But if that is the case, then they should also be twice as wide, so that the actual *area* of the drawing, which is what strikes the eye, will be four times as great. Indeed, if the drawing is skilful and gives a three-dimensional impression, we might even make our assessment of the growth in sales from the *volume*, which will be eight times as great! In this way, the increase is made to appear much more impressive than it actually is. The honest way, of course, would be to represent the '88 sales by *two* pairs of trousers, each the same size as that used for the 1986 figure; and in general, you should always decide on a standard 'unit' for a pictogram, and not alter its size.

## The pie chart

The second type of diagram, the *pie chart*, is also much used in newspapers, government publications and so on. The word 'pie' in a mathematical context probably conjures up vague recollections of the formula for the area of a circle, but in fact here it refers to the ordinary concept of a pie as a round thing with apples or mincemeat in it! The idea is that we use the whole 'pie' or circle to represent some set of data, and break it down into various 'slices' to illustrate how the data breaks down into different categories. For example, if we want to show how the 1988 profits of 'Weatherguard' were made up (Table III) we will need to divide our 'pie' into four 'slices', one for Hailguard (male), one for Hailguard (female), and one each for Rainguard male and female. In the past, the major drawback to constructing a pie chart was that it involved certain amount of calculation. If we want to find what angle the 'slice' representing Hailguard (male) should contain, we have to note that the entire circle, containing 360°, is to represent the total profits for the year, £161,000. So, since Hailguard (male) contributed £53,000 of this, its 'slice' should contain an angle which is 53,000/161,000 of the 360°. Thus we have:

$$\text{angle for Hailguard (male)} \quad = \frac{53}{161} \times 360 = 119°$$

and similarly:

$$\text{angle for Hailguard (female)} = \frac{40}{161} \times 360 = 89°$$

$$\text{angle for Rainguard (male)} \quad = \frac{46}{161} \times 360 = 103°$$

$$\text{angle for Rainguard (female)} = \frac{22}{161} \times 360 = 49°.$$

However, since a computer package is likely to be used today to plot the chart this no longer applies. The chart for the 'Weatherguard' data is shown in Fig. 5.2 using the convention (fairly common but by no means universal) of drawing the 'slices' in decreasing order of size, starting from a horizontal line on the left of the 'pie'. The chart certainly brings out the differences in size between the contributions of the different

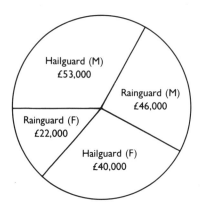

**Fig. 5.2** Pie chart of data in Table III

categories, but the criticism which we applied to the pictogram is even more relevant here: for conveying accurate information, the pie chart is useless. In fact, whereas with the aid of the key the pictogram did at least give us a vague idea of the size of the figures involved, the pie chart can do no such thing unless we actually write the numbers in each sector, as has been done here.

One difficulty with pie charts is that the human eye is not very good at judging small differences in angles, particularly if there are many small angles of almost the same size. It's therefore not a good idea to use this as a way of displaying the data if there are more than about six categories involved.

But perhaps the most limiting factor about this method of data representation is that it really isn't suited to a comparison of the breakdown of several different sets of data – for instance, the profit breakdowns in Table III over a number of years. The reason for this is easily seen if you recall that the total area of the 'pie' in each case would represent the total profits for the year; so the circle we drew for, say, 1986 would represent a total profit of £90,000. But in that case the circle for 1987 would have to have an area representing a profit of £128,000; so the ratio of the *areas* of the two circles would be 90:128. However, we draw circles not to a given area, but with a given *radius*, and you may remember that the connection between area and radius is that area = $\pi \times$ radius squared. You can perhaps begin to see that determining the radii we should use in order that the areas of our two circles should be in the ratio 90:128 is going to involve some messy calculations!

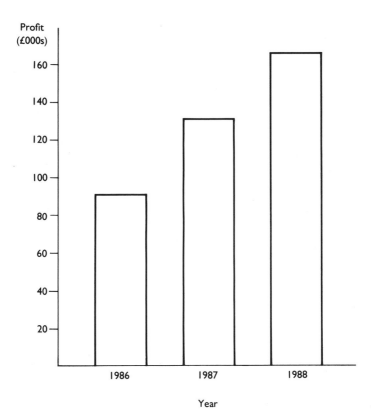

**Fig. 5.3** Bar chart of data in Table I

Roughly then, we can say that a pie chart will give a reasonable impression of the break-down of one set of data into not more than about half a dozen categories, but if we want to compare the way in which several sets of data break down, we need to adopt an alternative method.

## The bar chart

This is provided by the various forms of *bar chart*. The simplest of these is shown in Fig. 5.3, which represents the data of Table I. The diagram is almost self-explanatory, but a couple of points are worth mentioning. The width of the bars has no significance at all – it is simply chosen for convenience, as is the size of the gaps between the bars. It is a good idea always to leave *some* gap, and not put the bars directly next to each other, as this aids the clarity of the diagram. The other thing to note is that the vertical scale *must* start at zero; however tempting it may be to save paper by beginning at, say, £80,000, to do so would be quite misleading, as it would distort the relationship between the heights of the different bars. You can easily see this by placing a sheet of paper across

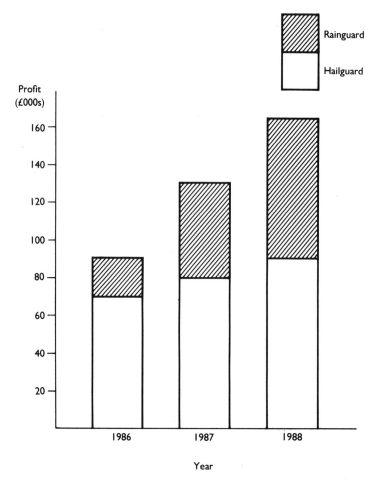

Fig. 5.4 Compound bar chart of data in Table II

Fig. 5.3 at 80 on the vertical axis, and seeing how the apparent relationship from year to year is altered.

The strength of the bar chart, however, lies not so much in this simple type as in the facility with which the bars may be subdivided to illustrate more complex classifications of the data. For example in Fig. 5.4 we have a *compound* bar chart showing the data of Table II. In this format we retain the information about *total* profit each year in easily-read form, since the height of each bar overall represents that total. If, however, we were less concerned to retain this information, but more anxious that the individual 'Hailguard' and 'Rainguard' totals should be easily accessible, we might prefer the *multiple* bar chart format shown in Fig. 5.5. Note there also the use of gaps to distinguish one year's data from the next, while the bars *within* each year are placed next to each other. Yet a third option is provided by the *percentage* bar chart (Fig. 5.6) where, of course, each year's bar has the same height, representing as it does a total of 100 per cent, but the changing balance between the two product ranges is clearly brought out.

You will realise by now that the bar chart is by far the most versatile, as well as the most accurate form of statistical diagram that we have looked at so far. Precisely because of this versatility, there is rarely one 'right' way of presenting data such as this, and you should find plenty of scope for imagination in deciding which method best suits the use which you wish to make of the diagram.

Again, use of a computer package greatly facilitates experimenting with different types of diagram – see the section 'Tables and diagrams with MINITAB and LOTUS', p. 79.

There are, of course, many other types of diagram by which we can convey numerical information; if you look in the publication *Regional Statistics* issued from time to time by the Government Statistical Service, for instance, you will find plenty of examples of *statistical maps*, and *Which?*, the Consumers' Association magazine, is a rich source of less orthodox ways of getting facts across by means of diagrams. But although you can enjoy yourself inventing your own original methods, don't lose sight of the essential objective of the exercise – to make the data more easily and attractively accessible to the reader.

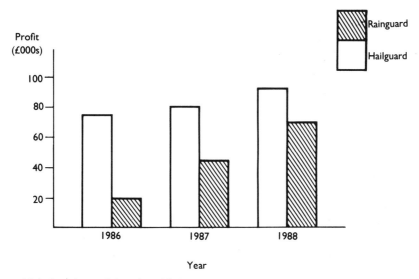

**Fig. 5.5** Multiple bar chart of data in Table II

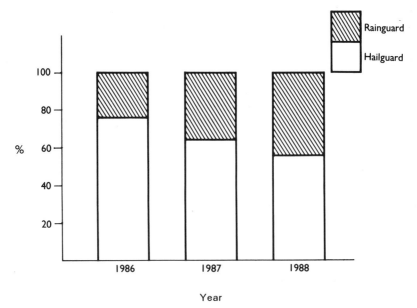

**Fig. 5.6** Percentage bar chart of data in Table II

## TABULATING QUANTITATIVE DATA

### Ungrouped frequency tables

Thus far, almost everything we have said on the subject of data presentation has applied to qualitative data – we have drawn up tables for the descriptive categories 'Hailguard' and 'Rainguard', 'Male' and 'Female', and so on, and then constructed diagrams from these tables. The position is rather different, however, if we are dealing with actual measurements, and we need to devise new types of table to deal with the difference.

Take the following statement from the 'Weatherguard' report as an example:

I contacted a sample of 25 department stores who stock our products, and asked them to tell me how many ladies' anoraks they had sold during the winter quarter. The results are given below:

| 4 | 7 | 10 | 11 | 14 | 18 | 19 | 20 | 20 | 22 |
|---|---|----|----|----|----|----|----|----|----|
| 23 | 25 | 25 | 27 | 28 | 30 | 33 | 34 | 37 | 37 |
| 38 | 45 | 48 | 50 | 52 | | | | | |

Now, as it stands, this data is not particularly easy to assimilate. You can see that the largest number sold was 52, and the smallest 4, but apart from that it would be hard to draw any conclusions as to the pattern of sales. The data has been arranged in ascending order of size, but that isn't really enough; we will have to make much more drastic simplification if we are to make the figures really easy to grasp.

This is, in the terminology of the section on multifarious measurements in Chapter 3, a set of *discrete* data; since the shops presumably do not deal in fractions of an anorak, the sales figure has to be a whole number. So we could write down a list of all the sales figures which *might* arise, and then count how many times each of them *did* arise. There's not much point in starting below 4, as we've already observed that is the lowest value in the data; equally we can stop at 52. That still leaves us with a lot of possibilities, though, many of which never occur at all:

| No. sold | No. of stores | No. sold | No. of stores | No. sold | No. of stores |
|---|---|---|---|---|---|
| 4 | 1 | 20 | 2 | 36 | 0 |
| 5 | 0 | 21 | 0 | 37 | 2 |
| 6 | 0 | 22 | 1 | 38 | 1 |
| 7 | 1 | 23 | 1 | 39 | 0 |
| 8 | 0 | 24 | 0 | 40 | 0 |
| 9 | 0 | 25 | 2 | 41 | 0 |
| 10 | 1 | 26 | 0 | 42 | 0 |
| 11 | 1 | 27 | 1 | 43 | 0 |
| 12 | 0 | 28 | 1 | 44 | 0 |
| 13 | 0 | 29 | 0 | 45 | 1 |
| 14 | 1 | 30 | 1 | 46 | 0 |
| 15 | 0 | 31 | 0 | 47 | 0 |
| 16 | 0 | 32 | 0 | 48 | 1 |
| 17 | 0 | 33 | 1 | 49 | 0 |
| 18 | 1 | 34 | 1 | 50 | 1 |
| 19 | 1 | 35 | 0 | 51 | 0 |
|  |  |  |  | 52 | 1 |

This arrangement is known as an *ungrouped frequency table*, the *frequencies* being the number of times each value in the table occurs. For example, 25 has a frequency of 2. We often denote the frequencies by the letter $f$, and the values themselves − in this case, the numbers of items sold − by $x$. An arrangement like this can be quite useful if we have to deal with a fairly small number of discrete possibilities confined to a limited range; but in the present case the values cover far too large a range for this kind of table to effect much simplification, and we resort to the further step of *grouping* the values.

## Grouped frequency tables

By 'grouping' the data we mean constructing a set of non-overlapping groups or classes, which between them cover the whole range of the data we are interested in. We can then count how many of the data values fall within each class.

In order to decide where each class shall begin and end, we recall that we must cover the range of the data − from 4 to 52 − but there is no reason why we need actually start at 4, or finish dead on 52. Life is considerably simplified, especially later on when we come to calculate means and so on, if we choose nice round numbers as our class boundaries as far as possible. We don't want, either, to have too many classes, otherwise the final table won't be much simpler than the original data. On the other hand, if we have too *few* classes, we will have thrown away too much information about the data − for make no mistake, we *are* throwing away information, however we group the figures. If the classes are sensibly chosen, however, we will effect considerable simplification while retaining the essential features of the data.

Suppose, then, that we choose to make our classes 0 to 9, 10 to 19, and so on. This will give us six classes to cover the data, which is perhaps a little on the low side, but is probably preferable to the eleven we should need if we used 0 to 4, 5 to 9, and so on. There will be just two values in the first class − 4 and 7 − as we can see by reference to the original data. Similarly, counting up the numbers of items in the other classes, we arrive at the following *grouped frequency table*:

**Table IV**

| Class | Frequency |
|-------|-----------|
| 0–9   | 2 |
| 10–19 | 5 |
| 20–29 | 8 |
| 39–39 | 6 |
| 40–49 | 2 |
| 50–59 | 2 |

You can see how this arrangement of the data immediately makes it clear that, for example, the commonest number of anoraks sold was between 20 and 29, and that values in the two highest classes didn't occur very often. If this table were given, however, to someone who did not have access to the original data – which would probably be the case in practice – they would have no way of knowing whether the '2' in the frequency column for the first class indicates that there is one store which sold no anoraks at all, or whether both those two in fact sold nine anoraks. This is what was meant by the loss of information which is the price we pay for simplification.

There are several things which we have taken for granted in drawing up this table but which aren't really essential. The first is that all the classes are the same size. We will discover later that this does have many advantages, but there is no reason why, for instance, we should not choose to have classes 20–24, 25–29, 30–34 and 35–39 in the middle of the table where a lot of the values occur, but larger classes 0–9, 10–19 and 50–59 at the ends where the values are more scattered. The second point is that here we *knew* where to start and end the table, because we had the data in front of us and could see that it ranged from 4 to 52. If, however, we had been sending someone out to collect the data, and wished to give him the table so that as he went along he could enter the data values he found into the appropriate class, then we would have very little idea where to stop the table. It's pretty clear that we must begin, at worst, at zero, since no store can sell less than that number of anoraks; but the easiest way to cope at the upper limit is to make use of an *open* class, such as '50 and upwards', to ensure that, whatever the highest value encountered may be, it will find a place in our table.

One final matter before we leave this set of figures: we can easily check that we have included all the data when constructing the table, by making sure that the 'frequency' column adds up to 25, the total number in our sample. The information given in the frequency table is often referred to as a *frequency distribution*, since it shows how the frequencies are distributed among the various classes.

## Another example

The frequency table above was easy to construct because we knew, since the data was discrete, exactly what values we might expect to occur. If, however, we have continuous data, the situation is rather different. Consider, as an illustration, this set of data, again taken from the 'Weatherguard' report, representing the average number of miles travelled by salesmen for each effective call they make:

| | | | | | | | |
|---|---|---|---|---|---|---|---|
| 10.1 | 43.6 | 12.9 | 37.4 | 33.2 | 27.4 | 39.7 | 36.3 |
| 34.0 | 47.0 | 25.5 | 51.7 | 37.6 | 28.5 | 47.9 | 36.8 |
| 37.9 | 28.0 | 33.8 | 38.5 | 39.6 | 33.7 | 32.0 | 22.6 |
| 25.9 | 17.3 | 55.0 | 44.7 | 32.5 | 11.2 | 37.0 | 36.4 |
| 31.1 | 24.0 | 46.8 | 43.3 | 58.0 | 44.1 | 35.0 | 40.0 |

It is clear that these values have been quoted to the first decimal place only, but of course they are actually values of a continuous variable. So the kind of class boundaries which we used in our first frequency table won't cover this case; there, we were able to specify a class as, for example, '10–19' because, knowing that the data represented numbers of anoraks sold, we could be sure that we would never encounter a value of 19.5 which might, as it were, fall down the hole between these two classes. But in the present case, if we had classes '30–39' and '40–49' then the value 39.7 occurring in the table above would not be covered by either.

Nor can we take the apparently obvious step of making the classes '30–40' and '40–50', because that would give us an ambiguity as to where the value 40.0 should be placed. So we resort to the rather long-winded but safe expedient of making our classes '10 but under 20', '20 but under 30', and so on; that way, every value up to 20, including 19.9999 should we happen to be working to that level of accuracy, would be placed in the first class, but 20 would definitely belong in the second. (Of course, there is nothing to stop you always using this system, even when the data is discrete – though that can lead to problems later in working out averages, as we will see.)

Having got round this problem, there is another minor difficulty associated with tabulating this data. In the previous example, the data was already arranged in increasing order of size, so that it was easy to count how many values there were in each class. Here, we have a haphazard arrangement of the data, but there is no need to rearrange it in order before drawing up the frequency table if we make use of a *tally*.

This means that, rather than dotting about the raw data trying to count say, all the values in the '20 but under 30' class, we proceed through the table in an orderly manner, either going down columns or along rows, and for each value encountered we place a tally or mark opposite the appropriate class. When the table has been completely covered in this way, we simply have to count the number of marks opposite each class to arrive at the frequency – the process of counting up being considerably easier if we place every fifth tally across the preceding four, so that a count in multiples of five can be made quickly. The whole process is illustrated below.

**Table V**

| No. of miles per effective call | Tally | No. of salesmen |
|---|---|---|
| 10 but less than 20 | IIII | 4 |
| 20 but less than 30 | JHT II | 7 |
| 30 but less than 40 | JHT JHT JHT III | 18 |
| 40 but less than 50 | JHT III | 8 |
| 50 but less than 60 | III | 3 |

Again, the accuracy of our tabulation can be checked to a certain extent by making sure the frequencies total to 40, since that was the number of items in our raw data.

Tables of this kind are useful in showing such features of the data as its range, whereabouts the majority of values occur, and so on. But often we want answers to a somewhat different type of question: not 'How many salesmen did between 30 and 40 miles per call?' but 'If we define an efficient salesman as one who has to travel under 40 miles per effective call, how many of this sample count as efficient?' In other words what we want is the number of items *less than* a certain value, and the question is most conveniently answered by converting the table above into a *cumulative* frequency table.

We will begin this table with a class 'under 10', which will, of course, contain none of the salesmen, since they all did at least ten miles per call. In the next class, 'under 20', we have just the four salesmen who did 10 but under 20 miles per call. In the next class, however, which is 'under 30', we have both the 4 in the '10 but less than 20' group, *and* the 7 in the '20 but less than 30' group – that is, 11 salesmen altogether. You can now see why we call this a cumulative frequency table – as we proceed through the table, we accumulate more and more of the frequencies until we end up with all 40 salesmen in the 'under 60' class. The complete cumulative table is shown below:

**Table VI**

| No. of miles per effective call | No. of salesmen |
|---|---|
| Less than 10 | 0 |
| Less than 20 | 4 |
| Less than 30 | 11 |
| Less than 40 | 29 |
| Less than 50 | 37 |
| Less than 60 | 40 |

We could have constructed the table from the opposite end, as it were, by asking how many salesmen did 50 or more miles, 40 or more, and so on; but as this arrangement would effectively convey the same information as the 'less than' table above, it is not usually used, and if a 'cumulative frequency table' is referred to, you are safe in assuming that a 'less than' table is meant.

A word of caution needs to be said on the subject of constructing cumulative tables for *discrete* data. If we revert to our data concerning numbers of anoraks sold, where the classes used were 0–9, 10–19, etc., then the first class in a cumulative table produced from these figures would be, not 'less than 9', but 'less than 10', because the value 9, should it occur, is actually included in the first group. For this reason, try not to succumb to the temptation to turn the ordinary frequency table into a cumulative one by merely tacking on the cumulative frequencies down the side; it really is worthwhile, particularly to avoid confusion in this sort of discrete situation, going to the effort of writing out a *separate* cumulative table.

## DIAGRAMS FROM FREQUENCY TABLES

The kinds of diagrams we discussed in the section 'Easily digested diagrams', p. 60 – bar charts, pie charts and so on – are very well suited to the presentation of qualitative data, but we need to develop rather different methods to cope with quantitative data such as we have tabulated in the preceding section. We will look specifically at two such methods

— the *histogram*, by means of which an ordinary grouped frequency table may be represented, and the *ogive*, constructed from the cumulative frequency table.

## The histogram

Probably the easiest way to introduce the histogram is to discuss the one in Fig 5.7, which displays the data on salesmen's mileages per call discussed above. At first sight this may appear to you to differ very little from a bar chart, but a closer examination should reveal some important differences. Most significant is the fact that the width of each 'block' in the histogram is no longer simply a matter of convenience; there is a genuine numerical scale on the horizontal axis, and the width of each block relates to this. If one of our classes happened to be twice the width of the others, then the block representing that class would also be twice as wide. For the same reason, there are no gaps between the blocks; the first represents all values from 10 up to 19.99999 . . . ., which takes us right up to 20, the beginning of the next block.

If you inspect the vertical axis of the histogram, you may well suspect that the printers – or the author! – have forgotten to include the label for this axis. The numerical scale is there, but why no explanation as to what it's measuring? But in fact the omission is deliberate because the vertical scale itself isn't measuring anything. If you give a histogram a cursory glance, what surely makes the impression on your eye is not so much the *height* of each block as the overall *area* occupied by the histogram, and the shape of that area. This doesn't make much difference if all the classes are the same width, in which case the height of each block and its area are proportional; but it becomes absolutely crucial if we have one or more non-standard classes.

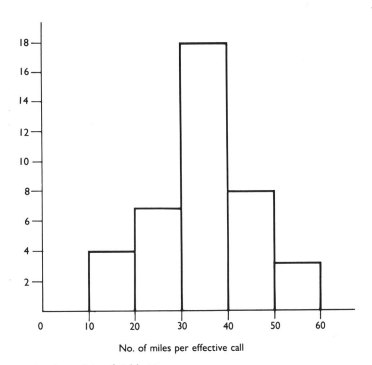

Fig. 5.7 Histogram to show data of Table V

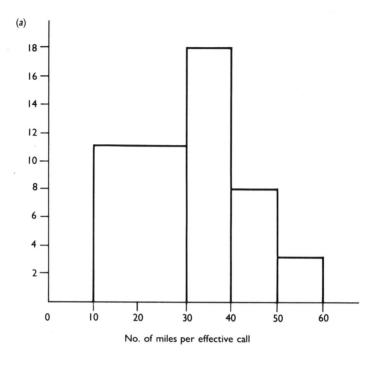

No. of miles per effective call

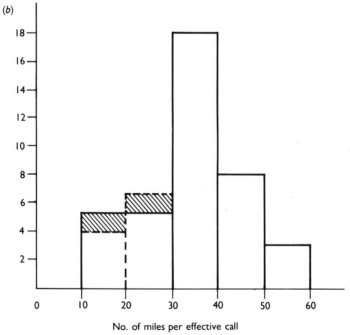

No. of miles per effective call

**Fig. 5.8** Combination of classes (a) incorrect; (b) correct

To see why this should be, imagine that the first two classes of the data in Table V are combined, giving a class '10 but less than 30' with a frequency of 11. If we were to represent this combined class in the histogram by a block extending from 10 to 30, and having a height of 11, as shown in Fig. 5.8(*a*), we would give a very misleading impression that a large proportion of the salesmen did under 30 miles per sale; this impression is conveyed by the large area occupied by the 10–30 block. What we want to do is combine the blocks in such a way that the overall area of the new 'combined' block is exactly equal to the areas of the original two blocks added together, so that the impression of area given by the diagram does not alter.

This can be done by adjusting the height of the new combined block in such a way that its area represents a frequency of 11 on the same scale as all the other blocks. Since this class is now twice as wide as all the other classes – we might say it has a width of two standard classes – we need only plot a block 5.5 units in height to produce an area of 11 units. This is shown in Fig. 5.8(*b*) where you can also see how the area of the new combined block is just the same as that of the two original blocks, the added and removed pieces (shaded in the figure) being equal.

In general then, if we have a class which is twice the width of the other, 'standard' classes in the distribution, we must plot that block of the histogram with a height equal to half the frequency; if we have a class three times as wide as the standard, the height of its block will only be one-third of the frequency, and so on. It would clearly be quite wrong, then, to label the vertical axis of the histogram 'frequency' or 'number of salemen' – that would suggest that there were 5.5 salesmen who did 10 but under 30 miles per call! You will sometimes find the label 'relative frequency' used, but there is really no need for any label; if you feel you *must* show the scale, then an *area* scale is the right way to do it.

This histogram represented data which was definitely continuous, but there is something of a 'grey area' between histograms and bar charts when it comes to discrete data. For an ungrouped frequency table like that in Table VII, we really are back with bar charts, as shown in Fig. 5.9.

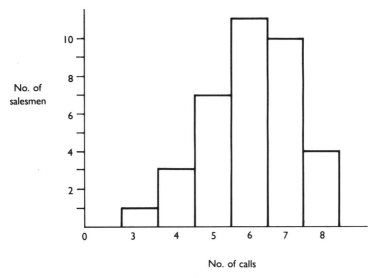

**Fig. 5.9** Bar chart of data in Table VII

**Table VII. Distribution of numbers of calls made by salesmen in one day**

| No. of calls | No. of salesmen making this no. of calls |
|:---:|:---:|
| 3 | 1 |
| 4 | 3 |
| 5 | 7 |
| 6 | 11 |
| 7 | 10 |
| 8 | 4 |

With a grouped discrete table, however, such as that in Table IV, you will find several versions of the labelling of the horizontal axis, as shown in Fig. 5.10, in use. Certainly the diagram should be treated like a histogram in terms of the adjustment needed if there are some non-standard classes.

One final headache about drawing histograms is the problem of open classes: how does one show a class '60 and over' on a histogram? The simple answer is that one doesn't; if you really want to draw a histogram for a distribution which has such a class, you will have to begin by assuming some upper limit to the open class – usually on common sense grounds. For example, a class '90 and over' in an age distribution might well be closed at 100 on the grounds that hardly anyone lasts longer than that. Sometimes, if such a 'closing assumption' has had to be made, the corresponding block of the histogram will be enclosed by a broken line, intended to show that the point of closure is only conjectural.

By now you are probably beginning to think that histograms are more trouble than they are worth – a point of view with which I would, on the whole, concur. They provide a useful picture of the general shape of a distribution, but cannot be used to give any further information about its characteristics – a defect which renders them very much inferior to graphs of cumulative frequency tables, to which we now turn.

## The ogive

Such a graph for the data of Table VI, is shown in Fig. 5.11. It is termed an *ogive*

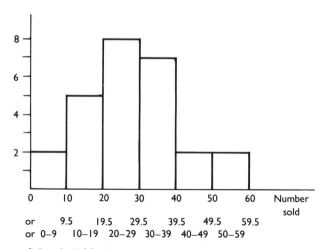

**Fig. 5.10** Histogram of data in Table IV

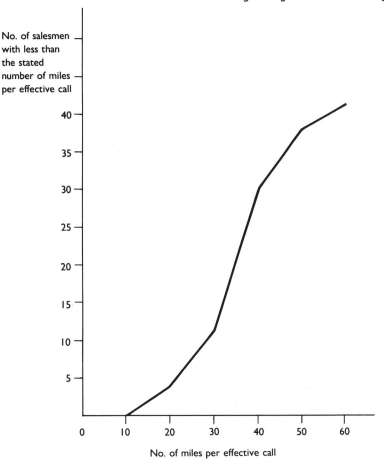

**Fig. 5.11** Ogive of data in Table VI

(pronounced variously with hard or soft 'g'), from its characteristic shape, which is similar to that of half of an ogival arch in architectural terminology. It always has this upward-climbing shape, of course, since the cumulative frequencies grow steadily larger.

The ogive is easy to plot, as it's just an ordinary graph of the cumulative frequencies. The only possible confusion will arise if you have neglected the advice given in the section 'Tabulating quantitative data', p. 66, and added the cumulative frequencies to the side of your ordinary frequency table like this:

|  | f | Cum. f |
|---|---|---|
| 10 but less than 20 | 4 | 4 |
| 20 but less than 30 | 7 | 11 |

and so on. In that case you may well wonder whether to plot the cumulative frequency 11 opposite to 20, or 30, or somewhere in the middle. If, however, you had taken the trouble to write out a new table:

| Less than 20 | 4 |
|---|---|
| Less than 30 | 11 |

etc., it would be quite clear to you that the frequency 11 is to be plotted above 30 on the horizontal axis. Incidentally, the convention of putting the class boundaries on the horizontal axis and the cumulative frequencies on the vertical axis is absolutely standard – an ogive plotted the other way round looks very funny to a statistician.

There are two things about the ogive of Fig. 5.11 which may strike you as funny, particularly if you have come across such graphs before. One is that the points of the graph are connected by straight lines rather than a smooth curve. This is not merely because the author is incapable of drawing a 'smooth curve' which does not look like a string of telegraph wires; there is a logical reason for it. When we connect up the points of the graph in *any* way we are making some kind of assumption about how the points within each class are distributed. But at least, with a straight line, we *know* what we are assuming – namely, that the values in each class are spread uniformly throughout the class. With a so-called smooth curve, there is no knowing *what* assumptions are involved – and probably no two people's curves will be the same anyway; hence the author's preference for straight lines.

The second thing is that the label on the vertical axis of the graph no doubt strikes you as very long-winded; and indeed, you *could* simply label it 'cumulative frequency'. But, labelled as in Fig. 5.11, we have a clear statement of exactly *what* the graph is designed to show – and, incidentally, a demonstration of why the ogive is so much superior to the histogram in terms of the information it can convey. Suppose, for example, that we wish to determine how many salesmen are efficient, if efficient is defined as doing 45 miles per effective call or less. We can't find this directly from Table VI, since 45 is midway between class boundaries; but if we go along the horizontal axis to 45, and then up the graph and across to the corresponding point on the vertical axis, we can read off that the number of salesmen doing less than 45 miles per effective call is about 33.

We will find in the next chapter that the ogive, once plotted, can give us measurements which form a useful summary of the behaviour of the entire distribution, by very much the same simple procedure we've just carried out. So by plotting it you are not merely giving a useful display of the data, but preparing for further operations on that data in the future.

Although histograms and ogives are still the types of statistical diagram most widely used and included in examination syllabuses, there are several more recent arrivals on the scene, generally included under the title of Exploratory Data Analysis (EDA). You will find a discussion of these approaches in reference (17) in Suggestions for Further Reading in Appendix 1, and one of them, the oddly-named 'box-and-whisker' diagram, is illustrated in the next chapter.

## SOME SIMPLE GRAPHS

We have already discussed a few graphs in Chapter 1, in the sections on straight line and other types of graph, and we will be encountering many more in later chapters. But the graphs examined in Chapter 1 were those of algebraic expressions, particularly straight lines, whereas the object of the present section is to look at some numerical graphs which can be used as an effective way of presenting data. In particular, we will get away from the idea of a graph as a smooth or continuous curve, and discover that in many cases, it would be quite wrong, even impossible, to try to draw such a curve through a set of points.

## A 'spiky' graph

Take the following set of figures, again abstracted from the 'Weatherguard' report mentioned at the beginning of the chapter, which give the total revenue generated by the sales of 'Hailguard' outerwear for the years 1985–87, summarised quarterly. The figures are in £000s:

| Year | Quarter | Sales revenue |
|------|---------|---------------|
| 1985 | 1 | 256 |
|      | 2 | 220 |
|      | 3 | 130 |
|      | 4 | 283 |
| 1986 | 1 | 260 |
|      | 2 | 225 |
|      | 3 | 137 |
|      | 4 | 288 |
| 1987 | 1 | 264 |
|      | 2 | 227 |
|      | 3 | 141 |
|      | 4 | 290 |

It is clear simply from a glance at the figures that there is a pattern in the sales for each year, which vary in a fairly regular manner from quarter to quarter. However, the pattern is made much clearer by plotting the data on a graph, with time on the horizontal axis and revenue on the vertical axis, as in Fig. 5.12. But it is certainly not possible to join the points of this graph by smooth curves; nor should we try to do so. The lines connecting the points here have no function except to emphasise the shape of the pattern produced by the figures; there can be no question, for example, of reading off an intermediate figure of 181 as the sales half-way between the second and third quarters of 1986, as one might do with the sorts of graph we looked at in Chapter 1. Nevertheless,

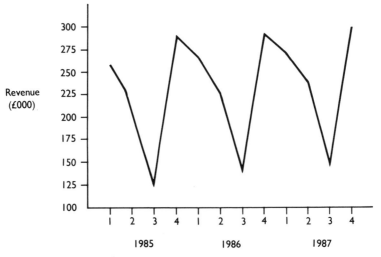

**Fig. 5.12** Graph of 'Weatherguard' quarterly revenue

such graphs are very useful if we wish to identify the kind of patterns inherent in data of this kind; we will be encountering them again in Chapter 14.

## A 'stepped' graph

In other cases, the appropriate way of connecting the points of the graph is not by jagged straight lines, as in Fig. 5.12, but by a 'stepped' form of line. If, for instance, 'Weatherguard' want to show graphically the interest rates which they have been charged by their bank on loans over the past few years, they could do so as shown in Fig. 5.13. The graph takes this 'stepped' shape because the interest rate will remain constant for a certain length of time, then change suddenly and immediately to a new value. The vertical parts of the graph again have no significance – they are there merely to connect the horizontal sections. It would be very misleading here if we tried to connect the points in some other way, perhaps as shown by the dotted lines in Fig. 5.13. These would suggest that an interest rate of 15 per cent was being charged on November 15th, whereas of course such a rate never applied – the rate actually decreased at one jump from 16 per cent to 14 per cent.

## A scattergraph

There is a third type of graph, more extreme than either of the two we have looked at so far, where we make no attempt to connect the points in any way whatsoever. Such a graph is shown in Fig. 5.14, and you can see at a glance why it goes by the name of *scattergraph*. The object of the graph is to demonstrate what sort of relationship, if any, exists between two quantities – in this case, the amount 'Weatherguard' spends on advertising 'Hailguard' outerwear and the sales revenue generated by that product group. The firm presumably hopes that larger advertising expenditures will result in larger sales, and the scattergraph showing both quantities over a period of five years suggests that something of the kind is indeed true; the larger values of sales revenue occur at larger values of advertising expenditure, and the smaller sales revenues at smaller advertising

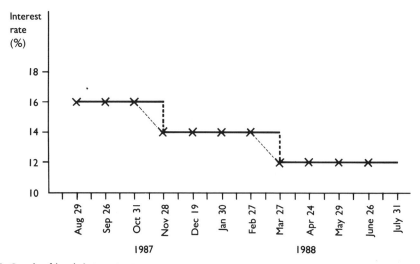

**Fig. 5.13** Graph of bank interest rate

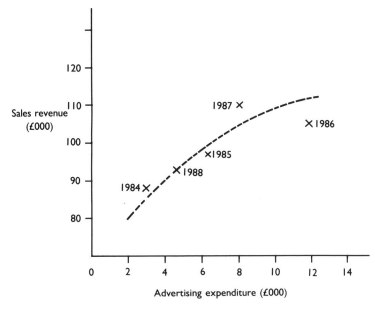

**Fig. 5.14** Scattergraph of relationship between advertising and revenue for 'Hailguard' outerwear

expenditures. The points also seem to cluster around a curve of the approximate shape indicated by the dotted line, which might suggest a further line of investigation if we wanted to determine the relationship between the two quantities more exactly. We will be pursuing this topic in Chapter 12; at present we mention the scattergraph simply as yet another example of a graph far removed from the smooth graphs which are probably most familiar to you from school work.

## ◪ TABLES AND DIAGRAMS WITH MINITAB AND LOTUS

If you already have your data stored as either a MINITAB or a LOTUS worksheet, you can make use of the facilities they offer for tabulation and graphing, though these are not always ideal, as we will see.

### MINITAB

The command TABLE C1 C2 will produce a cross-tabulation of the values in columns 1 and 2, as long as these are integers. Row and column totals are automatically shown. Moreover, by the use of subcommands such as COUNT, ROWPERCENT, COLPERCENT and TOTPERCENT, we can also display the frequency for each cell, and the percentage which each cell represents out of the row, column or overall total. And with the subcommand MEAN C3, we can insert into each cell the mean of the C3 values for that cell.

For example, refer to the worksheet EMP.MTW described in Chapter 2, which contains columns as follows:

C1, named 'STATUS', contains the status of an employee – 0 = full-time, 1 = part-time

C2, named 'SEX', contains the gender of the employee – 0 = male, 1 = female
C3, named 'AGE', contains the employee's age in years last birthday.

Then Table VIII at the bottom of this page shows the results of the command

MTB⟩ TABLE C1 C2;
SUBC⟩COUNT;
SUBC⟩ROWP;
SUBC⟩MEAN C3.

The table shows a cross-tabulation of status (rows) against sex (columns), with each cell containing a count of the number of people falling in that cell, what percentage they constitute of that row, and what the mean age is for this group. Thus the top left-hand cell, for example, shows that there are 10 female full-timers, who constitute 23.81 per cent of all full-timers, and whose average age is 36.6 years.

By judicious use of combinations of sub-commands, it is possible to produce a great variety of tables very easily. One thing which MINITAB does *not* do easily, however, is to construct a grouped frequency table – you can see the result of the command TABLE 'AGE' in Table IX on p. 81; it is merely a list of all the ages with their frequencies.

MINITAB also offers a number of diagrams. You can see the results of the commands HIST (for histogram – remember that only the first four characters of a MINITAB command are read) and DOTPLOT in Figs. 5.15 and 5.16, using the AGE data; as you can see, the histogram is turned sideways, while the dotplot looks very much like a histogram. It is possible to alter the scales of these plots, but left to its own devices, MINITAB will select a default scale which always uses equal class intervals.

One particularly handy feature is the BY subcommand, which enables us to construct dotplots for different subgroups of the data on the same scale, so that comparison is easy. For example, the command

MTB⟩ DOTPLOT 'AGE';
SUBC⟩BY 'STATUS';

gives the picture in Fig. 5.17, making it clear that the age-distributions of full- and part-time workers do not differ greatly.

**Table VIII**

| *ROWS: status* | | *COLUMNS: sex* | |
| --- | --- | --- | --- |
| | 0 | 1 | ALL |
| 0 | 10 | 32 | 42 |
| | 23.81 | 76.19 | 100.00 |
| | 36.600 | 38.750 | 38.238 |
| 1 | 14 | 4 | 18 |
| | 77.78 | 22.22 | 100.00 |
| | 35.000 | 39.250 | 36.722 |
| ALL | 24 | 36 | 60 |
| | 40.00 | 60.00 | 100.00 |
| | 36.250 | 38.806 | 37.783 |

CELL CONTENTS —
COUNT
% OF ROW
age:MEAN

**Table IX**

| ROWS: age | |
|---|---|
| | COUNT |
| 17 | 1 |
| 20 | 1 |
| 23 | 1 |
| 27 | 1 |
| 28 | 2 |
| 29 | 1 |
| 30 | 3 |
| 31 | 2 |
| 32 | 1 |
| 33 | 2 |
| 34 | 3 |
| 35 | 1 |
| 36 | 5 |
| 37 | 4 |
| 38 | 8 |
| 39 | 1 |
| 40 | 3 |
| 41 | 2 |
| 42 | 2 |
| 43 | 3 |
| 44 | 2 |
| 45 | 3 |
| 47 | 1 |
| 48 | 2 |
| 49 | 2 |
| 50 | 1 |
| 51 | 1 |
| 57 | 1 |
| ALL | 60 |

```
Histogram of age    N = 60

Midpoint    Count
      15        1   *
      20        1   *
      25        2   **
      30        9   *********
      35       15   ***************
      40       16   ****************
      45        9   *********
      50        6   ******
      55        1   *
```

**Fig. 5.15**

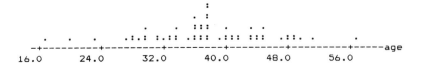

**Fig. 5.16**

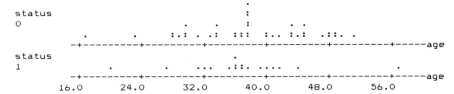

**Fig. 5.17**

Finally, if a straightforward scatter plot is required, the command

MTB〉 PLOT C1 C2

will produce a graph on which the values in the worksheet are plotted with C1 as the *y*-axis and C2 as the *x*-axis.

## LOTUS

It is particularly easy to set up one-way frequency tables in LOTUS, but you need to think ahead and set up a column containing the class limits. For example, if we want to tabulate the numbers of full- and part-time employees from the data in EMP.WK1, we put the numbers 0 and 1 into two cells one below the other in the worksheet (say, E1 and E2), making sure that the cells in the next column to the right are not occupied. We then select the sequence

/ data distribution

from the menu, after which we are prompted for the *values range*. In our case, this is cells A2 to A61, so we enter this range, either directly or by pointing. We are then asked for the *bin range*, which means the specification of the class limits, so we enter the range E1 to E2. LOTUS then counts how many 0s and 1s are in the values range, and inserts the corresponding frequencies into cells F1 and F2 – plus a zero in cell F3 indicating that there are no higher values. Thus we see that there are in fact 42 full-time and 18 part-time employees in the dataset.

If we are constructing a grouped frequency table, the LOTUS convention is that all values up to and including the bin limit are included in the frequency count. So if we were tabulating the age data; our first step might be to use LOTUS @MAX and @MIN functions to examine the range of ages involved. If we then enter a bin range 20, 30, 40 and so on, the frequency placed opposite 20 will be the count of all employees aged 20 or under, that opposite 30 will be all those aged 21–30, etc. Such a frequency table can then easily be turned into the cumulative format – I leave it as an exercise for LOTUS users to work out the most efficient way of doing this. One point to beware of is that the frequencies are always placed in cells immediately to the right of the corresponding bin limit, so if you have two sets of data which you wish to tabulate using the same bin limits, you will need to copy the limits, otherwise the second lot of frequencies will overwrite the first. Once the table has been constructed, of course, the limits can be overwritten with something more meaningful, such as our '21 and up to 30' format, and the columns given suitable titles.

LOTUS certainly has the edge over MINITAB where diagrams are concerned, since it provides simple and compound bar charts and pie charts as well as ordinary *xy*-graphs.

All are constructed by selecting

/ GRAPH

from the menu, followed by the specification of the required type of graph. There are also many facilities for improving the layout of graphs by adding titles, legends, labels on axes and so on. Figures 5.18 and 5.19 show respectively a pie chart of the employee status figures from EMP.WK1, and an ogive of the age data from the same dataset; see if you can reconstruct these for yourself. If you wish to print the diagrams, you will need to save them using the sequence

/ GRAPH SAVE

and giving them different names. They will be stored as NAME.PIC and can then be printed via the PRINTGRAPH module. More recent issues of LOTUS have simpler ways of printing graphs.

One thing version 2.3 of LOTUS cannot do is to produce a proper histogram; Fig. 5.20 is the nearest we can get with the age data, using the bar-chart specification, but as you

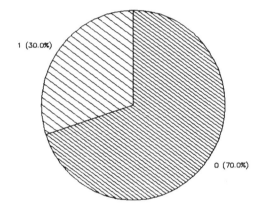

**Fig. 5.18**

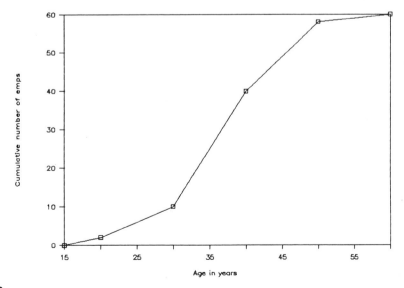

**Fig. 5.19**

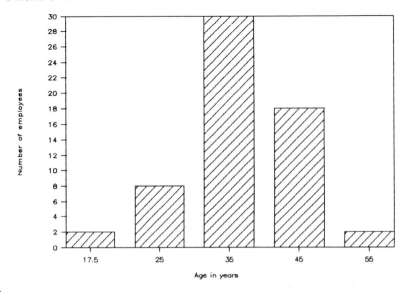

**Fig. 5.20**

can see no allowance has been made for the unequal class widths, and gaps have been left between classes. This would be fine if we were charting, say, the discrete equally-spaced STATUS or SEX columns, for which a bar chart would be adequate, but for continuous data it is not very satisfactory.

The great strength of using a computer package to do your tables and diagrams is that you can try lots of different versions very quickly on the screen, and decide which you prefer before printing. However it's important not to be persuaded to use a particular format simply because it is provided by your software. For example, it is now quite easy to produce '3-dimensional bar-charts', with shadow effects to enhance the solidity of the bars, but this rarely improves the clarity of the information communicated by the diagram. Use it only if you are more interested in impact than in conveying quantitative information.

## HOW *NOT* TO DO IT

Before we leave the topic of visual presentation of data altogether, one final note of caution: we have been discussing the *honest* presentation of figures by means of diagrams, and I hope that is what you are interested in doing, but it *is* possible to make use of these methods in a deliberate attempt to *mis*represent a situation. Beware, for instance, of the graph with no label on the vertical axis, perhaps even no scale at all, as in Fig. 5.21(*a*); treat with caution the graph in which the vertical axis is broken without any indication to the reader, as in Fig. 5.21(*b*) (sometimes one is forced to do this, but the reader's attention should be drawn to the fact by showing a deliberate break in the scale, as Fig. 5.21(*c*) illustrates). Not everyone will be as honest as you! For more illustrations of the dishonest use of statistical data, look at reference (3) in the Suggestions for Further Reading in Appendix 1; for some examples of both good and bad data presentation, see also reference (13).

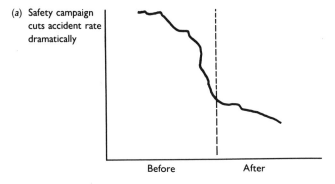

(a) Safety campaign cuts accident rate dramatically

Before     After

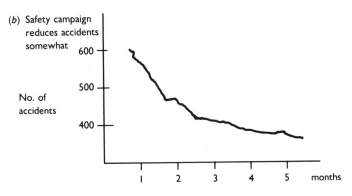

(b) Safety campaign reduces accidents somewhat

No. of accidents

600

500

400

1   2   3   4   5   months

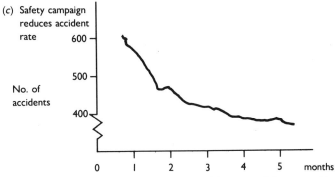

(c) Safety campaign reduces accident rate

No. of accidents

600

500

400

0   1   2   3   4   5   months

**Fig. 5.21** Right and wrong way of presenting information: (a) wrong; (b) wrong; (c) right

## Practical exercises

1  Tabulate the data contained in the following extract from a company report:

'This year saw an increase of 20 per cent over last year's total of 11,000 customers. We classify our customers, one quarter of whom are overseas, as 'regular', 'occasional', or 'dormant', according to the number of orders they have placed in the past year. Overall, 'regular' customers formed 60 per cent of the total, and only 10 per cent were classed as 'dormant', though among overseas customers the proportions in the three categories were 3 : 2 : 1.'

2  Produce a diagram illustrating the data of Problem 1 suitable for inclusion in the report.

3   A sample of 1,000 receipted bills was taken from a firm's files, and checked for errors. Of the bills 105 contained errors which were classified as follows:

In firm's favour by
| under 5p | 32 |
| 5p but under 10p | 11 |
| 10p but under 15p | 4 |
| 15p but under 20p | 1 |
| 20p or more | 1 |

In customer's favour by
| under 5p | 29 |
| 5p but under 10p | 18 |
| 10p but under 15p | 7 |
| 15p but under 20p | 0 |
| 20p or more | 2 |

Construct a diagram to represent this data.

4   The council of a seaside resort has carried out a small-scale survey to find out how far day visitors travel to the resort. The raw results are as follows (figures in miles):

12, 23, 14, 27, 14, 8, 19, 27, 25, 11, 17, 32, 22, 25, 42, 13,
9, 36, 16, 5, 13, 22, 28, 6, 29, 37, 24, 24, 7, 28, 34, 56, 21,
39, 12, 18, 25, 45, 33, 31.

Tabulate these figures in a manner which could be used at a council meeting.

5   Get hold of a list of postal charges for first-class letters and from it draw a suitable graph showing charge against weight, which could be used in a firm's post room.

6   Look at *Social Trends*, *Economic Trends*, *Regional Statistics*, or other government statistical publications, noticing what kinds of diagrams are used to present particular types of data. Be critical!

7   Collect examples of bad or misleading diagrams from the press (pseudo-scientific advertisements are a rich source), and look out, too, for articles in which numerical information is presented in narrative style.

8   ⏚ For the data in the file STUD.MTW/STUD/WK1/STUD.DAT, draw up (*a*) a frequency distribution of ages for male and female students; (*b*) a table showing subject of first degree and gender. For each of these tables, construct a diagram suitable for use in a presentation to potential students of the course in question.

9   ⏚ For the data in the file MACH.MTW/MACH.WKI/MACH.DAT, produce a cumulative frequency table of weights of packets for the three machines, and display the results on a single ogive.

10   ⏚ For the data in the file QUAL.MTW/QUAL.WK1/QUAL.DAT, plot a scattergraph of floorspace against takings. What can you conclude from the graph?

## Case study problem

Dear X,

Well, here I am at the end of my first year of trading, still in business! But now I have to produce a report on the first year of operation for my bank manager, and I want it to be a professional effort, with lots of nice diagrams.

I've summarised the basic facts for you, and I wondered if you could help me to present them in a more attractive way? By all means use the graphics on your computer, if you wish.

Many thanks – you must come and stay sometime soon.

Best wishes,

Jane

### Personal Touch Catering

The business was started in July 19XX, just under a year ago, with capital of £2000 (from my legacy) plus a loan of £1000 from the bank. I spent £1500 of this on equipment and materials, (crockery, cutlery, glasses, etc.) and a further £1000 on advertising and publicity material; the remainder I kept as a contingency fund for emergencies.

I have catered for 180 functions of various kinds in that period – 30 per cent business functions (directors' lunches, etc.) and the rest private. Total income from these was £33,750, and the number of people catered for totalled around 5,500; there's a detailed breakdown of the sizes of functions below. My expenditure totalled £18,000 for purchase and cooking of food, £2000 for travelling expenses, £1500 wages for help with cooking, and a further £4000 for various expenses (legal and financial advice, insurance, interest charges, etc.). I paid myself a salary of £4000, and the balance is profit!

| Number of people catered for | Number of functions |
|---|---|
| Under 10 | 26 |
| 10 but under 20 | 11 |
| 20 but under 30 | 53 |
| 30 but under 50 | 71 |
| Over 50 | 19 |

## Case study question

Present the information contained in this report in the form of suitable tables and diagrams, including derived statistics (percentages etc.) where appropriate.

## CHAPTER 6

# Summarising the figures: measures of location and spread

**Objectives**

Before starting work on this chapter, make sure you are happy with the following topics:

(a) construction of frequency tables (*see* Chapter 5, pp. 66–70);
(b) construction and interpretation of histograms and ogives (*see* Chapter 5, pp. 70–6).

By the end of your work on this chapter you should be able to:

(a) define and calculate the mean, median, mode, standard deviation, quartiles and range, for a given set of data;
(b) select the most appropriate measures for use with a particular set of data, and explain your choice.

## THE TRADE UNION LEADER'S PROBLEM

The Grimchester plant of the Northern Motor Company has for many years enjoyed good management–employee relations, but now this happy state of affairs is threatened by increasing industrial unrest. The root of the problem is that workers feel that they are under-paid, compared with their colleagues at Northern's nearby Greentown plant, and claim that this difference is due to differing ways of interpreting piecework pay agreements.

Northern's management are quite prepared to listen to the workers' grievances, but first they wish to see some evidence on paper that the wages of the two groups really *are* different. So, full-time union official Arthur Hughes has been called in to try to put together some figures.

He realises immediately that, as each plant employs several thousand workers, it isn't going to be practical to collect details about how much every single one of them earns – especially as some of them are unwilling to give him the information. Moreover, the firm's payroll is not yet computerised, so he will have to collect all the information himself. He therefore decides to use a sample of 150 workers from each factory. After consultation with a friendly statistician, he comes up with a *stratified sample* (*see* Chapter 3) designed so as to cover all groups in the work force; management examines this design and agrees to accept the samples as representative.

Arthur therefore goes ahead and collects from all the people in his two samples the amount of take-home pay they received last week. This gives him two sets, each of 150 figures, all different due to differing amounts of tax, allowances and so on, and varying in size from £82 a week to £177 a week. He knows enough about data presentation to arrange the two sets into two frequency tables which are shown below.

| Weekly take-home pay (£) | No. of Grimchester workers | No. of Greentown workers |
|---|---|---|
| 80 but under 90 | 3 | 4 |
| 90 but under 100 | 7 | 12 |
| 100 but under 110 | 33 | 17 |
| 110 but under 120 | 26 | 23 |
| 120 but under 130 | 24 | 38 |
| 130 but under 140 | 20 | 26 |
| 140 but under 150 | 18 | 16 |
| 150 but under 160 | 15 | 12 |
| 160 but under 180 | 4 | 2 |

However, he realises that this will not convey a great deal to Northern's management – in fact, in some ways it makes it appear that the Greentown workers are worse off, since there are more of them in the bottom class and fewer at the top! What he really needs is a few simple numbers which will *summarise*, in an easily understood fashion, the behaviour of the two samples.

## WHAT NEEDS TO BE MEASURED

To help us decide what kind of measurements would be useful to Arthur, it is a good idea to look at the histograms of the two samples. These are drawn in Fig. 6.1; in interpreting them remember that because the last group has a range of £20, whereas all the others have ranges of only £10, the height of the last blocks in the histograms must be adjusted accordingly.

The most noticeable feature of the two histograms is perhaps the fact that the peak of the 'Grimchester' histogram is further over to the left than the peak of the 'Greentown' one, although both are contained within the same interval. Associated with this is the fact that the 'Greentown' one is much more symmetrical. And these facts really pinpoint the three properties of the distributions which need to be measured: the *location*, or roughly where on the pay-scale the values in the sample tend to be situated; the *dispersion*, or how scattered the values in the sample tend to be; and – rather less importantly – the *skewness*, or degree of asymmetry of the sample values.

We will find, however, that it is not sufficient to devise just one way of measuring each of these characteristics of a frequency distribution. Because different distributions behave in different ways, and because different types of measurement are suited to those different types of behaviour, quite a variety of ways of measuring the three characteristics has been developed. We are going to look at three ways of measuring location and three ways of measuring dispersion – measurements of the two features tend to go together in pairs. We will not actually calculate any measures of skewness, since these are much less standardised than the other two types, but will merely look at skewness in a descriptive sort of way.

## MEASURING LOCATION

### The mode

We have already, in fact, looked at one measure of location without being explicit about it, when we said in the previous section that 'the "Grimchester" histogram has its peak

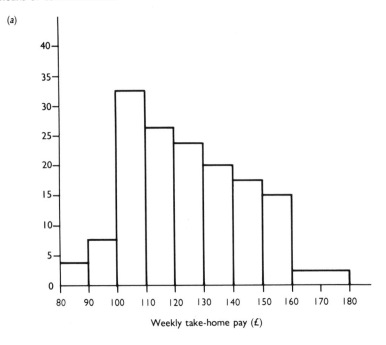

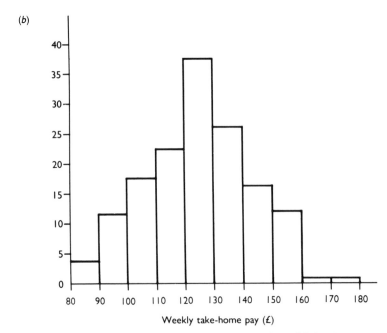

**Fig. 6.1** Histograms of wage distributions (a) for Grimchester workers; (b) for Greentown workers

further over to the left'. We were suggesting here the idea that the 'peak' or most common value in a distribution gives us a clue to the 'typical' value for the distribution as a whole. The technical name for this most common value is the *mode*, and it's very easy to see, either by looking at the histogram or by inspecting the frequency table to find the highest frequency, whereabouts it occurs.

Actually, what we find in the case of a grouped frequency table like the ones here is not a *single* figure for the mode, but rather a modal class; in the case of the Grimchester data, the modal class is £100–£110, while for Greentown it is £120–£130. These certainly seem to support the Grimchester workers' idea that they are worse off – but let's look at some of the criticisms which could be levelled at this way of measuring the 'typical' wage.

First of all, it's rather imprecise – we have a range of £10 in each case. There *are* ways of deciding whereabouts in the modal class the actual mode must lie, but for the sort of data you are likely to encounter these methods give purely theoretical figures which may not in practice have much to do with the 'most common' value. This is clearly undesirable; so, too, is the fact that there may well be more than one mode in a distribution. Consider, for instance, the distribution you would get if you classified into 2-inch wide groups the heights of all the members of your course. There would almost certainly be two 'peak' values if your course contains a mixture of males and females – one peak at around the average height for girls, and another at the average height for men. There might even be exactly equal numbers in each of these 'peak' classes. So we should have two modes, which would lead to a good deal of ambiguity in talking about *the* mode. And there are situations where *more* than two modes exist – even where *all* values are modal!

Perhaps, though, the most serious drawback of the mode as a way of measuring the 'typical' value in a distribution is the fact that it completely ignores the data in the rest of the distribution. With the wages data, for example, it takes no account of the very considerable numbers of both groups who earn amounts quite a long way above or below the modal group. Indeed if the data had been grouped in a different way – perhaps in classes running £75 but under £85, and so on – we might have come to a completely different conclusion about where the mode is, which is altogether an unsatisfactory state of affairs.

All these reasons combine to make the mode the least useful of the three measures of location we are going to examine. We certainly could not recommend it to Arthur Hughes as anything but a preliminary way of looking at his data, simplicity being about its one redeeming feature.

## The mean

### How to calculate the mean

The most familiar measure of the 'typical' wage in the two groups is, of course, the ordinary 'average' which is obtained by adding together the wages of all the people in the sample and dividing by the number of people involved. Another way of interpreting this procedure is to say that the average wage is the amount each worker would be getting if all their earnings were pooled and then shared out equally among them. The statisticians' term for this way of calculating the typical value in a distribution is the *mean* – strictly the *arithmetic* mean, to distinguish it from other kinds of mean which are sometimes used. As we are not going to encounter those other kinds, we will refer simply to the mean, an abbreviation which is generally understood to signify the arithmetic mean.

Although most people probably feel that they know what an average wage is, and could find one quite easily with the aid of a calculator, in practice for large amounts of data it may not be quite such a simple matter as it appears at first. Look again at the wage data for Grimchester, reproduced overleaf.

| Weekly take-home pay (£) | No. of workers |
|---|---|
| 80 but under 90 | 3 |
| 90 but under 100 | 7 |
| 100 but under 110 | 33 |
| 110 but under 120 | 26 |
| 120 but under 130 | 24 |
| 130 but under 140 | 20 |
| 140 but under 150 | 18 |
| 150 but under 160 | 15 |
| 160 but under 180 | 4 |

We certainly can't 'add up all the wages' as the simple description of calculating an average would suggest because we don't actually know what all the individual wages are! Of course, at some stage in the construction of the table Arthur Hughes must have had that information, but for the sake of simplifying the presentation of the information he has given up that level of detail, and – let's suppose – thrown the original figures away. So he has to begin by *choosing* a single wage to represent all the workers in each class; it may not be what each one is actually earning but the errors involved shouldn't be too great. The most sensible representative value to choose is the *middle* wage in each group; so it is assumed that all the workers in the '£80 but under £90' class earn £85 per week, and so on. In fact, the assumption needn't be quite so sweeping; all we really need, in order for this £85 figure correctly to represent all the workers in the '£80 but under £90' class, is that they should be evenly spread throughout the class (can you see why this is?).

So we now have a single value to represent each wage-group, and this class *mid-point* is often denoted by the letter $x$. A foolproof way of finding the $x$s, in cases where the class boundaries are not so easy to deal with as here, is to add up the upper and lower class boundaries and divide the result by two. Thus a class '26 but under 34' in a distribution of ages would have mid-point $(26 + 34)/2 = 30$, a class '20–29' in a discrete mark-distribution would have mid-point $(20 + 29)/2 = 24.5$, and so on.

We also have a letter which is commonly used to denote the number of workers in each wage-group – the letter $f$, standing for 'frequency'. You will recall that this was the term applied in Chapter 5 to the number of items occurring in each group.

But having names for the various quantities involved doesn't help us to do the calculation. For that we need to return to our definition of the mean: 'add up all the wages and divide by the number of workers in the sample'. Does this mean add up all the $x$-values? That would certainly be the case if there were just *one* worker earning £85, one earning £95, and so on, but in reality there are *three* with £85, *seven* with £95, etc. So the total wages of all the workers in the sample *could* be found by taking £$(85 + 85 + 85 + 95 + 95 + 95 + 95 + 95 + 95 + 95 + 105 + \ldots)$ – in all, 150 figures to be added together, since there are a total of 150 workers in the sample.

However, doing the calculation of the total this way is a bit inefficient – especially when someone has gone to the trouble of arranging the data into a frequency table. The clue to a better method lies in realising that $85 + 85 + 85$ is the same thing as $3 \times 85$ – in other words, successive addition is equivalent to multiplication. (It may be of interest to note in passing that this is how old-fashioned electro-mechanical calculators actually did multiplications. If one asked such a machine to multiply 37 by 42, one could watch it adding 37 to itself 42 times – which is why it took so long!)

Thus, to find the total wages of all workers in the sample, what we need to do is to take each wage, $x$, $f$ times over: $3 \times 85$, $7 \times 95$, etc. The neatest way of doing this is to set out the calculation in three columns as shown below.

| Weekly take-home pay (£) | Class mid-point, x | No. of workers in class, f | fx |
|---|---|---|---|
| 80 but under  90 | 85 | 3 | 255 |
| 90 but under 100 | 95 | 7 | 655 |
| 100 but under 110 | 105 | 33 | 3465 |
| 110 but under 120 | 115 | 26 | 2990 |
| 120 but under 130 | 125 | 24 | 3000 |
| 130 but under 140 | 135 | 20 | 2700 |
| 140 but under 150 | 145 | 18 | 2610 |
| 150 but under 160 | 165 | 15 | 2325 |
| 160 but under 180 | 170 | 4 | 680 |
| | | 150 | 18,690 |

So the total income of all the 150 workers in the group is £18,690 – the total we get by adding up the '$fx$' column. (Remember that $fx$ means $f$ multiplied by $x$, only we don't usually bother to write the multiplication sign.) Now, we want to share out this £18,690 equally among the 150 workers, so the mean wage per worker would be:

$$\frac{18,690}{150} = £124.60.$$

(It's worth reminding ourselves that this figure is an approximation to the true mean, since we've used the class mid-points rather than individual wages in calculating it.)

### Expressing the mean symbolically

This calculation is easy to carry out, but takes quite a long time to explain in words, as you can see! Fortunately, with the help of a symbol which may be new to you but which will prove very useful throughout our statistical work, we can summarise the process of finding the mean by one simple formula. The symbol is $\Sigma$ – a capital sigma, the Greek form of $s$ – standing for *summation*. It doesn't mean anything on its own, but can be read as 'add up all the', so that if, for example, we write $\Sigma x$, this is to be understood as meaning 'add up all the $x$s'.

What we have to do in finding the mean is to add up all the '$f$ multiplied by $x$' terms, and then divide that total by the total number of items in our sample. With the aid of our $\Sigma$ sign we can write 'add up all the $fx$s' as $\Sigma fx$; and the total number of items in our sample is just $\Sigma f$, the sum of the numbers of items in each class. We therefore arrive at the *formula for the mean*:

$$\bar{x} = \frac{\Sigma fx}{\Sigma f}.$$

We have used the letter $\bar{x}$ (pronounced '$x$-bar') here to stand for the mean; it is standard practice to denote the mean of a sample of values $x$ as $\bar{x}$. Similarly, if the values were denoted by $y$ then the mean would be $\bar{y}$, and so on. When we are talking about the mean of an entire population, rather than just a sample, we use the Greek letter $\mu$ (pronounced 'mew') – this is the Greek version of $m$, standing for mean. The convention of using ordinary Roman letters for sample values and Greek ones for population values is used for many measures other than the mean, as we will see later.

Of course, in the case where we *don't* have a frequency table but just a set of *x*s, we may regard the 'frequency' with which each *x* occurs as being 1, so that the formula then reduces to:

$$\bar{x} = \frac{\Sigma x}{\text{No. of items}}$$

– the old familiar average.

One point worth noticing here is that the mean has the same units as the original data – the mean of a distribution of wages in £s will also be a wage in £s. This is not just a detail, but can actually help you to notice if you've made a silly mistake in the calculation. For example, suppose in finding the mean wage of the Grimchester workers we had got our decimal point in the wrong place and arrived at an answer of 1246.00. A 'mean' of 1246 doesn't look too bad – but an average wage of £1246 for a group of workers, none of whom gets more than £180, looks very unlikely indeed!

Before going any further, you might like to test your understanding of the story so far by calculating the mean for the Greentown workers. You can do this by repeating the calculation we have done above, making best use of the 'memory' facility on your calculator to total the *fx* terms as you work them out. Alternatively, if you have a statistical calculator you may be able to compute the mean directly – read your instruction booklet to find out how to enter the data. And if you are going to use MINITAB, LOTUS, or another computer package, read the last section of the chapter to find out more about how to obtain the mean in that way.

Whichever way you do the calculation, if you get it right, you should reach an answer of £124.60 – exactly the same figure as for the Grimchester sample! So for Arthur Hughes' purposes the mean certainly isn't a very satisfactory measure of the typical wage, since it seems to suggest that there is no difference between the two groups. From our more dispassionate standpoint, however, let's try to find out *why* two such apparently different distributions should have the same mean.

### What does it tell us?

The root of the matter really lies in the fact that the mean is very much affected by the extreme values in a distribution. To see this, one need only consider the set of figures 2, 4, 6, 8, 80, which has mean 20. The mean here is clearly *not* a good representative value, either for the 'majority' values, which are all below 10, or for the 'rogue' value 80. It has been 'pulled over' towards the one very high value in the distribution, which makes it a rather unreliable measure in such a case.

Something similar is going on with the Grimchester data. Although a lot of the workers earn less than £120 per week, there is a substantial number with much higher wages, which is why the mean turns out to be identical to that for the Greentown data, although the peak or modal group for the latter data is twenty pounds higher. So it looks as if the mean might not be quite suitable as a measure of the 'typical' value in the case of a very *un*symmetrical distribution, but is certainly a good guide with fairly symmetrical data like the Greentown wages.

There are one or two other factors which also need to be taken into account when deciding whether to use the mean as one's measure of location. If we had had an open class (such as 'over £160') at either or both ends of our data, we would have had difficulty in assigning a mid-point to that class, and in fact we would have had to make some *assumption* as to where the class ended (perhaps at £190) before we could get any further with the calculation of the mean. But, of course, such an assumption might be quite wrong, introducing an element of unreliability into our mean value.

On the 'pro' side, one strong point in favour of the mean is that it does take into account every item of data, which was certainly not the case with the mode. It is also easy to calculate automatically – we've seen how to do it with a calculator, and later we will see how simply it can be found using a computer package. Moreover, it lends itself well to further calculations – for example, if we know the means of two separate samples (and their sizes), we can combine them to get an overall mean for the two samples together, as the following example demonstrates.

Suppose a firm has taken samples from its receipted bills in order to find out how many contain errors, and has discovered that there are 80 which contain errors favourable to the customer (that is, the bill is *lower* than it should be). The average size of these errors is 4p. Among the 120 errors which are in favour of the firm (the bills are too *high*), the mean size of error is 3p per bill. The problem is to find out if taken overall, the errors produce a surplus or a deficit for the firm. Now, it would be quite wrong to say, '4p on average for the customer and only 3p on average for us – that means an average of 1p for the customer altogether'; what we *must* take into account is the relative *size* of the two groups of erroneous bills. Eighty bills each with an average error of 4p give a total of £3.20 in favour of the customers, while 120 bills each with an average error of 3p give a total of £3.60 in favour of the firm, so in fact over the whole 200 bills the average error is (£3.60–£3.20)/200 = 0.2p per bill in favour of the firm.

But perhaps the most important reason why the mean has become the standard measure of location lies in the fact that, given the mean of a sample, it is relatively easy to make sensible deductions about the mean of the entire population from which the sample was taken. We will look in detail at how this works in Chapter 11.

On the whole then, the mean has more 'pro' than 'con' properties, and certainly is the measure of location you will encounter most commonly. But for use in the cases we have pointed out where it *does* have drawbacks, we need a third type of measure.

## The median

If you were to give a well-shuffled pack of cards to someone and ask them to choose one at random, my guess is that 99 people out of 100 would *not* choose the bottom or the top one, but would take one from somewhere in the middle of the pack; they would feel that the top or bottom card might somehow be more special than one in the middle. In the same way, if you were a sociologist conducting a piece of research, and wanted to interview a 'typical' child out of a family of three, I expect you would prefer to use the middle child as being in some way more representative, less extreme than either of the other two.

This intuitive feeling we have that a middle value should be in some sense a representative value has been made use of by statisticians in devising the third measure of location we are going to examine – the *median*. We define the median of a set of data as the middle value when the data has been arranged in order of size (either increasing or decreasing). For example, if seven metal bars produced by a machine have lengths as follows:

6.2, 4.9, 8.7, 3.4, 6.6, 5.2, 5.2 cm

then in order to find the median length we would first of all rearrange the lengths in, say, ascending order:

3.4, 4.9, 5.2, 5.2, 6.2, 6.6, 8.7.

Then the median would be the length of the middle, that is the fourth bar, which is 5.2 cm.

If we had had eight bars rather than seven, the situation would be slightly different. Suppose that an extra bar is added to the seven above, giving:

$$3.4, \ 4.9, \ 5.2, \ 5.2, \ 5.7, \ 6.2, \ 6.6, \ 8.7$$

as the eight lengths. The mid-point of the data now occurs *between* the fourth and fifth lengths – between 5.2 and 5.7 cm in other words. We take as the actual median the length which is half-way in between these two – in this case it will be $(5.2 + 5.7)/2 = 5.45$ cm.

It was easy enough with such small sets of data to see whereabouts the median was going to be, but if we have a very large amount of data it may not be quite so simple, so it is useful to have a standard way of finding the position of the median. We have seen that with seven numbers the median is the 4th; with eight it is the $4\frac{1}{2}$th. In general, if we have a set of $n$ numbers, the median will be the $(n + 1)/2$th number. You can check that this does indeed give 4 when $n = 7$ and $4\frac{1}{2}$ when $n = 8$. Actually if we have a very large amount of data, so that $n$ is big, then adding 1 to $n$ isn't going to make a lot of difference; if $n = 500$, for example, then the median should strictly be the $(500 + 1)/2$th $= 250\frac{1}{2}$th item – halfway between the 250th and the 251st – but we won't be much in error if we take it as the $500/2$th $= 250$th item instead. In the remainder of the chapter we won't worry about adding the 1 to $n$ as long as $n$ is over 50.

With this in mind, we can now look at the wages data on page 89 again with a view to finding the median wage for each group. As there are 150 workers in each sample, the median in both cases will be the wage earned by the 75th worker. So all we need do is to arrange the individual wages in increasing order and pick out the 75th . . . but we don't *know* the individual wages! As we already found when calculating the mean, the loss of that individual information was the price we paid for the simplification produced by grouping the data.

It is quite easy to find out which *group* the median wage falls into; if we convert the data to a *cumulative* frequency table (*see* the section on tabulating quantitative data in Chapter 5) we can see immediately where the 75th wage will lie:

| Weekly take-home pay (£) | No. of Grimchester workers | No. of Greentown workers |
| --- | --- | --- |
| less than   80 | 0 | 0 |
| less than   90 | 3 | 4 |
| less than 100 | 10 | 16 |
| less than 110 | 43 | 33 |
| less than 120 | 69 | 56 |
| less than 130 | 93 | 94 |
| less than 140 | 113 | 120 |
| less than 150 | 131 | 136 |
| less than 160 | 146 | 148 |
| less than 180 | 150 | 150 |

As only 69 Grimchester workers are getting less than £120 week, but 93 of them are getting less than £130 week, the 75th wage must be somewhere in the £120–£130 bracket.

We would, however, like to be more precise about this. Fortunately there is a very simple way to find out a more specific value for the median. The cumulative frequency table should remind you of the *ogive* – the graph we discussed in Chapter 5 (p. 74), which showed how many items were below a given value. The ogive plotted from the wage data above is drawn in Fig. 6.2 and it is a simple matter to read off from the graph the

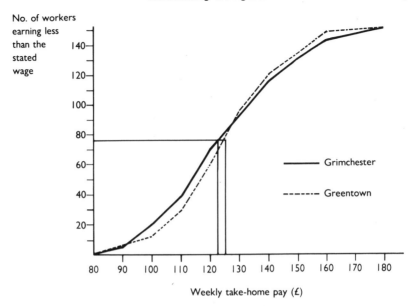

No. of workers earning less than the stated wage

Weekly take-home pay (£)

Grimchester

Greentown

**Fig. 6.2** Ogives for wages of Grimchester and Greentown workers

wage earned by the 75th worker in each group. The *median wage* is £122.50 for the Grimchester workers, and £125 for the Greentown workers.

So there is a difference between the two groups if we use the median as our measure of location, even though the two mean wages were the same. Again, we can see why this occurs by taking some rather simpler figures as an illustration. If we return to the set of figures 2, 4, 6, 8, 80 which we used above to show how the mean – 20 – isn't really a very good 'typical' measure for such lopsided data, we can see immediately that the median here is the third figure, 6. This is certainly more representative of the four low figures in the set than is the mean, demonstrating how the median, by ignoring the extreme values – in fact, ignoring *everything* but the middle value – manages not to be 'pulled' towards the odd untypically high or low item.

Hence in the wages case, the median is less affected than the mean by the minority of Grimchester workers who earn really high wages, and might be regarded as a fairer representation of the bulk of lower-paid workers. With the Greentown data, we have a much more symmetrical distribution, so there is far less difference between median and mean. This gives us the key to one way in which you can decide, for a particular set of data, which measure to choose: if the data has a marked degree of unsymmetry, the median may well be a better choice; if it is pretty symmetrical there will not be much to choose between the two and in such a case the mean would probably be chosen for the various reasons discussed above.

Two other factors which might cause us to opt for a median in preference to a mean are that its calculation doesn't require us to make any assumptions about closing open classes at the top or bottom of the distribution, and that it can be used even in situations where we can't get a proper measurement of the data, but can only rank it in order (*see* Chapter 3). For instance, if we arranged workers in order of their efficiency in performing a job, then the median efficiency would be represented by the middle worker, even though we could not perform any actual calculations on the data.

**Fig. 6.3** Calculating the median

For this reason the median is often used in areas such as sociology where it may be difficult to quantify data accurately.

One final point before we leave the topic of measures of location. For those of you who like calculations, and dislike plotting graphs, it *is* possible to find the median of a grouped distribution without drawing an ogive, by means of a straightforward proportion calculation. We decided that the median for the Grimchester data must fall in the group £120–£130. Now there are 69 workers earning less than £130, so person number 75, who gets the median wage, is the sixth person in a group which contains 24 people altogether; that is, he is a quarter of the way through the group. But the group covers a range of £10, so the median is a quarter of £10 *above* £120, at £122.50 as we already found from the ogive. Reference to Fig. 6.3 may help to clarify this argument and you are advised, if you wish to perform this calculation, always to draw a similar diagram.

## MEASURING SPREAD

### The range

The second feature of frequency distributions which we decided it would be useful to be able to measure was the degree to which the values in the distribution were spread out or squashed together – the degree of *spread* among those values. If you were asked the question, with reference to our two sets of wage data, 'how spread out are the wages in the two groups?' you might well reply 'Both samples contain wages ranging from £80 to £180 a week'.

This, the simplest measure of spread, is called, not surprisingly, the *range*, and might be defined as the distance from the highest to the lowest value in the distribution. So here we would say the data ranges from £80 to £180, or that there is a range of £100 in each of the samples. But immediately we see one of the chief drawbacks to the range: it gives us the same answer for both groups, even though we can see by looking at the ogives in Fig. 6.2 that actually the Greentown wages are a good deal more compact than those for Grimchester.

The cause of this, and the consequent unreliability of the range, is that it ignores all but the two extreme items in the distribution, so what is going on in the middle makes no difference at all to it. Moreover, just one 'rogue' value in a set of data – maybe due to an error in measurement – can produce a quite misleading value of the range. Our old example of the figures 2, 4, 6, 8, 80 has a range of 80 − 2 = 78, even though the first four numbers only have a range of 8 − 2 = 6 among themselves.

So, like its companion measure the mode, the range is really only useful when we want a quick idea of the variability in a set of data without having to go to the trouble of doing any calculations. For more precise information, other forms of measure of spread are needed.

## The standard deviation

One of the defects of the range is that it is a sort of absolute measure – it tells us about the variation between the highest and lowest items in a distribution, but gives us no idea how those items relate to the mean. And yet this is just what we would like to know if we want to assess the usefulness of the mean as a 'typical' value for the distribution – if all the items in the distribution are pretty near to the mean then clearly it represents them well; if some of them are quite a long way from the mean, then it isn't such a good representative for those items.

The measure which has been devised precisely to do this job of telling us how near, on the whole, the values in the data are to the mean, is called the *standard deviation*, and because it is a measure which may seem a bit complicated at first sight, we will see how it is devised first of all for a very easy set of numbers – the figures 1, 2, 3, 5, 9.

## An easy example

We obviously need to find the mean of these numbers first before we can start looking at how the numbers relate to this mean. The numbers add up to 20, so their mean is 4. If we refer to the numbers in the distribution, as we did earlier in the chapter, as $x$, then the simplest way to find out how far the $x$ is from the mean is to look at $x - \bar{x}$ for each $x$. This will actually tell us, not just how far $x$ is from $\bar{x}$, but also which side of $\bar{x}$ it is; numbers *below* $\bar{x}$ will give a negative $x - \bar{x}$, those above, a positive one. So we get $x - \bar{x}$ values of $1 - 4$, $2 - 4$, $3 - 4$, $5 - 4$, and $9 - 4$, or $-3$, $-2$, $-1$, 1 and 5. These are shown in the second column of Table X.

**Table X**

| $x$ | $x - \bar{x}$ | $(x - \bar{x})^2$ |
|---|---|---|
| 1 | $-3$ | 9 |
| 2 | $-2$ | 4 |
| 3 | $-1$ | 1 |
| 5 | 1 | 1 |
| 9 | 5 | 25 |
| | | 40 |

What we really want is not just these individual values, but something which will tell us how far, *on the average*, an $x$ is from the mean. So if we add up all the $x - \bar{x}$ terms – the usual name for these is *deviations* because they tell us how much the $x$s *deviate* from the mean – and then divide by 5, we should get the kind of measure we are after. But when we total the deviations, we find $-6 + 6 = 0$! And this isn't just a freak of the set of numbers used; if you repeat the process with *any* set of numbers you will find the same thing happening – roughly because the mean is 'in the middle' of the data. So as a sensible measure of spread, this is rather a non-starter.

The problem was, of course, caused by the $-$ signs, which cancelled out the positive deviations to give a zero total. We *could* try just ignoring them, but in a way that would be ignoring a fact about the data, namely, which side of the mean a point comes. So a better way of eliminating them has been devised; we are going to *square* each of the deviations. That will certainly get rid of the troublesome $-$ signs (the square of a negative number is always positive) and at the same time, we won't lose any important information about the deviations. If an $x$ is a long way from $\bar{x}$, then $x - \bar{x}$ will be big, and so will $(x - \bar{x})^2$; if $x$ is near to $\bar{x}$, then $x - \bar{x}$ and $(x - \bar{x})^2$ will both be small.

This process gives 9, 4, 1, 1 and 25 as the squared deviations, totalling 40 altogether. The figures are also shown in column 3 of Table X.

The average squared deviation per point is thus $40/5 = 8$, and we *could* use this as our measure of spread. In fact, it *is* sometimes used, and so has been given a special name – the *variance*. But it has one snag: because we squared all the deviations, the units in which the variance is expressed are the square of the original units. For example, if we started out with a set of lengths in inches, the variance will be in square inches; if our original data was percentage marks in an exam, the variance is in squared percentages (!) and so on. This is clearly not desirable – we would like our measure of spread to have the *same* units as our original data, so the last step in constructing it is to take a square root, in our case $\sqrt{8}$ or 2.828. And this finally, is the standard deviation.

## Expressing it symbolically

We can build up a formula for calculating the standard deviation for other sets of data if we recap the process we've followed in terms of $x$ and $m$. What we did was to take the sum of the $(x - \bar{x})^2$ terms, average them out among the items of our distribution, and then take the square root of the result. So using the $\Sigma$ sign we introduced in the section 'Measuring location', p. 93, we can write standard deviation:

$$s = \sqrt{\frac{\Sigma(x - \bar{x})^2}{\text{No. of items}}}.$$

Doing the calculation like this was quite easy for our set of data 1, 2, 3, 5, 9, because the mean was a simple whole number. You can imagine, however, that if we had a set of data whose mean was a complicated decimal, subtracting it from each data value separately, then squaring the differences, and so on, would be rather a messy business. Fortunately, with a little algebraic manipulation we can put the formula into a more convenient form. We will not give the details, though if you are mathematically-minded you might like to verify the result for yourself by multiplying out the term $(x - \bar{x})^2$ in the formula above. After doing so, and rearranging terms, we find:

$$s = \sqrt{\frac{\Sigma x^2}{\text{No. of items}} - \bar{x}^2}.$$

In other words, rather than having to subtract the mean from each $x$-value individually and then square the resulting differences, we square the $x$s alone and then just subtract $\bar{x}^2$ once at the end. For our data 1, 2, 3, 5, 9 this gives us

$$s = \sqrt{\frac{1 + 4 + 9 + 25 + 81}{5} - 4^2}$$

$$= \sqrt{\frac{120}{5} - 16} = \sqrt{24 - 16}$$

$$= \sqrt{8}$$

exactly as before.

As you can see, we have used $s$ to denote the standard deviation of the sample; in line with what we said earlier in connection with the mean, the Greek version of $s$, which is $\sigma$ (pronounced sigma) would be used if we were talking about the standard deviation of an entire population.

You can of course compute the standard deviation using the statistical functions on your calculator, or a computer package. If you do this, you may come across some puzzling discrepancies between the hand-calculated version using the formula above, and the value obtained from the calculator or computer. Indeed, you may discover that you have a choice of two standard deviation buttons on your calculator, probably labelled 'SDn' and 'SDn-1' or something similar. The reason for this is that the formula we used above, where the sum of the squared deviations is divided by $n$, is fine if we have data about an entire population; but if we only have a sample, then the value we get from this formula is likely to be a slight underestimate of the population standard deviation – we say the sample value gives us a biased estimate of the population value.

Commonsense suggests why this might be; if we take a sample – particularly a small one – from a population, we may end up with values which are closely bunched together, and therefore don't fully reflect the variability in the population as a whole. To correct for this, the sum of squared deviations should be divided, not by $n$ but by $n - 1$ (this can be proved mathematically – it isn't just a 'fiddle factor'!). Actually if $n$ is bigger than about 30 there is very little difference in the two figures, so it is not worth getting too excited about which version you use. But the idea of estimating population values from sample data is an important one, which we will be encountering again in Chapter 10.

There is one further modification which we must make to the formula, before we can try to calculate the standard deviation for the wage-distributions with which we began the chapter. In the case of those distributions, we had not *one* item in each class, but $f$ items, where $f$ was the frequency of that class. Consequently, when we come to calculate the standard deviation the $x^2$ term for each class will contribute to the total not just once, but $f$ times – a total contribution of $fx^2$; precisely the same argument as when we found in calculating the mean that each class would contribute $fx$ to the overall total wages. We also saw at that point that the number of items altogether is equal to $\Sigma f$; thus we can write the formula for standard deviation for a frequency distribution as:

$$s = \sqrt{\frac{\Sigma fx^2}{\Sigma f} - \bar{x}^2}.$$

This is the version of the formula which we will use in all subsequent work, and which you are recommended to commit to memory, though you will find slight variations on it also used by other authors.

## Returning to the problem

We are now in a position to calculate the standard deviation for the wages of the Grimchester factory workers. For the sake of completeness, since one is in practice nearly always calculating a mean and standard deviation simultaneously, the calculation of the mean is shown again.

The $fx^2$ column here was calculated not by squaring $x$ and then multiplying by $f$, but by noticing that $fx^2 = fx \times x$, so we can find each $fx^2$ term by multiplying the $fx$ figure once more by $x$. Again, you can make use of the memory facility on your calculator to add up the $fx^2$ column as you go along.

| Weekly take-home pay (£) | Class mid-point, x | No. of workers in class, f | fx | fx² |
|---|---|---|---|---|
| 80 but under 90 | 85 | 3 | 255 | 21,675 |
| 90 but under 100 | 95 | 7 | 665 | 63,175 |
| 100 but under 110 | 105 | 33 | 3,465 | 363,825 |
| 110 but under 120 | 115 | 26 | 2,990 | 343,850 |
| 120 but under 130 | 125 | 24 | 3,000 | 375,000 |
| 130 but under 140 | 135 | 20 | 2,700 | 364,500 |
| 140 but under 150 | 145 | 18 | 2,610 | 378,450 |
| 150 but under 160 | 155 | 15 | 2,325 | 360,375 |
| 160 but under 180 | 170 | 4 | 680 | 115,600 |
| | | 150 | 18,690 | 2,386,450 |

As already calculated, we have the mean $\bar{x} = 18,690/150 = £124.60$. Then the standard deviation is given by:

$$s = \sqrt{\frac{2,386,450}{150} - 124.60^2}$$

$$= \sqrt{15909.66 - 15525.16}$$

$$= \sqrt{384.507}$$

$$= £19.60.$$

At this point, your reaction may well be 'So what?' One of the difficulties experienced by most people on encountering the standard deviation for the first time is that the calculation is rather complex, and when finally one arrives at the answer it is not straightforward to interpret. Bear in mind first of all that it is a measure of *spread around the mean*: the bigger the standard deviation, the more spread-out the distribution. To develop more of a feeling for what it means, however, it will help if we look at it in the context of a companion between two distributions.

To that end, and in order to practise carrying out the arithmetical procedures, you should now verify that the standard deviation of the Greentown wage distribution is £18.28 – that is, over £1 less than for the Grimchester workers (remember that if you do the calculation with a calculator or computer package, you may get a slightly different answer, for the reasons explained above). This fact demonstrates that though both groups have the same average wage, the Grimchester group are less consistent than the Greentown group, there being more of the former who have wages quite a long way from the mean. This will be confirmed by looking again at Fig. 6.1, which brings out the more compact form, dropping off quite sharply into the two 'tails', of the Greentown distribution.

The Greentown figures also exhibit another fact about the standard deviation which is useful in learning to interpret it. If we take a range of three standard deviations both above and below the mean, we arrive at an upper limit of approximately £124.60 + 3 × £18.28 = £180, and a lower limit of about £124.60 – 3 × £18.28 = £70. Between these two limits, the entire Greentown data is included; and you will find in fact that for any reasonably symmetrical set of data, a range of three standard deviations either side of the mean should include all but a few data items. We will come to understand more clearly why this should be when we examine the normal distribution in

Chapter 9. Meanwhile, the fact will give you a very rough check on the correctness of your calculations, at least to the extent of showing up errors such as misplaced decimal points.

By now you may well have lost track of the fact that we originally set out to assist Arthur Hughes with his problem of comparing the wages of the two groups of workers. Let us therefore recap at this point, making use of the various measures we have developed so far. We have seen that, while both sets of workers have wages ranging from £80 to £180, and both earn the same average or mean wage, the differences in the way the wages are scattered within those ranges are reflected by the greater standard deviation of the Grimchester workers, while the fact that their distribution 'peaks' farther to the left (that is, at a lower value) is shown by their lower median and modal wages.

We have seen how the standard deviation can show how spread out the data is around the mean, but what it *won't* tell us is whether the top end of the distribution tends to be more 'stretched out' than the bottom, or vice versa. To give that information, we need to introduce our third measure of spread.

## The quartiles

One of the criticisms we levelled at the range as a measure of spread was the fact that by using the extreme upper and lower limits of the data it might well fail to give us an adequate indication as to how the main part of the data was spread out. One way to avoid this is to look at the range, not among all 100 per cent of the data, but among, for instance, the central 50 per cent. We therefore ignore the extreme upper and lower 25 per cent of the data, on the grounds that these values might in some way be untypical, and we examine the amount of scatter between the values 25 per cent of the way and 75 per cent of the way through the distribution.

These two values are called respectively the first and third *quartiles*, being one-quarter and three-quarters of the way through the data; the second quartile is, of course, the mid-point of the data, which we have already encountered in the guise of the median. This suggests that, as we were easily able to find the median by looking at the ogive of the data, we should be able to do the same for the quartiles. For the Grimchester workers, of whom there are 150, the lower quartile will be the wage earned by the $150/4 = 37.5$th worker, and the upper quartile the wage of the $3 \times 150/4 = 112.5$th worker. Reference to Fig. 6.2 then shows that the lower quartile, often written $Q_1$, is £108.30 approximately, while $Q_3$ is £139.75. You can confirm that for the Greentown wages the figures are $Q_1 = £111.95$ and $Q_3 = £137.15$, as accurately as can be read from the graph. Of course, we could always use a proportion calculation, like the one illustrated on pp. 97–8 rather than resorting to the ogive to find the quartiles.

Whatever means we have used to calculate them, the quartiles can convey a good deal of information to anyone who knows how to interpret them. First and most simple, they tell us that the central 50 per cent of Grimchester workers have wages ranging from £108.30 to £139.75, an *interquartile range* of £31.45, while for the Greentown workers this is £111.95 to £137.15 or £25.20. There is thus less variability in the wages of the central 50 per cent of Greentown workers, confirming the picture we obtained by comparison of the standard deviations. (You may also encounter the semi-interquartile range, which as its name suggests is half the interquartile range, in this case £15.73. Its interpretation is similar.)

But the quartiles can tell us more. Looked at in conjunction with the median they can convey information about how unsymmetrical or *skew* the data is, and in what direction. For instance, if you look at the relationship between $Q_1$, M and $Q_3$ for the Grimchester data, you will notice that $Q_1$ is closer to the median than $Q_3$, whereas for the Greentown data the quartiles are much closer to being equidistant on either side of the median. For a perfectly symmetric distribution they would, in fact, be exactly equidistant; the more skew the distribution is, the more the median will tend to be closer to one of the quartiles and further from the other. The more distant quartile is on the side of the longer 'tail' of the distribution, as you can see by relating the quartiles for the Grimchester data to the histogram of that data shown in Fig. 6.1. The high value of $Q_3$ in this case is due to the effect of the quite large number of Grimchester workers receiving wages in the higher groups, who tend to 'pull' the upper quartile over to the right. Conversely, of course, a distribution which had a long *left*-hand 'tail' would exhibit a $Q_1$ which was noticeably further from the median than $Q_3$.

Thus, to the informed person, the simple statement 'The Grimchester workers have a median wage of £142.50, lower quartile £108.30 and upper quartile £139.75' conveys information as to the general position, degree of variability, and overall shape of the wage distribution. For this reason, it is particularly useful to use the median and quartiles as one's measures of location and dispersion in cases where the data is markedly unsymmetric. Where there is a reasonable degree of symmetry, however, the advantages already mentioned earlier for the mean, most of which also apply to the standard deviation, make these the usual choice.

An interesting way of presenting all the information contained in the median, quartiles and range of a set of data is provided by the *box-and-whisker diagram*. A diagram of this kind based on the Grimchester/Greentown data is shown in Fig. 6.4; it consists of a 'box' extending from the first to the third quartiles, with 'whiskers' stretching to the full extent of the range in each direction. Within the 'box', the position of the median is shown by an asterisk (or sometimes a vertical line). Thus a small box with long whiskers indicates a distribution with its central values very bunched, but long tails; a median much nearer to one end of the box than the other, a degree of skewness, and so on. In the particular case shown, the observations we have already made about the greater skewness of the Grimchester figures and the more compact centre of the Greentown ones are summed up in a neat and easy to understand way.

Such diagrams are not, as yet, very widely used, but they are now available on packages such as MINITAB and will probably become more popular as users begin to see their advantages over the conventional histograms and ogives covered in the last chapter.

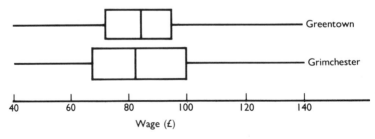

**Fig. 6.4** Box-and-whisker plot

## ◨ SUMMARY MEASURES WITH MINITAB AND LOTUS

### MINITAB

Finding means, standard deviations and so on couldn't be easier than in MINITAB, as long as you have the raw data and not a frequency table. Assuming that the raw data is in column C1, the following are the required commands:

MEAN C1 will give you the mean.
STAN C1 gives standard deviation.
MEDIAN C1 gives the median.
MAX C1 and MIN C1 give the greatest and smallest values in the column.

From MAX and MIN you can easily calculate the range. Only the mode is not available – if you try typing MODE C1 you will get a polite message indicating that MINITAB doesn't know what you are talking about!

Perhaps simplest of all is to use the command DESCRIBE C1 to get a full range of information about C1, including its mean, truncated or TMEAN (the mean with the top and bottom 5 per cent of data excluded – just in case it is untypical), the standard deviation, median and quartiles, maximum and minimum values, as well as the number of values in the column, and a further measure called the standard error of the mean which we will be learning about in Chapter 10. You'll find an example of the output from the DESCRIBE command in the case-study problem at the end of this chapter.

MINITAB will also do you a box-and-whisker plot, as described in the last section – the command for that is BOXPLOT C1, and you can use it with the subcommand BY C2 to get comparable box plots of different subsets of the data one below the other (rather like the DOTPLOT BY described in Chapter 5).

### LOTUS

There are standard LOTUS @ functions for many summary measures:

@AVG gives the mean,
@STD gives standard deviation,
@MAX and @MIN give the maximum and minimum,

so assuming that you have the raw data in a column all you need do is specify the appropriate range of cells. To find median and quartiles, sort the data into ascending or descending order using the sequence

/ DATA SORT

and it will be easy to pick out the required values from the sorted column (make sure you carry along any other columns in the sorting process, though, otherwise your data will become hopelessly muddled!).

LOTUS is also well suited to computation of the mean and standard deviation from a frequency table, using the basic process described in the section 'Measuring spread', p. 102. By exploiting the way in which formulae can be copied around a spreadsheet using the relative addressing property, the table with columns for $f$, $x$, $fx$ and $fx^2$ can be set up very quickly. You will find an example of this kind of spreadsheet in the file MSD.WK1 on the diskette; the data used there is the Grimchester/Greentown wage data discussed in this chapter, but you can overwrite it with other values of $f$ and $x$. You should explore the contents of the various cells to make sure you understand what is going on.

## WHICH SHOULD WE CHOOSE?

You may feel by now that poor Arthur Hughes is no better off than he was at the beginning of the chapter, having passed from a situation where he has no means of summarising his data to one where he has perhaps too many methods to choose from. And we have only looked at the three most popular measures of location and dispersion – there are several more of each which we have not even touched on! Although one cannot lay down hard and fast rules for the use of these various measures, there is usually one which seems more appropriate than the rest in a given situation. We have already indicated that the mode and range are really only suited to giving us a quick idea of position and variability; the median and quartiles are the ones to choose if you have a noticeably skew distribution, while in most other situations the mean and standard deviation, by long historical usage as well as for the other reasons noted above, are the ones to use.

In the case of the wage data with which we have been mainly concerned in this chapter, my personal choice would be the median and quartiles – and it should certainly be Arthur Hughes' choice if he wants to support the idea that the Grimchester workers are worse off, since their median wage really is £2.50 less than that of their colleagues in Greentown. On the other hand, if management know anything about statistics they will realise that the high upper quartile for the Grimchester workers means that some of them are really getting rather highly paid, so maybe their complaint isn't justified after all!

## PRACTICAL EXERCISES

1 The following sets of data represent the distribution of house prices in two counties. By calculating all three measures of location and dispersion for the two distributions, compare the position in the two counties:

| Price range (£000s) | No. of houses in Barsetshire sample | No. houses in Cokeshire sample |
|---|---|---|
| 65 but under 70 | 2 | 4 |
| 70 but under 75 | 5 | 11 |
| 75 but under 80 | 12 | 19 |
| 80 but under 90 | 20 | 15 |
| 90 but under 110 | 14 | 6 |
| 110 but under 140 | 6 | 4 |
| 140 and upwards | 1 | 1 |

2 Calculate the standard deviation for the two distributions 2, 5, 7, 8, 10 and 22, 25, 27, 28, 30, using the standard deviation key of your calculator or a suitable computer package if possible.

What do you notice about the means and the standard deviations of the two sets of data? Can you suggest a generalisation of this result? Confirm your guess by examining other sets of data of your own devising.

**3** Do the same as in Question 2 for the two sets of data 2, 5, 7, 8, 10 and 6, 15, 21, 24, 30.

**4** Look out for mentions in the press, TV and radio of the word 'average' (for example, in accounts of wage negotiations) and discuss what particular form of 'average' or typical value might actually be being used in each case.

**5** Can you think of any practical situations in which a modal value might actually be the best one to use?

**6** ◘ Using the software to which you have access, calculate suitable summary measures to describe the data on weights of tea packets stored in the files MACH.WK1/ MACH.MTW/MACH.DAT. Incorporate these measures into a brief report comparing the performance of the three filling machines.

## Case study problem

Dear X,

The new computer has arrived! It is a great help with accounting and so on – it has really idiot-proof programs – but when I tried analysing the results of a little customer survey I did recently, using the MINITAB statistical package, I did not understand all the figures which came out! Perhaps you could give me some guidance – even if you haven't used this particular package, I think the printout which I have attached is fairly self-explanatory.

Glad to hear about your new job – it sounds very exciting!

Best wishes,

Jane

## Case study question

Write a short report interpreting the information given in the MINITAB printout in practical terms, and making recommendations for action as a result.

```
MTB > note 0 = business customers
MTB > note 1 = private customers
```

| | type | N | MEAN | MEDIAN | TRMEAN | STDEV | SEMEAN |
|---|---|---|---|---|---|---|---|
| amount | 0 | 40 | 230.30 | 234.00 | 227.94 | 55.33 | 8.75 |
| | 1 | 57 | 206.44 | 199.00 | 205.29 | 60.30 | 7.99 |

| | type | MIN | MAX | Q1 | Q3 | | |
|---|---|---|---|---|---|---|---|
| amount | 0 | 138.00 | 398.00 | 180.25 | 263.75 | | |
| | 1 | 97.00 | 338.00 | 160.00 | 248.50 | | |

| | type | N | MEAN | MEDIAN | TRMEAN | STDEV | SEMEAN |
|---|---|---|---|---|---|---|---|
| size | 0 | 40 | 25.150 | 25.000 | 25.278 | 4.246 | 0.671 |
| | 1 | 57 | 40.667 | 41.000 | 40.765 | 7.398 | 0.980 |

| | type | MIN | MAX | Q1 | Q3 | | |
|---|---|---|---|---|---|---|---|
| size | 0 | 14.000 | 34.000 | 23.000 | 28.000 | | |
| | 1 | 24.000 | 54.000 | 35.000 | 46.500 | | |

| | type | N | MEAN | MEDIAN | TRMEAN | STDEV | SEMEAN |
|---|---|---|---|---|---|---|---|
| avperhd | 0 | 40 | 9.145 | 8.984 | 9.128 | 1.347 | 0.213 |
| | 1 | 57 | 5.047 | 4.925 | 5.031 | 1.028 | 0.136 |

| | type | MIN | MAX | Q1 | Q3 |
|---|---|---|---|---|---|
| avperhd | 0 | 6.429 | 12.192 | 8.099 | 10.075 |
| | 1 | 2.917 | 7.348 | 4.276 | 5.694 |

Note: amount  = amount spent at last transaction (£)
size       = number of people catered for
avperhd  = average expenditure per head (£)

## CHAPTER 7

# Measuring changes: index numbers

## Objectives

Before starting work on this chapter make sure you are happy with:

(a) the ideas of percentages (*see* Chapter 1, pp. 11–12);
(b) the use of the $\Sigma$ sign (*see* Chapter 6, p. 93);

By the end of your work on this chapter you should be able to:

(a) calculate a price index according to the Laspeyres (base-weighted) or Paasche (current-weighted) methods;
(b) explain the difference between these two methods of calculation and the meaning of the indices obtained;
(c) outline the purpose and use of the General Index of Retail Prices with the data upon which it is based;
(d) make use of a price index to 'deflate' a series of figures (profits, revenues, etc.).

## THE INVESTOR'S PROBLEM

Susan White has been left a small legacy by her great-aunt. It isn't enough to do anything very exciting with, and she doesn't need it for day-to-day living expenses or immediate purchases, so she has decided to invest it. But she feels she would like to have some fun out of her investment, so rather than placing the money somewhere 'safe' like a building society, she would prefer to buy a small number of shares in a reputable company.

However, she is finding it hard to decide which company to select. The amount concerned is too small to interest an investment consultant, so she has been to her bank manager for advice, and he has provided her with half a dozen company annual reports to study, so that she can form an idea of the financial health – or otherwise – of the firm she finally chooses.

Naturally these reports, while they must satisfy certain statutory requirements, are designed to present the company's performance in as favourable a light as possible. In particular, Susan has noticed that, although the Chairman's report will usually mention the effects of the recession, the other side of the coin, in the shape of the effect of inflation upon prices and profits, is rarely mentioned. She is understandably concerned that the return on her investment should, if at all possible, at least keep pace with inflation. She is also curious to know when, for instance one of the companies she is considering states that 'before-tax profits over the five years 1987–1991 were £12, £13.5, £15.1, £17 and £19 millions respectively', how much of this increase can be ascribed simply to the firm's prices increasing in line with everyone else's, rather than to a genuine expansion in business.

In order to satisfy her curiosity, what Susan requires is a 'measure of inflation' – some kind of overall, average figure which will tell her how rapidly prices are changing. The most easily available and widely accepted measure of this kind is the Retail Price Index (more properly known as the General Index of Retail Prices), but before we can discuss this particular index we need to examine the general concept of *index numbers*.

## WHAT IS AN INDEX NUMBER?

Many of the complications in constructing a measure of price increases for our economy arise from the fact that people are free to spend their money on a tremendous variety of goods and services, and probably no two households dispose of their income in precisely the same way. Suppose, however, we simplify the discussion by imagining a community living on a remote island, who subsist entirely on a diet of potatoes. Then the sole factor determining the purchasing power of a family's wage will be the price per pound of this staple commodity.

Let's say that the price of a pound of potatoes was 12 pence in 1991, and went up to 14 pence in 1992. It's no good simply stating that 'the price went up by 2 pence'; an increase of 2 pence which raised the price from 2 to 4 pence a pound would clearly have a more serious effect on people's standard of living than the present one which raises it from 12 to 14 pence per pound, since the former price increase would halve the amount of potatoes they could purchase for a given wage, whereas the latter would only reduce it by one-seventh. So what is needed is a measure of how the price per pound has increased *relative* to the price at some time in the past.

This is the basic idea behind all index numbers: they measure *changes* – in prices, quantities consumed, or whatever – *relative* to the situation at some period in the past. The period to which the changes are related is referred to as the *base period* (base year, base month, etc.).

We can construct a very simple kind of index, called a *price relative*, for the increase in the price of potatoes from 1991 to 1992, by defining:

Price relative for 1992 based on 1991

$$= \frac{1992 \text{ price/pound}}{1991 \text{ price/pound}} \times 100$$

$$= \frac{14}{12} \times 100$$

$$= 117 \ (\%) \ \text{(to the nearest whole \%)}.$$

There are several things to notice about this very basic kind of price index for a single item, because they apply also to the more complex types of index we're going to look at later. First, the index is expressed as a percentage – hence the ' × 100' in the calculation – but, because this applies almost universally, we don't usually bother to write in the % sign (which is why it is shown in brackets). There *are* one or two of the more obscure indices which use a 'per thousand' rather than 'per cent' form of expression, but you are not likely to come across them.

Second, and following on from this, we can deduce that the index for the base year will always be 100, since it will be calculated by:

$$\frac{1991 \text{ price}}{1991 \text{ price}} \times 100 = 100.$$

An index greater than 100 therefore shows that the price has increased since the base year, while one which is below 100 indicates a decrease in price. All that the 1991 index of 117 is telling us is that potato prices have increased by about 17 per cent from 1991 to 1992.

We must beware, however, in interpreting changes in the index from one year to the next. If, for instance, the price of potatoes were to increase to 16 pence per pound during 1993, then the index for 1993, still based on 1991 would be:

$$\frac{16}{12} \times 100 = 133.$$

We could thus say, quite fairly, that potato prices have increased by 33 per cent from 1991 to 1993. What we could *not* do, however, would be to say 'The index has increased from 117 to 133 between 1988 and 1989, an increase of 16 per cent'. Each index is a percentage *of the base year price*, so the increase is 16 per cent of *that* price; the distinction is sometimes made by saying 'The index has increased by 16 percentage points'. If we wished to speak of the percentage increase between 1992 and 1993 we would have to express 16 as a percentage of the 1992 figure of 117, which would give about 14 per cent.

## DIVERSIFYING THE DIET

The situation considered in the previous section was particularly simple because we didn't have to worry about *how* the residents of our imaginary island might choose to spend their money – the only thing to spend it on was potatoes! But now suppose that they have diversified their diet somewhat to include not only potatoes but also milk and fish. The prices of these items over the past two years have been as follows:

|                     | 1991  | 1992  |
|---------------------|-------|-------|
| Fish (per pound)    | £2.40 | £2.90 |
| Potatoes (per pound)| 12p   | 14p   |
| Milk (per pint)     | 27p   | 29p   |

There are two obvious ways of going about the construction of a price index taking all three commodities into account. First, we might try adding up the three prices and then constructing one overall price relative:

$$\frac{\text{Total cost of three items in 1988}}{\text{Total cost of three items in 1987}} = \frac{333}{279} \text{ (prices in pence)}$$

so the suggested index will be 119. Or we could try working out the three price relatives separately and then averaging them:

$$\frac{290}{240} \text{ (price relative for fish)}$$

$$+ \frac{14}{12} \text{ (price relative for potatoes)}$$

$$+ \frac{29}{27} \text{ (price relative for milk)}$$

$$= 345 \text{ giving an average of 115.}$$

Unfortunately, neither of these obvious methods is at all satisfactory, since both have the serious defect of completely ignoring the *amounts* of each item which people consume. The effect on a typical family's budget of an increase in the price of potatoes will be much more serious than the effect of a corresponding increase in the price of fish if they eat potatoes every day but fish only as an occasional special treat. Imagine, for example, that their annual consumption of fish is 20 pounds. Then the price increase on fish between 1991 and 1992 will add $20 \times 50p = £10$ to their annual food bill. But if they eat ten pounds of potatoes per week, then their annual consumption will be 520 pounds, so the additional cost produced by the potato price increasing from 12 pence to 14 pence per pound will be $520 \times 2$ pence $= £10.40$ per annum – rather greater than the effect of the fish price increase.

In other words, a small increase in the price of a heavily-used commodity may have an effect just as serious, if not more so, upon the typical family's budget as a large increase in the price of a less popular commodity. Any sensible price index, purporting to demonstrate the effect of increasing prices upon people's budgets, must take this into consideration; yet both the 'indices' devised above give an equal weight to each of the three items. What is needed is a method of constructing a *weighted* index which will take account of the differing importance of items in the overall budget.

## WEIGHTING THE INDEX

By far the simplest way to deduce the importance of a certain item in a family's budget is to note how much they spend on that item – in other words, the *value* of their purchases of the item. This in turn will depend on the *quantity* of the item which they purchase. So an index which would correctly reflect the relative importance of the various items which people use could be defined as a price relative for their whole 'shopping basket' over a certain period (year, month or whatever):

$$\text{Price index} = \frac{\text{Total cost of 'shopping basket' at present prices}}{\text{Total cost of 'shopping basket' at base year prices.}}$$

And the total cost of the 'basket', of course, will just be the quantity of each item bought multiplied by the price of that item, added together for all the items in the 'basket'.

But here we come up against a snag: when we say, 'the quantity of each item bought', which quantity are we referring to – the amount which people bought in the base year, or the amount that they are buying *now*? If the prices have changed, then doubtless the quantities purchased have, too; the dearer rump steak becomes relative to sausages, the more likely people are to transfer some of their spending from rump steak to sausages, thus altering the quantities of each which would be bought. How are we going to take account of this factor in devising an index?

### Base-weighting

There are actually two common systems in use, both of which involve the assumption that the quantities being purchased do not alter along with altering prices. The first system, sometimes known as the *Laspeyres* price index, after its inventor, assumes that people are still buying *now* the quantities which they bought in the base year. For this reason, the name I prefer for this method is the *base-weighted price index*. A verbal definition would be:

$$\text{Base weighted price index} = \frac{\text{Total cost of base-year quantities at current prices}}{\text{Total cost of base-year quantities at base-year prices}}$$

expressed, as usual, as a percentage. If you are a formula-lover, you can easily devise one in this case, using the notations $p_0$, $p_n$ to stand for the old and new prices, and $q_0$ to stand for the old or base-year quantities. The amount spent on one item during the period would be quantity $\times$ price for that item; so, using the $\Sigma$ symbol which was introduced in the last chapter, and which in this case we interpret as 'add up for all the items in the basket', we could say that the total cost of the base-year quantities at current prices is $\Sigma q_0 p_n$, and that of the base-year quantities at the base-year prices is $\Sigma q_0 p_0$. Thus, including the conversion to percentages, we have:

$$\text{Base-weighted price index} = \frac{\Sigma q_0 p_n}{\Sigma q_0 p_0} \times 100.$$

However, a much better way to remember how to calculate the index is to think of it simply as a price relative for the whole shopping basket, the quantities bought being those for the base-year.

### Current-weighting

You probably won't be too surprised to learn that the alternative method of calculation, known as a *Paasche* or, more meaningfully a *current-weighted price index*, makes the alternative assumption that people were buying in the base year the same quantities as they are buying now. The verbal definition of this index is:

$$\text{Current-weighted price index} = \frac{\text{Total cost of current quantities at current prices}}{\text{Total cost of current quantities at base-year prices}}$$

once again expressed as a percentage. Using the notation previously introduced, together with the additional symbol $q_n$ to represent the current (new) quantities, we can write this as:

$$\text{Current-weighted price index} = \frac{\Sigma q_n p_n}{\Sigma q_n p_0} \times 100.$$

## CALCULATING THE INDICES

Before we discuss the pros and cons of these two methods of calculating an index, let's see how the calculations are actually done for the situation we've previously been discussing. The prices for the three commodities being consumed by our islanders are repeated below, together with the amounts of each which they consumed in the two years in question:

|  | 1991 | | 1992 | |
|---|---|---|---|---|
|  | price | quantity | price | quantity |
| Fish | 240 | 20 | 290 | 25 |
| Potatoes | 12 | 520 | 14 | 500 |
| Milk | 27 | 200 | 29 | 190 |

The 1991 prices and quantities will be our $p_0$s and $q_0$s, and those for 1992 will be the $p_n$s and $q_n$s. If you examine the formulae for the two types of index you will see that we need to calculate four combinations of $p$s and $q$s: $p_0q_0$, $p_0q_n$, $p_nq_0$ and $p_nq_n$. The best way to lay out the calculation is in columns as follows:

| $p_0$ | $q_0$ | $p_n$ | $q_n$ | $p_0q_0$ | $p_0q_n$ | $p_nq_0$ | $p_nq_n$ |
|---|---|---|---|---|---|---|---|
| 240 | 20 | 290 | 25 | 4800 | 6000 | 5800 | 7250 |
| 12 | 520 | 14 | 500 | 6240 | 6000 | 7280 | 7000 |
| 27 | 200 | 29 | 190 | 5400 | 5130 | 5800 | 5510 |
|  |  |  |  | 16,440 | 17,130 | 18,880 | 19,760 |

◖ If you are used to using a spreadsheet, it is very easy to carry out this calculation – simply enter the appropriate formula into the top cells of the product columns, and then copy it down the entire column. You will find a LOTUS worksheet for doing this calculation at INDEX.WK1 on the diskette.

So the base-weighted price index will be:

$$\frac{\Sigma p_nq_0}{\Sigma p_0q_0} = \frac{18,880}{16,440} = 1.15$$

which when expressed as a percentage is 115. The current-weighted index is:

$$\frac{\Sigma p_nq_n}{\Sigma p_0q_n} = \frac{19,760}{17,130} = 1.15$$

which in percentage terms is also 115. So in this case the two systems give virtually the same result; we would have to go to more than two decimal places before we could distinguish any difference between them.

Why is this the case? After all, both prices and quantities have changed quite a bit over the two years. But the *proportion* of total expenditure which is taken up by each item remains very similar. Had these proportions changed drastically, we would have got values for the two indices which were more noticeably different. For example, you might like to confirm that if the rise in the price of fish had caused people to cut their consumption down to only 10 pounds per year, then the current-weighted index would become 114, because the effect on the budget of the fish price increase would be relatively less important.

## DECIDING WHICH TO USE

How, then, should we decide which system to use in a given situation? The chief drawback of the base-weighted system is that it uses weights which are out of date, since they refer to spending patterns in the base year. However, we have also seen that, if the changes in quantities purchased are not too drastic, the use of old quantities doesn't result in serious inaccuracy; so this drawback need not be taken too seriously as long as we are not *too* far from the base year, nor in a very rapidly-fluctuating situation. And the base-weighting system has some very powerful compensating advantages.

First of these is the fact that we don't require a knowledge of the quantities used in the current period in order to calculate a base-weighted index, which means that it can be calculated as soon as the current prices are known; a current-weighted index, on the other hand, could not be calculated until the end of the period, when information about current quantities becomes available. Second, and perhaps even more important, the *denominator* of the base-weighted index – the $\Sigma p_0 q_0$ term – remains the same from year to year, since it doesn't involve any current figures. So it can be calculated once and for all, then simply stored away in the computer or wherever, to be used each time a new index is calculated. This may seem a trivial saving in effort when only three items are involved, but if you realise that the real-life Retail Price Index involves hundreds of items, the saving in calculation time becomes quite significant.

Moreover, because the denominator of every price index based on the same year will be exactly the same, a series of index numbers calculated in this way can be compared directly with each other. The current-weighted index, in contrast to this, has a denominator which contains the term $\Sigma p_0 q_n$, and which therefore changes from one year to another, so that a series of index numbers of this kind can only be compared with the base-year figure, and not directly with each other. Also, as already indicated, we must wait until the end of the period when the current quantities are known before computing a current-weighted index; so the disadvantages of the current-weighted index generally outweigh the advantages, except in situations where the quantities are changing substantially from one period to the next.

Several other more complex types of index number have been devised in an attempt to combine the advantages of base-weighting with those of current-weighting, or to provide various other, rather theoretical, advantages, but the two we have examined remain by far the most widely used and useful.

## THE RETAIL PRICE INDEX

The government's General Index of Retail Prices, which has been in existence – though with substantial modifications – since 1914, measures the changes in the prices of a 'basket' of some 350 or so goods and services bought by the 'average family' from one month to the next. In this context the buying patterns of the 'average family' are deduced by means of the Family Expenditure Survey, an ongoing enquiry in which about 7,000 families throughout the country keep a continuous record of all their spending. The sample is carefully structured so as to cover all sections of the population with the exception of one- and two-person pensioner households, and those in the top three or four per cent when classified by weekly income. These two categories of households are excluded because it is considered that their spending patterns differ substantially from those of the majority of households.

The actual method of calculation of the Retail Price Index, or RPI as it is often called, is closely related to the base-weighted system which we examined in the sections, 'Weighting the index', p. 112, and 'Calculating the indices', p. 113. The weightings for the various items included are obtained from the information provided by the Family Expenditure Survey, while the information as to the prices each month is gathered by numerous investigators throughout the country, who cover a wide range of types of retail outlet from hypermarkets to small travelling grocery suppliers. Some items, of course, don't vary over the country, and can be collected centrally; these include things like postage and telephone charges. The overall weights total 1000, and in 1990 the weight for food was 158, for alcoholic drink, 77, and so on.

When all the information has been gathered the index can be calculated, but as you can imagine this is quite a substantial task. By the time all the collating and computation has been done, the index is about four-and-a-half weeks out of date when it is announced. Naturally, deciding what items should go into the index, what base-year should be used, when it should be changed, and so on, is an important part of producing the index, and so a standing advisory panel, consisting of members from a wide range of interested bodies, has been set up to guide the government in this respect.

As well as the overall index, separate indices are published – which together comprise the general index. The 'pensioner households' also have their own index, published separately from the main one.

For more details of how the RPI is calculated, particularly since its re-basing in January 1987, see the April 1987 edition of the 'Employment Gazette'.

It would not be fair to leave the topic of the RPI, however, without a mention of some of the criticisms which have been levelled at it. The monthly announcement of the latest rise in the RPI has attained an almost mystical significance as inflation has gained a hold on the economy and so, not surprisingly, efforts to 'debunk' it have been made. It is certainly true, as many critics point out, that it is *not* a 'cost of living' index, since some items which have a very significant effect on people's standard of living are excluded from its calculation. Moreover, it makes no attempt to include any reflection of the *quality* of the goods or services purchased – admittedly a very difficult thing to quantify. The most sweeping criticisms – and the most difficult to respond to – are made by those who claim that the index is totally oriented to the standards of the 'consumer society', that it describes the requirements of a mythical 'typical family', and that it makes no attempt to reflect more imponderable, but possibly more important, factors than how many pounds of potatoes people can buy with their wages, such as how much pollution they have to put up with, or what educational and employment opportunities are open to them. There is also scope for argument about the *interpretation* of the index – you have probably heard or read discussions about the 'headline' and 'underlying' inflation rates.

Here, however, we are straying into the realms of the economist and sociologist. Certainly, within the limitations of its design, the RPI remains probably the most useful measure we have of the effect of inflation upon the purchasing power of the majority of the population.

## WHAT'S THE USE OF THE RPI?

You are probably far better informed as to the applications to which the RPI and index numbers in general, can be put, than your counterparts would have been not many years ago. The idea of 'index-linked' savings, designed to keep pace with inflation as measured by the RPI, is now a very familiar one. The principle here is quite simple: if the general level of prices as indicated by the RPI, rises by say 35 per cent over a period of three years then you are guaranteed a minimum return of 35 per cent on your savings, so that at least you will be no worse off, in terms of what you can buy with your money, than you were at the time you invested it. The RPI is also often referred to in wage negotiations, the Government wishing at present to discourage wage increases greater than the inflation rate as measured by the RPI.

In an inflationary situation we should really make use of the RPI whenever we wish to compare amounts of money – profits, incomes, and so on – being paid at different points in time. This can be done very simply, as the following example will illustrate.

Suppose a worker was earning £180 per week in 1989 and this rose to £225 per week in 1990 – an apparent increase of 25 per cent. How much better off is he in real terms when the effect of inflation is taken into account?

Published values for the RPI give 115.2 as the average for the year in 1989, and 126.1 in 1990, both figures being based on January 1987. In other words, goods and services which would have cost £115.20 in 1989 would cost £126.10 in 1990. So what he could buy for £1 in 1990 would have cost only £115.2/126.1 = 91p in 1989; that is, the 1990 £1 is worth only 91p or 91 per cent of what £1 was worth in 1989. The £225-a-week wage in 1990 is therefore worth only about £205 in 1989 terms, and so the real percentage increase in the worker's wage, looked at in terms of what he can buy with his money, is only 25/180 or about 14 per cent.

## ADVISING THE INVESTOR

We are now in a position to return to the problem mentioned in section 1 above, and to advise the potential share-purchaser of the *real* behaviour of her chosen company's profits, when the effect of inflation is removed. You will recall that the quoted profits for the five years 1987–1991 were, in millions of pounds, 12, 13.5, 15.1, 17 and 19. What has happened to the retail price index, our 'measure of inflation', in the meantime? The published values for the annual average retail price indices for the five years in question are 101.9, 106.9, 115.2, 126.1 and 133.5 respectively, all based upon January 1987. So we can 'deflate' the quoted profit figures to their value in terms of the 1987 pound as follows:

The 1987 figure, of course, is unaltered. The 1988 figure must be multiplied by a factor of 101.9/106.9:

$$13.5 \times \frac{101.9}{106.9} = 12.87.$$

For 1989 we have $15.1 \times \dfrac{101.9}{115.2} = 13.36.$

You should verify for yourself that the remaining calculations give 13.74 for 1990 and 14.50 for 1991 so the increase in the 'deflated' profits is not nearly so impressive as the original figures would lead us to believe. If you care to calculate the percentage changes in the profit quoted and also those in the retail price index from year to year, the reason for this will be brought home to you: the quoted profits are increasing at 11–12 per cent per year but simultaneously the RPI is increasing by 5–8 per cent per year. Thus a part

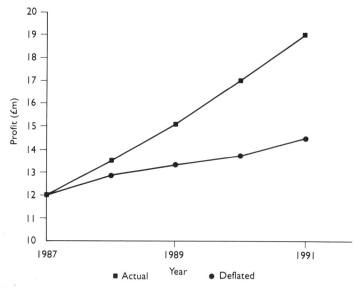

**Fig. 7.1** The effect of inflation on profits

of the increase in profits is accountable for simply by price increases in line with inflation. Figure 7.1 emphasises this.

## SOME TECHNICAL CONSIDERATIONS

There are one or two rather technical points which we should consider before leaving the subject of index numbers. We have discussed the arguments for and against the two systems of weighting, but there are other decisions to be made in arriving at an index, notably as to what items should be included and what base year should be chosen. With the RPI, for example, it is clearly impossible to include every single item which people buy, while, with regard to the base year, if you look at the published values of the RPI you will find that within recent years it has been based successively on 1956, 1962, 1974 and currently 1987.

The choice of items to be included is crucial, since different selections could give quite different results. Clearly the items must be in fairly general use – one would not include in a food price index caviar or strawberries in January. From time to time they will need to be altered so that the index keeps pace with changing consumer tastes; as items such as colour television sets or calculators become more widely purchased, the index will be modified to take account of such changes. Beyond this, it can only be said that some items are known to be good 'indicators' of inflation, responding more quickly to pressures for price rises. Ideally one should have a balance between this type of item and those which are more stable and less susceptible to sudden price increases.

The choice of a base-period, and in particular the decision as to when the base-period should be changed, is often problematical. The conventional wisdom states that a base year should be 'typical', neither a period of economic boom nor recession, and not exceptional in any other way; thus, for example, a year during which there has been a great deal of industrial unrest, reducing production levels or cutting down on public services, would not be a good candidate for a base period. It is obviously undesirable to let the index run for too long with the same base period; items in the index become out of date, comparisons are being made with a far distant point in time, and eventually the index becomes very large and unwieldy for calculation purposes. This was actually the situation quite recently, when in 1987 the base of the index was changed. At the time of the change the 'old' index series, based on January 1974, stood at 394.5. When the change was made, the government took the opportunity also to make some changes in the calculation of the index, including a number of items and categories of expenditure which had not appeared in the index hitherto, such as expenditure on leisure activities.

The changes naturally led to some criticism, particularly with regard to the applicability of the new index to the 'average' or 'typical' household. In fact, whenever the base year of the index is changed, political capital can be made of the decision, particularly now that regular announcements in the news media of the monthly values of the index have made the public more 'index-conscious'. The suggestion can be made that the party in power hopes to make the rate of inflation look better by exploiting the public's erroneous view that an RPI of 102 is 'better' than one of 302. In practice, however, though it is the minister with responsibility for employment who actually takes decisions regarding the RPI, he or she is strongly influenced by the views of the non-party advisory panel already mentioned, so it is unlikely that such a decision could be taken on purely political grounds.

## OTHER KINDS OF INDEX

We have concentrated so far almost entirely on price indices and on the Retail Price Index in particular, because these are the ones you are most likely to encounter, and which have the most obviously useful applications. You have probably heard of the Financial Times Ordinary Share Index which measures price movements on the Stock Exchange in London, and the Dow Jones Index which does the same sort of thing for the New York stock market.

But there are many other index numbers which are not price indices, as a glance at the contents page of any issue of the *Monthly Digest of Statistics* will show you. Index numbers of output, index numbers of retail sales, and index numbers of basic wage rates of manual workers are just three examples. These all have their individual mode of calculation, details of which you can find, should you need to know, in the specialised government publications dealing with these topics, but all have in common with the price indices we have looked at the fact that they are designed to examine how a situation has *changed* when referred to some base period in the past, and that they consist of some form of *weighted average* over a whole collection of different items.

### Practical exercises

**1** Customers of the *Statisticians Arms* have a rather limited choice of beverages, being restricted to beer, whisky or tomato juice. The prices of these items, and the consumption by customers, for 1991 and 1992 are as follows:

|  | 1991 | | 1992 | |
| --- | --- | --- | --- | --- |
|  | Price | Quantity | Price | Quantity |
| Beer (pint) | 130 | 60,000 | 140 | 55,000 |
| Whisky (single) | 165 | 20,000 | 180 | 21,000 |
| Tomato juice (small) | 55 | 15,000 | 75 | 18,000 |

Calculate a base-weighted and a current-weighted price index for this data in 1992, using 1991 as base-year. (Use INDEX.WK1 if you wish.)

2  A firm quotes turnover figures of £16,000,000, £18,000,000 and £22,000,000 for the three years 1988, 1989 and 1990. Use the values of the Retail Price Index given in the section, 'Advising the investor', p. 117 to deflate these turnovers to constant 1988 values, and hence find out if they are keeping pace with inflation.

3  'The Retail Price Index went up from 245 to 265 over the last six months, but we haven't had a twenty per cent rise to keep up with it, so we're worse off now.' Criticise and correct this statement.

4  Get hold of an Annual Report and Accounts for a large public company, which usually includes a summary for the past five years of key figures such as turnovers and profits. By finding the values of the Retail Price Index for the corresponding period from the *Monthly Digest* or other published source deflate the five-year series of profits or turnovers, and deduce whether the company's performance is actually improving or not. You might also like to compare the performance of two companies in the same industrial sector on this basis.

5  By keeping a record of your expenditure, and noting the prices of 'typical' items which you buy, you can construct your own personal 'cost of living index'. Ideally you need to carry out the exercise over a period of about three months. The procedure would be as follows.

(a)  Choose two or three items for each of the eleven major categories in the RPI which you feel are 'representative' items for you, and make a note of their prices on a single fixed date at the beginning of your three-month period.

(b)  Keep a record of *all* your spending over a period of about a fortnight. If there are some items, such as rent, which happen not to be included during your chosen fortnight, you should add in an appropriate proportion to the fortnight's budget. From this expenditure record you can find what percentage of your budget goes on food, alcoholic drink, and the rest of the eleven RPI categories – in other words, the *weighting* of each of these categories within your personal 'basket' of goods and services.

(c)  At the end of your three-month period, collect the new prices of your selected items. Many of them may not have altered – don't worry!

(d)  The easiest way to calculate your index from this data is by means of a *weighted average of price relatives*, which is effectively identical with the kinds of indices we've discussed in the chapter, but avoids your having to collect information about the quantities you use. The method is best shown with some simple figures. Suppose your chosen items are only three: a small tin of baked beans, representing food, which has increased in price from 23 pence to 24 pence over the period; a return bus-ticket to college, representing transport, which has stayed the same at 90 pence; and a pair of jeans, representing clothing, which have gone up from £19.95 to £21.45. Suppose too that your expenditure record shows that you spend 60 per cent of your budget on food,

30 per cent on transport and 10 per cent on clothing. Then you would calculate your index by:

(i) finding the price relative for each of the three items:

$$\text{Food } 24/23 = 104.3$$

$$\text{Transport } 90/90 = 100$$

$$\text{Clothing } \frac{21.45}{19.95} = 107.5$$

(ii) finding the appropriate weighted average of these:

$$60\% \times 104.3 + 30\% \times 100 + 10\% \times 107.5 = 103.3.$$

Your personal index would therefore be 103.3.

(e) Having calculated your index, you might like to consider these further points.

(i) How does it compare with the official RPI for the same period? (You'll have to wait for a few weeks to find this.)

(ii) What sort of difficulties have you come across in constructing the index? Do you think the producers of the RPI have the same difficulties and if so, how do they resolve them?

(iii) If your 'personal inflation rate' as measured by your index continued at the same level for the next year, how much grant would you need to receive for the corresponding period next year?

## Case study problem

Dear X,

You'll be thinking I only write to you when I want to ask for help! This time I am concerned about the prices I am charging – material costs go up so fast, and many food prices are very seasonal, but it's a year since I increased my prices.

I imagine the 'cost of living index' would give me some idea of the amount by which I should raise my prices – but I am confused by the different figures which are published. I can find the General Index of Retail Prices, and there is a special section for 'Meals bought and consumed outside the home', which fits my situation. But then there are different indices for the various foods, and some of them are 'de-seasonalised' which doesn't help.

Can you explain just what the various numbers measure, and work out for me how much I should put up the price of my basic Finger Buffet (currently £4.50 excluding drinks) to allow for price increases over the past year, using the most suitable index as a guide?

Thanks again for all your help,

Jane

## Case study question

Obtain the most up-to-date information you can about the Retail Price Index and its various components, and use this information to draft a reply to the above letter.

# PART 3

# Numbers – a basis for deduction

Throughout Part 2 we have been concerned only with *descriptive statistics* – we have presented data in tables and diagrams, we have summarised it with the aid of means, standard deviations, index numbers, and so forth, but we have always confined our attention to the sample of data actually available.

In many situations, however, what we wish to do is go *beyond* the available sample of data, and use that data as a basis for making deductions about the entire population from which the sample was drawn. This is the case, for example, in a market research enquiry, where having discovered that 60 per cent of a sample of 500 housewives will purchase our product, we want to find out what this implies about the percentage of the entire buying population who will buy the product. It is the case in controlling the quality of output from a production line: if a machine is producing 5,000 screws a minute, it is clearly impossible to inspect every single one, so only a sample will be inspected and deductions about the quality of the whole production will be made on the basis of the sample.

We could, of course, content ourselves with saying 'Well, the figure for the whole population buying our product will be near enough 60 per cent too', or 'This sample of screws is OK – I expect the rest are as well'. But 'near enough' isn't really good enough in many such cases; we want to know just *how* near – and how likely we are to be wrong in our estimate. It's that word 'likely', in fact, which gives the clue as to how we should proceed. What we need to deal with such problems effectively is a proper mathematically-based theory with which we can pin down statements of the 'likely' or 'near enough' kind. So we start our work in this part, the rest of which will be concerned with the drawing of conclusions from statistical information, with a discussion of probability theory.

## CHAPTER 8

# A firm foundation: elementary probability

## Objectives

Before starting work on this chapter make sure you are happy with:

(a)  addition, subtraction and multiplication of fractions (*see* Chapter 1, pp. 7–8).
(b)  conversion of fractions to decimals or percentages and vice versa (*see* Chapter 1, pp. 10–11);
(c)  calculation of the arithmetic mean (*see* Chapter 6, pp. 91–95).

By the end of your work on this chapter you should be able to:

(a)  define a probability in a given situation using *a priori* or empirical methods as appropriate;
(b)  solve problems involving the calculation of simple probabilities and their combination in 'or' and 'and' situations;
(c)  say what is meant by the expected value of a process, and calculate expected values for simple processes;
(d)  construct decision tables and trees, and make use of expected values to arrive at decisions;
(e)  know the limitations of this approach to decision-making.

## THE PRODUCT DEVELOPMENT MANAGER'S PROBLEM

Harold Black is responsible for the development of new product lines for Shoddier Toys Limited, an old-established firm which manufactures dolls and other small plastic toys. He has recently been working hard to develop and promote a line of 'Flash Spockman' toys, which will be marketed to coincide with the introduction of a new television series of that name, so he is naturally very upset when an acquaintance who is employed by the television company producing the series telephones him with the news that the series may, after all, not be broadcast.

Although he reckons this rumour has only about a 40 per cent chance of being true, it presents him with a difficult choice. Sales during the product's first year on the market had been estimated at 12,000 units, each generating a profit of £2, but this projection was based on the assumption that the TV series would be going ahead. If this is not the case, Mr Black reckons that the sales might be as low as 2,000 units. He is therefore forced to consider whether it might not be better to abandon development of the new product now, even though £5,000 has already been invested in its development.

To make matters worse, no sooner has he digested this piece of bad news than the firm's managing director rings to tell him that if the TV series appears, a rival company, Nastitoys, may be planning to produce a 'pirated' competitive product, which will sell at a cheaper price and cut down Shoddier's sales to 8,000 units. Admittedly, the managing director reckons the chance of Nastitoys getting away with this piracy to be only 50–50, but the possibility still has to be taken into account. Shoddier thus have the choice of two alternatives: to abandon the new product altogether, or to go ahead and market it regardless of whether the TV series comes off or not, and take the risk that, if it does, Nastitoys will bring out their competing product.

There are two clear requirements if Mr Black is to be able to tackle his problem logically. First of all, he needs to understand precisely what the statements 'the chances are 50–50' and 'a 40 per cent chance' mean, and to be able to find the chances of various sequences of events happening; and secondly, he needs to be able to tie together the *chance* of something happening with the *financial result* of that occurrence.

## RECKONING THE CHANCES

Whether wittingly or unwittingly, we are making assessments of chances, or *probabilities* as statisticians prefer to call them, all the time. For example, when you look out of the window in the morning and decide not to wear a raincoat to go out, you are making a decision based on your estimate of the chance of rain during the day; if you learn that in past years 95 per cent of students on your course have passed the first-year examination, and accordingly feel somewhat encouraged, it is because you recognise that your chance of passing is presumably about the same; and of course, if you do the football pools or place bets on horses, you are making assessments of the chance that a particular horse or team will be successful.

Probably, in these cases, you would not like to be pinned down to an actual numerical statement of the chance involved, but in order to make use of probabilities in dealing with problems such as that outlined at the beginning of this chapter, that is just what we need to do. We will therefore begin by looking at the various ways in which a quantified probability might be arrived at.

### Working it out in advance

Imagine that the Queen is coming to open a new factory for a firm with 600 employees, and that one worker is to be chosen to present her with a souvenir book. So that this is done fairly, 600 pieces of paper, of which 599 are blank and one marked with a cross, are put into a hat, and each worker is invited to take one (you may be reminded of what we said about simple random samples in Chapter 3). Then I think you will agree that, if the hat is well shaken and all the pieces of paper are indistinguishable, the chances of any one individual, say Fred Smith, being chosen are 1 in 600 or 1/600.

In other words, we have found the probability of the event 'Fred Smith is chosen' by taking the number of ways this may happen – just one – as a fraction of the total numbers of possible events. We often denote the probability of an event occurring by writing $p$(event); so here we would say:

$$p(\text{Fred Smith chosen}) = 1/600.$$

We call this an a *priori* method of finding the probability, because we are able to assess the probability of the event *prior* to its actual occurrence simply by using our knowledge of the situation. Before generalising this definition to *any* event, however, we should look again at the assumptions we made in reaching our figure of 1/600. We said: '. . . the hat is well shaken and all the pieces of paper are indistinguishable'; in other words, the chances of each person being chosen are exactly the same, or, in statistical terms, all the outcomes are equally likely. Of course, if this were not the case − if the piece of paper bearing the cross were blue, say, so that the first person offered the hat could be sure of taking it − then, far from having a 1 in 600 chance of selection, poor old Fred, unless *he* were the lucky first, would have no chance at all!

With the proviso, then, that all outcomes *are* equally likely, we can define a probability *a priori* as follows:

$$p(\text{event}) = \frac{\text{Number of ways that event can occur}}{\text{Total number of possible outcomes}}.$$

So if we know that out of the 600 employees, 250 are women, we can say that the chance of the chosen individual being a woman is given by:

$$p(\text{woman}) = \frac{250}{600}$$

since there are 250 ways in which the selected person could be a woman.

## Doing an experiment

Unfortunately, there are many situations in which we just don't have the requisite prior knowledge to calculate probabilities in this way. Suppose, for example, that a firm wants to know what is the probability of an item produced by a particular automatic machine being defective. It's a perfectly reasonable question to ask: presumably a small proportion of defective items is unavoidable, whereas a large proportion would need to be remedied; but there is no way in which we can find this probability by *a priori* means. To ask 'How many ways can an acceptable item occur?' is a question no more meaningful than 'How long is a piece of string' − the item either *is* defective or it isn't, so the whole basis of the *a priori* method breaks down.

The obvious course to adopt here is to monitor the output of the machine over a reasonable period of time and actually find out how often it produces a defective item. Note that proviso 'over a reasonable period of time' − it's clearly no good just looking at two or three items; a sample of a few hundred items will give a much clearer picture of what's going on. If among 200 items say, we found 12 defectives, then we might estimate the probability of a defective item being produced by the machine as 12/200. This is the experimental or empirical approach to probability, based on looking at what actually happens in practice rather than theorising ahead of the event. We might define probability in this way as:

$$p(\text{event}) = \frac{\text{Number of times event occurs}}{\text{Total number of experiments}}$$

where we are using 'experiment' in a rather loose sense to mean the occasions on which the event *might* have occurred.

It might well happen, of course, that if we were to take a second sample of 200 items we would find 14 defectives, or perhaps only 11; for this reason a probability arrived at in this way can really only be regarded as an estimate. However, the larger the number of experiments, the more accurate we should expect the estimate to be. There are cases where we can actually verify this expectation by finding out how closely the experimental probability agrees with an *a priori* figure. For instance, we know that the chance of obtaining a six on a single throw of an unbiased dice is theoretically 1/6. If we perform the experiment of actually throwing the dice a number of times, we don't expect to get exactly 1/6 of the throws producing sixes, but the greater the number of throws, the nearer the proportion should get to the theoretical figure of 1/6. For this reason we say:

> experimental probability approaches theoretical probability as the number of experiments becomes very large.

## Trusting to instinct

If you think back for a moment to the problem posed at the start of this chapter, you will realise that neither of the two definitions of probability given so far is likely to be the basis for a statement such as 'the chance of Nastitoys getting away with piracy is 50–50'. A probability of this kind is almost certainly the product of someone's intuition – hopefully backed by experience and information – and in many business situations it is this third, *intuitive*, method of quantifying probabilities which we have to fall back on.

By whatever means we arrive at a probability figure, we will end up with something which is a fraction, either expressed as such (Fred Smith's chance of selection is 1/600), or as a percentage (like Nastitoys' 50–50 chance of getting away with piracy). Probabilities are thus measured on a scale from zero – representing, in terms of our three definitions, an event which cannot occur in any way, which has never been known to occur, or which we feel is impossible – to one – representing an event which is bound to occur, which has always happened so far, or which we feel to be inevitable.

This fact gives us a useful check on the correctness of our arguments in future, more complex probability calculations. An answer which is supposed to be a probability, and which is greater than 1, must be wrong!

Before we go on to consider how these definitions of probability apply to more complicated problems, let's apply them in a few simple cases. (You will often receive the impression in studying basic probability that statisticians are obsessed with gambling – all the problems seem to be about dice, cards and roulette wheels – but that's mainly because these are easy problems to consider.)

## SOME EASY EXAMPLES

Suppose first that you have a dice* which, instead of the usual numbered faces, has two green, two red and two yellow. What is the chance that, when it is thrown at random, a yellow face will show? The *a priori* definition gives two yellow faces out of six faces altogether, or 2/6. Notice, incidentally, that it often isn't worth cancelling probability fractions like this one, particularly if you need to combine them later; you will often find yourself cancelling and then putting them over a common denominator, thus going round in circles!

If we had two such dice, and tossed them simultaneously, what would be the chance of obtaining one yellow and one green face? There are thirty-six combinations altogether, since any of the six faces of the first dice can be combined with any of the six faces of

---

* Strictly, the singular term is die: one die, two dice, but I will adopt the popular usage of 'dice' for both singular and plural.

the second. Of these, how many fall into the category we are interested in? Either of the two yellow faces on the first dice could be combined with either of the two green ones on the second, so there are four possibilities there; or we could have either green face of the first dice combined with either yellow face of the second – another four possibilities. Altogether, then, there are eight possibilities in the category we are looking for, out of 36 possibilities in all, giving a probability of 8/36.

Now consider how you would determine the probability that it will be a wet day tomorrow. This is one which we need to approach via the experimental method, since there is no way we can count 'how many ways it might rain tomorrow'. If tomorrow is February 28th, then one way of approaching the problem would be to look up the weather records over the past, say, ten years, and find out, among all the February days in the ten-year period, what proportion have been wet. This will then give at least an approximate idea of the figure, though of course there's always the possibility that *this* year is exceptionally wet – or exceptionally dry!

Finally, what happens if someone asks you what you reckon to be the chance that you will pass the examinations at the end of your course. How would you reply? You *could* adopt an experimental approach, and look up the percentage of students on your course who have passed the examination over the past few years; but ultimately only you know whether you have done sufficient work, written good lecture notes and so on, so your best bet is probably to give some kind of intuitive assessment of the probability based on that knowledge.

## PUTTING PROBABILITIES TOGETHER

If you glance again through our solution of the problem above concerning the two coloured dice tossed simultaneously, your reaction may well be 'There must be an easier way!' The business of counting the number of ways the thing we are interested in might happen is certainly very tedious. The problem is really a combination of two separate problems – throwing the first dice, and throwing the second – each of which is very easy on its own. So isn't there some way we can combine what we know about the two separate problems to give us the answer to the combined one?

There are actually *two* ways in which separate events may be combined in order to give a composite event, and fortunately there are ways of dealing with both forms of combination. If we refer to the two separate events as A and B, then we may ask what is the probability of either A *or* B happening, or alternatively what is the probability of A *and* B happening at once.

### The 'or' rule

Taking the first of these forms of combination, let's ask what would be the probability, in throwing just one of our coloured dice, that we get either a yellow or a red face showing? The probability of a yellow face is 2/6, and that of a red one is 2/6 also, and since it is easy to see that altogether four faces fall into the category of 'yellow or red', the probability of this latter event is clearly 4/6. It looks, then, as if we have combined the separate probabilities in this case by adding them. In fact, it would appear that this is a general rule, for if we return to the *a priori* definition of probability, then:

Probability of A or B happening

$$= \frac{\text{Number of ways A or B can happen}}{\text{Total number of possibilities}}$$

$$= \frac{\text{Number of ways A can happen} + \text{number of ways B can happen}}{\text{Total number of possibilities}}$$

$$= \frac{\text{Number of ways A can happen}}{\text{Total number of possibilities}} + \frac{\text{Number of ways B can happen}}{\text{Total number of possibilities}}$$

= Probability of A happening + Probability of B happening.

However, we must be a little careful when applying this result. The step we have taken in saying that the number of ways A or B can happen is the sum of the ways A can happen and the ways B can happen is only true if A and B can't both happen at once − if, in statistical jargon, they are *mutually exclusive*. If A and B *can* occur simultaneously, then we will, in adding up the two sets of cases like this, be counting twice over those occasions on which both A and B happen.

This will be clear if we consider another example. If we throw an ordinary dice and ask what is the probability that an even number or one divisible by three will show, the addition rule in its simple form would suggest that the answer should be $p(\text{even}) + p(\text{divisible by three}) = 3/6 + 2/6 = 5/6$. In fact, of course, the answer should be $4/6$: one of the even numbers − 6 − is also divisible by three, and so the events 'even' and 'divisible by three' are not mutually exclusive. The simple rule fails because it causes us to count 6 twice over.

There *are* ways of dealing with 'or' problems when the events are *not* mutually exclusive, as we'll see later. For the time being, we state the rule in its simple form:

When A and B are mutually exclusive events
$$p(\text{A } or \text{ B}) = p(\text{A}) + p(\text{B}).$$

## The 'and' rule

Now consider the other type of combination, where we wish to find the probability of A *and* B happening at once. The problem discussed on p. 128 of throwing the two coloured dice so as to obtain a combination of one yellow and one green face, can be broken down into the probability of getting a yellow on the first dice *and* a green on the second, *or* vice versa. The first of these, a yellow on the first and a green on the second, we saw could occur in four ways, giving a probability of 4/36. Now the chance of a yellow on the first is 2/6, as is the chance of a green on the second, so it looks as if what we have done here is to *multiply* the two separate probabilities to get the combined one:

Probability of A and B happening
= Probability of A × Probability of B.

But once again, there is a cautionary note to be sounded in the application of this result. In the example we have just looked at, the colour which showed on the second dice was clearly independent of what showed on the first; the fact that the first produced a yellow face did not make it any more, or any less, likely that the second would show a green one. But situations arise quite frequently in which the outcome of the second event does depend on what has happened on the first attempt — where, in other words, the events are *dependent*. This, while it doesn't actually alter the form of the 'and' rule, does mean that we have to be careful to take into account the event which has already occurred in finding the probability of the other event.

Imagine, for example, that in a certain firm 40 per cent of the work force are women — in other words, the probability that a worker chosen at random is a woman is 2/5. Only 25 per cent of the female work force are management grade, whereas for male workers the figure is 30 per cent. What is the probability that a worker selected at random is both female *and* management grade? Here the probability of selecting a management grade worker varies according to whether the worker is male or female, so we must modify the 'and' rule slightly and say:

$$p(\text{female and management})$$
$$= p(\text{worker is female}) \times p(\text{worker is management}$$
$$\textit{given that} \text{ worker is female})$$

$$= \frac{2}{5} \times \frac{1}{4} = \frac{2}{20} \text{ or } \frac{1}{10}$$

With this reservation we can write the 'and' rule for combining probabilities as:

$$p(\text{A } \textit{and} \text{ B}) = p(\text{A}) \times p(\text{B}).$$

These two rules are really all one needs to know in order to solve quite a wide range of probability problems. If you find it difficult to remember '*and* means multiply and *or* means add', which may seem a bit back to front at first — after all, it's usually 'and' which means add — ask yourself how big you would expect your combined probability to be, relative to the two separate probabilities. If we insist on two things happening at once — the 'and' case — this is surely less likely to occur than either of the separate events alone, so multiplying the two (fractional) probabilities gives an answer which is *smaller* than either of the figures being multiplied. If on the other hand we want one or another of two events to occur, and we aren't fussy which it is, this is *more* likely to happen than either of the events alone, so adding the two separate probabilities gives an answer which is *bigger* than either of the individual figures.

Before we go on to solve some problems using our two rules, there is one useful consequence of the 'or' rule which should be pointed out: if we have a set of mutually exclusive events which between them cover all possible outcomes of a situation — let's call them A, B, C ... — then the probabilities of all these events together must add up to one, for one or another of them is *bound* to occur — in other words it's a certainty, with probability 1. The probability of A or B or C or ... happening is $p(\text{A}) + p(\text{B}) + p(\text{C}) + \ldots$, so this must be equal to 1. We call such events exhaustive, because between them they exhaust all the possible results of a process.

This fact can save a lot of arithmetic if recalled at the appropriate time. It is particularly useful if we want to find the chance of something *not* happening. Between them 'A happens' and 'A does not happen' are exhaustive events, and so:

$$p(\text{A happens}) + p(\text{A does not happen}) = 1,$$
whence $p(\text{A does not happen}) = 1 - p(\text{A happens}).$

Thus, for example, if the probability that you will pass the examination at the end of your course is reckoned at 9/10, then the probability that you will fail (i.e. *not* pass) must be 1/10.

## TACKLING PROBLEMS

Although the definitions of probability, and the two basic rules for combining probabilities, are very simple, it is only fair to recognise that many students find it quite difficult at first to deal with problems involving them. The English language is, I think, at least partly to blame for this difficulty. There are many different ways in which, for instance, an 'and' type of combination may be expressed – as 'both', 'neither', or 'also', to name but three possibilities. Unfortunately there is really no foolproof 'method' for tackling such problems – practice is the only way to acquire facility. So, here are a few illustrations to get you into the right frame of mind.

## Example I

A production line involves the use of three machines consecutively. The chance that the first machine will break down in any one week is 1/10, for the second the chance is 1/20, and for the third 1/40. What is the probability that at least one of the machines breaks down in a certain week?

Here is a case where it pays to recall that exhaustive probabilities add up to one. To count the number of ways in which at least one of the machines may break down is very time consuming; it might be the first which breaks down, while the second and third are working; or the second could break down while one and three are working, or the third break down while one and two are working. But 'at least one' also includes the possibility that any *two* of the machines are broken down and only one is working – or, for that matter, that all three machines are broken down. So there are, in fact, seven different possibilities to examine. However, the *opposite* of at least one being out of action is that all three are working, in other words:

$$p(\text{at least one not working}) + p(\text{all three working}) = 1$$

so that:

$$p(\text{at least one not working}) = 1 - p(\text{all three working}).$$

Now the chance that all three are working is easily found, for this means that the first is working and the second is working *and* the third is working:

$$p(\text{all three working}) = p(\text{1st working}) \times p(\text{2nd working}) \times p(\text{3rd working}).$$

If the chance that the first is *not* working, as given in the statement of the problem, is 1/10, then the chance that it *is* working will, of course, be 9/10. Applying a similar argument to the other two machines, we have:

$$p(\text{all three working}) = \frac{9}{10} \times \frac{19}{20} \times \frac{39}{40} = \frac{6,669}{8,000}.$$

So

$$p(\text{at least one not working}) = 1 - \frac{6,669}{8,000} = \frac{1,331}{8,000}.$$

Of course, the solution could be written down in a much more abbreviated way; we have dotted the *i*s and crossed the *t*s rather laboriously here for the sake of illustrating the method.

## Example 2

In a certain firm, when a worker arrives late there is a one in four chance that he will be caught by the foreman. On the first occasion he is caught, he is given a warning; the second time he is dismissed. What is the probability that a worker who is late three times is not dismissed?

Here we have a situation involving conditional probabilities: what happens to the worker on the second and third occasions he is late depends on what happened the previous time. Such problems can often be presented most simply by means of a *probability tree*, as shown in Fig. 8.1. The extreme left-hand branch of the tree stops after two stages because, since this corresponds to the case when the worker is caught on the first two occasions, he will then be dismissed and so the possibility of his being caught a third time does not arise.

The tree makes it easier for us to see the ways in which the case we are interested in − when the worker is late three times but caught at most once − may arise. There are in fact four possibilities: he may be caught just once, either on the first, second or third occasions, or he may not be caught at all. Each of these cases involves an 'and' combination of probabilities; for example:

$$p(\text{caught the first time but not the second or third})$$

$$= \frac{1}{4} \times \frac{3}{4} \times \frac{3}{4} = \frac{9}{64}$$

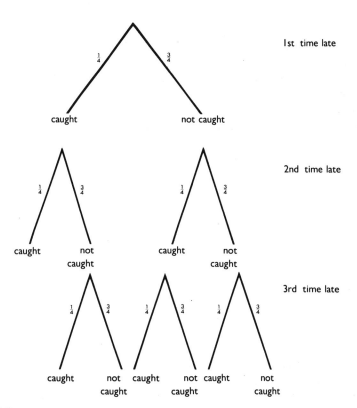

**Fig. 8.1** Probability tree

You should check that $p$(caught only on second occasion) and $p$(caught only on third occasion) are also equal to 9/64, while $p$(not caught at all) = 3/4 × 3/4 × 3/4 = 27/64. The four cases are linked together in an 'or' combination to give the answer we require:

$$p(\text{late three times but not dismissed})$$
$$= 9/64 + 9/64 + 9/64 + 27/64 = 54/64.$$

It might actually have been slightly quicker here to have worked from the opposite end, i.e. find the probability that he *is* dismissed, and take that away from 1 to find the probability that he isn't – but there is little saving of effort.

## Example 3

Two firms compete for contracts, and on past performance firm A has a probability of 3/4 of obtaining any one contract, while firm B has probability 1/4 (there are no other firms bidding). What is the probability that, when they bid for two contracts, firm A will obtain either the first or the second?

At first sight this looks like a straightforward 'or' combination:

$$p(A \text{ gets first or A gets second}) = 3/4 + 3/4 = 6/4$$

which immediately tells us that something has gone wrong, because we can't have a probability greater than 1. What has gone wrong is that we have ignored the restriction in using the 'or' rule – the events must be mutually exclusive – and of course in this case they aren't. There is nothing to stop A getting the first *and* second contract. Our wrong 'method' has resulted in our counting twice over the occasions when this happens.

So what argument will give the correct answer? There are various possibilities; we may say, since we are looking for the probability that A gains the first or the second, *or both*, the only case we are *not* interested in is that in which B gets both the contracts. The probability of this is $p$(B gets first) × $p$(B gets second) = 1/4 × 1/4 = 1/16 (assuming that bids are independent). So $p$(A gets one or the other or both) = 1 – 1/16 = 15/16.

Alternatively, we can split up 'A gets the first or the second or both' into the three separate cases 'A gets the first but not the second' or 'A gets the second but not the first' or 'A gets both', which gives as before:

$$p(A \text{ gets first or second or both})$$
$$= \left(\frac{3}{4} \times \frac{1}{4}\right) + \left(\frac{1}{4} \times \frac{3}{4}\right) + \left(\frac{3}{4} \times \frac{3}{4}\right) = \frac{15}{16}$$

## Example 4

Refer to the firm we discussed at p. 131 where 40 per cent of the work force are female, 25 per cent of the female workers are management grade and 30 per cent of the male workers are management grade. If a management-grade worker is selected at random from this firm what is the probability that it will be a female?

The first point to note here is that we are *not* asking 'What is the probability that a worker is a female management grade'; we are saying 'We *know* this worker is management; what's the probability that it's a female?' In other words, rather than selecting our sample workers from the entire work force, we are restricting ourselves to look at the management-grade workers only. The safest way of dealing with this situation is to draw up a table, with two dimensions representing the two quite separate divisions of the workers into male/female and management/non-management:

|  | Male | Female | Total |
|---|---|---|---|
| Management | 18 | 10 | 28 |
| Non-management | 42 | 30 | 72 |
| Total | 60 | 40 | 100 |

In drawing up this table we have assumed for simplicity that the total workforce is 100 people, since this makes the calculations a bit easier. As we are only concerned with probabilities – that is, with proportions – it really doesn't matter what size work force we assume.

It is now a simple matter to pick out of the table the figures we need: there are 10 female management workers out of 28 management workers altogether, so the probability that a management-grade worker is female is 10/28.

This tabular arrangement of the data is the one safe way of obtaining probabilities in this type of situation where we are looking, not at the entire population but at a restricted group within it. The key point to look for is that we are *given* some additional piece of information about the cases we are looking for, which enables us to narrow down our interest from the whole population to one of its subgroups – in this case, the management-grade workers.

Before reading the remainder of this chapter, you are strongly recommended to try Practical Exercises 1–5 in order to practise handling probabilities.

## GIVING PROBABILITIES A CASH VALUE

If you go back and re-read the problem posed at the beginning of this chapter, you will realise that, although we would now be in a position to advise Mr Black as to the probability of various combinations of events in which he might be interested, we still have no way of linking the probabilities of events with the financial results of those events. It is to this problem that we now turn our attention.

Let's begin with a very simple problem. A vendor sells cups of tea on a railway station at 35p per cup, and by keeping records of his sales over several weeks finds that they vary as follows in convenient multiples of 10:

| No. of cups sold | Percentage of days |
|---|---|
| 40 | 20 |
| 50 | 20 |
| 60 | 30 |
| 70 | 20 |
| 80 | 10 |

What can he expect his average takings per day to be, assuming that this pattern persists? He brews the cups of tea separately on demand, so that there's no problem of trying to predict the sales in advance of each day's business.

Clearly we can calculate his average takings per day by considering the distribution of takings over a period of, say, 100 days, and calculating the mean as in Chapter 6:

| Takings (£) (x) | No. of days (f) | fx |
|---|---|---|
| 14 | 20 | 280 |
| 17.50 | 20 | 350 |
| 21 | 30 | 630 |
| 24.50 | 20 | 490 |
| 28 | 10 | 280 |
| | | 2030 |

So mean takings per day = 2030/100 = £20.30.

We call this the *expected value* of his daily takings. Of course, he doesn't actually expect to get this precise amount on any one day – he gets either £14, or £17.50, or £21, or £24.50, or £28. But this is what he would expect, *in the long term*, his average daily takings to work out to.

Now we would have got exactly the same figure of £20.30 if, rather than taking an imaginary sample of 100 days as our averaging period, we had simply said that there's a twenty per cent chance that on any given day he'll take £14, a twenty per cent chance that he'll make £17.50, and so on. In other words, his expected average daily takings would be:

$$0.2 \times 14 + 0.2 \times 17.5 + 0.3 \times 21 + 0.2 \times 24.5 + 0.1 \times 28 = £20.30.$$

So the expected value of his daily takings can be calculated as:

probability of selling 40 cups × financial result of selling 40 cups + probability of selling 50 cups × financial result of selling 50 cups + . . .

and we can generalise this to define the expected value of any process as $\Sigma$ (probability of outcome × financial result of outcome), where the $\Sigma$ sign means 'added up over all the possible outcomes of the process'.

Before going on to apply this idea to decision-making problems, let's see how it can be used in a couple of simple cases.

Suppose an insurance company finds, by examining its past records, that on 80 per cent of its policies there is no claim, on 15 per cent there is a small claim, typically £50, and on the remaining 5 per cent there is a large claim, typically £500. In order to make a profit, it must make the premium per policy larger than the expected value of the claim per policy; but this, using the theory just developed, will be $0.8 \times 0 + 0.15 \times 50 + 0.05 \times 500 = £32.50$. It is really a much-elaborated version of this calculation which insurance companies actually use in deciding how much their premiums should be.

As a second illustration, imagine that you have watched people playing a fruit machine in a certain pub, and have noticed that over a long period it gave a £1.00 payout on average every 20 turns. Is it worth your while playing the machine, if the charge per turn is 10p?

Your expected winning per turn is
$p$(winning) × gain if you win + $p$(losing) × loss if you lose
= 1/20 × 90 + 19/20 × (−10)
= 4.5 − 9.5 = −5.

So on the average, you stand to make a loss of 5 pence per turn, and therefore it is not worth playing.

Really, without saying so explicitly, we have moved here into the realm of decision-making, for you have to make a decision — to play or not to play — and on the basis of your expected winnings, the sensible decision would be not to play. The problem also highlights one of the defects of this approach to decision-making, in that someone with a well-developed gambling instinct would probably argue that it is worth something to him simply to have the *chance* of winning £1.00. The rather detached way in which we have looked at the decision takes no account of this; nor, being essentially a 'long-term' view of things, can it allow for the possibility that the machine will pay out on your very first turn, and you will have the strength of mind to quit at that point!

## DECISION TABLES

When we have a large number of possible courses of action among which a decision has to be made, and a large number of possible consequences to consider, the process can be made more systematic by drawing up a *decision table* (sometimes given the more technical-sounding name of decision *matrix*). To illustrate how it works, let's return to the problem of our railway-station tea vendor, and imagine that he has decided to diversify his business by also selling fruit pies. Unlike the cups of tea, however, these can't be prepared on demand as each customer arrives; they have to be ordered in advance, and the supplier doesn't like the size of order changing from day to day — he will only accept orders for a week at a time. In other words, if our vendor decides to order 40 pies a day this week, he will be stuck with 40 per day for the whole week, and can't change the number until next week.

Once again, the vendor begins by keeping a record of demand for the pies over a period of a few weeks and finds that it is as follows:

| No. of pies demanded | Percentage of occasions |
|---|---|
| 25 | 10 |
| 30 | 20 |
| 35 | 25 |
| 40 | 20 |
| 45 | 15 |
| 50 | 10 |

Of course, in practice there would probably be some kind of pattern of variation discernible from one day of the week to the next which might help him to plan his supplies. But for the moment, let's suppose that there's no such pattern and furthermore that the supplier insists that for the good of his reputation only fresh pies are sold; any left at the end of a day are to be returned to the bakery for a nominal refund of 5p. The vendor buys the pies from the supplier at 15p each, and sells them at 25p; thus every pie sold represents a profit of 10p, while every unsold pie represents a loss of 10p.

The vendor's problem is an example of decision-making *under uncertainty*; if he *knew* what the demand for pies each day would be, then he could buy just the right number and maximise his profits, but he doesn't have that knowledge. How then can he decide the 'best' number of pies per day to order?

The decision table for the vendor's problem is shown below: the possible decisions are at the left-hand side, and the uncontrollable factor – in this case, the demand for pies – across the columns of the table, the probability of each demand also being shown. There is clearly no point in considering buying fewer than 25 pies, since this number can *always* be sold; by the same token, as more than 50 are never required, to order such quantities would be pointless. So only the quantities actually demanded will be considered.

| | | | Demand | | | | Expected |
|---|---|---|---|---|---|---|---|
| | 25(0.1) | 30(0.2) | 35(0.25) | 40(0.2) | 45(0.15) | 50(0.1) | value |
| 25 | 2.5 | 2.5 | 2.5 | 2.5 | 2.5 | 2.5 | 2.5 |
| 30 | 2.0 | 3.0 | 3.0 | 3.0 | 3.0 | 3.0 | 2.9 |
| 35 | 1.5 | 2.5 | 3.5 | 3.5 | 3.5 | 3.5 | 3.1 |
| Buy 40 | 1.0 | 2.0 | 3.0 | 4.0 | 4.0 | 4.0 | 3.05 |
| 45 | 0.5 | 1.5 | 2.5 | 3.5 | 4.5 | 4.5 | 2.8 |
| 50 | 0.0 | 1.0 | 2.0 | 3.0 | 4.0 | 5.0 | 2.4 |

The figures in the body of the table are arrived at as follows. Consider the occasions when 35 pies are demanded and only 25 have been bought; obviously in this case only 25 can be sold, which at a profit of 10p per pie will give a total profit of £2.50. The same will apply, in fact, to all other combinations in the top row (we are ignoring any question of the cost of lost goodwill through turning customers away). If however, 35 pies are demanded and 40 have been bought, then although the sale of the 35 will produce £3.50 profit, we must offset against this the 5 pies which have to be returned at a loss of 10p per pie – a total loss of 50p. Thus the actual profit resulting from the '40 bought, 35 demanded' combination is only £3.00. You should verify in a similar way the calculation of the rest of the figures in the table.

The table, once completed like this, provides us with all the information we need to calculate the *expected value* of the vendor's profits resulting from each possible decision. For example, if he decides to buy 30 pies then his expected profit will be, using the method developed in section 6 above:

$$0.1 \times 2 + 0.2 \times 3 + 0.25 \times 3 + 0.2 \times 3 + 0.15 \times 3 + 0.1 \times 3 = £2.90.$$

You can see the expected values of the remaining decisions in the right-hand column of the table.

Thus, if the vendor wishes to maximise his expected profits, then he should choose to buy 35 pies per day. What this means is that if he persists in this strategy and the pattern of demand also remains as established, then in the long run this will give him an average profit of £3.10 a day – better than that achieved by any other choice.

This basis for decision-making is sometimes known as the *expected monetary value*, or EMV, decision criterion; we will return to a discussion of its suitability in particular cases, and alternative criteria which might be adopted, below.

## DECISION TREES

We were able to deal with the problem in the last section by means of a simple decision table, because it involved only *one* set of 'uncontrollable circumstances' which applied with the same probabilities whatever the decision selected. Where there are different sets of consequences, with different probabilities, dependent upon which decision is made, such a method will not do and we must resort to drawing a *decision tree*. This, as its name suggests, is somewhat akin to a probability tree, with the incorporation of the financial outcomes which will result from each set of circumstances.

We will at last return to the problem posed at the start of the chapter to see how the method is used. You will recall that the choice which we left confronting Mr Black was whether to abandon development of the new product now, incurring a loss of £5,000, or to go ahead and market the new product immediately, thus possibly achieving sales of 12,000 units if the associated TV series appears, but only 2,000 units if it does not. If the series does appear he also has to consider the possibility of the 'pirate' competitive product appearing and cutting sales down to 8,000 units. The probability of the TV series appearing was reckoned at 60 per cent, and the probability of the rival product being marketed, at 50 per cent.

In Fig. 8.2 you will see the probability tree representing the various decisions and their consequences, without as yet the inclusion of any of the profits or costs. Notice that the tree *begins* with the decision to be made – this is the general rule. This decision *node* as it is often called is represented by a square box, to distinguish it from 'chance nodes' represented by circles. Of course, the decisions 'abandon' and 'go ahead' don't have probabilities attached to them like the other branches of the tree, because unlike 'rival markets' or 'series appears' they are not subject to uncontrollable, probabilistic forces; one of them definitely *will* happen, and the other definitely *won't*, depending upon what choice is made.

We now begin to insert the profit figures into the tree, always starting from the *end* points of the branches, since it is these final consequences whose effects have been estimated. For example, the profit resulting from 'series appears, rival markets' will be $8,000 \times £2 - £5,000 = £11,000$, this is, the profit from the reduced sales, minus the development costs.

In the same way, 'series appears, no rival' yields $12,000 \times £2 - £5,000 = £19,000$, while 'no series' yields $2,000 \times £2 - £5,000 = -£1,000$ – a loss, in fact – and of course 'abandon now' gives simply a loss of £5,000.

We now use our definition of expected value to find first the expected result of the sequence of events, 'market now, series appears', taking into account both the possibilities, 'rival markets' and 'no rival'. This will be $0.5 \times 11,000 + 0.5 \times 19,000 = £15,000$. We insert that figure as the financial result of the event 'series appears'. Then we can work back further still, to the expected result of the decision 'market now'. This will be $15,000 \times 0.6 + (-1,000) \times 0.4 = £8,600$. We already know the expected result of the decision 'abandon now' which is a loss of £5,000. So, on the basis of selecting the

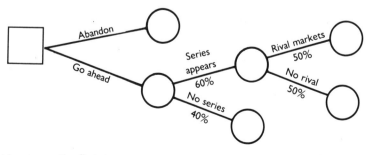

**Fig. 8.2** Decision tree – the first stage

decision which gives the highest expected profit, we would recommend Mr Black to go ahead and market his product. The completed tree is shown in Fig. 8.3.

This decision has turned out to be the 'best', in the sense of yielding the greatest expected profit, primarily because there is a pretty good chance of the series appearing. If the chance of this were very much smaller, then it might be better for the firm to cut its losses and abandon the project now.

Briefly then, the procedure for constructing a decision tree was as follows: draw the tree representing the logical sequence of events, always beginning with the decision to be made; insert at the terminal points of the branches the financial results of each sequence of events; work back towards the decisions, using the expected value method to calculate the financial result at each junction of branches; and finally select the decision with the greatest expected profit (or, of course, smallest expected cost, if that is the question of interest).

We will finish this section with another example of the process. I am about to buy a new calculator, and have the choice of a cheap unbranded model at £4.50, or a well-known make at £7.50. There is no guarantee with the cheap model, so if it breaks down during the first year of usage I will simply have to buy another, at the same price. Friends who have similar calculators tell me this happens with about one in five of them. The more expensive calculator is much less likely to break down – the manufacturer states that the proportion which do so is only about one in 50 – and if it does, the guarantee means that I will only have to pay the 50p postage to return it to the factory. Is it worth buying the dearer machine?

The tree for this problem is shown in Fig. 8.4, starting at the left with the decision 'dearer' versus 'cheaper' machine. The total cost to me of having a cheap machine which breaks down is £9, since I have no choice but to buy another at £4.50. The cost of an expensive machine which breaks down is only £8 – the initial cost of £7.50 plus the 50p postage. If the machine does *not* break down, of course, then in either case the cost is merely the initial purchase price.

As you can see, the expected cost of buying a cheap machine is $0.2 \times 9 + 0.8 \times 4.5 = £5.40$, whereas for the dearer machine it is $0.02 \times 8 + 0.98 \times 7.5 = £7.51$. So it would appear that the cheaper machine is the better bet – though of course you might ask, since the chance of a breakdown is so high in this case, what is the chance that your replacement machine will break down – and so on!

Both the examples we have considered here involve only a single decision. However, many real decision problems involve sequences of decisions; they can be tackled in the

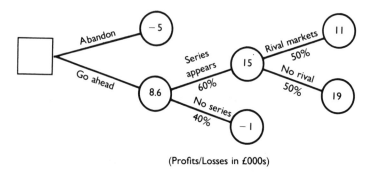

(Profits/Losses in £000s)

**Fig. 8.3** The completed decision tree

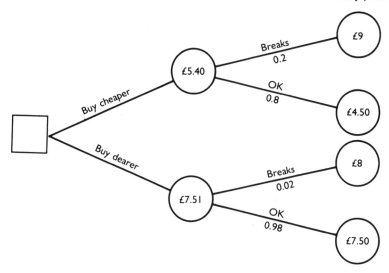

**Fig. 8.4** Decision tree – buying a calculator

same way as our simpler examples, as you will find if you work Practical Exercise 13 at the end of the chapter – a more complicated version of Mr Black's problem. When the decision tree becomes very large and complex, it is often necessary to use computer software for the analysis; this will generally speaking be a 'dedicated' package specifically designed for decision analysis, rather than an application of a multi-purpose package such as MINITAB or LOTUS.

Such packages often offer additional facilities to the user. They may allow a manager to give a range of options, such as 'most likely, pessimistic, optimistic', rather than a single figure as the financial consequence of a decision. They may also help to answer questions such as 'How much should I be prepared to pay for further information about this situation which will help to improve my decision-making?'

## DRAWBACKS OF THE METHOD

Strictly speaking decision theory belongs in a later section of this book, since it is definitely 'a tool of planning', and a very important one at that. However, we have really only scratched the surface of the topic here, to illustrate how probability theory can be applied to some very real problems. In practice, problems would rarely be as simple as the ones we have solved, and would often involve not just one decision but a whole sequence. For further reading on this topic, see references in the Suggestions for Further Reading in Appendix 1.

It would not be fair to leave this topic without mentioning some of the defects of this whole approach to decision-making. We have already touched on this in the section on decision tables, where we mentioned that the EMV as a decision criterion is really most appropriate in a situation where the process is going to be repeated numerous times, since it is in such a case that the EMV can guarantee us the best possible overall return. In a 'one-off' type of situation – such as the marketing decision discussed in the section on decision trees – it is by no means clear that EMV will give the 'best' solution.

The other major drawback to using EMV as our criterion is that it requires at least estimated values for the probabilities of the various uncontrollable circumstances which may arise. Where no such estimates are available, the whole method fails, and other criteria have been developed for coping with such cases. For example, in the case of the vendor's problem examined on p. 137, had the vendor had no idea of the pattern of demand for fruit pies, other than that the most he'd ever been asked for was 50 in one day, and the least 25, he might adopt the pessimistic viewpoint that, if the worst comes to the worst, he will sell 25 pies in a day. From that standpoint, his best decision would clearly be to buy 25 only, as this gives him the maximum possible profit if 25 are demanded. This 'pessimistic' strategy is sometimes referred to as 'maximin', since it maximises his profits in, as it were, the 'minimum' circumstances.

An optimistic vendor, on the other hand, would hope that he might sell 50 pies – the maximum which has ever been demanded of him in one day. His choice therefore would be to buy 50, since that will give him the maximum profit under the circumstance he is hoping for. The 'optimist's' strategy is often called 'maximax', since it maximises profits under the 'maximum' circumstances which may arise.

This by no means exhausts the possible choices of decision criteria, but unfortunately, in the absence of any idea what the probabilities of various contingencies may be, some of them are little more than shots in the dark. A further defect of the method as a whole is that we need to be able to put at least an approximate cash figure on the outcome of various sequences of events, but some of the figures used may be no more than inspired guesses. How, for instance, does Mr Black of Shoddier Toys *know* that sales of his new product will be 12,000 items if the TV series appears? And if he's got his estimates wrong, will he end up by making a disastrously wrong decision? It's easy to visualise a situation in which the expected results of two or more possible decisions could be so finely balanced that just a small change to one of the profit estimates – or, for that matter, to one of the probabilities – would completely alter the decision. You'll have a chance to think about this question of the *sensitivity* of the decision to changes in the figures a bit more in some of the Practical Exercises at the end of the chapter, and this whole topic of how small errors in the data of a problem may alter the solution is one which will become familiar if you read Part 4.

Finally, as pointed out earlier, we've taken a very coldbloodedly financial point of view throughout our decision-making. But frequently where business decisions are concerned there are other, less quantifiable, but equally important factors to be considered. Suppose a firm is considering re-siting its plant on a green-belt industrial estate; how can it measure in cash terms the benefits to its workers of a healthier working environment, or the inconvenience of being more distant from a railway station, or the effect on production of workers having much longer journeys to reach the plant? And yet these are precisely the kind of questions the firm *should* be considering when trying to decide whether to make the move. There are ways of attempting to attach nominal cash values to factors of this kind, but naturally the subject is much less cut-and-dried, and much more open to controversy than anything we have considered in this chapter.

## Practical exercises

1  A public health inspector is visiting the Squalorama supermarket, and inspects the staff washroom. The manager knows that one day on average out of every three the sink is blocked, and two days out of five there is no towel available. If the inspector will only pass the premises if the sink is clear and a towel is available, what is the chance that he will do so?

2 Half the workers in a certain factory are women, but among part-time workers they represent a much higher proportion, in fact four-fifths. A quarter of the overall work force consists of part-timers. What is the probability (a) that a worker is male; (b) that a part-time worker is male; (c) that a male worker is a part-timer?

3 The probability that Martin Moribund will die during the ten-year term of a life insurance policy is assessed by the insurance company at 1/5. Arthur Average's probability of living to the end of the ten-year period is reckoned at 95 per cent. What is the probability that at the end of the ten years (a) both (b) one or the other, but not both, is living?

4 As part of a very strict auditing procedure, every audit document is examined first by an articled junior accountant, then by a qualified accountant, and finally by one of the partners in the accounting firm. If there is an error in the document the chance that the junior will detect it is 4/5: if he finds the error, he will not bother passing on the document to his senior. The chance of the qualified accountant detecting an error in the documents *he* examines is 3/5, and once again he passes on only those documents which appear to him to be correct. Finally, when the partner examines the documents which reach him, his chance of detecting an error is 1/2.

(a) What is the probability that an erroneous document will be detected by one or other of the three examiners?
(b) Do the three probabilities for the three personnel quoted suggest that the junior is better at detecting errors than the partner?

5 An unscrupulous manufacturer knows that in a box of a dozen light bulbs which he is selling to a customer four are in fact not working. He watches nervously as the customer insists on removing three and testing them. What is the probability that only one of the three tested fails to work?

6 I am trying to decide whether to move house or stay in my present one. I must decide immediately, but unfortunately there is an element of uncertainty in the situation, as my firm is in the middle of reorganisation, and may shortly move me to another site, closer to my present home than to the house I am considering buying. I reckon the chances of my being moved at about 40 per cent. If I am moved, I estimate that annual fares from my present home would cost £200, as opposed to £250 from the new house. To reach the site where I work at present, on the other hand, currently costs me £300 per year from my present house, but would cost only £200 a year from the new house. If there is no price-difference between the two houses, so that I make neither a profit nor a loss on the transaction, what would you advise?

7 If I don't put any money in a parking meter when I park, there's a one-in-ten chance that a warden will notice, and I will be fined £25. If I pay now, it will cost me 20p. Is it worth trying to get away without paying?

8 I have an old tea set inherited from my great-aunt. At the moment I would get £50 for it if I sold it, which can be invested to give me £65 in a year's time. If I hang on to the tea set for a year, an antique dealer friend tells me there's a one-in-five chance that this particular type of pottery will become fashionable and I will be able to sell the tea set for £125. Otherwise the value will remain the same, though my cleaning lady is very clumsy and there's always the chance, if I do decide to

keep the tea set for another year, that she will smash it during that year. On past performance I assess the chance of this happening at 10 per cent. What should I do?

9 Discuss how you would assess the probability that:

(a) a candidate of a given party, standing in a by-election in a given constituency, will be elected;

(b) the baby your elder sister is expecting will be a girl;

(c) a consumer, presented with two otherwise identical packages, will take the red one in preference to the blue;

(d) the aeroplane on which you are flying to Majorca for your holidays will crash on the way.

10 Demonstrate for yourself how the probability given by the experimental approach becomes closer to that given by the *a priori* approach as the number of experiments becomes larger. You can do this by tossing a coin over and over, keeping a running record of the cumulative number of heads obtained, and the cumulative probability, and seeing how the latter figure approaches 0.5 (assuming, of course, that the coin is fair!).

As an example, suppose your first ten tosses gave H, H, T, H, T, T, H, T, H, H. Then your running total of heads would be 1, 2, 2, 3, 3, 3, 4, 4, 5, 6, and the cumulative probabilities would be as follows:

$$1/1 = 1, 2/2 = 1, 2/3 = 0.67, 3/4 = 0.75, 3/5 = 0.6,$$
$$3/6 = 0.5, 4/7 = 0.57, 4/8 = 0.5, 5/9 = 0.55, 6/10 = 0.6.$$

If you choose to plot the cumulative probabilities on a graph against the number of experiments, you will see in an even more striking way how as the number of experiments becomes larger, the probability tends to 'home in' upon 0.5.

11 Referring to the problem posed on p. 125 and the decision tree in Fig. 8.3, all other things being equal, how small would the chance of the TV series appearing have to be, before it would be worthwhile abandoning the project?

12 In Problem 7 above, what chance of discovery by the traffic warden would make it worth your while trying to get away without paying the meter? Given the probabilities as in the question, what increase in the standard charge for the meter would convince you that it is worthwhile not to pay?

(In questions 11 and 12 we are investigating the *sensitivity* of our decision to changes – a topic to which we will be returning in later chapters).

13 Upon further investigation, Mr Black discovers that his problem, considered in the section 'Decision trees', p. 138, is more complicated than he had realised. The company is actually faced with a choice of *three* alternatives: abandon the project now, go ahead immediately with a full-scale product launch, or carry out a market survey first, at a cost of £2,000. For the first two alternatives, the consequences remain as they were before. If a survey is carried out, and is positive (the chance of this is estimated at 70 per cent based on pilot studies), the product will be launched and will lead to profits of £13,000 (irrespective of the status of the series or the rival product). However, if the survey is deemed to give negative results, then a further decision must be taken: whether to go ahead anyway, or abandon the project at that point. If the project goes ahead in spite of the negative survey,

there is a 20 per cent chance that it will still bring in a profit of £10,000, otherwise it will make only £3,000 profit.

(a)   Draw the modified decision tree taking account of these additional factors.
(b)   By calculating EMVs, advise Mr Black as to (*i*) if he carries out the survey, whether he should go ahead in spite of negative results, and (*ii*) should he choose the survey, the full launch or abandonment of the project?

## Case study problem

Dear X,

Happy Christmas! I hope you like the enclosed present – with thanks for all your help over the past year. A fairly short query this time: I am currently trying to decide if it would be a good idea to continue working from home, and build an extension to my kitchen to provide the extra space I need, or to buy (or rent) other premises and convert them for my purposes. I understand there is something called 'decision theory' which puts this kind of thing on a more solid basis than sheer intuition, and I wondered whether I should try to use it. I haven't got any very firm figures worked out yet, so perhaps the best way would be for you to invent some – just as an illustration – to show me how the ideas work.

What always worries me with these mathematical methods is, what if they give you the wrong answer! So could you include a bit of explanation as to how disastrous it might be if things *did* go wrong that will help me decide whether I want to use this approach or not.

Hope to see you in the New Year,
Best wishes,

Jane

## Case study question

Draft a reply to this letter, using the basic situation and inventing your own data to illustrate the ideas of decision theory. You may assume that Jane understands the basic concepts of probability.

## CHAPTER 9

# Patterns of probability: some distributions

## Objectives

Before starting work on this chapter make sure you are happy with:

(a)  the definitions of probability and the rules for combining elementary probabilities (*see* Chapter 8, pp. 126–31);

(b)  the ideas of frequency distributions and histograms (*see* Chapter 5, pp. 66–76);

(c)  the definition and meaning of mean and standard deviation (*see* Chapter 6, pp. 91–5, 99–103);

(d)  the conversion of decimals to percentages and vice versa (*see* Chapter 1, p. 11);

By the end of your work on this chapter you should be able to:

(a)  recognise problems which can be modelled by the binomial, Poisson and normal distributions;

(b)  solve such problems with the use of the appropriate tables;

(c)  recognise when the use of these distributions involves approximations in the original problem;

(d)  outline the connections between these three distributions.

## THE QUALITY MANAGER'S PROBLEM

Bennetts is a small firm which manufactures 'wholefood' cakes and confectionery. Originally something of a 'cottage industry', started in the premises behind a wholefood retail store by the wife of the proprietor, the business has expanded rapidly in line with the entire wholefood business, and now employs some thirty people manufacturing around two dozen product lines and distributing to wholefood and healthfood stores over quite a large area.

When the business was started, the control of the quality of the product presented no problems, as output was so small that every item could be individually checked. With expansion, however, it has been increasingly difficult to maintain this standard of checking, particularly since some automatic packing machinery has been purchased. Moreover, now that goods are more widely distributed the weights and measures inspectorate is likely to become involved. One of the staff has therefore been designated – along with his several other job functions – 'Quality Manager', and has been given overall responsibility for ensuring that products generally come up to scratch, that the packing machines are not producing large numbers of underweight packs, and so on.

We will concentrate on just three of the problems he has encountered in his new role. First, there is the Crunchy Flapjack situation: these rather fragile biscuits are packed by machine in boxes of half-a-dozen; in the interests of customer goodwill, Bennetts will replace any box in which more than half of the biscuits are broken. The quality manager has monitored the machine and found that it tends to break, on average, one biscuit in every twenty. So what sort of proportion of returned boxes are Bennetts likely to have to deal with? He's assuming, of course, that the biscuits are so well packed that once they get inside the box, no more will be broken – in other words, all breakages can be ascribed to the packing machine.

The second problem concerns the Natural Molasses Coated Toffee Apples. These are supplied to retailers packed in boxes, but as the boxes are filled by weight, and of course the weight of individual apples varies, there is no knowing exactly how many are in a given box (though it's a pretty large number – around 144). Inevitably, now that the apples are produced in large numbers, the occasional one isn't properly dipped in the toffee. One important customer has suggested that, if as the apples are being unpacked in his shop there appear to be an exceptionally large number with faulty toffee coatings, he should have the option of returning the whole box for replacement. While Bennetts agree to this in principle, the quality manager would like to know just what should be agreed on as 'an exceptionally large number'. He knows that the average number of faulty apples per box is 6, and he'd like to fix the agreement in such a way that he'll only need to replace one box in 100.

Finally, the machine which fills bags of Carrot Candy has been causing problems. The nominal weight of these bags is 500 g, but of course in practice there is a certain variation in the exact weights produced by the machine. The current procedure is to set the machine to an average weight, slightly higher than 500 g – at present 510 g – and then check-weigh the bags and refill by hand any which are underweight. However, this is wasting a great deal of time as it turns out that about 20 per cent of all the bags have to be manually refilled. So the quality manager would like to know what setting he should use for the average weight on the packing machine if he wants to cut this proportion down to 5 per cent.

You will not be surprised to learn that all three of these problems are connected with probability. The manager wants to know, for example, what is the probability that a box of Crunchy Flapjacks will contain more than three broken out of six; he wants to know what the probability is of various numbers of faulty toffee apples per box, so that he can make an informed decision about the agreed number for an automatic replacement of the consignment; and if he knew the probability, for a given setting of the packing machine, that a bag of Carrot Candy weighing less than 500 g will be produced, then he could adjust the setting to give the required proportion of underweight bags.

But these are not the sort of probability questions with which we have dealt in Chapter 8. The first one *could* be dealt with 'from scratch', as it were, since we know the probability of a single biscuit being broken, and want to find the probability that more than three biscuits out of six will be broken. Even this, however, would be very tedious, since we would have to work out all the different ways in which four biscuits out of six might be broken (there are in fact 15 of them!), or five out of the six might be broken, or all six might be broken – rather a daunting task. And when it comes to the remaining two problems the methods we've used so far fail completely.

However, what these three problems have in common is that each belongs to a well-established *pattern* of problem – patterns which recur so often and in so many different situations that to save our having to develop the theory for such a problem every time it is encountered, the required probabilities have been calculated once for all, and provided in the form of tables. Thus all that you, the user of the established theory, need to be able to do is, firstly to recognise *which* of the established patterns your problem conforms to – or can be made to conform to, since sometimes a bit of approximation is needed – and secondly to make use of the appropriate set of tables in the context of your problem to obtain the probability you need.

These standard patterns of probability are called *probability distributions*, which may ring a bell in your mind; we've already come across that word distribution, though in a different context, in Chapter 5. There we were discussing frequency distributions; is this one of those confusing cases where the same word is used to mean different things in two different contexts?

There is actually a very close link between the idea of a probability distribution, which will form the main topic of this chapter, and the familiar frequency distribution; but in order to establish this link, we will have to abandon for a moment the *theoretical* probability distributions – the standard patterns of probability which we've just been talking about – and take a look at a more practical example.

## THE IDEA OF A PROBABILITY DISTRIBUTION

We will return, for this section, to the frequency distribution which became very familiar in Chapter 6 – the wage distribution of the Grimchester motor-workers, which for simplicity is repeated below:

| Weekly take-home pay (£) | No. of Grimchester workers |
|---|---|
| 80 but under 90 | 3 |
| 90 but under 100 | 7 |
| 100 but under 110 | 33 |
| 110 but under 120 | 26 |
| 120 but under 130 | 24 |
| 130 but under 140 | 20 |
| 140 but under 150 | 18 |
| 150 but under 160 | 15 |
| 160 but under 180 | 4 |

Suppose we now ask, not how many of the workers in this sample earn between £80 and £50 per week, but what is the *probability* of a Grimchester motor-worker earning between £80 and £90 per week. Then, assuming this sample of workers is representative, we can easily calculate the required probability using the familiar definition:

$$\frac{\text{Number of workers in the £80–£90 bracket}}{\text{Total number of workers in the sample}} = 3/150 = 0.02.$$

In the same way we could convert all the other frequencies to probabilities simply by dividing by 150, and so convert our frequency distribution into a probability distribution

— a table which tells us how the probabilities are distributed between the various wage-groups:

| Weekly take-home pay (£) | Probability |
|---|---|
| 80 but under 90 | 0.02 |
| 90 but under 100 | 0.047 |
| 100 but under 110 | 0.22 |
| 110 but under 120 | 0.173 |
| 120 but under 130 | 0.16 |
| 130 but under 140 | 0.133 |
| 140 but under 150 | 0.12 |
| 150 but under 160 | 0.1 |
| 160 but under 180 | 0.027 |

This is an example of an *experimental* probability distribution, since it was obtained by actually taking a sample of workers and noting their wages. Many of the features with which we are familiar in the frequency distribution carry over into the probability distribution. It will, for instance, have a mean and a standard deviation, which are identical with those we calculated in Chapter 6 (can you see why?). Just as the frequencies in the original distribution added up to 150, the total number of workers in the sample, so the probabilities in the new distribution add up to 1; between them they cover all the possible wages for the sample.

We can also convert the diagram which represented the frequency distribution — the histogram — into one which represents the probability distribution. You can see this in Fig. 9.1 — apart from the vertical scale, the diagram is identical with Fig. 6.1(*a*). But whereas in the ordinary histogram the area of each block represented the frequency of the corresponding class, in what we might call the probability histogram the area of the blocks represents the probability that a value falls in the corresponding class. It follows from this that the overall area under the probability histogram must add up to 1, the sum of the probabilities. This is a point we shall be returning to later.

Although this experimental probability distribution serves quite well as an introduction

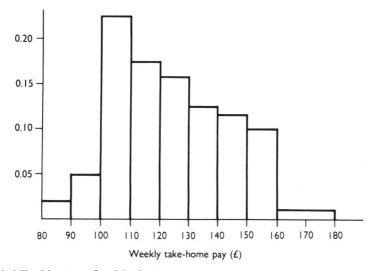

**Fig. 9.1** Probability histogram for Grimchester wages

to the idea of a probability distribution, it is not very useful in terms of working out probabilities, since it applies only to the particular sample of 150 workers included in the survey (although if the survey was well designed it presumably has some degree of applicability to the population from which the sample was taken). But far more useful in general terms are the *theoretical* probability distributions which relate to the kind of experimental distribution we've just looked at rather as the *a priori* definition of probability relates to the experimental definition. They are distributions worked out on general, theoretical grounds, which retain many of the features we've observed in the experimental distribution, but which are applicable to a much wider class of problems.

## THE BINOMIAL DISTRIBUTION

### Recognising the pattern

The first of the quality manager's problems was, you will recall, concerned with the fragile Crunchy Flapjacks. He has determined that the packing machine breaks, on average, one biscuit in twenty – which is another way of saying that the probability of a biscuit being broken is one-twentieth or 0.05. What he needs to know is the proportion of boxes which will contain more than three broken biscuits; this is, again, equivalent to knowing the probability that a box of six biscuits will contain more than three broken.

Let's try to summarise the things which we know about this problem. The most obvious, perhaps, is that we are concerned with a situation in which there are only a finite, discrete number of possibilities: there could be 0, 1, 2 ... up to 6 broken biscuits in a box, but it doesn't make any sense to think of the probability that there are, say two-and-a-half broken ones! Furthermore, we are in an either/or situation: either a biscuit is broken or it isn't – there is no such thing as a partly broken biscuit. The remaining information we are supplied with is, first the number of biscuits in a box, which is known and fixed, and second the probability of an individual biscuit being broken by the machine, which presumably if the machine is warmed up and running steadily will again be fixed.

The facts about this problem which we have just summarised make it a typical example of a *binomial* probability situation, which can be tackled with the aid of the binomial distribution. The name *bi*nomial gives a clue as to one major feature of this distribution; it applies in cases where there are just two possible outcomes to a process – here, the individual biscuit is broken or it isn't. We could summarise the requirements for a problem to fit this binomial pattern as follows:

(a)   either/or situation;
(b)   number of trials (usually called $n$) is known and fixed;
(c)   probability of success on each trial (usually called $p$) is known and fixed.

We're using the terms 'trials' and 'success' fairly loosely here, to mean respectively the number of times a thing might have a chance of occurring, and the times when it actually *does* occur. This means that, in the problem of the biscuits, a 'success' consists of a biscuit being broken by the machine!

Before looking at the actual probabilities obtained in binomial situations, it's a good idea to practise recognising a binomial problem when you see one. We'll look at three further examples.

(a)  Five coins are tossed simultaneously; what is the chance of obtaining three heads?

The either/or requirement is clearly met here, since the coin must come down showing either heads or tails. The number of 'trials' is the number of coins being tossed, so $n = 5$; and if the coins are all fair ones, then the probability of 'success' (i.e. getting a head) each time is $\frac{1}{2}$. All the requirements for a binomial problem are thus present.

(b)  By looking up weather records for the past ten years I've discovered that the proportion of wet days in the current month of the year has been 60 per cent. What is the probability that next week there will be 5 or more wet days?

If a day is defined as wet (it rains sometimes during the day) or dry (it doesn't), then we have our either/or situation. We can use the 60 per cent figure to give an approximate value of 0.6 for $p$, the probability of 'success' (a wet day) but there's a certain amount of approximation here in assuming that $p$ is fixed; wet days, corresponding to periods of atmospheric low pressure tend to come in twos and threes, so you might argue that if it rained today the probability of rain tomorrow is higher than if it had been dry today. However, we won't be making too serious an error if we treat $p$ as having a fixed value of 0.6. Of course, $n$ will be 7, the number of days in the week.

(c)  An unscrupulous shopkeeper has packed up light-bulbs into crates of 144 and is selling them off at a bargain price; what his customers don't know is that in each box, 24 are in fact faulty bulbs which won't work. A customer insists on trying a sample of 6 bulbs before he buys; what is the probability that they will all work?

Here the either/or corresponds to the bulbs working/not working, and $n$ is 6, the number being tried. As for $p$, it's clearly 24/144 – or is it? When the first bulb is taken, there are 24 ways of picking a dud bulb out of 144 bulbs altogether. But presumably the customer won't replace the first bulb before taking a second one, so that on his second choice the chance of getting a dud is either 23/143 – if the first was a dud – or 24/143 if the first was working. So the requirement that $p$ is known *and fixed* appears to break down again. However, the difference between 24/144, which as a decimal is 0.167, and 23/143 (0.161) or 24/143 (0.168) is so small that in practice we would not be making too sweeping an approximation if we took $p = 24/144$ and used the binomial distribution.

This is only the case, however, because the 'population of bulbs from which we are sampling is relatively large (144). If the whole case of bulbs contained only, say 30 bulbs, then the differences between the values of $p$ as successive bulbs were taken would be a good deal greater, as you can easily verify, and the use of the binomial distribution would hardly be justified.

From this it should be clear that frequently, in 'squeezing' our practical problem slightly to fit the binomial pattern, we are using the theoretical distribution as a reasonably good but easier-to-handle imitation of the real-life situation. We are in fact using the binomial to *model* the practical problem, a process with which you will become increasingly familiar as you read later sections of this book.

## Using the tables

As mentioned earlier, we could in principle solve problems of the binomial pattern by means of the basic rules for combining probabilities introduced in Chapter 8. To see how this can be done, and also how much simpler the process is with the aid of the tables of the distribution, let's return to the first of the problems examined above. If five coins are tossed simultaneously, what is the probability of obtaining three heads? We can, somewhat laboriously, write down all the different ways in which three heads out of five coins might occur:

| | | | | |
|---|---|---|---|---|
| HHHTT | HHTHT | HHTTH | HTHHT | HTHTH |
| HTTHH | THHHT | THHTH | THTHH | TTHHH |

In other words, there are ten different ways in which the case we are interested in might arise. The probability of any one of these will be 1/32; for example, $p(\text{HHHTT}) = \frac{1}{2} \times \frac{1}{2} \times \frac{1}{2} \times \frac{1}{2} \times \frac{1}{2}$, and so on. So the probability we are looking for will be $10 \times 1/32$ or 10/32, which as a decimal is 0.3125.

In fact, we could say that in general for a binomial problem, the chance of getting $r$ successes out of $n$ trials will be:

Probability of $r$ successes × probability of the remaining $(n - r)$ failures
× the number of ways in which $r$ successes out of $n$ trials can happen.

However, as you can see, the process of working out binomial probabilities in this way, particularly the business of determining the number of different ways in which a certain number of successes can occur, is quite complicated, even though there are short-cut methods which can help. We will therefore rely for our solution of binomial problems on the tables in Appendix 4.

You will find the tables headed '*Cumulative* Binomial Probabilities' – in other words, they give the probability of getting *r or more* successes out of $n$ trials in a binomial situation. The values of $n$ – from 2 to 10 – correspond to the main blocks of the table, while the values of $p$ – from 0.05 to 0.5 – are to be found at the heads of the columns. Where there are blanks in the table, for instance for $n = 5$ with $r = 4$ and $p = 0.05$, this simply means that the probability is so small that it would not show up in these tables which are given only to four decimal places.

To see how the tables are to be used, let us first deal with the coin-tossing problem we've just been looking at 'by hand'. We had $n = 5$ and $p = 0.5$, and we were interested in the chance of getting three heads. Now if we look in the block $n = 5$ of the tables, under the column $p = 0.5$ and in the row $r = 3$, what we find – namely 0.5000 – is the probability of getting 3 or more heads. This, of course, is not exactly what we want. However, the figure opposite $r = 4$ – that's 0.1875 – is the probability of getting 4 or more heads. Now '4 or more' heads out of 5 means 4 heads or 5 heads, whereas '3 or more' means 3 or 4 or 5. So the difference between these two figures must give the probability of getting *exactly* three heads.

Thus $p$ (three heads in five throws) $= 0.5000 - 0.1875 = 0.3125$, just as we calculated at the beginning of this section.

You may wonder *why* the tables are arranged in this way, which means we have to perform subtraction sums to find the probability of getting an exact number of successes. But in practical situations it is often more useful to answer questions like 'What's the chance of more than three eggs being smashed?' or 'What's the probability this salesman will make at least six sales?', so on balance, I think this cumulative method of presenting the tables is preferable.

Let us now solve the problem (b) posed above, where the probability of rain on a particular day is 60 per cent, giving $p = 0.6$, and we wish to know the probability of 5 or more wet days next week, so $n = 7$. It is easy enough to find the block of tables headed

$n = 7$, but where is $p = 0.6$? The values of $p$ at the heads of the columns only go as far as $p = 0.5$ so how are we to deal with the remaining values between 0.5 and 1? The answer is, by turning the problem on its head and asking, not what is the probability of 5 or more wet days if $p$(wet day) = 0.6, but rather what is the probability of 2 *or less* dry days if $p$(dry day) = 0.4 – which of course amounts to exactly the same thing. Because of the either/or nature of binomial problems, a problem involving a value of $p$ greater than 0.5 can always be re-expressed in terms of the *opposite* situation, for which $p$ is less than 0.5. That's why the tables need only go as far as $p = 0.5$.

To solve this problem, then, we want $p$(2 or less dry days out of 7), with $p$(dry day) = 0.4; we are still not quite home, however, for the tables are arranged to give the probability of $r$ or more events, not $r$ or less. But here the fact that probabilities add up to 1 comes to our rescue:

$$p(\text{2 or less dry days}) + p(\text{3 or more dry days}) = 1$$

because between them the two situations cover all possibilities, so we have:

$$p(\text{2 or less dry days}) = 1 - p(\text{3 or more dry days}).$$

If we look in the $n = 7$ block of the tables, under $p = 0.4$ and opposite $r = 3$, what we find is the probability of 3 or more dry days, which turns out to be 0.5800. So $p$(2 or less dry days) = $1 - 0.5800 = 0.4200$, which is therefore also the chance of 5 or more wet days in the week.

You will realise by now that one often has to do a certain amount of juggling with a problem before it appears in the right form for use with the tables. Here again, as with the elementary probability problems in Chapter 8, I am afraid the English language is very much to blame. It is worth spending a little time looking at the various ways in which questions of this kind can be posed, and how they relate to each other. For this purpose it is useful to make use once more of the 'number line' which we encountered in Chapter 1 and which is repeated below:

The probabilities given directly by the tables are, as we have seen, of the 'or more' variety – for example, 5 or more wet days out of seven. The *opposite* of this can be found from the number line by drawing a division which cuts off the 'five or more' cases from the rest, as shown; then it is clear that the remaining possibilities are '4 or less'. (The precise position of the division does not matter since we are dealing with a discrete situation where values between 4 and 5 cannot occur.) But there are other ways of expressing these two fundamental cases: '5 or more' is the same as 'more than 4', or 'not less than 5', or 'at least 5', while '4 or less' can also be stated as 'less than 5', 'not more than 4', and 'at most 4'. So you really need your wits about you in untangling this sort of problem, and the use of the number line, though it may seem a bit infantile, can be a great help. You can always write it on a scrap of paper and throw it away afterwards, so no one need know you resorted to such basic methods!

There are two other points about the binomial tables worth noting. First, you have probably observed that the figures in the $r = 0$ row for every block of the tables are all 1.0000. This is not surprising, if you recall that these figures represent the probability of

0 or more successes out of $n$; there are *bound* to be 0 or more successes, so this probability corresponds to a certainty, whatever the value of $n$. Hence it is always equal to 1.

The second fact is that the set of tables provided in Appendix 4 is very limited. It is taken in the main from a more extensive set given in *Statistical Tables for Science Engineering Management and Business Studies*, by J. Murdoch and J. A. Barnes (Macmillan), which also contains all the other sets of statistical tables to which we are going to be referring later in the book. You are strongly advised to equip yourself with a copy! But in fact even the most extensive tables don't run to very large values of $n$, since in that case there are approximations which can be made to render use of the binomial distribution unnecessary.

We will now conclude our use of the binomial tables by returning to the quality manager's problem with the Crunchy Flapjacks: given $n = 6$, and $p = 0.05$, what is the probability of more than 3 broken biscuits in a box? $p$(more than 3) = $p$(4 or more), so we should be looking up the block $n = 6$, the column $p = 0.05$ and the row $r = 4$; the probability then turns out to be 0.0001 within the accuracy of the tables, so apparently the proportion of replacements demanded will be only 1 in 10,000. This isn't too surprising if you ask what would be the average number of broken biscuits you'd expect to find in a box; if the proportion of broken ones is 1 in 20, and boxes contain six, then the average proportion broken per box will be one-twentieth of six, which is 0.3. So the chance of getting a box with more than three broken will indeed be very small.

# THE POISSON DISTRIBUTION

## Recognising the pattern

If you were approaching the second of the quality manager's problems from scratch, you might well, armed with your new knowledge of the binomial distribution, try to fit it into that pattern. Remember that the difficulty with the toffee apples was that small number with faulty toffee coating – an average of three per box. The number of apples in a box wasn't known exactly, since they are packed by weight, but it's fairly large.

We certainly have the binomial-type either/or situation here: either an apple has a faulty coating or it hasn't. But we look in vain for the other two requirements, $n$ and $p$: we don't know $n$, as we've just observed; nor do we know what the probability of an individual apple being faulty may be. All we have is the average or *mean* number of faulty apples per box. What we can say however, is that the faulty ones are pretty unusual – there are only three of them in a box containing round about 144 – so the value of $p$, whatever it may be, must be quite small.

The information which we have here characterises a *Poisson* problem, for which probabilities are given by the Poisson distribution (called after its French discoverer). These characteristics may be summarised:

(a) either/or situation;
(b) mean number of successes per unit, $m$, known and fixed;
(c) $p$, chance of success, unknown but small, (the event is 'unusual').

As with the binomial problems, we'll begin our study of Poisson problems by learning to recognise this pattern in particular cases.

(a)   Attendance records at a large factory show that on average there are seven absentees on any day. What is the probability that on a certain day there will be more than eight people absent?

Here the either/or situation is provided by absent/present. The mean to be used is clearly seven, and if the factory is large and only seven people per day on average are absent, the chance of an individual being absent is clearly small. The only assumption we need to make is that the average number of absences is fixed, in other words it doesn't vary with, for instance, the day of the week or the time of year. This might lead to slight inaccuracies if we are actually interested in a day in February which falls in the middle of a 'flu epidemic, or the day after a public holiday when some workers may decide unofficially to extend their time off.

(b)   An automated production line breaks down on average once in every two hours. A certain special production run requires uninterrupted running of the line for eight hours. What is the probability that this can be achieved?

Our two-way outcome here is breakdown/no breakdown, but when we come to identify the mean we have to be a bit careful about the relevant unit over which to average. As stated in the problem, there is a breakdown every two hours; that's an average of 0.5 breakdowns per hour. But we are actually interested in the numbers of breakdowns over an *eight*-hour period, so the mean relevant to this period will be *four* breakdowns. At this rate, the chance of the machine breaking down at any particular point in time is pretty small, so we have the 'unusual event' requirement.

(c)   It is known that an automatic packing machine produces, on average, one in a hundred bags which is underweight. What is the probability that a case of 500 bags filled by the machine will contain less than three underweight?

Although the magic word 'average' occurs in this problem, it is strictly speaking, a binomial problem. We have the bags classified as either underweight or not; we know $n$, which is the 500 bags per box; and $p$, the probability that a bag is underweight, is 1/100 or 0.01. However, we certainly can't use the tables in Appendix 4 to solve the problem since they don't go anywhere near $n = 500$.

What we *can* do though, is to make use of the Poisson distribution as an approximation to the binomial. As $p = 0.01$ is certainly small, the 'unusual event' requirement is satisfied, and the mean number of underweight bags per crate is easily calculated as 5 (1 in 100 is underweight, and there are 500 in the crate). So we have the necessary conditions for using the Poisson distribution.

You may say 'Well, in that case where does the approximation come in?' It arises from the fact that, in a binomial problem, there is an *upper limit* to the number of successes which can occur; there is no way we could have 501 underweight boxes if the crate only contains 500. But strictly speaking, in a Poisson situation, as we don't know $n$ there is *no* upper limit to the number of successes which might occur. It's pretty unlikely, in problem (b), that the machine would break down 20 times, or even 100 times, over the eight-hour period; nevertheless, it just *might* happen and the Poisson distribution takes account of this.

However, in a case like the present one, where $n$ is very big and $p$ is very small, these probabilities at the 'top end' of the range of possibilities are going to be so tiny that the difference between the two distributions, over the range of practical interest, is not important.

From what's been said it will be clear that in many cases, as with the binomial problems, we are using the Poisson pattern as a model, which *may* fit our problem exactly, or may involve a certain amount of approximation.

## Using the tables

Tables of the probabilities which apply to problems of the Poisson pattern will be found in Appendix 5. In many respects these resemble the binomial tables: they are cumulative, giving the probability of *r or more* successes; the probabilities are quoted to four decimal places, so that a blank doesn't indicate that something is impossible, merely that the chance of its occurrence is too small to show up in the tables; and all the entries for $r = 0$ are 1.0000, since '0 or more successes' is an event which is bound to occur. The tables are, however, simpler in that, as the Poisson pattern only requires the knowledge of a single quantity $m$, they are arranged throughout in columns corresponding to the various values of $m$.

You can see, too, how the point made above about the absence of an upper limit to the number of successes shows up in the tables. The column of the table with $m = 2.0$, for instance, stops at $r = 9$ only because that is where the probabilities cease to show up in four-figure tables. There is no reason why, given more accurate tables, the possibility of $r = 10$ or higher values should not be considered.

So much for the theoretical aspects of the tables; we can now make use of them to solve the problems posed in the preceding section. Let's start with problem (a) where we had $m = 7$, and wished to know $p$(more than 8 people absent). Before the tables can be used, 'more than 8' has to be rephrased as '9 or more'; then all we need do is look in the column $m = 7$ and the row $r = 9$, to obtain a probability of 0.2709.

For problem (b), we found that the relevant mean, the number of breakdowns per eight-hour period, was equal to 4, and we were interested in the chance of obtaining such a period with no breakdowns. We can find this in a manner similar to the one we used in section 9.3 with reference to the binomial tables:

$$p(\text{no breakdowns}) = p(0 \text{ or more breakdowns}) - p(1 \text{ or more})$$

$$= 1.000 - 0.9817, \text{ looking under } m = 4$$

$$= 0.0183.$$

Finally, problem (c) had $m = 5$, and we need the chance of less than three underweight bags: $p$(less than 3 underweight) + $p$(3 or more underweight) = 1, so $p$(less than 3 underweight) = $1 - p$(3 or more underweight). Looking in the tables under $m = 5$ and $r = 3$ we find the figure 0.8753, so

$$p(\text{less than 3 underweight}) = 1 - 0.8753 = 0.1247.$$

Having practised the use of the tables with these examples you will realise that many of the points raised in connection with the binomial tables – particularly the way in which the wording of a question may need adjustment to the precise form given in the tables – apply equally well here.

Let's now return to the quality manager's second problem which concerned the faulty toffee apples. These were averaging out at six per box – in other words $m = 6$. But he doesn't want to know a probability; rather he has *decided* what probability he is interested in – the one-in-a-hundred replacement rate which he is prepared to accept – and needs to know what number of faulty apples that probability corresponds to. That is, he wishes to find the value of $r$, with an $m$ of 6, such that the probability of $r$ or more 'successes' (i.e. faulty apples) is 1/100 or 0.01.

We are, in effect, using the tables 'backwards' here; we look under $m = 6$ and run down the column of probabilities until we meet 0.01. Actually that precise value doesn't occur;

the probability of 12 or more 'successes' is 0.0201, while that of 13 or more is 0.0088. Thus if the quality manager agrees to replace the entire box if 13 or more badly-coated apples are encountered, he can be confident that he will have to do this with a probability of only 0.0088, which represents less than one box in 100.

As with problems (a) and (c) above, strictly speaking the Poisson is only an approximation here, since there is an upper limit to the possible number of 'successes'. However, since this limit is large, the approximation will be good.

## THE NORMAL DISTRIBUTION

### The pattern

When we turn from the two distributions we have looked at so far in this chapter to consider the quality manager's last problem concerning the weight of bags of Carrot Candy, one major difference should strike you immediately. Whereas with both binomial and Poisson problems we were talking about either/or situations where the number of times a thing occurred could be *counted*, in the Carrot Candy problem we are talking about something – weight – which is not being counted but *measured*. The distinction is more or less the same as the one made in Chapter 3 between discrete and continuous variables, and so the binomial and Poisson distributions are referred to as *discrete* probability distributions. What we need to deal with the Carrot Candy problem is a *continuous* probability distribution – one which will tell us (given of course a certain amount of data) what is the probability that a continuous variable, such as the weight of a bag of Carrot Candy, will take certain values.

We approached the idea of a probability distribution in the section 'The idea of a probability distribution', p. 148, by way of frequency distributions, so let's try to shed some light on the current problem by doing the same thing. If the quality manager were to take a sample of 100 bags filled by an automatic machine (let's assume it's a different one from the one which is causing his problems) he might get the following frequency table:

| Weight of bag (g) | No. of bags |
|---|---|
| 503 but under 505 | 2 |
| 505 but under 507 | 12 |
| 507 but under 509 | 21 |
| 509 but under 511 | 29 |
| 511 but under 513 | 23 |
| 513 but under 515 | 11 |
| 515 but under 517 | 2 |

This could, of course, be turned into an experimental probability distribution by dividing all the frequencies by 100. The probability histogram for this distribution is shown in Fig. 9.2(*a*). It shows a certain degree of symmetry, as we might expect, the machine apparently producing roughly equal proportions of bags above and below the average weight. It is also clear that weights a very long way from the centre of the distribution occur much less often than those close to the central value.

This histogram, however, is not likely to be very representative of the entire output of the machine since it applies only to one particular sample of 100 bags. Were the sample

(a)

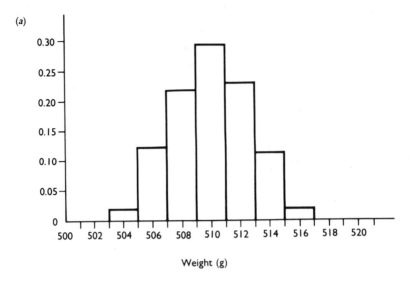

(b)

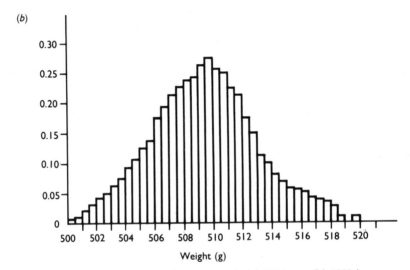

**Fig. 9.2** Probability histogram for weights of Carrot Candy (a) 100 bags; (b) 1000 bags

to consist of 1,000 rather than 100 bags, we could expect to find a good deal more regularity in the behaviour of the distribution, resulting in something like the histogram in Fig. 9.2(*b*). You can see that as there is so much more data, it has been possible to subdivide it into classes with a width of only 0.5 g rather than the 2 g interval used in Fig. 9.2(*a*). Altogether the histogram exhibits a much smoother appearance, though the feature of symmetry about a central peak value is still noticeable.

By now you should find it quite easy to imagine that, were we to take more and more bags in the sample and subdivide the intervals of the histogram with increasing precision, we would ultimately obtain a histogram with steps so small and so close together as to be almost indistinguishable from the smooth curve shown in Fig. 9.3. This is what is known as the *normal distribution* curve, and it will become very familiar to you in the course of the next few chapters.

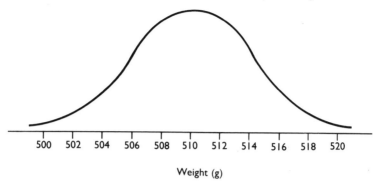

Weight (g)

**Fig. 9.3** Normal distribution curve

## How the normal distribution works

Before proceeding to ask how the normal distribution can help us in calculating probabilities, we should take note of some of its important features. The symmetry which we noticed in the histograms is apparent also here; if the curve were folded down the centre, the two halves would lie exactly on top of each other. The curve is often described as 'bell-shaped', expressing the fact that it drops on either side of a central peak. But it never actually touches the horizontal axis though it gets closer and closer to it the further away from the peak we go. And here is where the element of 'modelling' comes in again – the normal distribution is a *theoretical* distribution, so we can't expect that our real-life distributions will conform to it exactly. The weight distribution, for example, will have a lower limit; the samples of 100 and 1,000 bags contained no bags weighing less than 500 g, and even if we admit the possibility that the machine may occasionally omit to fill a bag at all, thus producing an item with zero weight, it certainly can't produce negative weights. Yet the theoretical distribution carries on, in principle, indefinitely to the left as well as to the right, so clearly it doesn't fit our real-life situation very well at these extremes. However, over the part which matters – the bit between about 500 and 520 g – it fits very well, and the part of the distribution in the region where it *doesn't* fit is so tiny that it isn't very important. We'll be returning to this question of how well a particular practical case fits the theoretical normal curve later on.

Two very important facts about the probability histogram which were noted in the section 'The idea of a probability distribution', p. 148–50, apply equally well to the smoothed-off histogram which gives the normal curve. First, the *area* occupied by the histogram represented probability; so it is for the areas under the normal curve. Second, the total area of the histogram was 1; similarly with the total area under the normal curve.

We are happily talking about 'the' normal curve, but of course what we've got in Fig. 9.3 is only one of an infinite number of possible normal curves, all basically the same shape, but varying in their position and amount of spread; several such curves are shown in Fig. 9.4. So what information do we need in order to distinguish one normal curve from another? If we know the *mean* of the relevant distribution we will know the position of the 'peak' of the curve, while the standard deviation is the easiest way of characterising how spread out the distribution is. For the weight distribution in Fig. 9.3 the mean is 510 g as shown, and the standard deviation, as you can check from the distribution for 100 bags, is about 2.5 g.

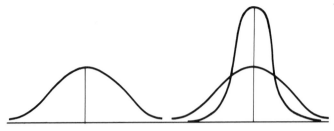

**Fig. 9.4** Normal curves with different means and spreads

Now that we know how the normal distribution behaves and have the mean and standard deviation to describe our particular normal distribution, we can begin to ask questions about probabilities. Suppose, for example, that we want to know what proportion of these bags weighs more than 515 g; this will be given by the proportion of the area under the curve to the right of 515 g, as shown in Fig. 9.5(*a*). (You are strongly recommended always to draw such a diagram when tackling normal distribution problems.)

But how are we to determine this area? True, we know that the total area is 1, but that doesn't help us to find exactly what fraction of the area falls to the right of 515. We could try plotting the curve accurately on graph paper and finding the area by counting squares, but apart from being very slow, that would require a knowledge of the equation of the curve, which is so unpleasant that I won't alarm you by writing it down. Anyway, such an answer wouldn't be very accurate. So we resort to the expedient which has come to

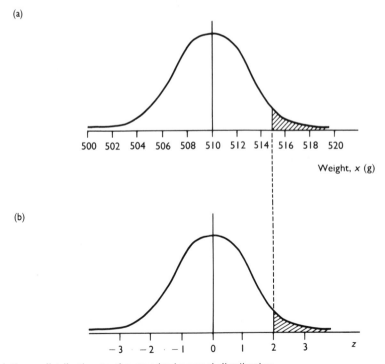

**Fig. 9.5** Relating a distribution to the standard normal distribution

our aid with the previous two distributions: we make use of a set of tables of the areas under the normal curve, which have already been computed accurately by someone else. All we need know, once again, is how to use them.

## Using the tables

That insidious phrase '*the* normal curve' has slipped in again in the last paragraph, but we now know that there are any number of normal curves with different means and different standard deviations. This is rather a depressing thought: does it mean we're going to need an infinite, or at least a very large, set of tables to cope with all the different combinations of mean and standard deviation which we might come across? Happily the answer is no. Since all these different normal curves are the same fundamental *shape*, tables are provided for just one such curve, called the *standard* normal distribution, and all other normal distributions are then related to that.

You'll find a table of areas under the standard normal curve in Appendix 6. It really is the simplest normal distribution that one could have since its mean is 0, as shown in the sketch at the top of the tables, and its standard deviation is 1. The table, as its heading tells us, gives the areas in the 'tail' of the distribution – the bit to the right of a given value. The horizontal axis is called the $z$-axis, and $z$ is often referred to as the *standard normal variable*. So, the tables work like this: to find the probability, say, that $z$ is greater than 2 – perhaps more meaningfully interpreted as finding the proportion of the values in the standard distribution which are bigger than 2 – we simply look down the left-hand side of the tables until we find $z = 2$, and then read off the probability under the column headed 0.00. This tells us that the probability of a value greater than 2.00 is 0.02275. Had we wanted a value greater than 2.05 we would have located 2.0 in the left-hand column first, and then proceeded across the tables to the column headed 0.05 to obtain a probability of 0.02018.

This, you may say, is all very well, but how does this highly theoretical distribution, referring to nothing in particular, help us to answer questions about the weight distribution of bags with a mean of 510 g and a standard deviation of 2.5 g? How can we connect our practical distribution with the standard one in the tables? The clue is provided in Fig. 9.5(*a*) and (*b*). Remember that the *shape* of the two normal distributions is the same; all that varies is their means and standard deviations. So the necessary connection will be provided if we can determine what points in the theoretical distribution – on the $z$-axis – correspond to what points in the practical distribution – on the $x$-axis. For instance, to take a concrete case, what $z$-value lies directly under $x = 515$?

It's easy enough to see that $z = 0$ will coincide with $x = 510$, these being the peak values, that is, the means, of the two distributions. As we move out from the means, it is the standard deviation which indicates how far from the mean the rest of the values in the distribution tend to be. By the time we reach $x = 515$, we are two standard deviations away from the mean of the weight distribution (the standard deviation was 2.5 g, remember). Thus $x = 515$ must correspond to a point on the $z$-axis two standard deviations away from the mean. But the standard deviation of *this* distribution is 1; so $x = 515$ will correspond to $z = 2$. In other words, $z$ tells us *how many standard deviations away from the mean* the point we are interested in lies.

If you like formulae rather than words, we can translate this fact as follows: the distance from the mean, 510 g, to the value we're interested in, 515 g, is 515–510; then

$z$ is the number of standard deviations in this distance, so:

$$z = \frac{515 - 510}{2.5} = 2$$

as before. In fact for *any* point $x$ in a distribution with a mean $m$ and a standard deviation $s$:

$$z = \frac{x - m}{s}.*$$

The process of calculating $z$ from $x$ is sometimes called *standardisation*.

Once we have made this transition from $x$ to $z$, the rest is easy. We set out to find the proportion of the bags which have weight in excess of 515 g, represented by the area under the standard curve to the right of $z = 2$, which we have already looked up in the tables and found to be 0.02275. Because five-figure decimals don't say much to most people, I prefer to convert this to a percentage and say that 2.275 per cent of all bags filled by this machine will weigh more than 515 g.

## Using the normal distribution in practice

Setting up the machinery for using the normal tables has taken rather a long time, but really the process is quite simple: we sketched the normal distribution for our problem, and identified on it the mean and the particular value we are interested in. Then we made the transition from our $x$-distribution to the standard $z$-distribution by using the fact that $z$ is the number of standard deviations from the mean up to our $x$-value. Finally, we used the tables to tell us the required probability. When we apply this process to a few more sample problems you will see how quick it is. For simplicity we will stay with the weight distribution, mean 510 and standard deviation 2.5 g.

(a)  What percentage of the bags filled by the machine will weigh less than 507.5 g?
The area we require is shown in Fig. 9.6(*a*); it is the shaded area beyond one standard deviation to the *left* of the mean, so that it corresponds, as the sketch at the top of Appendix 6 shows, to a *negative* value of $z$. (You should find the same thing if you use the formula for calculating $z$.) But there aren't any negative values of $z$ given in the tables, and a minute's thought should suggest why not. The symmetry of the distribution means that if the areas at the left-hand end of the distribution, where $z$ is negative, *were* tabulated, they'd be exactly the same as those at the right-hand end, so the exercise would be a bit of a waste of time.
We can, then, find the area we are interested in, to the left of $z = -1$, by ignoring the fact that $z$ is negative and looking up the area to the *right* of $z = +1$, which is 0.1587. So 15.87 per cent of bags weigh less than 507.5 g.

(b)  What is the probability that a bag filled by the machine weighs less than 512 g?
As you can see from Fig. 9.6(*b*), the area we want here isn't the right shape for looking up directly in the tables. What we *can* find directly, though, is the probability that a bag weighs *more* than 512 g. The $z$-value corresponding to $x = 512$ is $\dfrac{512 - 510}{2.5}$ or 0.8, and the tables give the area to the right of 0.8 as 0.2119. So $p$(bag weighs more than 512 g) = 0.2119. But of course $p$(bag weighs

---

* You will also encounter this formula with the Greek letters $\mu$ and $\sigma$ used in place of $m$ and $s$, in other textbooks and sets of statistical tables.

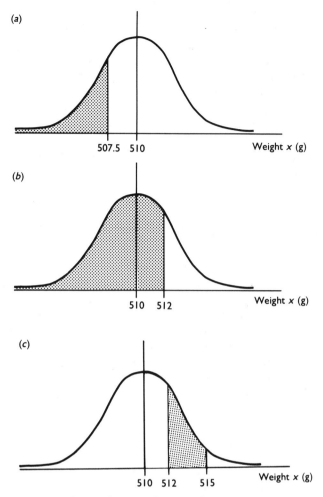

**Fig. 9.6** Areas under the normal curve (see text for details)

more than 512 g) + $p$(bag weighs less than 512 g) = 1, so $p$(bag weighs less than 512 g) = 1 − 0.2119 = 0.7881.

At this point you may feel a bit worried about the bags which weigh *exactly* 512 g, which seem to have got left out of our analysis. In fact the normal distribution can't deal with the probability of obtaining a single exact value, like for instance $p(x = 512$ g). In terms of the diagram it's not too difficult to see why this is: the 'area' corresponding to a single value like this is zero. In practical terms this can be interpreted by saying that, when there is an infinite range of possible weights for the bags, as there is with any continuous distribution, the chance of any one precise *value* occurring is so small as to be effectively zero; we might get a bag which we think weighs 512 g, but no doubt if we weighed it more accurately we would find it actually weighed 511.97 g, or 512.01 g. So whether we write $p$(bag weighs less than 512 g) or $p$(bag weighs less than or equal to 512 g) is really immaterial.

(c)   What percentage of the bags will weigh between 512 and 515 g?

Again, the area as illustrated in Fig. 9.6(c) can't be looked up directly. What we have to do in this case is express the required area as the difference of two areas which *can* be looked up: namely, the area to the right of 512 and that to the right of 515. We've just found, under (b), that the area to the right of 512 is 0.2119, and earlier in this section we determined the area to the right of 515 as 0.02275. So $p$(bag weighs between 512 and 515 g) = 0.2119 − 0.02275 = 0.18915, which means nearly 19 per cent of bags fall between these two limits.

These examples don't cover all the possible types of area which may arise, but by now you should realise that the way to tackle any area which isn't suitable for direct use with the tables is to split it into several which *are* suitable, not forgetting the useful facts that the total area under the curve is 1 and the areas on either side of the mean are each 0.5.

## SOME GENERAL POINTS ABOUT THE NORMAL DISTRIBUTION

Before returning to and solving the quality manager's third problem, there are a few more general points worth making about the normal distribution. The first takes us back to Chapter 6, where in our efforts to get a 'feel' for the meaning of the standard deviation, we noted that most of the values in a fairly symmetric distribution will lie within three standard deviations either side of the mean. The reason for this becomes clear if we now interpret 'reasonably symmetric' as meaning 'approximately normal', and examine the normal tables. Three standard deviations away from the mean gives $z = 3$, and sure enough the tables show that only 0.135 per cent of the distribution lies beyond this point. At the same time, you can verify the statement made earlier in this chapter that the normal curve never actually hits the $z$-axis. By the time we get out to $z = 4$, only 0.003 per cent of the distribution is excluded, but no matter how large the value of $z$, we would find, given sufficiently accurate tables, that there would always be a tiny bit 'left over'.

If you are observant you may have wondered why the sub-heading on p. 157 was only 'the pattern' rather than 'recognising the pattern', the expression which was used in the corresponding sections on the binomial and Poisson distributions. The fact is that we rather tend to *assume* that distributions of continuous variables such as weights, people's heights, IQs and so on will be normal. The very name of the distribution reflects this assumption: it's what we 'normally' expect to occur; and in most of these cases the assumption is fairly well justified, as long as we are talking about a pretty big population. Take IQs, for example. The majority of people have IQs somewhere near the mean; the further away from the mean an IQ is, the less likely one is to encounter someone with that IQ, and the proportions of the population with IQs above and below the average are, in principle, roughly the same – the numbers of Einsteins being balanced by people at the other end of the distribution. Thus we'd expect the shape of this distribution to be something close to the normal. The same will apply to *any* variable which is the result of the accumulative effect of a large number of random influences (this can actually be demonstrated mathematically).

Nevertheless, there *are* other continuous distributions of importance – we'll encounter one of these in Chapter 11. There are even other symmetrical distributions with infinite tails on either side, looking to the naked eye indistinguishable from normal curves. So it doesn't do to be *too* ready to assume that a variable is normally distributed, but a method of deciding whether this is the case or not will have to wait until Chapter 11.

### Solving the original problem

As the grand finale to our discussion of the normal distribution, we will now tackle the quality manager's third problem. The machine filling bags of Carrot Candy is set to a mean weight of 510 g, but this setting is producing rejects – bags weighing under 500 g – at a rate of 20 per cent of total production which is unacceptably high. So what should the new average setting of the machine be if the rate of rejects is to be cut down to 5 per cent?

We will assume that the weights of bags as filled by the machine are normally distributed with a mean of 510 g. A sketch of the distribution is given in Fig. 9.7. But this problem differs from all those we've solved so far in that we aren't trying to find a probability, or percentage, or whatever one likes to call it. Instead we are *given* the proportion of bags weighing less than 500 g – in other words, we are told that the shaded area in Fig. 9.7 is 20 per cent of the whole or 0.2. So what *do* we need to find?

What we don't know at this point is the variability of the weights being produced by this machine as measured by the standard deviation. However we can deduce this via the known proportion of rejects being produced. The problem is the reverse of the ones solved earlier, in that we know the area and want to work backwards from there. So when we consult the tables, we look among the areas – the figures in the body of the table – for something as near as possible to 0.2000. The nearest is 0.2005, corresponding to a $z$ of 0.84 (you should be following this in the tables).

Recalling that $z$ tells us 'how many standard deviations from $x$ to the mean', we can therefore deduce that from 500 to 510 is 0.84 standard deviations. That means 10 g is $0.84 \times s$, so that $s$ must be 10/0.84 or 11.9 g. (If you find this hard to follow, try asking yourself how you'd work out $s$ if 10 g had turned out to be 2 standard deviations.)

This is a rather high value for the standard deviation. However, it is generally much more difficult – and expensive – to adjust the variability than the mean. So we therefore ask: given this degree of variability, what should the mean setting on the machine be if only 5 per cent of the bags are to fall below 500 g?

A new sketch is required, since the distribution produced by the adjusted machine will centre on the new, unknown mean, $m$, as shown in Fig. 9.8. Again, what we know is the area to the left of 500 g, but now this area is reduced to 5 per cent or 0.05. The same 'backward' use of the tables as before shows that such an area is cut off by the value $z = 1.65$ (this actually gives an area of 0.0495, but that's the nearest we can get within the accuracy of these tables). So the distance from 500 to the mean must be 1.65 standard deviations, hence the mean is 1.65 standard deviations above 500:

$$m = 500 + 1.65 \times 11.9 = 519.64 \text{ g}.$$

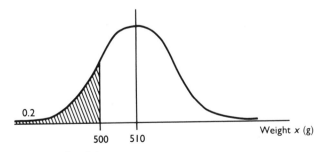

**Fig. 9.7** Present distribution of weights

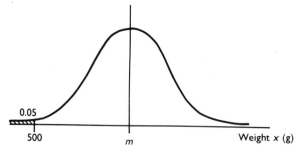

**Fig. 9.8** Required distribution of weights

This is therefore the average weight to which the machine would have to be set to give only 5 per cent of bags below 500 g, with its existing variability.

One final point about all these problems. You will find that many textbooks and sets of tables use notation in such situations which bristles with Greek letters, brackets, < and > signs. It is quite unnecessary for you to try to use such notation; as long as you explain what you are doing clearly, and don't just produce numbers like rabbits out of a hat with no indication as to whether they are areas, standard deviations or what, there is no one 'right' way of writing out these problems.

## SOME FURTHER POINTS

The distributions – two discrete and one continuous – which we have studied in this chapter are only three, though arguably the three most important, out of the large number of probability distributions which have been investigated and tabulated. As already mentioned, we will be coming across two other continuous distributions, called the *chi-squared* distribution and the *t*-distribution, in Chapter 11, and a glance through a book of statistical tables will show several others. With all of them, however, the same two-stage process is needed: first the recognition of the type of situation to which the distribution in question applies, and second the use of the tabulated probabilities associated with the distribution.

Although we have made the distinction between the continuous normal distribution and the discrete binomial and Poisson, there are in fact links between them. We've already seen how the Poisson can be used as an approximation to the binomial, but both of these can be approximated by the normal under certain circumstances. If you recall how we approached the normal curve in the first place by taking histograms with larger amounts of data and smaller class intervals, you should not be surprised to learn that when *n*

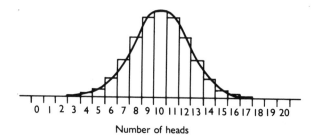

**Fig. 9.9** Normal approximation to a binomial situation

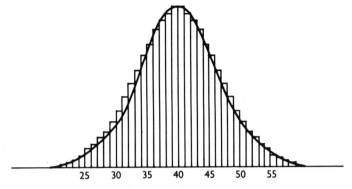

**Fig. 9.10** Normal approximation to a Poisson situation

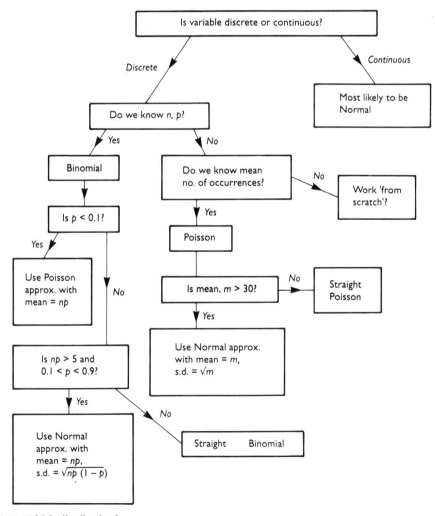

**Fig. 9.11** Which distribution?

becomes large and $p$ is not too far from $\frac{1}{2}$, the binomial is approximated quite well by the normal; the requirement that $n$ should be large means that 'smoothing off' the histogram does not introduce too much inaccuracy, while the need for $p$ to be near to 0.5 is occasioned by the symmetry of the normal curve. It's impossible to lay down hard and fast rules as to how large is large, but roughly speaking if $p$ is between 0.1 and 0.9, and $n \times p > 5$, the approximation is a reasonable one. Fig. 9.9 shows a binomial distribution histogram resulting from tossing twenty coins together 1,000 times and recording the number of heads (so $n = 20$, $p = 0.5$). You can see from the superimposed normal curve how closely the approximation works; an example of its use will be found in the Practical Exercises at the end of the chapter.

The Poisson, too, can be approximated by a normal curve if $m$, the average number of successes, is large (bigger than about 30). Again, there's a problem below which illustrates this, and Fig. 9.10 shows how well the normal curve fits a Poisson probability histogram with $m = 40$. This is why most tables of binomial and Poisson probabilities don't cover a very wide range; over a large part of the range the normal approximation is quite adequate. This tendency of other distributions to become normal when large amounts of data are involved is one reason why the normal is so important, and explains why it crops up again and again in more advanced statistical work.

The major problem which most students have when tackling probability distribution problems for the first time is deciding on the appropriate distribution to use in a given situation. The critical question is 'What information do I have?', since this will generally determine the distribution to be used, even if some approximation is called for. You may find the diagram in Fig. 9.11 helpful in dealing with this difficulty.

## ◩ PROBABILITIES FROM THE COMPUTER

MINITAB has two functions which can be useful in finding probabilities. The function CDF stands for Cumulative Distribution Function, and gives you a cumulative probability; a subcommand allows you to specify the distribution you wish to use. Thus the command

    CDF 6;
    NORM 5 1.

requests the cumulative probability up to the value 6 for a Normal distribution with mean 5 and standard deviation 1, and so returns the value 0.8413.

The related command INVCDF denotes Inverse Cumulative Distribution Function, and gives the value associated with a given cumulative probability level for the specified distribution. So

    INVCDF 0.8;
    POIS 4.

will return the information

| K | P(X LESS OR = K) | K | P(X LESS OR = K) |
|---|---|---|---|
| 5 | 0.7851 | 6 | 0.8893 |

indicating that for a Poisson distribution with mean 4, the probability of obtaining a value less than or equal to 5 is 0.7851, while the probability of a value less than or equal to 6 is 0.8893. The value we specified, 0.8, actually falls between these limits – since the

Poisson is a discrete distribution, we cannot expect to find a value of K which will give a probability of *exactly* 0.8.

These functions can be useful particularly since they generally cover a wider range of values than can be obtained from printed tables (for example, by using INVCDF you can find that the $z$-value which cuts off an area of 0.00001 in the tail of a Normal distribution is 4.2649, a much more accurate figure than is obtainable from most sets of statistical tables).

## Practical exercises

In this section you will find a hotch-potch of problems of all three types, so that you get used to recognising each distribution.

1  A greengrocer has checked six trays of tomatoes and found that they contain respectively 2, 0, 1, 4, 3 and 2 bad fruit. What is the probability that a tray will contain (a) 2 or more; (b) no bad fruit?

2  A manufacturer of Christmas crackers knows that three crackers in every twenty don't contain a paper hat and a customer complains that his box of ten crackers contained three without paper hats. What is the probability of this occurrence?

3  A machine produces small metal components whose lengths are normally distributed with a mean of 5 cm and a standard deviation of 0.2 cm. What is the probability that a component will have a length (a) less than 4.7 cm; (b) more than 4.8 cm; (c) between 4.6 cm and 5.3 cm?

4  A worker is late, on average, one morning in four. If he works a five-day week, what is the probability that he will be late less than three times next week? What is the most likely number of times he will be late?

5  A work-study engineer times a certain operation, and discovers that the average time it takes is 10 minutes, but on 15 per cent of occasions it takes more than 13 minutes. Assuming that times for the operation follow a normal distribution, what is its standard deviation?

6  Nine times out of ten a quotation made by a firm to a customer leads to a definite order. What is the probability that a batch of five quotations leads to four definite orders?

7  A small internal switchboard can cope with up to six incoming calls per minute. The average number of incoming calls received is twelve every five minutes. What is the probability that in a two-minute interval the switchboard receives more calls than it can cope with?

8  An automatic packing machine is filling bags of sugar to a nominal weight of 1 kg. Fifty thousand bags per week are produced by the machine, which at present is set to a mean of 1,005 g. All bags below the nominal weight are rejected, this policy resulting at present in a reject rate of 1,500 bags per week. (a) What is the standard deviation of the bags filled by the machine? (b) To what mean should the machine be re-set if the standard deviation cannot be changed, if each rejected bag costs the company 8p, and a saving of £40 per week is to be made?

**9** Ten coins are tossed together and the number of heads is counted.

   (a) Using the binomial distribution, find the probability of getting six or more heads.

   (b) Now see how close to this figure the normal approximation comes. The appropriate mean to use will be 5, since that's the average number of heads we'd expect to get in 10 tosses of a fair coin. It can be proved that the standard deviation of a binomial distribution is $\sqrt{np(1-p)}$, so here it will be $\sqrt{10 \times 0.5 \times 0.5}$ which is 1.58. You need to be careful, too, as to what '6 or more' means in terms of a continuous distribution like the normal. Everything from 5.5 upwards has to be included, since 5.5, 5.6 etc. would all be rounded off to 6 when treated as discrete.

**10** Now try the same sort of thing with the Poisson as an approximation to the binomial. Suppose 5 per cent of items produced by a machine are defective in some way, and a sample of 10 items is taken.

   (a) Use the binomial to work out the probability that at least one of the ten is defective.

   (b) Now use the Poisson to work out the same thing. The mean to use is, of course, 0.5, since if 5 per cent of the items are faulty, the number of defectives to be expected out of 10 would on average, be 5 per cent of 10.

**11** Very large reels of electrical cable may have quite large numbers of small flaws without their usefulness being seriously impaired. Suppose the average number of such flaws per 2000 metre reel is 36. What is the probability that if you purchase such a reel it will have fewer than 30 flaws? This is strictly a Poisson problem, but since the mean is large (36) we can use the Normal as an approximation. It can be proved that the standard deviation of the Poisson is the square root of its mean, so that here s.d. $= \sqrt{36} = 6$. Use Normal tables to solve the problem (remember that as in question 9 above, we are approximating a discrete situation by a continuous one).

## Case study problem

Dear X,

I'm hoping you can settle an argument for me! I buy packs of cheese biscuits from the local market, usually 10 at a time. They are labelled 'Weight 1 kg net', but because I suspect the stall-holder is a bit of a cowboy, I usually weigh them. Last week, out of the 10 I had bought, there were two weighing less than 980 gm – so I had been done out of over 40 gm of biscuits, which is nearly two ounces!

When I tackled the stall-holder about it, he blustered and said that the bags were filled by a machine, and you couldn't expect every one to be exactly the same. He said that the machine was set to give an average weight of 1015 gm, and that a quarter of bags actually weigh more than 1025 gm. What I want to know is, if this is true, what's the chance of getting a bag weighing under 980 gm? – or for that matter, two of them in a batch of ten, as I did?

Of course, I know the weights and measures legislation is supposed to deal with this kind of thing. Could you find out just what it says about when something is underweight – I know the system changed a few years ago, and now a lot of packets have the 'e' showing that they conform to the EC system, but I don't really know what this implies for me as a consumer – and I feel I should!

   Yours in some annoyance,

      Jane

## Case study question

Reply to this letter, including if possible getting hold of a copy of the Weights and Measures Act 1979, or information from your local Trading Standards Officers, and explaining the current system used for weight labelling on packages of food etc.

## CHAPTER 10

# Estimating from samples: inference

## Objectives

Before starting work on this chapter, make sure you are happy with:

(a) simple random samples (*see* Chapter 3, pp. 40–1);
(b) the binomial distribution (*see* Chapter 9, pp. 150–4);
(c) the normal distribution (*see* Chapter 9, pp. 157–66);
(d) solution of equations (*see* Chapter 1, pp. 14–16);

By the end of your work on this chapter you should be able to:

(a) estimate a population mean or percentage from the mean or percentage in a large simple random sample taken from the population to any required level of confidence;
(b) determine the minimum sample size needed to estimate a population percentage or mean to a given level of accuracy with a prescribed level of confidence;
(c) find the probability that a sample of a given size from a known population will have a certain mean or percentage;
(d) state the conditions under which the above processes are valid.

## THE DISSATISFIED CUSTOMER'S PROBLEM

Radio Supplies Ltd is a firm which supplies small components to the electronics industry. A particular type of connection is normally dispatched in boxes of 500, and as a small number of faulty items is unavoidable with this type of component, customers have agreed that a rate of 2 per cent defectives is acceptable. However, Radio Supplies has recently received a complaint from one of its major customers, suggesting that as a recent consignment of 500 of these connections contained 25 which were faulty, the quality of the product must be deteriorating, and threatening cancellation of future orders unless the previous quality can be maintained. Naturally Radio Supplies' management are very concerned that this should not happen, and wish to investigate the contention that quality is deteriorating.

If you recall what was said about sampling methods in Chapter 3, you should realise that the first question to be asked is 'Was this box of 500 representative of production as a whole?' Perhaps the batch all came from one machine which was causing problems at the time; perhaps they were produced after at weekend or a holiday period when machines had not warmed up or workers were not operating at maximum efficiency. It may not be very easy, several weeks or even months after the event, to discover the answers to these questions, but if a valuable order depends on obtaining the information it is clearly worth making the effort.

However, even if all these possibilities can be ruled out, and the batch genuinely appears to be a random sample of the entire output of the connections, it does not necessarily follow that the quality is deteriorating. The box of 500, after all, only constitutes a *sample* from the whole output, and we have already seen that samples, even random ones, can be very unrepresentative of the populations from which they are taken. Maybe another lucky customer has received a box with no defective items at all – but he would be foolish to deduce that Radio Supplies has managed to produce a 100 per cent perfect product.

These *sampling variations* are to be expected. It would be naive to imagine that every sample will reflect the proportion of defective items in the population *exactly*. The relevant question is, if the overall proportion of defective items *hasn't* increased, just how likely is it that a box of 500 with 25 defectives will occur – or, to look at the problem another way, what proportion of all the boxes of 500 sent out will contain as many as 25 defectives, or maybe even more? These are clearly questions which should vitally concern the management of Radio Supplies, and, as you will have realised by now, they are questions concerned once again with *probabilities*.

## A SIMPLE EXAMPLE

To be able to answer questions of the kind posed in the previous section we need to know quite a lot about how samples of a particular size taken from a given population may vary. (We say 'of a particular size' because it's intuitively clear to most people that a big sample is 'more reliable' or 'more representative' than a small one, so the size of the sample should be an important factor.) We can get some useful preliminary ideas about this if we begin by considering a very simple situation in which the entire population contains only six members.

Let us suppose, then, that a market researcher is carrying out a survey on a small Hebridean island with only six households, in order to determine which of them consume that staple Scottish breakfast-food, porridge. Of course, in this situation he could easily carry out a census (a survey of the entire population) but instead he has decided to take a sample of three of the six households. We will further suppose that we already have, from some other source, perfect information as to the diets of the six families, which reveals the following facts:

$$\left.\begin{array}{l} \text{Adams} \\ \text{Brown} \\ \text{Carter} \\ \text{Davies} \end{array}\right\} \textit{do} \text{ breakfast on porridge;} \qquad \left.\begin{array}{l} \text{Evans} \\ \text{Finch} \end{array}\right\} \text{ do not.}$$

Now, because the population is so small, we can actually list all the possible samples which the researcher might obtain, and thus find the percentage of each sample possessing the required characteristic – in this case, porridge consumption. The samples are listed below, together with the percentage for each, using A, B, C . . . to denote the six families:

| Sample | Percentage eating porridge | Sample | Percentage eating porridge |
|--------|---------------------------|--------|---------------------------|
| ABC | 100 | BCD | 100 |
| ABD | 100 | BCE | 67 |
| ABE | 67 | BCF | 67 |
| ABF | 67 | BDE | 67 |
| ACD | 100 | BDF | 67 |
| ACE | 67 | BEF | 33 |
| ACF | 67 | CDE | 67 |
| ADE | 67 | CDF | 67 |
| ADF | 67 | CEF | 33 |
| AEF | 33 | DEF | 33 |

So, out of the twenty possible samples, 4 contain 100 per cent, 12 contain 67 per cent and 4 contain 33 per cent with the required characteristic. Moreover, *if* the researcher chooses his sample randomly (in the technical sense in which we defined that term in Chapter 3), then each sample is equally likely to arise, and so we can say that the probability of his getting a sample with 100 per cent porridge-eaters is 4/20, for 67 per cent it's 12/20, and for 33 per cent, 4/20 again. We can summarise this in the table below:

| Percentage in sample | Probability |
|----------------------|-------------|
| 100 | 4/20 or 0.2 |
| 67 | 12/20 or 0.6 |
| 33 | 4/20 or 0.2 |

What we have here is, of course, a *probability distribution* of the kind we discussed in Chapter 9. However, because this particular distribution refers specifically to the probability of obtaining various percentages in a sample, we give it the more descriptive name of a *sampling distribution* – the sampling distribution of percentages in samples of three items, in this case.

Although this is such a simple example there are certain features of the sampling distribution which are worth noticing because they will appear again later when we look at other more realistic sampling situations. Firstly, if we work out the *mean* of the distribution in the usual way, we have:

$$\text{Mean} = 100\% \times 0.2 + 67\% \times 0.6 + 33\% \times 0.2 = 67\%.$$

In other words, the mean of the sampling distribution is the true percentage for the population as a whole. This seems intuitively reasonable; we would expect samples containing the population percentage to crop up more often than samples with any other percentage (unless, of course, the samples are deliberately biased).

Secondly, we can see that if the investigator were simply to assume that the percentage obtained in his sample automatically reflects that in the entire population, he might be led very seriously astray – depending on which sample he obtains, he could get the impression that as many as 100 per cent of the households, or as few as 33 per cent, consume porridge for breakfast. In order to get a fair impression of what the population figure might be, he obviously has to make some allowance for the variability of the samples.

You may like, before going further, to try constructing for yourself the distribution of percentages in samples of *four* households from this same population. There will be 15 possible samples and you should find that, while the mean is still 67 per cent, the sample percentages this time only vary between 50 and 100 per cent, reflecting the feeling we have that the bigger a sample is, the more 'reliable' – that is, the closer to the true population figure – it's likely to be.

## THE SAMPLING DISTRIBUTION OF PERCENTAGES

In the example given above we could actually explicitly construct the sampling distribution because the number of possible samples was very small. Normally, however, we are going to be considering populations which are so large that we certainly won't be able to do this. In fact, we shall generally be able to assume that the population is so big in comparison with the size of the sample that removing the sample makes no effective difference to the population – that, for all practical purposes, the population is infinitely large.

This being so, it follows that when we start choosing our sample, the percentage of the population having the characteristic we are interested in will remain the same whether the items we remove have the characteristic or not; the probability of selecting an item with the required characteristic remains constant throughout the selection of the sample. So, in the process of selecting the sample, these three conditions apply:

(a) the number of items in the sample, say *n*, is fixed and known in advance;
(b) as each item of the sample is selected there are two possible outcomes – either it has, or does not have, the characteristic we are interested in;
(c) the probability of selecting an item *with* the characteristic remains constant, and is known to be P per cent.

These three conditions should be familiar to you already; they are, of course, the conditions under which the binomial distribution is applicable (see Chapter 9, p. 150, if you have forgotten this). The sampling distribution of percentages is, in fact, a binomial distribution, as long as the assumptions we've made – simple random samples, taken from a population which is effectively infinite – are satisfied.

We aren't, however, going to use the binomial distribution directly in answering questions like the one posed in the first section of this chapter. If we are prepared to make one further assumption, we can instead use the normal approximation to the binomial, which is a great deal more convenient. That assumption is that the samples are large – an assumption which is certainly likely to be justified in many of the applications of sampling, such as the analysis of market research surveys, that we'll be looking at. We saw in Chapter 9 that if *n* is 'large', then the binomial is very well approximated by a normal distribution, though what exactly constitutes 'large' in this context depends on how symmetrical the binomial we're concerned with is; roughly speaking, the more *un*symmetrical the binomial, the bigger *n* needs to be before the normal approximation becomes valid. A sort of rule-of-thumb answer for the question 'How big is big?' in this context is that samples should contain 30 or more items, though for fairly symmetrical situations – that is, percentages near to 50 – we can often get away with a smaller sample, and occasionally we have to be rather careful with values of P near to 0 or 100 per cent.

Once we have accepted that the sampling distribution of percentages for large samples is more or less normal, there are two further things we need to know before we can begin to apply this fact to the solution of problems – namely the *mean* and *standard deviation* of this normal sampling distribution, which as we saw in Chapter 9 are the two *parameters* which define a normal distribution. If you did Practical Exercise 9 in Chapter 9 you will know that the mean *number* of items with the characteristic we are interested in, in samples of $n$ items chosen at random, will be $np$, where $p$ is the probability of an item having the characteristic. In the same exercise we saw that the standard deviation of this number was $\sqrt{np(1-p)}$. This isn't quite what we are after, however, because what we've been talking about so far isn't the *number* of items per sample, but rather the *percentage*, which is usually a much more useful concept.

The transition from numbers to percentages isn't difficult to make: if the mean number of items in a sample with our characteristic – let's call it characteristic X – is $np$, then the mean percentage is $\dfrac{np}{n} \times 100 = 100p = P$, where P is the percentage of the population with characteristic X. In the same way, the standard deviation expressed in percentage terms will be:

$$\frac{\sqrt{np(1-p)}}{n} \times 100 = 100 \sqrt{\frac{p(1-p)}{n}} = \sqrt{\frac{P(100-P)}{n}}.$$

This quantity – the standard deviation of the sampling distribution – is so important that it has been given a special name. Remember that the standard deviation measures how spread out around the mean the points of a distribution are. So this particular standard deviation will tell us, more or less, how the sample values differ from the mean P, which is the population value. It could therefore be thought of as giving an idea of the *error* we might be making if we were to use a sample value instead of the population value. For that reason it is called the *ST*andard *E*rror of *P*ercentages – subsequently referred to in this book as STEP.

We now have all the information we need to begin applying sampling theory to practical problems, but as there's been quite a dose of theory to swallow in the last few pages, let's pause before we carry on to summarise what we have shown so far, and to see how it fits in with common sense.

We have seen that the sampling distribution of percentages in samples of $n$ item ($n \geqslant 30$ approximately) taken at random from a population in which P per cent of items have characteristic X, will be:

a NORMAL distribution
with MEAN P%
and STANDARD DEVIATION (STEP) $= \sqrt{\dfrac{P(100-P)}{n}}$ %.

The % signs are put in here to remind you that, just as for a distribution of heights in centimetres the mean and standard deviation are in centimetres, so for this distribution of percentages the mean and standard deviation will also be percentages.

Now, how does this fit in with the intuitive feelings most of us have as to how samples 'ought' to behave? Let's think about the shape of the distribution first: the normal curve is symmetrical, so that there will be equal chances of obtaining samples with, say, over 30 per cent and under 20 per cent of 'characteristic X' items from a population where the actual figure is 25 per cent. This seems fair enough – we've no reason to suppose, unless the samples are chosen in a biased way, that they will have any tendency either to lower-than-average or to higher-than-average percentages.

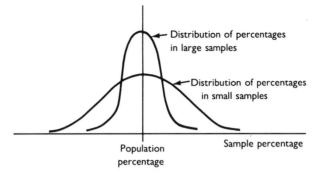

**Fig. 10.1** How sample size affects the sampling distribution

In saying 'lower-than-*average*' here we are really making the second point – the average or mean percentage occurring in the samples will be P, the percentage which applies to the population as a whole. This again is reasonable – if we are going to use samples as a guide to the situation in the entire population, then although we have to realise that they *will* vary somewhat, it is reassuring to think that 'the average sample' will actually contain the same percentage as the population.

Finally, the standard deviation, which we have called STEP, depends *inversely* on the size of the sample – that is, as *n* increases, STEP will decrease, so that the distribution becomes more compact – in other words, all the sample values will tend to be closer to the population value. (You can see an illustration of this in Fig. 10.1.) This merely confirms what we already noted in relation to the porridge-eaters example above, namely that bigger samples are more reliable as a guide to the population than smaller ones. To put it another way: a small sample could be very misleading because just a few untypical items could give it a strong bias. This is much less likely to happen in a large sample.

We have gone into some detail over these points because they are probably some of the most subtle you will be required to deal with. However, if you haven't followed all the details, don't worry – they will probably begin to fall into place as we proceed with practical applications of the theory.

## APPLICATIONS OF STEP

We are going to use the results of the preceding section to examine three categories of problem:

(a) those where a straightforward probability is required – we want to answer a question of the type 'What is the probability that such a sample will arise?';
(b) those where we wish to estimate the percentage P in the population from information obtained from a single sample; and
(c) those where we want to know how large a sample would be required in order to estimate a population percentage with a given degree of accuracy.

There is a fourth type of problem, that in which we want to test some theory concerning a population by taking a sample from it, but this latter type is a topic of such importance that we have reserved Chapter 11 for its discussion.

## Finding a probability

An example of the first type of problem described above might be the following. Suppose the personnel records of a firm show that a quarter of its workforce consists of women, and imagine that a random sample of 80 workers is to be selected to take part in a work-study exercise. How likely is it that this sample will contain 25 or more women?

We know that the distribution of percentages of women in these samples will be normal, with a mean of 25 per cent (one quarter, the population value) and a standard deviation of STEP, where:

$$\text{STEP} = \sqrt{\frac{25 \times 75}{80}} = 4.84 \text{ per cent.}$$

We want to find the probability that there will be 25 or more women in a sample, which means the sample contains 31.25 per cent or more of women (since 25/80 is 31.25 per cent). This will be represented by the area shaded in Fig. 10.2, so we have exactly the same type of problem as we were solving when we discussed the normal distribution in Chapter 9, the only difference being that the standard deviation in this case is the special one we've called STEP. So, as usual, we begin by calculating $z$, the number of standard deviations from the mean to our figure of interest:

$$z = \frac{31.25 - 25}{4.84} = 1.29.$$

The normal tables in Appendix 6 then show that the probability we require is 0.0985. That is, nearly 10 per cent of all the possible samples of 80 workers will contain 25 or more women.

Of course, there are several unrealistic features to this problem. First of all, it's fairly unlikely that a sample, particularly in connection with a work-study exercise, would be selected completely randomly in this way – it's much more likely that it would be stratified in some way so as to reflect, among other factors, the male/female composition of the work force. We haven't, either, said anything about how big the work force is altogether, but to satisfy the assumptions we made in building up the theory, it must be very much larger than the 80 in the sample. Most seriously, perhaps, we have chosen here a rather unusual situation in which the population percentage P is actually known, but it is far more often the case that we are taking a sample precisely because we *cannot* find P for the whole population – either because it would take too long, or cost too much, or because it simply isn't worth the effort of getting an accurate answer. It is this sort of circumstance which is covered by the kind of problems outlined under (b) above.

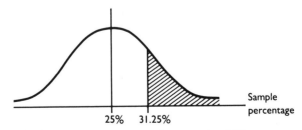

**Fig. 10.2** Probability of finding 25 or more women in a sample of 80

## Estimating a percentage

Such a problem might be confronted by a market researcher who wishes to conduct a survey to determine what percentage of consumers purchase his company's products. If he selects a sample of 400 consumers at random, and finds that 280 of them are purchasers of the products, what can he conclude about the percentage of *all* consumers who buy them?

It is helpful to start by saying what he definitely *cannot* conclude – namely, that the figure 280/400 or 70 per cent will be exactly representative of the population as a whole. We know from the example of the porridge eaters how misleading *that* assumption might be. The figure will be somewhere *around* 70 per cent – but it would help to be a bit more precise as to how far away from 70 per cent 'around' might mean. We can get some ideas as to how we could achieve this precision by looking at some populations from which such a sample *could* have come.

First, could it have come from a population in which the actual percentage buying the products is 72 per cent? This is equivalent to asking what is the probability of obtaining a sample with a percentage of purchasers as low as 70 from a population with 72 per cent. This is, of course, just the type of problem we looked at under (a). We therefore leave you to check that here, with P = 72 per cent and $n = 400$, STEP is 2.24. So $z = 0.89$, and the normal tables then tell us that the chance of getting a sample with a percentage as low as 70 per cent or even less is 0.1867 (represented by the shaded area in Fig 10.3($a$)). So more than 18 per cent of all samples would contain a percentage as low as or lower than 70; such a sample would not be at all unusual, and therefore might well have come from a population for which the figure *is* 72 per cent.

If, on the other hand, we ask whether it could have come from a population with P = 60 per cent, the answer is certainly that it's most unlikely. STEP in this case would be 2.45, so that $z = 10/2.45$ (*see* Fig. 10.3($b$)), and this $z$-value is well beyond the range of our

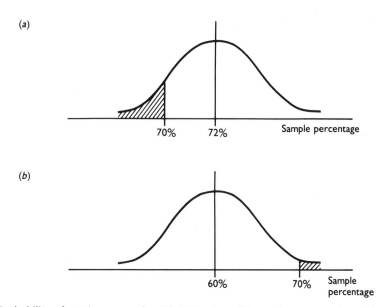

**Fig. 10.3** Probability of getting a sample with 70% where (a) population contains 72%; (b) population contains 60%

tables, showing that the chance of getting a sample with as high a percentage as 70 or more from a population which contains only 60 per cent is so small as to be virtually zero.

So, 72 is quite likely; 60 is very *un*likely. But we obviously can't proceed in this haphazard manner; what we need are some limits between which we can be reasonably confident that the population value will lie.

It seems sensible, first of all, that these limits should be symmetrically placed on either side of the sample figure of 70, since we've no reason to assume that this sample is biased either upward or downward. So what we are looking for, as illustrated in Fig. 10.4, are two possible population percentages, one on either side of 70, which represent the lowest and highest population percentages from which such a sample could reasonably be supposed to come. What we mean by reasonably, of course, will depend on the circumstances, but for many purposes a convention has grown up, that to demand that we can be '95 per cent confident' in our estimate is a reasonable requirement.

By 95 per cent confident we mean that in view of our symmetry requirement, the limits must be so arranged on either side of 70 as to exclude only $2\frac{1}{2}$ per cent in each 'tail' of the normal sampling distribution (see Fig. 10.4). As a decimal $2\frac{1}{2}$ per cent is 0.025, and if we consult the normal tables again we find that a $z$-value of 1.96 will cut off an area of this size. Thus the two extreme values we are looking for will lie 1.96 standard deviations away on either side of 70. If, in other words, we give as the limits for our estimate points which are 1.96 standard deviations above and below 70, we can be 95 per cent confident in our estimate, since we have excluded only the extreme 5 per cent of possibilities.

There's one further slight complication: we know that the standard deviation in question is STEP, but how are we to find it? To do so, we need to know the population percentage, P, but this is precisely what we *don't* know at this stage, otherwise we wouldn't be going to all this trouble! However, we do know the *sample* percentage, 70, and if we use that as an approximation to P in calculating STEP we shouldn't go far wrong. So we can say:

$$\text{STEP} \sqrt{\frac{70 \times 30}{400}} = 2.29\%$$

and thus we would give our estimate for the population percentage, with 95 per cent confidence, as $70 \pm 1.96 \times \text{STEP}$ or $70 \pm 1.96 \times 2.29$ (the $\pm$ indicating the two limits equal distances each side of 70). When we do the arithmetic this gives 65.51 per cent and 74.49 per cent as the two limits, and 65.51 to 74.49 is often referred to as the 95 *per cent confidence interval*, though you may find it more helpful to think of allowing 1.96

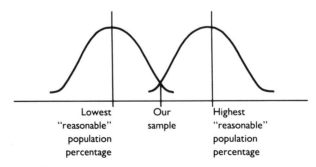

|  | | |
| :---: | :---: | :---: |
| Lowest | Our | Highest |
| "reasonable" | sample | "reasonable" |
| population | | population |
| percentage | | percentage |

**Fig. 10.4** The idea of confidence limits

standard deviations 'margin of error' around the sample value in estimating the population figure.

No doubt, at a first reading this seems a very involved process, but in fact, in practice it can be simplified in a number of ways. First of all, having once established the fact that for 95 per cent confidence one must go 1.96 standard deviations either side of the mean for the normal distribution, we can simply quote this in future – there is no need to go to the normal tables every time. Secondly, for many purposes it is sufficiently accurate to round off 1.96 to 2. With these two assumptions, we can state very succinctly that if a sample of $n$ items contains P per cent with characteristic X, then with 95 per cent confidence we estimate the population percentage with that characteristic as lying in the interval P $\pm$ 2 STEP. For instance, if a sample of 60 students contained 12 who were left-handed – that's 20 per cent – then we could estimate with 95 per cent confidence that the percentage of left-handers in the student population as a whole will be in the range:

$$20 \pm 2 \times \text{STEP} = 20 \pm 2 \times \sqrt{\frac{20 \times 80}{60}}$$

or between 9.67 per cent and 30.33 per cent. So the actual mechanics of the estimation process are quite simple.

Of course, there is nothing sacrosanct about 95 per cent confidence; we could in theory use any level we wished, but there are a few others which are generally used, of which 99 per cent is perhaps the next most common. If we think of the confidence interval as a sort of 'margin of error' around the sample value, then it's clear that in order to have greater confidence in our estimate, we must allow a wider margin of error – the interval for 99 per cent confidence will be bigger than for 95 per cent. By using the normal tables as before, but now looking for the $z$-value which cuts off only $\frac{1}{2}$ per cent in each tail (*see* Fig. 10.5), we find that in this case we need to go 2.58 $\times$ STEP either side of P. Conversely, a lower confidence level will result in a narrower interval – though this *isn't* a good way of achieving what might at first sight seem a more precise, because a smaller, range in our estimate. If we need a smaller interval, the correct way to achieve it would be to take a bigger sample, thus reducing the size of STEP.

Incidentally, although we can increase the confidence level to 99.9 per cent or even 99.99 per cent if we so wish, we cannot ever achieve 100 per cent confidence in our estimate – or at least, only if we are prepared to accept the rather obvious estimate of the population percentage as somewhere between 0 and 100! The point is that when we quote a confidence level, we aren't saying 'The probability that the population percentage is in this interval is 95 per cent' – or whatever confidence level we're using. The percentage for the population either *is* in the interval or it *isn't*. What we *are* saying is that if we make a habit of estimating population figures from sample figures in this way, then 95 per cent

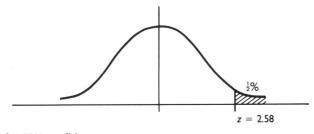

**Fig. 10.5** Looking for 99% confidence

of the time we are going to be right, in the sense that our confidence interval *will* contain the true population figure. This may seem like playing with words, but it's the misunderstanding of points like this which causes statements such as 'You can prove anything with statistics' to be made!

## Finding a sample size

Finally in this section on the uses to which sampling of percentages may be put, we examine the question posed in (c) at the beginning of this section, which is of very real practical importance to market researchers designing sample surveys: How large a sample is needed to estimate a population percentage to some predetermined degree of accuracy? Sampling costs money and takes time, so clearly it is pointless to interview 6,000 people if 600 would have been enough to give us a sufficiently accurate figure; equally, however, it is no good interviewing 600, processing all the results and then finding that the answers aren't accurate enough. Fortunately, with the aid of STEP both these dangers can be avoided.

Imagine, then, that you have been asked to conduct a survey to determine the percentage of full-time students who own cars. How many students must you interview? This will naturally depend on (a) how accurate you want your answer to be, and (b) how confident you want to be in that answer. Let's be fairly generous and say that a figure within 5 per cent either way from the true percentage will do, and as usual let's take a 95 per cent confidence level. Furthermore, suppose that a rough pilot survey suggests the figure is somewhere around the 30 per cent mark. Then, referring to Fig. 10.6 it becomes apparent that we have two quite separate expressions representing the distance *d*. First, in order to satisfy the 95 per cent confidence requirement, it must be equal to $2 \times$ STEP; second, to achieve the desired accuracy it must also be no more than 5 per cent. So, at worst, these two things must be equal to each other: $2 \times$ STEP = 5, whence STEP = 2.5. Using the rough value for P obtained in the pilot survey, we can now say

$$\text{STEP} = \sqrt{\frac{30 \times 70}{n}}$$ where $n$ is, of course, unknown – the sample size is what we are

trying to find. So we have an equation for $n$, namely $\sqrt{\dfrac{30 \times 70}{n}} = 2.5$. The details of

how this can be inverted to find $n$ shouldn't cause you any problems if you revise the solution of equations in Chapter 1, pp. 14–16 (as a hint, begin by squaring each side of the equation). The final result is $n = 336$. That is, we must interview 336 people to be 95 per cent confident that our estimate is within 5 per cent of the true answer.

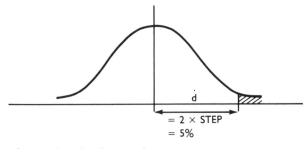

**Fig. 10.6** Two ways of expressing the distance *d*

This process can easily be adapted to deal with other levels of confidence and/or other required accuracies. The only small defect in the method is that we had to have a rough idea what P was likely to be – in the example above, obtained from a pilot survey. This isn't generally too difficult to arrange, but if you *should* be in the position of trying to find out what size sample you need without any idea at all of what you expect the answer to be, then you must, as it were, assume the worst. The 'worst', in this case, is the value of P which, should it occur, would give rise to the largest error, and you can easily verify by calculating STEP for, say, samples of 100 items with P = 10 per cent, 20 per cent, etc., that STEP has a maximum when P = 50. This is true for any sample size, in fact, and so, if you have no prior information as to roughly what P might be, assuming it's 50 per cent will give you a sample which is more than big enough to cope with any other value of P.

We have now covered the three types of problem mentioned at the start of this section. One final word of warning before we leave the topic of sampling percentages: you will have noticed that we have worked throughout with *percentages*, even when the original information was perhaps given in terms of actual *numbers* in a sample. Where necessary, we converted to percentage terms at the start of the problem and converted back at the end. There *are* alternative versions of the theory designed to deal with numbers or proportions in a sample, but by far the safest principle is always to use figures in percentage form, thus avoiding confusion; then the only point in the theory at which an actual *number* occurs is the sample size $n$ in the denominator of the STEP formula.

## THE SAMPLING DISTRIBUTION OF MEANS

Although we have chosen to discuss the sampling of percentages in order to introduce you to the theory of sampling, *every* statistic which is calculated from a sample will have its own sampling distribution. So, for example, we could talk about the sampling distribution for standard deviations or for quartiles, or indeed for any of the measurements we discussed in Chapter 6. The trouble with many of these situations, however, is that they do not follow simple distributions such as the normal, and are therefore difficult to examine theoretically, though we could of course build them up experimentally by actually taking lots of samples from a known population and using them to calculate the measurement we are interested in.

One measurement which fortunately *does* follow a straightforward pattern is the *mean*. (Remember from Chapter 6 that the mean is what's colloquially called the 'average'.) We could define the sampling distribution of means in much the same way as we defined that for percentages, as the distribution we would get if we were able to take all possible random samples of a given size from a particular population and calculate their means. It would seem that the resulting distribution is bound to depend on what the population we're sampling looks like. After all, surely a population in which all values occur the same number of times (*a uniform* distribution of values) is going to give us very different looking samples from, say, a normal population where some values are much more likely to arise than others.

The extraordinary thing is, however, that although this is undoubtedly true if the samples are small, if the samples are big enough the distribution of their means turns out to be near enough normal *regardless of what kind of population they are taken from*! (You can see an illustration of this in Fig. 10.7.) This remarkable fact is a consequence

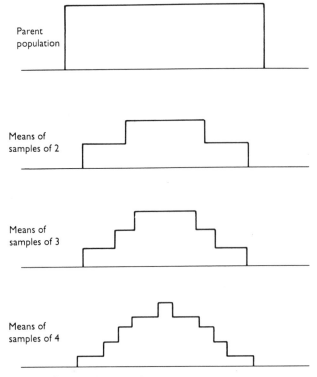

**Fig. 10.7** The Central Limit Theorem in operation

of a result called the Central Limit Theorem, the proof of which need not concern us; what we are going to concentrate on is the use of the result.

So, if we accept that for large enough samples – and again, as with sampling percentages, 30 is generally considered to be 'large' – the distribution of sample means is normal, then we also need to know its mean and standard deviation. The fact that the mean of the sampling distribution is equal to the overall population mean doesn't take much swallowing; it seems reasonable that there should be more samples with the same mean as the whole population than with any other mean. (This is a point at which newcomers to this topic often get a sort of mental indigestion, due to the multitude of 'means' encountered. However, if you remind yourself that we are talking about a distribution all of whose members are means, so that the mean of *this* distribution is a mean *of means*, you shouldn't be confused.)

As for the standard deviation, it will come as no surprise to you to learn that it is called the *ST*andard *E*rror of the *M*ean, which we will abbreviate to STEM. Once again, as with the Central Limit Theorem, we are not going to give a proof but simply state that:

$$\text{STEM} = \frac{s.d.}{\sqrt{n}}$$

where *s.d.* denotes the standard deviation of the population and *n* is, as usual, the size of the sample. Like STEP, and for the same common-sense reason, STEM decreases as the samples get bigger. The fact that it gets larger as the population *s.d.* gets larger is also in accordance with common-sense, for clearly the more variation in the population, the more varied will be the samples taken from it, and hence their means.

Armed with a knowledge of the shape, mean and standard deviation of the sampling distribution of means, we can now use it to solve all the types of problems considered in the previous section on the application of STEP in relation to percentages. We give just two examples below.

(a) What is the probability that if we take a random sample of 64 children from a population whose mean IQ is 100 with a standard deviation of 15, the mean IQ of the sample will be below 95?

Here, $s = 15$, $n = 64$, and population mean $= 100$, so:

$$\text{STEM} = \frac{15}{\sqrt{64}} = \frac{15}{8} = 1.875.$$

In Fig. 10.8 the probability we want is represented by the shaded area, and by calculating:

$$z = \frac{100 - 95}{\text{STEM}} = \frac{5}{1.875} = 2.67$$

and then using the normal tables, we find that the required probability is 0.0038. So the chance that the average IQ of our sample is below 95 is very small indeed. Note that this is a fact about the *average* IQ of the sample – it does not say anything about the individual children who make up the sample.

(b) The problem in (a) was a bit unrealistic in that we actually *knew* the population mean and standard deviation. In many situations we'll be taking a sample precisely because we *don't* have that information, and trying to estimate the population figures from the sample as we did with percentages in the preceding section. Exactly the same argument we went through there tells us that we can estimate with 95 per cent confidence that the population mean will lie in the interval: sample mean $\pm 2 \times$ STEM.

For example, suppose that an inspector, wishing to check the weight of tins of baked beans but unable to weigh every single one which comes off the production line, contents himself with weighing a random sample of 100 tins. He finds that the sample mean weight is 225 g with a standard deviation of 5 g. Now to calculate STEM we really need to know the *population* standard deviation, but in the absence of that information we can use the sample value, 5 g, instead without serious error (again, as long as $n$ is large). If we do this then STEM $= 5/\sqrt{100} = 0.5$, and so our 95 per cent confidence interval for the mean of the whole population will be $225 \pm 2 \times 0.5$, or from 224 to 226 g.

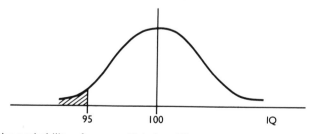

**Fig. 10.8** Finding the probability of a mean IQ below 95

## THE PROBLEM REVISITED

If you now go back and re-read the section at the beginning of this chapter on the dissatisfied customer's problem you will realise that Radio Supplies' problem is connected with sampling of percentages; they want to know how likely it is that a box of 500 connections would contain 25 – that is, 5 per cent – faulty items if overall only 2 per cent faulty were being produced. Has the customer just been unlucky? Here we have $P = 2$ per cent, $n = 500$, so STEP $= \sqrt{2 \times 98/500} = 0.626$. To find the probability that the sample percentage is 5 per cent or over, we need to find the area shown in Fig. 10.9. Thus we have $z = (5 - 2)/\text{STEP} = 3/0.626 = 4.79$. Now the normal tables show that the area to the right of $z = 4.79$ is negligible, so the chance of such a sample occurring if the population only contains 2 per cent defectives as claimed is very small indeed. It would be hard for Radio Supplies to convince the customer that he's just been unfortunate – particularly if he knows any statistics!

We ought to think for a moment here about the effect on this 'solution' to Radio Supplies' problem of the assumptions we've made in the process of deriving the theory. We saw earlier that the more unsymmetrical the binomial – that is, the further away $P$ is from 50 per cent – the bigger the sample needs to be before the normal becomes an adequate approximation. Now, here we have $P = 2$ per cent, which is certainly a long way from 50 per cent by any standards. However, the fact that we have such a very large sample should ensure that even so, we are safe with the normal approximation.

More serious, not just for this particular problem but in general terms, is the assumption that the sample is a simple random one. We discussed briefly in the first section of this chapter why it might be hard, particularly investigating the customer's complaint in retrospect, to ascertain whether the 'sample' represented by the box of 500 connections really was random, and in Chapter 3 we noted a number of very good reasons why it might be impossible or undesirable to take a simple random sample. In most market research enquiries, for example, some kind of stratified sample is preferred because it ensures adequate and representative coverage of the population in a way that a simple random sample does not.

So have we wasted our time in discussing STEP and STEM? Are they just elegant pieces of theory with no real application in practice? Well, of course the answer is no. Sampling theory such as we have examined in this chapter is the basis for the theory of obtaining estimates and so on from samples of more complicated structures. For stratified samples, for instance, it is often a question simply of modifying our version of the estimation procedure slightly to make allowance for the effect of the stratification (students of marketing may recall the term 'design factor'). Equipped with your knowledge of STEM

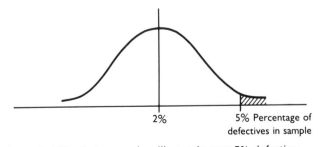

Fig. 10.9 Finding the probability that a sample will contain over 5% defectives

and STEP, you are in a good position, should the need arise, to understand the theory dealing with more complex types of sample.

The assumption that the population from which we are sampling is infinite (or at least very large compared to the sample size) is also easily overcome, by the insertion of what is called a *finite population correction factor*. If your sample constitutes more than about 10 per cent of the population, then STEM and STEP should be multiplied by

$$\sqrt{1 - \frac{n}{N}}$$

where N is the size of the population. You can check that if *n* is less than 0.1N this factor won't make much difference. When it *is* used, it has the effect of reducing the standard error; this is sensible, since a sample which constitutes a large portion of the population is more reliable, and hence should result in a lower degree of uncertainty about the true population.

What about the assumption that the sample size is greater than 30? If we are sampling proportions, we can go back to the exact binomial if sample sizes are small. For sampling of means, we will see in the next chapter that a modification to our sampling distribution enables us to deal with small samples by methods very similar to those of this chapter.

Finally, let's return briefly to Radio Supplies and their faulty connections. In fact what we have done in tackling this problem is to examine a theory about the population – in this case, the customer's theory that the 2 per cent defective rate is not being maintained – and decide, with the aid of STEP and our knowledge of normal probability, whether that theory holds water or not – in this case, the customer may well be right. We have really been testing a *hypothesis* about the population – and a more detailed examination of such *hypothesis tests* forms the subject of the next chapter.

## Practical exercises

1 A survey of 400 voters contains 208 who will vote for the Regressive candidate at the next election. How likely is he to receive more than 50 per cent of the vote? What additional information would you like to have about the sample of 400 to ensure that your conclusion is justified?

2 A quick count in the college car park tells me that out of 40 cars parked there, 15 are hatch-backs. Assuming that these cars are representative of the entire population of vehicles on the road, estimate the percentage of that population which are hatch-backs (a) with 95 per cent, and (b) with 99 per cent confidence.

3 An advertiser claims 'Eight out of every ten housewives can't tell Albatross margarine from butter!' A consumers' group sets out to test this claim, and finds that among 75 of their members, 21 *can* distinguish between Albatross and butter. Would this cause you to doubt the advertiser's claim?

4 An Office Efficiency expert times 60 secretaries typing a page of text and finds that the average time for the task is 5.5 minutes with a standard deviation of 0.4 minutes. Estimate the average time taken by all similarly-qualified secretaries to type a comparable page of text. (Use 95 per cent confidence.)

5 Your managing director demands that you determine, with 99 per cent confidence and to an accuracy of 1 per cent either way, the percentage of bills sent out by your firm which are in error. At present no one has any idea what this figure may be. How many bills would you need to examine?

6 Carry out a small survey to estimate a percentage such as, for example, the percentage of shoppers at a local supermarket who are male. This is information which might be of interest, if say, the supermarket were considering stocking a new line of male toiletries. There will be problems as to how you get a representative sample. What time of day should you collect your data? What day of the week? And how big should your sample be?

7 Construct a population with a known mean and standard deviation by writing numbers on identical slips of paper. For instance, use a uniform distribution by writing 20 1s, 20 2s and so on up to 9. Put the slips in a bag and use the population to build up a sampling distribution of means by taking, perhaps, samples of 9 and 16 slips at a time and finding their means. Strictly speaking these samples are too small for the theory to apply exactly, but nevertheless if you take a reasonable number of samples – say 50 to 100 of each size, you should get distributions with means close to the population mean, and standard deviations not too different from the values given by the STEM formula.

8 Look out for claims made by advertisers, in newspaper articles, etc., which are based on samples, and get into the habit of being sceptical about them. Ask 'How big was the sample? Was it really random? What confidence level might they have been using?'

9 Look up in some source of published statistics a figure such as the percentage of imported cars in Britain (you can find this in the *Motor Industry of Great Britain*) and then compare this with the percentage from a sample you yourself have taken. How consistent are the two figures?

10 Build up an experimental sampling distribution of percentages by taking a large number of identical slips of paper, say about 300, and marking 75 per cent of them with a cross, so that P = 75 per cent. Shake them up in a bag and then remove samples of, perhaps 20 or 30 at a time. Count the number of crossed slips in each sample, and thus build up the sampling distribution. Or you can do it more conveniently with dried butter beans, some of which are marked with a spot of paint. Although, again, the sample size is a bit on the small side, the salient features of the distribution as discussed in section 3 should emerge. Put the slips/beans back between samples! You can think of this experiment as *simulating* a market research enquiry if, instead of marking a known percentage of the population, you mark an arbitrary number and then try to deduce what percentage they represent by taking samples.

◼ This exercise can also be carried out using MINITAB's random generation facility. Use the commands:

RANDOM 50 C1;
BERNOULLI 0.2.

to generate a random sample of 50 0s and 1s into column C1, from a population in which the probability of obtaining a 1 is 0.2 or 20 per cent. By repeating this, and noting the numbers of 1s you obtain each time, the sampling distribution can be built up.

**11** ◨ Using the data set STUD.WK1 (or STUD.MTW), and assuming that the students whose details are given constitute a random sample of all students on similar courses, estimate (a) the average age of all male students on such courses, and (b) the proportion of all such students who are from overseas.

## Case study problem

Dear X,

Do you remember that nearly a year ago you helped me out with some data from a customer survey? Well, I've just done a similar survey again, and although I can now interpret the descriptive statistics for myself, I'd like to go a bit further this time. I've attached the summary of the relevant part of the results, and what I would like to know is (a) what you would estimate the average amount spent by our business customers, and by our private customers, to be, (b) how many customers from both groups combined I would need to survey in order to estimate the average amount they spend accurately to within £5 either way, (c) your estimate of the proportion of customers from each group who are either dissatisfied or very dissatisfied with our service.

Does it make a difference to your conclusions if I tell you that I don't think my survey was done on a proper random sample? And how do I decide, in general, what is a big enough sample – should I always try to ask as many people as possible, or isn't it worth the effort above a certain number? (I notice that lots of surveys seem to use 500–1000 people, even when they are supposed to apply to a much bigger group, which seems a bit odd.)

I think there may be a few more queries about this data when I've thought about it more, so don't throw it away! I hope you enjoyed your French holiday – we are off to Italy next Friday, thank goodness!

Best wishes,

Jane

## Personal touch catering

Results of customer survey, 20/719XX

| Type of Customer | Average amount spent | Standard deviation | Size of sample |
| --- | --- | --- | --- |
| Business | £420 | £37 | 47 |
| Private | £343 | £42 | 55 |

| | Very satisfied | Satisfied | Indifferent | Dissatisfied | Very dissatisfied |
| --- | --- | --- | --- | --- | --- |
| Business | 16 | 19 | 7 | 3 | 2 |
| Private | 25 | 16 | 5 | 6 | 3 |

## Case study question

Draft your reply to this letter; note that you will have to think about how to combine the 'business' and 'private' figures to get an overall mean and standard deviation, in order to answer part (b).

## CHAPTER 11

# Checking a theory: hypothesis testing

## Objectives

Before starting work on this chapter, make sure you are happy with all the material on sampling distributions covered in Chapter 10. By the end of your work on this chapter you should be able to:

(a) formulate and test an appropriate null hypothesis in situations involving percentages in large samples, means and differences of means in large or small samples;

(b) recognise situations in which a chi-squared test can be applied, and carry out the test.

## THE TRAINING MANAGER'S PROBLEM

Mrs Field is the training manager of a light engineering firm which employs a considerable number of skilled machine operators. The firm is constantly making efforts to improve the quality of its product, and so recently Mrs Field has introduced a new 'refresher' training course for workers who have been on the same machines for a long time. The first group has now completed the course and returned to normal work, and Mrs Field would like to assess the effect, if any, which the retraining has had upon the standard of its work so that she can decide whether to make such courses a regular event.

There are three particular questions which she would like to answer:

(a) is the *quality* of the product produced by the retrained workers, as measured by the proportion of reject items they produce, better than that produced *before* retraining;

(b) has the *speed* at which they operate their machines increased; and

(c) do some classes of workers respond better to retraining than others – for example, younger workers, or female operatives?

In each of these cases, Mrs Field is not, of course, asking the question in a vacuum. She has some idea what was going on before the training course, and she wants to compare the new situation with that established position. Moreover, she clearly hopes that the course *will* have produced improvements all round. She wants, in fact, to test a theory or *hypothesis* about the effect of the course.

## TESTING HYPOTHESES ABOUT PERCENTAGES

### Pinning down the problem

Take first the question regarding the proportion of defective items which the workers produced before and after the course. As far as the position *before* the course is concerned, there will undoubtedly be records available which show what percentage of reject items had been produced over a period by each worker. The amount of data available is probably so large that we can regard this as giving the percentage of defective items among the entire *population* of items produced by the worker in question.

But when it comes to the position *after* the course, there won't be nearly such a large amount of data available – or at least, not if Mrs Field wants to make her assessment fairly soon. She will have to rely on taking just a *sample* of items produced by a retrained worker, and base her assessment of the efficacy of the course on that sample. Suppose, for instance, that worker X, before the course, had been producing 4 per cent of reject items; after the course, his performance is monitored during the production of 400 items, and 14 of them are found to be defective. This represents a rate of only 3.5 per cent, which is certainly an improvement. So Mrs Field can congratulate herself that the course seems to have worked. Or *can* she?

We know from our work on sampling distributions in the last chapter that, just because the *population* percentage of reject items was 4 per cent, it doesn't follow that every single sample of 400 items taken from that population would also contain exactly 4 per cent rejects; there would be quite a bit of variation among the samples. So perhaps the 3.5 per cent figure doesn't demonstrate an improvement at all, but is simply the product of a random sampling variation. Maybe, in fact, if we continued to monitor this worker's output, we would find that he's still producing 4 per cent rejects overall – or even, perhaps, that having been away from the job during the retraining, he's deteriorated in efficiency and is now producing *more* than 4 per cent rejects!

In order to draw a sound conclusion on the basis of the sample evidence, then, we have to take sampling variations into account. It's also important that we don't begin by assuming what we are trying to prove. Mrs Field obviously hopes that her course will have produced an improvement, but to convince her sceptical superiors she must begin with the assumption that it hasn't produced any change at all. This initial assumption is called the *null hypothesis*, often abbreviated to NH; you may find it helpful to think of it as the 'boring hypothesis' – everything's the same, nothing's changed, the population is just as it always was.

The implication of the null hypothesis is that the sample of 400 items taken after the course has been drawn from a population in which the percentage of reject items is still 4 per cent, so using the notation of Chapter 10, P = 4. From this point of view, the null hypothesis is the only logical assumption we *can* make, since the 4 per cent figure is the only one we're sure about. (If the figure isn't 4 per cent, then what on earth is it? Not 3.5 per cent – that only applies to a sample, which may turn out to be an untypical one.)

With this value of P, and knowing that $n = 400$, we can proceed to calculate STEP:

$$\text{STEP} = \sqrt{\frac{4 \times 96}{400}} = 0.98\%.$$

We could now go ahead and calculate the probability that a sample such as we've got – with 3.5 per cent of rejects or even less – could arise from a population in which the proportion of rejects is 4 per cent. This is very much the sort of thing we did in Chapter 10, and in many ways it has a lot to recommend it. But a rather more systematic procedure has grown up for deciding whether or not the sample is consistent with the truth of the null hypothesis.

## Setting out the procedure

Remember that we found in Chapter 10 that 95 per cent of all the possible samples from a population with 4 per cent defective items will be contained within two standard deviations – that's $2 \times$ STEP – either side of 4 per cent. So the great majority – 95 per cent or 19 out of 20 – of all the samples of 400 items which we might get if the population percentage were 4 per cent will contain percentages of rejects in the range $4 \pm 2 \times 0.98$; that's between 2.04 per cent and 5.96 per cent. You can see this illustrated in Fig. 11.1.

This suggests that the sample taken after the course, containing 3.5 per cent rejects, isn't at all inconsistent with the assumption that overall the worker is still producing 4 per cent rejects. In fact, quite often before the course he would have been producing samples as good as this or even better. So really we've no grounds, at least from this sample, for deciding that the percentage of defective items he's producing has changed at all. However, being naturally cautious, statisticians don't say anything so definite as, 'The null hypothesis is correct', or, 'We've proved that the worker hasn't improved'. All that can be fairly claimed is that, on the strength of this sample, we have no grounds for rejecting the null hypothesis.

Of course, as always in sampling situations, we have to accept the fact that this conclusion *may* be incorrect. The usual way of expressing the conclusion is to say that the difference between the sample and the population percentage is not significant at the 5 per cent level; the 5 per cent refers to the leftover portion of the sampling distribution, the 'odd 5 per cent of samples', as it were, among which our sample would have to fall before we would be justified in rejecting the NH.

It's easier to understand why the conclusion is expressed in this way if we take another example. Suppose that a second worker had been producing 5 per cent reject items before the course, and afterwards his sample of 400 items contains only 10 rejects – that's 2.5 per cent. Has *this* worker changed?

In this case the null hypothesis is that P = 5 (i.e. there's been no change). So

$$\text{STEP} = \sqrt{\frac{5 \times 95}{400}} = 1.09$$

and 95 per cent of all samples of 400 would fall in the interval $5 \pm 2 \times 1.09$, or 2.82 per cent to 7.18 per cent. However, this time when we compare the sample taken after the course with this interval, we find that it lies outside the limits; in other words, if it *does* come from this population, it's a pretty unusual sample – one of only 5 per cent which differs from the mean by more than 2.18 per cent. So we'd be quite justified here in concluding that the sample is so different from what we would expect to get most of the time were the null hypothesis true, as to cast doubt on that hypothesis.

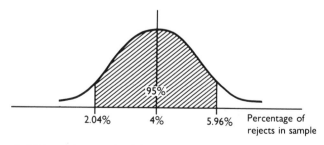

**Fig. 11.1** Samples of 400 items from a 4% defective population

We would therefore conclude that the null hypothesis should be *rejected*. Again, note the word used – we don't say, 'The null hypothesis must be wrong' – and we must qualify our statement, as usual, according to the particular interval we used to make the decision. We would say in this case that the difference between the sample and the population *is* significant at the 5 per cent level; there probably *has* been a change in the proportion of rejects being produced by this worker.

It's important to realise that we have *not* proved at the 5 per cent level that the worker has improved. By taking a symmetrical confidence interval, and dividing the 'leftover' 5 per cent equally between the two tails of the sampling distribution, we have considered the possibility of either an improvement *or* a deterioration in the quality of the worker's output. So all we have shown is that there is a difference since the worker went on the course. We'll be returning to this point in the next section.

As always, setting up the procedure for carrying out a hypothesis test has made it appear much more lengthy than it really is. The process can be summarised as follows:

(a) Formulate a null hypothesis, which will give you the value of P.
(b) Calculate STEP, and hence the appropriate interval (2 STEP on either side of P if you're using a 5 per cent significance level).
(c) Compare the sample percentage with this interval to see whether it's inside or outside.
(d) If the sample value falls *outside* the interval, reject the null hypothesis – the sample differs significantly from the population percentage (at the 5 per cent level if you've used the 95 per cent interval).

    If the sample value lies *inside* the interval, do *not* reject the null hypothesis – the difference is not significant at the 5 per cent level.

If you find it difficult to remember which way the decision rule works, remember that the bigger the difference between the sample and the population percentages, the less likely the population percentage is to be applicable; when the difference gets so big that the sample actually falls outside the 95 per cent interval, then we are forced to conclude that the population percentage *can't* be applicable, so the null hypothesis must be rejected. If, on the other hand, the sample is one of the 'majority' – the 95 per cent of samples which fall within the limits – then there are no grounds for doubting the null hypothesis.

(It has probably struck you that embedded in this process for testing hypotheses is the construction of what looks very much like a 95 per cent confidence interval. It is *not*, however, a confidence interval – we are not trying to estimate anything – and so the word 'confidence' is strictly barred from our discussion. We are *not*, for instance, 'rejecting or accepting a null hypothesis with 95 per cent confidence', but at a certain *significance* level. To avoid the possibility of confusion, the interval in a hypothesis test is sometimes called the 'acceptance region', and the part outside the interval the 'rejection region', since we reject the null hypothesis for a sample in this region.)

## FURTHER POINTS ABOUT HYPOTHESIS TESTING

This section contains some rather more theoretical considerations. Don't skip over it, but don't, either, worry too much if you don't grasp all the details; they will probably fall into place later.

Just as there was nothing special about the 95 per cent confidence level, merely conventional popularity, so there is nothing sacred about the corresponding 5 per cent significance level. By using a 99 per cent interval when carrying out the test (which, you will recall, requires an interval of 2.58 STEP either side of the population percentage), we could obtain conclusions at the 1 per cent level of significance instead. Of course, the 99 per cent interval is wider than the 95 per cent one, so we would be less likely to conclude that a result is significant. In that sense, it is 'harder' to prove something significant at the 1 per cent than at the 5 per cent level – the lower the significance level, the less likely we are to conclude that something is significant when it isn't.

Perhaps the best way to understand what these significance levels mean is to think about the times when we'll make a *wrong* decision in a hypothesis test. There are two ways we might do this: we might conclude that there *is* a significant difference when there isn't one, or we might decide that there is *no* significant difference when in fact one does exist. The first of these possibilities is by far the easier to consider – we conclude that something is significant at say, the 5 per cent level if our sample falls outside the 95 per cent interval. But 5 per cent of the perfectly respectable samples from the null hypothesis population will be outside this interval anyway; how do we know that the sample we've got doesn't just happen to be one of those 5 per cent? The answer is, or course, that we *don't* know that, so the chance of making a mistake of this kind is precisely 5 per cent: in 5 per cent of the cases when the null hypothesis is true, we will reject it. A mistake of this kind is known technically as a Type 1 error, so the significance level with which we make our decision is just the chance of making this kind of error – concluding that something is significant when it isn't.

The second kind of mistake is much more difficult to think about. The chance that we'll fail to spot a real difference between the null hypothesis and the true situation depends on a lot of factors. For example, it's clear that a big difference is much easier to spot than a small difference, so that the chance of making this kind of error – called Type 2 – will depend on how close the true population is to the null hypothesis population. But of course, we don't *know* about the true situation; if we did we wouldn't be doing the test in the first place!

That's only one of the problems in considering the second sort of error – an error which we risk making, remember, every time we fail to reject a null hypothesis. It's partly because of the difficulty in assessing the chance of being wrong in this situation that we are only prepared to make the very cautious statement 'No grounds for rejecting null hypothesis'.

When we conclude, on the basis of a test of the kind we did in the section on testing hypotheses about percentages, that there *is* a significant difference between the sample and the null hypothesis population, we can't, as indicated already, draw any *statistical* conclusions as to which direction the difference is in, since we have apportioned the 'leftover' 5 per cent of the sampling distribution equally between the two tails. So it would be wrong, in the second case above, to say that 'There has been a significant improvement at the 5 per cent level'; although common sense suggests that an improvement is more likely than a deterioration under the circumstances, all we've actually shown is that there is a difference, one way or the other, which is significant at the 5 per cent level.

It *is* possible to test for a difference in a predetermined direction, by using an unsymmetrical confidence interval. For example, in the case we've just been considering we could refuse to contemplate the possibility that the course has caused a decline in the quality of the workers' efforts, and look only for differences in the direction of an improvement. In practice that would mean putting all the 'leftover' 5 per cent of the sampling distribution under the left-hand tail of the distribution, where the percentages are lower than average, and forgetting all about the higher-than-average end. This is what is meant by 'one-tailed test', which you will encounter if you read other textbooks. However, as you can imagine, the grounds for looking for changes in one direction only have to be pretty strong before this kind of test can be justified, and so we will concentrate on the two-tailed type.

It may also have struck you that it must be possible, by juggling about with the significance level of your test, to prove that almost *anything* is significant. However, this is 'not the done thing' – or at least, it *is* done but it's not desirable! You should decide before you start doing a test what level of significance you are looking for and stick with it.

## TESTING HYPOTHESES ABOUT MEANS OF LARGE SAMPLES

Having established the routine for hypothesis testing on percentages, we can apply it also to tests on means of samples, just as we were able to adapt the inference procedures of Chapter 10 quite easily to this situation. So, we have really got two types of test for the price of one.

As an example, take Mrs Field's second requirement: she wants to test whether the time taken by the workers to produce items has been reduced since they went on the course. As with the percentage of rejects, there should be plenty of pre-course data to give us a population figure for the mean time taken, and the standard deviation of the times (presumably each worker doesn't always take exactly the same time). But for the post-course information, she'll have to rely on a sample only.

Worker X took a mean of 2.5 minutes to produce one item before the course, and the standard deviation of his times was 0.5 minutes. After the course, he is timed over the production of 64 items, which take him 2 hours 45 minutes to make; that's a mean of 2.58 minutes – actually slower than before. But again, this may not be indicative of any change; it may simply be the result of sampling variations, which if we took another sample of 64 items might produce a value *better* than 2.58 minutes.

In order to decide whether this is the explanation, we begin with the null hypothesis that there has been no change in the mean time taken by the worker for the job. So we're assuming that the population mean is 2.5 minutes just as it always was. The distribution of means of samples of 64 items taken from this population would then, as we saw in Chapter 10, be normal, with a mean of 2.5 minutes and a standard deviation of STEM, where

$$\text{STEM} = \frac{\text{population standard deviation}}{\sqrt{n}}$$

$$= \frac{0.5}{\sqrt{64}} = 0.0625 \text{ minutes.}$$

Ninety-five per cent of all the samples of 64 items taken out of this population at random would then fall in the range $2.5 \pm 2 \times 0.0625$ minutes, that is, between 2.375 and 2.625 minutes. The worker's mean after the course – 2.58 minutes – falls within this range; thus such a value could well arise even if there's been no change in his overall rate of working. We therefore have no grounds for rejecting the null hypothesis – there is no change significant at the 5 per cent level.

# AN ALTERNATIVE WAY OF CARRYING OUT HYPOTHESIS TESTS

In our tests with both STEM and STEP, we have chosen to calculate an acceptance region and see whether or not our sample value (mean or percentage) falls within this region. There is another, completely equivalent way of carrying out the test which is widely used; I mention it here because you may well come across it in other books.

Suppose to make things definite that we are going to repeat the test at pp. 191–4, where we wanted to know whether a sample of 400 items with 14 rejects produced by a worker after a training course enabled us to conclude that there had been a change from his previous rate of 4 per cent defectives. In this case our null hypothesis was that overall there had been no change, so the population percentage of defectives P was still 4 per cent. Then with $n = 400$, STEP turned out to be 0.98 per cent.

When we dealt with this problem earlier, we then worked out the interval $4 \pm 2 \times 0.98\%$, and found that 3.5 per cent lay inside this interval, furnishing no grounds for rejecting the null hypothesis. However, we can instead calculate a $z$-value based on our sample, exactly as we would if we were going to work out the probability of such a sample occurring using the normal tables. We would get

$$z = \frac{\text{our value} - \text{mean}}{\text{standard deviation}}$$

$$= \frac{\text{sample percentage} - \text{population percentage}}{\text{STEP}}$$

$$= (3.5 - 4)/0.98 = 0.51.$$

We then compare this with the $z$-value which would be needed to ensure that our sample falls in the 5 per cent 'tails' of the distribution; by now you will be very familiar with the fact that this critical $z$, as it is often called, is 1.96 or roughly 2. As our $z$ is much less than this, we can conclude that the probability of getting by random chance a sample which differs from the mean of 4 per cent as much as ours does, or even more, is quite high – certainly greater than the 5 per cent significance we are looking for. So, as before, the conclusion is that our sample is quite consistent with the null hypothesis, which should therefore not be rejected.

Had we been using a 1 per cent level of significance, the critical $z$-value would be 2.58. The process for doing the test in this way can be summed up as follows:

1 State null hypothesis.
2 Decide on significance level to be used and find corresponding critical value of $z$.
3 Calculate sample $z$ as (sample value – population value)/standard error (STEM or STEP as appropriate).
4 Compare sample $z$ with the critical $z$. If it is smaller, do not reject the null hypothesis; if greater, the sample provides grounds for rejecting the null hypothesis.

Because of the use of the letter $z$ to represent the standard normal variable, this type of hypothesis test has come to be known as a $z$-test. There is an increasing move among statisticians to encourage people to go further, and actually calculate the probability of getting a result such as their sample gives from the null hypothesis population. This probability is referred to as a $p$-value, and the point about insisting that it should be calculated is that this prevents the user of the test from blindly using a conventional figure such as 5 per cent or 1 per cent without thinking about the meaning of his results. You will therefore sometimes see statements like 'the result was significant ($p < 0.01$)', which is really just an alternative way of saying 'significant at the 1 per cent level'. And if you carry out hypothesis tests using a statistical computer package, you will find that the relevant $p$-value is given automatically (*see* the section, 'Hypothesis testing with MINITAB and LOTUS', p. 211).

## TESTING HYPOTHESES ABOUT THE MEANS OF SMALL SAMPLES

### The theory

As we noted when first encountering the sampling distribution of the mean in Chapter 10, this distribution will be normal only if the samples are large – 30 was mentioned as the conventional threshold size. But of course, people need to test hypotheses based on much smaller samples, because in many situations they only have a small amount of data to go on.

For instance, suppose that Mrs Field, the training manager of the company introduced in the first part of this chapter, wishes to determine whether the time needed to train workers who are recruited to a particular job is different for women. The mean training time required for a large number of men trained in the past was 10 days, but the only information she has about women recruits is based on a group of just 8 women trained in the last 6 months. They took an average of 9 days to train, so it looks at first sight as if they were quicker.

What we must remember, however, is that the variation might have been caused merely by sampling variations. After all, 8 is a very small sample indeed. So we need to know what the sampling distribution for the means of small samples looks like, before we can properly assess the implications of Mrs Field's data.

You may have noticed that we do not yet have the complete picture: there has been no mention of the standard deviation of the training times, or of what type of distribution the times might be expected to follow. This is absolutely crucial information. You will recall that, on p. 184, we met the Central Limit Theorem which assured us that whatever the form of the underlying distribution the means of *large* samples will be normally distributed. But this does *not* apply for *small* samples. We can only carry out tests of the kind we are studying here for small samples *if the underlying distribution is known to be normal*. (If it is not, there are other methods outside the scope of this book which can be resorted to.)

Even if we are sure that the underlying population *is* normal (and we will assume that that is the case here) there is still another complication. If we know the standard deviation of the underlying distribution, then the sampling distribution of the means is still normal, and everything proceeds as in the section earlier in the chapter on testing hypotheses about means, with STEM calculated in the usual way. But if we only know the standard deviation of the sample, and have to use that to approximate the population standard deviation, then more uncertainty creeps in. In this case the normal distribution of sample means will not apply, and instead we have to use a different distribution, called Student's $t$-distribution.

This curiously-named distribution (named after its inventor, an employee of Guinness breweries by the name of Gosset who used 'Student' as a pseudonym when writing statistical papers) looks very much like a normal distribution, in that it is symmetric and bell-shaped. However, it is in a way a mistake to talk about 'it' when referring to the *t*-distribution — we should really say 'them', because there is actually a whole family of *t*-distributions, their precise shape varying with the sample size we are using.

Some of these are sketched in Fig. 11.2 below. You can see that as *n* gets bigger, the *t*-distribution looks more and more like the normal curve, until by the time *n* = 30 or so, the two are pretty indistinguishable. That is why, for samples of size bigger than this, we can use the normal quite safely. For smaller samples, the distribution is wider than the normal, so that a 95 per cent confidence interval based on it would be correspondingly wider also; this reflects the greater degree of uncertainty in having to approximate the population standard deviation by that of the sample.

## The process

To get a clearer idea precisely how the *t*-distribution is used, let's go back to Mrs Field's problem where the mean training time for the population is 10 days, the sample mean for 8 women is 9 days, and let us further assume that we only know the sample standard deviation which is 2 days. First of all, we need to recall what was said in Chapter 6 about approximating a population standard deviation (s.d.) by a sample — really we get a better idea of the population figure if we divide the sum of the squared deviations in the s.d. calculation by $n - 1$ instead of $n$, before taking the square root. This did not matter with large samples, but here it does make a difference. So we'll assume that the $n - 1$ divisor was used in arriving at the sample s.d. of 2.

We can now say that STEM = $2/\sqrt{8} = 0.71$, and formulate our null hypothesis: there is no difference in overall mean training time between men and women. Instead of calculating a *z*-value, however, as we did at p. 197, we calculate a *t*-value in exactly the same way:

$$t = \frac{\text{sample mean} - \text{population mean}}{\text{STEM}} = \frac{9 - 10}{0.71} = -1.41.$$

The final stage of the process should be to compare this with a 'critical value' of *t*, to find whether or not it is significant. The critical values of *t*, like those of *z*, have to come from a table.

You will find the table of the *t*-distribution in Appendix 9. As you can see, it differs from the normal tables; because we need a lot of different values for different sample sizes, we cannot have each distribution tabulated in such detail otherwise the tables would

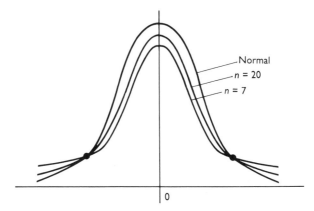

**Fig. 11.2** Student's *t*-distribution

be very bulky. Instead, we just have the $t$-values for a selection of the usual significance levels (across the table) and a variety of sample sizes (down the table).

Just to make life even more interesting, for reasons you do not need to go into, the rows of the table are labelled not according to sample size $n$ but according to $n - 1$, called the *degrees of freedom* of the distribution and often denoted by the Greek letter $\nu$ (pronounced 'new'). Note also that the significance levels at the tops of the columns refer to the area under one tail of the distribution, so to do our usual type of 2-tailed test we need to multiply them by 2.

Our sample with $n = 8$ means therefore that we should look in the row where $\nu = 8 - 1 = 7$. If we want a significance level of 5 per cent or 0.05, then as explained above we look in the 0.025 column and find that the critical $t$ is 2.365. What we calculated above was $t = 1.41$, which is smaller than this, so our decision would be *not* to reject the null hypothesis.

There are a few other things to notice while you are looking at the tables of the $t$-distribution. First, the $t$-value for a given significance level is always greater than the $z$-value would be, regardless of the value of $\nu$ – the $z$-value for 5 per cent significance, for example, would be the familiar 1.96 or roughly 2 – which confirms what was said earlier about the $t$-distribution being wider. Second, you can see the $t$-values getting closer to the normal or $z$-values as $\nu$ gets bigger. The tables indicate this by saying that the normal values apply to a $t$-distribution with 'infinite degrees of freedom' (bottom row of the table). Hence we can use the normal instead of $t$ with reasonable accuracy as long as the sample is not too small.

By now you have had to absorb quite a lot of information about testing hypotheses on sample means, so we will pause for a summary of the situation.

1 If the underlying population is normal and we know its standard deviation, then the distribution of sample means is normal with standard deviation = STEM = population s.d.$/\sqrt{n}$, whatever the value of $n$, and we can use a $z$-test.

2 If the underlying population is unknown but the sample size is large, the distribution of the sample means is approximately normal with standard deviation = STEM = population (or sample) s.d.$/\sqrt{n}$, and again a $z$-test can be used.

3 If the underlying population is normal, but we do not know its standard deviation, and we have data about a small sample, then we can use the sample s.d. to approximate that of the population (remembering to use the $n - 1$ divisor in the calculation of the s.d.). The distribution of sample means is then a $t$-distribution with $n - 1$ degrees of freedom, and standard deviation STEM = sample s.d.$/n - 1$. So a $t$-test can be used.

4 If the underlying population is not normal and we only have a small sample, none of the hypothesis testing procedures we have discussed can be safely used.

Of course, the use of the $t$-distribution is not confined to hypothesis testing; you can use it also to get confidence intervals. The process is no different to that using the normal distribution, except that $t$-values rather than $z$-values are used in the construction of the interval.

## TESTING THE DIFFERENCE BETWEEN TWO SAMPLE MEANS

You may have felt a certain sinking of the heart when reading the title of this section – not another hypothesis testing procedure! But one of the better things about hypothesis testing is that once you have the basic routine clear in your mind, many different types of test can be carried out with relatively few new ideas to grasp.

Suppose, for example, that we need not to test the mean of a single sample against a hypothesised population value, but to test whether there is a significant difference between two sample means. To be definite, let's imagine that the overworked Mrs Field has data on the wages of two groups of workers, both taken from large populations: a group of 30 taken from Production had a mean weekly wage of £120 after deductions, with a standard deviation of £10, while 50 workers from Maintenance had a mean of £130 with standard deviation £12. Does this evidence suggest that there is a difference in wages between workers in these two areas?

If we proceed in the usual way, the first step is to formulate the null hypothesis: here it will be 'There is no difference between the wages of workers in Production and Maintenance'. In other words, the two samples are effectively taken from the *same* population.

Secondly, we need to calculate the appropriate standard error, and it is here that the only real difference arises. The standard error we want here is that of the *difference* of two sample means, and it is calculated as

$$s\sqrt{\frac{1}{n_1} + \frac{1}{n_2}},$$

where $s$ is the standard deviation of the common population from which the samples are taken, and $n_1$ and $n_2$ are their respective sizes.

So here $n_1 = 30$, $n_2 = 50$ (it doesn't matter which way round we number the samples). However, there is a bit of a problem when it comes to the population standard deviation – namely, we do not know what it is. Instead, we have to estimate it by combining the information from the two samples (rather in the manner of a weighted average) according to the formula

$$s = \sqrt{\frac{n_1 s_1^2 + n_2 s_2^2}{n_1 + n_2}}.$$

$s_1$ and $s_2$ here are the sample standard deviations, and so we find $s = (30 \times 100 + 50 \times 144)/(30 + 50) = 11.29$. You can see that this estimate is nearer to the standard deviation of the larger sample than that of the smaller, just as we expect with a weighted average.

We can now proceed to calculate the standard error:
Standard Error of Difference in Sample Means (unpronounceably shortened to STEDM)

$$= 11.29\sqrt{\frac{1}{30} + \frac{1}{50}} = 2.60.$$

Thirdly, we need to know the relevant sampling distribution. For the difference of two large samples, just as with a single large sample, the distribution is normal. Its standard deviation is STEDM as calculated above, and of course its mean is zero, because if the null hypothesis is true there is *no* difference between the populations from which the samples come.

$$\text{All this enables us to calculate } z = \frac{\text{difference in sample means} - 0}{\text{STEDM}}$$

$$= \frac{120 - 130}{2.60} = -3.85.$$

This is well outside the critical $z$ for 5 per cent significance, which would be $-1.96$, so we have grounds for rejecting the null hypothesis, and concluding that there is a difference in wages between the two populations of workers.

Had we had small samples from normal populations instead, then as with a single sample we would have to replace the $z$-test by a $t$-test, this time with $n_1 + n_2 - 2$ degrees of freedom (the sum of the degrees of freedom for each sample separately). In this case too, we need to put in the correction factors for using sample standard deviations to estimate a population s.d., and remember to divide by $n - 1$ rather than $n$. The formula for pooling the s.d.s then becomes

$$s = \sqrt{\frac{(n_1 - 1)s_1^2 + (n_2 - 1)s_2^2}{n_1 + n_2 - 2}}$$

The STEDM formula remains unaltered and the process for completing the test is exactly as before with $z$ replaced by $t$.

By now you should be able to see that, whatever the context of your hypothesis test, the procedure can be summarised as:

1 State null hypothesis and decide significance level to be used.
2 Identify information given (number of samples, large or small, mean or proportion, etc.) and decide what standard error and what distribution are required.
3 Calculate required standard error.
4 Calculate $z$ or $t$ as difference between sample and population values divided by standard error.
5 Compare your $z$ or $t$ with the critical value from tables for the significance level you are using; if your $z$ or $t$ is greater than the critical value, reject the null hypothesis.

We will see in the next section, concerned with testing hypotheses about more than one proportion, how this procedure actually extends to further cases where neither $z$ nor $t$-tests apply, but the basic routine is still the same. Before going on to that, however, it would be a good idea to work through some of the Practical Exercises at the end of the chapter to make sure you have your ideas straight so far!

## TESTING HYPOTHESES ABOUT MORE THAN ONE PROPORTION

Mrs Field's third problem, about the relative effects of the course on different groups of workers, could be expressed in terms of the difference between the proportions of various groups who have, or haven't, improved. If she has collected some data broken down according to age, for example, she might be faced with something like the table below:

| Age group | Improved | Did not improve |
|-----------|----------|-----------------|
| Under 35  | 17       | 4               |
| 35–50     | 17       | 7               |
| Over 50   | 6        | 9               |

What she needs to test here is whether the proportion (or percentage) improving is consistent across all the age groups, or varies significantly from one to another. But the sort of test carried out at pp. 191–4 is no use to her here, since it dealt with just *one* sample percentage at a time. Even the tests of the last section for the difference of two samples are no good, since we have more than two. What we must develop is a method of testing the various categories simultaneously.

We begin, as always, by formulating a null hypothesis. In this case, the 'no difference' hypothesis takes the form of the assumption that the figures given are consistent with an improvement rate which is the same for all age groups; the variations which occur in practice between one age group and another are merely chance sampling fluctuations and not indicative of any real difference. This hypothesis can be expressed very succinctly by saying that there is *no association* between age group and improvement.

If this hypothesis were true, then we would expect the same rate of improvement to be found in all three age groups. Our best guide to what that overall rate may be is given by the combined rate for all groups together, and so we start by finding the totals for the various categories, as shown in the table below:

| Age group | Improved | Did not improve | |
|---|---|---|---|
| Under 35 | 17 (14) | 4 (7) | 21 |
| 35–50 | 17 (16) | 7 (8) | 24 |
| Over 50 | 6 (10) | 9 (5) | 15 |
| | 40 | 20 | 60 |

Thus overall, 40 out of 60 people improved – that's 2/3. Now, *if* the null hypothesis is true, then this rate applies equally to all three age groups. So we would have expected 2/3 of each age group to improve. We can therefore insert the *expected* numbers of people in each category into the table; these are the bracketed figures in the table above. They are easily calculated from the 2/3 improvement rate. For example, there were 21 people in the 'Under 35' age group; 2/3 of these would be expected to improve – that's 14. Similarly, in the '35–50' group, 2/3 of 24 people would be expected to show an improvement, whence we get the figure of 16.

These two 'expected' figures are the only ones which need to be calculated explicitly in this way. Once they are written into the table, the other 'expected' numbers can all be found using the known totals in each group. For instance, if the number of under-35s expected to improve was 14, and there were 21 altogether, then naturally 7 must be expected not to improve. We'll be returning to this question of how many 'expected' figures must actually be calculated later on.

It's now clear that *more* of the two younger age groups have improved than the null hypothesis would suggest, while for the 50+ group the figure is lower than expected. But are these differences significant? What we need is some way of measuring the disagreement between what actually happened (the 'observed' figures as they're usually called) and what the null hypothesis leads us to expect should happen. If we write O to denote the observed numbers and E for the expected numbers, then the obvious way to measure how much disagreement there is between them is to look at O − E for each category in the table. It's more convenient for this purpose to rewrite the data in columns – making sure we keep the pairs of Os and Es together correctly:

| O | E | O − E |
|---|---|---|
| 17 | 14 | 3 |
| 17 | 16 | 1 |
| 6 | 10 | −4 |
| 4 | 7 | −3 |
| 7 | 8 | −1 |
| 9 | 5 | 4 |

(Some of the (O − E)s are negative since E is bigger than O.)

Now, if we want a measure of the *overall* amount of disagreement for the entire table, between O and E, the sensible thing would seem to be to add up the O − E column. But unfortunately, if you try this you'll find the column totals to zero. This is no freak of the figures just for this set of data – the same thing will occur with *any* set of Os and Es worked out according to a null hypothesis. So this so-called 'measure of total disagreement' isn't much use.

Haven't we seen something like this before, though? In Chapter 6, when we were developing the method for calculating standard deviation, our first effort at a measurement of the spread of the points in a distribution around the mean broke down for exactly the same reason – the cancellation of positive and negative differences. The trick which solved the problem there was, you'll recall, to *square* the troublesome differences, thereby getting rid of the awkward minus signs without altering the relationship between the distances. Perhaps something similar is worth trying in this case.

Accordingly, we add a column for $(O − E)^2$ to our table:

| O | E | (O − E) | (O − E)² |
|---|---|---|---|
| 17 | 14 | 3 | 9 |
| 17 | 16 | 1 | 1 |
| 6 | 10 | − 4 | 16 |
| 4 | 7 | − 3 | 9 |
| 7 | 8 | − 1 | 1 |
| 9 | 8 | 4 | 16 |

The sum of the $(O − E)^2$ column should then give us a measure of the total amount of disagreement between O and E.

But is it really this *absolute* disagreement which is of interest? Suppose we had two sets of Os and Es, and worked out the corresponding values of $(O − E)^2$, as shown below:

| O | E | (O − E)² | O | E | (O − E)² |
|---|---|---|---|---|---|
| 1 | 2 | 1 | 101 | 102 | 1 |
| 2 | 2 | 0 | 102 | 102 | 0 |
| 3 | 2 | 1 | 103 | 102 | 1 |

The total of the $(O − E)^2$ column is the same in each case, but you will probably agree that the discrepancy between the Os and the Es is not nearly as serious in the second case. This, of course, is because it's not so much the actual *size* of the disagreement which matters, as the size of that disagreement *relative* to the figure which was expected. A disagreement of 1 on an expected figure of 2 represents a 50 per cent error, whereas the same disagreement on an expected figure of 102 is an error of only 0.98 per cent.

What we need, therefore, is a further column in our calculation giving the value of $(O − E)^2/E$ – the size of the squared disagreement relative to the corresponding expected figure:

| O | E | (O − E) | (O − E)² | (O − E)²/E |
|---|---|---|---|---|
| 17 | 14 | 3 | 9 | 9/14 = 0.643 |
| 17 | 16 | 1 | 1 | 1/16 = 0.0625 |
| 6 | 10 | − 4 | 16 | 16/10 = 1.6 |
| 4 | 7 | − 3 | 9 | 9/7 = 1.286 |
| 7 | 8 | − 1 | 1 | 1/8 = 0.125 |
| 9 | 5 | 4 | 16 | 16/5 = 3.2 |
| | | | | 6.92 |

The final measurement of the overall disagreement in the table between the Os and the Es is given by the sum of the last column (which can be calculated as the individual divisions are performed by using the memory on your calculator). Incidentally, it wasn't strictly necessary to bother putting in the minus signs in the third column, since they'll disappear when the quantities are squared; however, the fact that this column should add up to zero provides a useful check on the accuracy with which you have calculated the Es and the differences.

The measurement of disagreement which we have now constructed is known as chi-squared (pronounced 'ki-squared' and denoted by the Greek letter $\chi^2$). We can define it, according to the way we have worked it out, as:

$$\chi^2 = \sum \frac{(O-E)^2}{E}$$

where the $\Sigma$ sign indicates that we are to add up the values over all the categories in the table. By the way, $\chi$ on its own, without the square, means nothing and isn't used.

However, although we now have a way of measuring how well – or how badly – the Os and Es agree, we aren't yet in a position to say anything about the null hypothesis. We need some standard of comparison from which to judge whether a value of $\chi^2$ such as we have obtained is 'large' – i.e. indicating a lot of disagreement and therefore casting doubt on the null hypothesis – or 'small' – suggesting that the discrepancies noticed between O and E are merely the result of minor sampling variations. We want, in other words, to know what sampling distribution $\chi^2$ should follow.

## USING THE $\chi^2$ DISTRIBUTION

The distribution, not surprisingly, is known as the $\chi^2$ distribution. Like the normal distribution, it is continuous, though unlike the normal it isn't symmetric. We will look at its precise shape in a minute; first, turn to Appendix 7 where you will find this distribution tabulated.

The tables are arranged in a different manner from the ones for the normal distribution you are used to using and are similar to those for the $t$-distribution. They are, as it were, the 'opposite' of the normal tables in that, whereas with the normal tables the figures in the body of the table gave the probability associated with the $z$-value at the head of the column, in the chi-squared tables the probabilities are given at the heads of the columns and the corresponding values of chi-squared in the body of the table. The sketch at the top of the tables indicates just what is being tabulated: the table shows the value of $\chi^2$ which cuts off an area $\alpha$ under the right-hand tail of the distribution.

However, that isn't all we need to know to look up the tables; if you glance at the right-hand edge of the tables you will find the letter $\nu$ again. It tells you how the values of $\chi^2$ relate to the amount of data that we begin with. Our argument so far has gone something like this: $\chi^2$ measures the disagreement between O and E, so if $\chi^2$ is big, there's a lot of disagreement and the null hypothesis, from which the Es were calculated, must be wrong. But, of course, $\chi^2$ might also be big simply because we're adding up a lot of figures – because we had a big table to begin with. So the definition of what we mean by a 'big' value of $\chi^2$ must be related in some way to the size of the table.

The table we began with, before we added on the row and column totals, had six categories altogether – three for age and two for improvement/no improvement. But when we calculated the expected frequencies we found we couldn't just play around with these categories at will – once two of the Es were calculated, the rest were automatically fixed because of the totals in each class. We say that only two of the categories are *free*, or that the number of *degrees of freedom*, $\nu$, is two in this case. (You may recall this term from our work on $t$-tests in the section, 'Testing hypotheses about the means of small samples', p. 198).

You may feel that this is a rather hit-and-miss way of calculating the number of degrees of freedom. After all, if you picked the wrong categories you might find you had to calculate three of the expected figures before you could insert the rest, so you might wrongly conclude that $\nu = 3$. Fortunately, there is a more systematic way of working out $\nu$; if the original table had $r$ rows and $c$ columns, then once all expected values except those in the last row and the last column have been calculated, these could be filled in automatically. As shown in Fig. 11.3 then, only the categories in the top left-hand part of the table are 'free' in the sense described above, and so there are $(r-1) \times (c-1)$ degrees of freedom. In words, $\nu$ = number of rows minus 1 multiplied by number of columns minus 1. (Alternatively, you may like to obtain the number of degrees of freedom by crossing out one row and one column in the table, and then counting the remaining figures.)

Whichever way we look at it, then, $\nu$ is 2 in the present case, and so we should be consulting the second row of the table. Remembering that the $\alpha$ value tells us what area is left over in the tail of the $\chi^2$ distribution, we find that a $\chi^2$ of 5.991 will leave an area of only 5 per cent or 0.05 in the tail.

This fact can be interpreted as follows: if the null hypothesis were correct, and the variations between the O and E figures were merely due to chance, then we could expect 95 per cent of samples to yield a $\chi^2$ which is less than 5.991 and only the odd 5 per cent of samples to fall above that value. A sample yielding a $\chi^2$ less than 5.991, is therefore not unusual, and furnishes no evidence for disbelieving the null hypothesis. If, on the other hand, our sample produces a $\chi^2$ greater than 5.991, it is unlikely to have come from a population for which the null hypothesis holds good.

Because the $\chi^2$ value obtained from the tables (5.991 in this case) is the one which decides whether we are going to reject the null hypothesis or not, it is often referred to as the *critical* value of $\chi^2$, and denoted by $\chi_c^2$. We can interpret the meaning of all this in a way exactly analogous to our decision rule for other hypothesis tests, if we understand the interval from $\chi^2 = 0$ to $\chi^2 = 5.991$ as simply a 95 per cent interval – a one-sided interval, since we are not interested in the left-hand tail where $\chi^2$ is small, showing that the agreement between O and E is good. With this understanding, the rule becomes, as before: a sample value of $\chi^2$ *inside* the interval does not cause us to reject the null hypothesis – the differences between O and E are small enough to be accounted for by

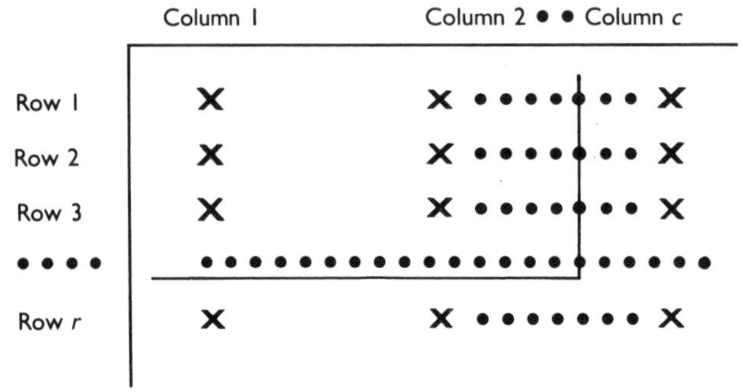

**Fig. 11.3** Finding the number of degrees of freedom

chance variations. If, however, the sample value of $\chi^2$ falls *outside* the interval, then the differences between O and E, as measured by $\chi^2$, are so large that the null hypothesis must be rejected. If we have used, in constructing the confidence interval, the $\alpha$ corresponding to a 'tail' area of 5 per cent, then of course these decisions will be made 'at the 5 per cent significance level'.

What then, after all this theory, is the implication of the value of $\chi^2$ we've obtained? Our sample $\chi^2$ there turned out to be 6.92, whereas the value of $\chi^2$ obtained from the tables was 5.99. So our sample falls outside the 95 per cent interval and we conclude that the null hypothesis should be rejected. There is an association between the age of workers and the improvement rate which is significant at the 5 per cent level.

Once again, this apparently lengthy process can be summed up in a few simple steps, now the method has been established.

(a) Formulate the null hypothesis (which, in this case, will always be of the 'no association' form).
(b) On the basis of this hypothesis, calculate the expected frequencies.
(c) Hence calculate $\chi^2$.
(d) Work out the number of degrees of freedom, $\nu$, as (rows minus one) $\times$ (columns minus one), and look up the critical $\chi_c^2$ in the tables under the selected significance level.
(e) Compare the value of $\chi^2$ calculated from your sample with $\chi_c^2$. If the sample $\chi^2$ is smaller (*inside* the interval) *don't* reject the null hypothesis, if it's bigger (*outside*) the null hypothesis can be rejected.

## MORE ABOUT $\chi^2$

To demonstrate how easy the process is to apply, we'll examine a second lot of data produced by Mrs Field. She suspects that whether workers show an improvement as a result of retraining may be connected with the length of time for which they have been doing the job. Accordingly she draws up the table below:

| Length of time on this job (months) | Improved | | Did not improve | | |
|---|---|---|---|---|---|
| 6 and under 12 | 6 | (8) | 6 | (4) | 12 |
| 12 and under 18 | 9 | (10) | 6 | (5) | 15 |
| 18 and under 24 | 13 | (12) | 5 | (6) | 18 |
| 24 and over | 12 | (10) | 3 | (5) | 15 |
| | 40 | | 20 | | 60 |

We've put the marginal totals in already, and as before the overall improvement rate is 2/3. The null hypothesis here will be: there is no association between improvement rate and length of time on the job. That being so, we would expect the 2/3 improvement rate to apply equally to all four groups, for example, we would expect 2/3 of the 12 people who have done the job for 6–12 months to improve, which gives E = 8 for the top left-hand category. You should verify for yourself the remaining E values; they are all shown in brackets in the table above.

As you can see, some of these Es are rather small. You should be accustomed by now to the idea that very small amounts of data can't be relied on to give a fair picture of a situation, so perhaps you won't be surprised to learn that we should really have Es which are all at least 5 before we can safely use $\chi^2$. However, that doesn't mean we have to give up in the present case. We can easily get round the difficulty by combining the two groups '6–12' and '12–18' into one group '6–18'. The new, contracted table is then as shown:

| Time on job (months) | Improved | Did not improve | |
|---|---|---|---|
| 6 and under 18 | 15 (18) | 12 (9) | 27 |
| 18 and under 24 | 13 (12) | 5 (6) | 18 |
| 24 and over | 12 (10) | 3 (5) | 15 |
| | 40 | 20 | 60 |

We can now go ahead and calculate $\chi^2$ as before. You should check that the value obtained is 2.95. The number of degrees of freedom (*after* we have done the necessary combining of classes) is $(3-1) \times (2-1) = 2$, so if we stick to the usual 5 per cent significance level, then $\chi_c^2$ is 5.991 as before. This time our $\chi^2$ is within the interval, being less then $\chi_c^2$, and so there is no reason to reject the null hypothesis; there is no evidence of an association between time on the job and improvement rate significant at the 5 per cent level.

Finally, let's test whether there is any evidence that men and women respond differently to the retraining, using the following data:

| | Improved | Did not improve | |
|---|---|---|---|
| Male | 21 (24) | 15 (12) | 36 |
| Female | 19 (16) | 5 (8) | 24 |
| | 40 | 20 | 60 |

The null hypothesis here will be: no association between sex of worker and improvement rate. Although in the previous two cases we worked out the Es using the fact that the overall improvement rate is 2/3, there's no reason why we shouldn't use instead the fact that here 36/60, or 60 per cent, of the workers are male, so we would expect 60 per cent of the improved workers – that's 60 per cent of 40 or 24 – to be males. In general, there is no rule as to whether one should use the column or the row totals to calculate the expected figures – pick whichever makes the calculation easier.

What we have here is a 2-by-2 table – two categories in each direction – which is, of course, the smallest table which can occur. With a table which *is* so small, a point becomes important which, for larger tables, we could afford to slide over. The $\chi^2$ distribution is, as we've already mentioned, a continuous distribution – but all the problems we've solved with its aid are discrete problems, involving as they do *counting* the number of items in each category of the table. So there's a certain amount of approximation involved in using $\chi^2$ – an approximation which fortunately is only really serious in this 2-by-2 case. We allow for it by making use of an adjustment to the value of $\chi^2$ known as *Yates' correction*, the application of which is very easy: reduce each O – E (ignoring the sign) by $\frac{1}{2}$. If this is applied correctly, all the resulting figures should be the same, as indicated in the table overleaf.

There is $(2-1) \times (2-1) = 1$ degree of freedom here, so the critical value, $\chi_c^2$, at the 5 per cent level is 3.84. As our sample $\chi^2$ is less than this, we have no grounds for rejecting the null hypothesis – women do not appear to respond to the course any better or worse than men. You may like to check that the *uncorrected* version of $\chi^2$ would be 2.81, so actually in this case the correction doesn't make any difference to the conclusion, but it's easy to envisage cases where it might.

| O | E | O − E | Corrected | (Corrected difference)$^2$ / E |
|---|----|-------|-----------|------|
| 21 | 24 | (−)3 | 2.5 | 0.26 |
| 19 | 16 | 3 | 2.5 | 0.39 |
| 15 | 12 | 3 | 2.5 | 0.52 |
| 5 | 8 | (−)3 | 2.5 | 0.78 |
| | | | | 1.95 |

## SINGLE-ROW TABLES

It was remarked towards the end of the last section that a 2-by-2 table is the smallest which can arise, but in some ways that isn't strictly true – the table might only have a single row. For example, if a firm wished to test whether numbers of absentees varied significantly from one day of the week to another, the data might be collected in the following way:

| Day of week | Mon | Tues | Wed | Thur | Fri |
|-------------|-----|------|-----|------|-----|
| Number of absentees | 17 | 12 | 11 | 12 | 18 |

Here we have a perfectly respectable set of observed frequencies; the null hypothesis will state that the numbers *don't* vary significantly from day to day (the usual 'no difference' hypothesis) and so we can work out the expected frequencies. There were 70 people absent altogether during the week, so if the null hypothesis were true we would expect to get the same number – one-fifth of 70, or 14 – absent each day. All the Es are therefore 14, and without going through the intermediate calculation, which you can check, we find that $\chi^2$ is exactly 3.

So far, apart from a slight difference in the method of obtaining the expected frequencies, there's been no difference between the method for this single row table and the bigger tables we had in previous examples. However, when you come to find the number of degrees of freedom, the formula we've used so far gives a silly answer in this case: (rows minus one) × (columns minus one) is zero, since the number of rows is only 1 to start off with. We therefore have to go back to the *meaning* of the number of degrees of freedom – how many of the daily frequencies are 'free'? The total number of absentees during the week is known to be 70, which means we can write down any old frequencies for Monday to Thursday, but then we have to give Friday a frequency which makes the whole lot add up to 70. So only four of the frequencies are 'free' in this sense; and more generally, for a single-row table of this kind with $n$ categories, there will be $n − 1$ degrees of freedom.

The $\chi^2$ tables, with $\nu = 4$, then tell us that $\chi_c^2$ is 9.488 at the 5 per cent level, which suggests, our sample $\chi^2$ of 3 being much less than this, that the null hypothesis should not be rejected: the sample provides no evidence that the number of absentees varies significantly from day to day.

What we have been doing here, in effect, is testing how well the observed frequencies fit a *uniform distribution* – one in which the frequencies of each category are expected to be the same. In a similar sort of way, $\chi^2$ can be used to test the *goodness of fit* of a set of observed frequencies to *any* theoretical distribution; in particular, it can help to answer the question, left unresolved in Chapter 9, 'How do we know when a distribution is normal?'.

The process in detail, however, is quite complicated, involving as it does first calculating the mean and standard deviation of the observed frequencies then using the normal tables to calculate the frequencies we'd *expect* to get from a normal distribution with that mean and standard deviation – all this before we even start on the $\chi^2$ calculation! Then the question of degrees of freedom is not straightforward; altogether, in fact, it is a messy business which we will not pursue further.

## A CAUTIONARY NOTE

Obviously $\chi^2$ provides an extremely useful and versatile kind of hypothesis test which is also relatively easy to apply. If I were going to be cast away on a desert island and could only take one set of statistical tables with me, I would certainly choose to take $\chi^2$! In the contingency table context, the test is useful in analysing the results of surveys, in assessing the efficacy of new manufacturing processes, in comparing the performance of different machines, to name but three areas. The single-row table, as we've seen, can be used to assess how well a set of observed data fits a theoretical distribution. And there are other uses of the tables, too, which we haven't even touched on. For example, you may have wondered why there are so many significance levels given in the tables; we might want to use 1 per cent or even 10 per cent, but why bother giving an $\alpha$ of 0.99 which corresponds to a significance level of 99 per cent?

The point of these very high significance levels is to enable $\chi^2$ to be used to test for 'fiddling' of results. A *very small* value of $\chi^2$ – less than the 99 per cent significance level critical value for the number of degrees of freedom in question – indicates an extraordinarily good agreement between O and E – an agreement *better* than would be found in 99 per cent of cases. Such *very* good agreement might, if we had suspicious minds, cause us to wonder about the Os involved – how come they are so good? Are these really random results? The high significance level values of $\chi^2$ help us to decide.

But just because $\chi^2$ *is* such a simple quantity to calculate, we must beware of using it *too* readily, perhaps in circumstances where it isn't really applicable. We've already seen that it won't do if some of the Es are below 5; it can't be used either if there is overlapping between some of the categories so that items may be counted more than once and the totals of rows and columns are meaningless.

Nor will $\chi^2$ tell us the *direction* of an association. In the example on pp. 202–7, we decided that there was evidence of an association between age and response to the retraining, but we have to look back at the data and use common sense to discover that it's the younger people who responded better. As far as the calculated value of $\chi^2$ is concerned, we could have obtained the same value from another set of data in which the situation was completely reversed and the *older* people were doing better. All $\chi^2$ tells us is that there is some kind of connection.

## ◨ HYPOTHESIS TESTING WITH MINITAB AND LOTUS

MINITAB offers several hypothesis testing procedures which can be carried out very simply.

(a) To test a hypothesised value K1 of the mean using a $z$-test on a single large sample (stored in C1) from a population with known s.d. K2, the command is

MTB⟩ ZTEST K1 K2 C1

For example, the output shown below gives the results of applying this test to the AGE column from the dataset EMP.MTW, with a hypothesised mean of 35 years and an s.d. of 7.5 years.

MTB ⟩ ztest 35 7.5 'age'

TEST of MU = 35.000 VS MU N.E. 35.000
THE ASSUMED SIGMA = 7.50

|      | N   | MEAN    | STDEV  | SE MEAN | Z     | P VALUE |
|------|-----|---------|--------|---------|-------|---------|
| age  | 60  | 37.783  | 7.591  | 0.968   | 2.87  | 0.0041  |

(b) Alternatively, we can perform a $t$-test, in which case we do not need to specify the s.d., since it will be estimated from the sample. Using the same data as above, we obtain:

MTB ⟩ ttest 35 'age'

TEST of MU = 35.000 VS MU N.E. 35.000

|      | N   | MEAN    | STDEV  | SE MEAN | T     | P VALUE |
|------|-----|---------|--------|---------|-------|---------|
| age  | 60  | 37.783  | 7.591  | 0.968   | 2.84  | 0.0062  |

If we wish to perform a 1-tailed test, we have to use the subcommand ALTERNATIVE = −1 (for an alternative hypothesis of the 'less than' form), or ALTERNATIVE = 1 (for a 'greater than' type of alternative). The subcommand can be used with either a $z$- or a $t$-test; the example below shows the same test as before, but now testing mean = 35 against mean > 35. Notice how the $t$-value is exactly the same, but the $p$-value is halved since we are only looking at one tail.

MTB ⟩ ttest 35 'age';
SUBC⟩ alternative = 1.

TEST of MU = 35.000 VS MU G.T. 35.000

|      | N   | MEAN    | STDEV  | SE MEAN | T     | P VALUE |
|------|-----|---------|--------|---------|-------|---------|
| age  | 60  | 37.783  | 7.591  | 0.968   | 2.84  | 0.0031  |

In each case, we need to compare the $p$-value with our significance level to decide whether or not the test is significant. For instance, in the last example if we are using a 5 per cent significance level then we would want $p$ to be less than 0.05 to be significant – which the calculated value of $p = 0.0031$ certainly is.

(c) A $t$-test for comparing two samples can be carried out using the command TWOT. This requires that we have all the data for both samples in a single column, while a second column contains subscripts indicating which sample each reading belongs to. An example will make this clearer: with the EMP.MTW data, we have ages in the column named 'AGE', and in the column 'SEX' we have subscripts 1 and 0 indicating whether the age belongs to a male or a female. (There is an alternative command TWOSAMPLE for use when the samples are in separate columns.) The result of carrying out the two-sample *t*-test on this data is as shown.

MTB ⟩ twot 'age' 'sex';
SUBC⟩ pooled.

TWOSAMPLE T FOR age

| sex | N | MEAN | STDEV | SE MEAN |
|-----|-----|-------|-------|---------|
| 1 | 36 | 38.81 | 7.50 | 1.3 |
| 0 | 24 | 36.25 | 7.62 | 1.6 |

95 PCT CI FOR MU 1 – MU 0: (– 1.4, 6.5)

TTEST MU 1 = MU 0 (VS NE): T = 1.28 P = 0.20 DF = 58

POOLED STDEV =        7.55

Notice how we have to use the subcommand POOLED to ensure that the separate s.d.s are pooled as they were in our hand calculation. We could also use the ALTERNATIVE subcommand, as described above, if we wanted to do a 1-tailed test. Notice too that we get a confidence interval for the difference of the two means, as well as the actual test result, which here, with a *p*-value of 0.20, suggests that the ages of males and females are not significantly different.

(d) Finally, chi-squared can be carried out with MINITAB – but we need to set up columns containing the contingency table. So if we want to carry out the test for association between experience of workers and improvement, which we did by hand in the section 'More about $\chi^2$', p. 207, we first need to read the observed values into two columns each of three rows. This process, and the resulting output, are shown below.

MTB ⟩ read c1 c2
DATA⟩ 15 12
DATA⟩ 13 5
DATA⟩ 12 3
DATA⟩ end
        3 ROWS READ
MTB ⟩ chis c1 c2

Expected counts are printed below observed counts:

|  | C1 | C2 | Total |
|-----|-------|------|-------|
| 1 | 15 | 12 | 27 |
|  | 18.00 | 9.00 |  |
| 2 | 13 | 5 | 18 |
|  | 12.00 | 6.00 |  |
| 3 | 12 | 3 | 15 |
|  | 10.00 | 5.00 |  |
| Total | 40 | 20 | 60 |

ChiSq = 0.500 + 1.000 +
        0.083 + 0.167 +
        0.400 + 0.800 = 2.950

df = 2

The computed value of chi-squared, 2.95, agrees with what we found by hand, but you still need to look up tables to find the critical chi-squared for 2 degrees of freedom, and deduce that there is no significant association here. So MINITAB does not quite do all the work for you!

With LOTUS, there are no automated hypothesis testing procedures, but the arithmetical drudgery can be considerably reduced. Chi-squared is particularly well suited to spreadsheet computation – a table can be set up with columns for O, E, and $(O - E)^2/E$, and then the calculation is very easily performed by copying the formulae down the necessary number of rows, and using the @SUM function to add the $(O - E)^2/E$ column. You will find a spreadsheet for doing this stored as CHI.WK1 on the diskette; it can be modified to carry out the calculation for other sets of data.


## CONCLUSION

From a theoretical point of view, the last two chapters have probably been the toughest in the book, but the actual application of the hypothesis testing procedure once you're used to it, is something of a sausage-machine – turn the handle, go through the appropriate steps and out pops the conclusion. Try *not* to apply *your* hypothesis tests in this way. A great help in thinking clearly about what you are proving is to write down a proper null hypothesis at the start of every test, and to draw your conclusion in terms of the particular problem you are dealing with. Don't, in other words, just write, ' .. significant' or 'there is no association'. Write: 'this sample probably did not come from such-and-such a population', or 'Sex of worker is not associated with response to retraining'. And don't get so accustomed to using 95 per cent intervals/5 per cent significance that you forget to state what level you are using. *Think* about the level used, and if necessary use something different. After all, if you were going to fly in an aeroplane, the engine of which had been tested to see if it was substandard, I think you might not be very happy to be told it had been passed as OK with 95 per cent confidence!


### Practical exercises

(Use 5 per cent significance unless otherwise indicated.)

1  The mean wage of workers in a certain industry over the whole country is £210 per week, with a standard deviation of £7.50. A sample of 100 workers from one particular factory is found to have a mean wage of £208 per week. Are the workers in this factory different from the rest of the industry?

2  It is known that 40 per cent of retail outlets in a certain area stock your product. An intensive marketing campaign is carried out, after which a survey of 80 outlets shows 41 stocking the product. Does this indicate a change significant at the 1 per cent level?

3  It has been suggested that women are less willing to join a trade union than men. A survey of 200 workers in a factory showed that, of 80 women, 53 belonged to the appropriate union; for men the figure was 97 out of 120. Is the suggestion supported by these figures?

**4** A factory employs three quality control inspectors, each of whom is asked to keep a record of the number of items he tests, and those he rejects, in the course of a day. The results are as below:

|  | Accepted | Rejected |
|---|---|---|
| Inspector A | 75 | 15 |
| Inspector B | 83 | 19 |
| Inspector C | 92 | 16 |

Do the inspectors differ significantly in the proportion of items they reject?

**5** An anthropologist is researching into hereditary factors in a certain country, and has formulated a theory that overall, 40 per cent of the population are fair-haired, 10 per cent are red-haired and the remainder are dark-haired. A sample from one particular tribe, however, contains 65 fair-haired, 19 red-haired and 66 dark-haired. Are these proportions consistent with the theory?

**6** Test a dice to see if it is fair: throw it 120 times and keep a record of the number of times each face occurs. Then test these observed values against the expected frequency of 20 for each face, by using $\chi^2$.

**7** Collect some data to enable you to formulate and carry out a hypothesis test about proportions. For instance, you might be able to find out from your college registry what percentage of students in your institution are girls. Then you could take a sample in, say the bar, or the college library, and test the hypothesis that the percentage of females using these facilities is the same as the percentage in the population as a whole. Alternatively, you can find out from the *Motor Industry of Great Britain* what percentage of the cars registered in Britain are foreign, and then test a sample of cars from your college car-park to see if it's consistent with this percentage. Again, you can probably think of other interesting hypotheses to test.

**8** ▣ Use the data file STUD.WK1 (or STUD.MTW) to test whether the age of the male students differs significantly from that of the females.

**9** You are monitoring the time taken to process orders in your organisation, and have found from examining a long run of historic data that the average time to process a certain type of order is 5.2 working days, with a standard deviation of 0.8 working days. This is regarded as acceptable, but you are anxious to make sure standards do not decline, so you examine a sample of 40 orders once a month. How high would the mean of such a sample need to be before you felt justified in concluding that standards are declining?

(The reasoning behind this question is an example of the ideas of *statistical process control*, which have made a considerable contribution to the Total Quality movement. The basic principle involves monitoring processes by periodically examining samples, and then using sampling theory to tell us when a sample is, or is not, within the bounds of what's 'OK'. If you would like to find out more about this important application of sampling theory, try reference (14) in the Suggestions for Further Reading in Appendix 1.)

## Case study problem

Dear X,

I knew I would have more questions about that survey! Now I need to know whether the average amount spent really differs between the private and business customers, and also whether there's a link between the different categories of customer and how satisfied or otherwise they tend to be. I think I gave you enough data to answer these queries last time I wrote.

Still on the subject of samples, I wonder if you can offer me some advice about an experiment I'd like to conduct concerning my advertising. I have a chance to advertise in colour in the local paper's special Wednesday 'Services Supplement', but I'm not convinced it's worth the extra expense. How could I carry out a little experiment to find out if the impact (in terms of what people remember) of a coloured advert is greater than that of a black-and-white one? And how would I go about analysing the results?

I've put in an example of the kind of advert we use at the moment, to give you some idea what's involved.

If I don't hear from you I'll assume you've been washed away in the terrible weather we've had lately – it's really getting me down! Still, keep smiling!

Jane

## Case study question

Draft your reply to this letter, including designing and if possible carrying out the experiment referred to, and analysing the results.

## CHAPTER 12

# Looking for connections: correlation

## Objectives

Before starting work on this chapter, make sure you are happy with:

(a)  the idea of a scattergraph (*see* Chapter 5, p. 79);
(b)  calculation and interpretation of mean and standard deviation (*see* Chapter 6, pp. 91–5, 99–103);
(c)  the concept of ranking (*see* Chapter 3).

By the end of your work on this chapter you should be able to:

(a)  recognise when a scattergraph suggests a relationship between two variables;
(b)  realise when the elimination of an outlier would make such a relationship more apparent;
(c)  calculate and interpret the rank correlation coefficient;
(d)  calculate and interpret Pearson's product-moment correlation coefficient.

## THE SALES MANAGER'S PROBLEM

Tim Newton is the sales manager of a firm which manufactures meat products (pies, sausages, etc.) and markets them directly to retail food stores via a large force of travelling salesmen. Recently, as the recession has begun to affect the business, Mr Newton has become aware of the need to monitor salesmen's performance more closely, but the trouble is that he doesn't have very much idea what factors may influence that performance. He feels, for example, that it wouldn't be fair to classify a salesman as inefficient on the basis of the comparatively low sales revenue he generates, if that particular salesman happens to cover a very sparsely populated area, in which he can't be expected to do as well as one of his colleagues who has been allocated to a well-populated urban sales region.

As a preliminary step, to help clarify his ideas, Mr Newton has collected some information relating to a random sample of ten salesmen. This information is shown in the table opposite.

| Salesman no. | Value of last quarter's sales (£000s) | Number of retail outlets visited regularly | Population of sales area (000s | Area covered (square miles) |
|---|---|---|---|---|
| 1 | 2 | 63 | 200 | 450 |
| 2 | 5 | 42 | 40 | 500 |
| 3 | 9 | 47 | 40 | 350 |
| 4 | 11 | 51 | 90 | 250 |
| 5 | 11 | 56 | 70 | 150 |
| 6 | 12 | 64 | 100 | 420 |
| 7 | 14 | 60 | 140 | 275 |
| 8 | 15 | 68 | 200 | 200 |
| 9 | 17 | 75 | 160 | 400 |
| 10 | 17 | 81 | 240 | 300 |

But this mass of figures, as it stands, doesn't convey much information to Mr Newton. He really has a twofold objective.

(*a*) *Control*: if he can demonstrate that there is a close connection between the value of the sales which a salesman generates – a variable which isn't directly within his control – and, for example, the number of retail outlets visited regularly by the salesmen – something which he *can* directly influence – then he can attempt to alter the sales revenue by making sure his salesmen visit more outlets in future. So he'd like a way of measuring how close a relationship there is between variables.

(*b*) *Estimation/prediction*: if he can go one step further and actually specify what the relationship between variables is, rather than merely stating that there is such a relationship, then he will be able to predict, with at least some degree of accuracy, what value of sales will be generated by, for example, a salesman who visits 80 retail outlets regularly. A knowledge of what the relationship *ought* to be will also help him to spot a salesman who seems to be 'the exception to the rule' – who, for instance, is failing to generate the appropriate sales volume considering the number of outlets he claims to visit. Such a salesman would merit further investigation to see if he is very inefficient for some reason, or if perhaps he is 'on the fiddle' and not actually visiting all the outlets he claims to visit. Conversely, if a salesman seems to be unusually successful when compared with the general pattern as established, it might pay dividends to follow him up and find out why this should be: has he got a new and more effective line of approach, perhaps?

You can see that the ability to spot a relationship between two quantities, to measure how close it is, and if possible to state explicitly what the relationship is, opens up all sorts of useful consequences, not just in this problem but in a more general context. The government would like to know the relationship between the rates of inflation and unemployment; a building society would be interested in a possible connection between the current interest rates it offers on investment and the number of new investors opening accounts; a travel agent would find it useful to be able to assess the link between the rate of exchange for the pound against the French franc and the numbers of people taking holidays in France; you yourself would no doubt be interested in a relationship which could predict for you, given your mark on assessed work during the year, what your examination mark is likely to be. And these are just four examples; you can probably think of dozens more straight away.

In a sense; though, we have been begging the question by talking vaguely about 'a relationship' without defining what exactly is meant by that. So before we go any further into investigating the closeness of relationships, let's try to be a bit more precise as to the meaning of the expression.

## WHAT KIND OF RELATIONSHIP?

It should already be clear to you from the examples mentioned at the end of the last section that we are not talking about *exact* relationships any more. By 'exact' I mean the sort of relationship which applies if you buy 5lb of bananas at 35p per pound; you can be quite certain that the price you have to pay will be $5 \times 35p = £1.75$, unless you are being overcharged! There is an exact relationship of the form: price = number of pounds bought × price per pound, which enables you to predict with complete accuracy what the price will be for any number of pounds purchased. No other factors, such as how tall the greengrocer is, or the temperature on the day you buy the bananas, will make any difference to this.

In the case of predicting your examination mark from your assessment mark, however, we have a completely different sort of problem. Presumably there *is* a link between the two marks – people with higher marks in assessment will probably get higher exam marks too – but there are a whole heap of other factors which will also have an influence on your examination performance: your basic ability in the subject, perhaps as measured by your A-level performance; your innate intelligence, maybe given by your IQ; the percentage of lectures you have missed during the year; and so on.

So there is no way in which you could establish a 'rule' for calculating the examination mark given the assessment marks in the way that we calculated the price of the bananas given the number of pounds bought. The problem is too complex and too full of imponderable factors for that, and the same goes for all the other examples mentioned above.

The banana problem can, however, give us some idea how we can start to tackle these more complex relationships. One good way to show the connection between the quantity

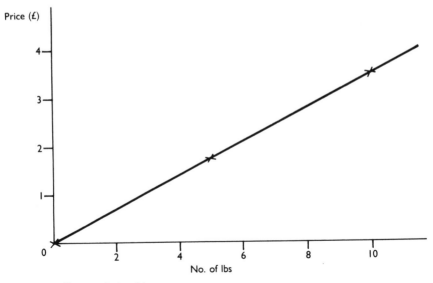

**Fig. 12.1** An exact linear relationship

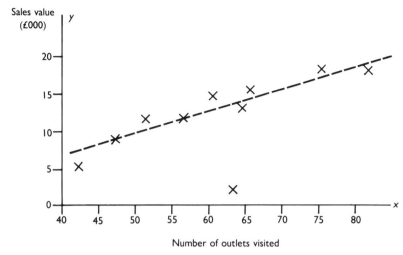

**Fig. 12.2** Scattergraph showing positive correlation

of bananas bought and the price paid would be to draw a graph, with the number of pounds bought on the horizontal axis and the price paid on the vertical axis. This would, of course, be a straight line as shown in Fig. 12.1. The three points marked are those which are used to plot the line, and represent the cost of 0, 5 and 10 pounds. Naturally, since the relationship is an exact one, the line passes precisely through all three points.

If we try doing the same thing for some of the sales data in the section on the sales manager's problem, we won't get a straight line, certainly, nor even any kind of smooth curve; but if we plot, as an example, the sales value for each salesman (on the vertical axis) against the number of retail outlets he visits regularly (on the horizontal axis), the points *do* seem to cluster fairly near to a line, even though they aren't all exactly on it. The graph is shown in Fig. 12.2 and it shouldn't be completely strange to you. It is a *scattergraph*, which we looked at briefly in Chapter 5.

## USING THE SCATTERGRAPH

Scattergraphs can be very useful as a preliminary step in investigating the existence of a relationship between two quantities. The kind of situation demonstrated by Fig. 12.2, where the points appear to cluster near to an upward-sloping straight line, is referred to as a *positive correlation*: as x (the horizontal variable) increases, so does y (the vertical one). So we expect to get such a relationship in situations where the two variables in question are rising or falling together: the more shops a salesman visits, the more sales he can hope to make, for example.

The converse situation, not surprisingly, is called *negative correlation*: one variable gets bigger as the other gets smaller. This produces a scattergraph in which the points are again near to a straight line, but this time one which slopes downhill from left to right. For instance, the more lectures you miss, the worse (I hope) your exam mark will be, producing a scattergraph resembling Fig. 12.3.

Of course, there is no reason why a relationship of this kind *must* be a straight line; in fact, if the data for sales value is plotted against the population of the salesman's region, the scatter graph produced (Fig. 12.4) suggests the existence of a curved

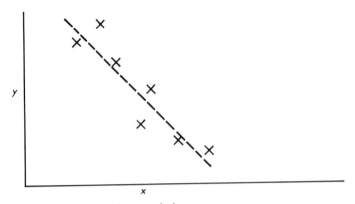

**Fig. 12.3** Scattergraph showing negative correlation

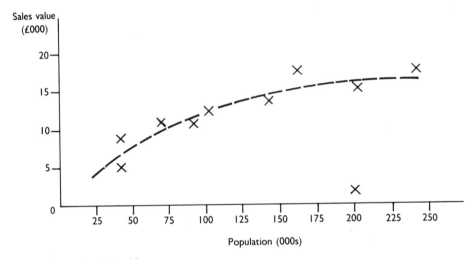

**Fig. 12.4** A curved relationship

relationship, as shown roughly by the dotted line. And it may turn out that our suspicions were wrong, and there's actually no relationship of any kind between two quantities: in this case the points of the scattergraph are indeed scattered, with no discernible pattern at all, like Fig. 12.5 which indicates the apparent absence of a link between the value of the sales generated by each salesman and the size of his sales region. (A bit of thought suggests that this is what we really ought to have expected: the area covered on its own isn't a significant factor; a salesman could cover thousands of square miles, but if they happened to be in the middle of the Scottish Highlands where nobody lives to buy his products, they wouldn't yield much in the way of sales revenue.)

Exact relationships, like the banana example we looked at earlier, can be tidily included among all the other types we've mentioned, if we regard them as cases of *perfect correlation*. The banana example gives a perfect positive correlation between price paid and number of pounds bought, and the resulting 'scattergraph', as we've seen, shows all the points lying exactly on the straight line.

Although it's easy enough to spot relationships of a curved type, like that in Fig. 12.4, by examining the scattergraph, curved graphs are, as we saw in Chapter 1, a much more complicated proposition than straight lines. A straight line graph is really the only kind

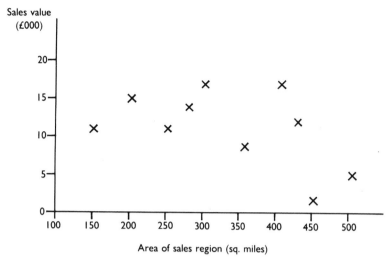

**Fig. 12.5** Two unrelated variables

one can be sure of plotting correctly, simply by using a ruler. From now on, therefore, we are going to limit our discussion to relationships like those shown in Figs 12.2 and 12.3, where the points seem to be near to a line. As far as all our future analysis in this chapter is concerned, a relationship like that shown in Fig. 12.4 is, almost as much as that shown in Fig. 12.5 is, an example of *zero correlation*.

The moral of all this is that, in investigating a suspected link between any two variables, your best bet to begin with is to draw a scattergraph. It will indicate if there is a correlation worth pursuing by more complex methods; if the relationship happens to be curved, it will indicate that too, and should that be the case your only course of action is to put in a freehand approximation to the relationship on the graph, trying to make your curve pass fairly 'through the middle' of the set of points.

There is a further piece of information which can be obtained from the scattergraph, as we can see by examining Figs 12.2 and 12.4 again. On each of these diagrams, there is one point which doesn't seem to conform to the general pattern. A point like this is often called an *outlier*, and if we go back to the original data in this case we find that the outliers in both diagrams are the points corresponding to salesman number 1. A closer look at his figures suggests that there is indeed something funny going on: he covers a well-populated area, seems to be visiting a fair number of outlets, yet his sales are lower than anyone else's. Maybe he is only *claiming* to have visited 63 outlets; maybe he *did* visit them but is simply a very poor salesman; but in either case, he needs investigating. And he shouldn't be included in any further analysis of the problem; whatever relationship may apply to the other salesmen in Fig. 12.2, it certainly doesn't apply to him, and his presence in our calculations will tend to make the relationship seem less clear-cut than it really is. We'll return to this point later in the chapter.

For all these reasons then, a scattergraph is a good start. Why, you may ask, do we need to go further? Can't we spot the relationship, if one exists, on the scattergraph and put in a reasonably good freehand line? For that matter, why do we need the line at all — we can *see* that there's a relationship, without having to specify exactly what it looks like.

There are two major drawbacks to this totally graphical approach. First, it's very hard to judge 'by eye' just how close a relationship is — the scale on which you choose to draw the scattergraph can make a lot of difference to the appearance of a relationship, as you'll discover if you try plotting Fig. 12.2 twice over, the second time with scales on both axes twice as big as the first time. So we could do with a proper numerical *measurement* of the closeness of the relationship.

Secondly, where exactly are we going to draw the freehand line on the graph? We must have such a line if we are to achieve the second objective mentioned on p. 217, the prediction of one variable given a value of the other. But if you make several copies of Fig. 12.2, and get different people to put in what *they* consider to be the line which fits the points best, you'll probably find you get some very varied results. Again, a proper systematic method of working out where the line should go is needed.

The second of these requirements we will defer until Chapter 13; the first will occupy us for the rest of this chapter.

## MEASURING THE STRENGH OF A RELATIONSHIP: THE RANK CORRELATION

We've actually already looked at one way in which we could assess the strength of the relationship between sales and number of outlets visited. Perhaps if that is rephrased as 'assess the association between sales and number of outlets visited' you will spot that we could use chi-squared. Sales could be classified as 'high', 'medium' or 'low', as could the number of outlets visited, and then chi-squared could be used to determine whether the association between the two is significant. But this is unsatisfactory in the present situation for a number of reasons: it involves throwing away quite a lot of information, since at present we have actual measurements for the two variables, which wouldn't be used if we simply lumped the items together into three broad categories. Nor would this method give us any idea whether the correlation is positive or negative. Chi-squared, as we noted in Chapter 11, doesn't tell us anything about the direction of an association. Finally, we are now specifically interested in looking for *straight line* relationships, which chi-squared certainly can't help with.

So we need a new way of measuring the strength of the relationship between two variables, in the specific sense of the closeness of points on the scattergraph to a straight line. Before actually calculating such a measurement, however, let's think about the characteristics we would like it to have. It would be sensible if it gave a positive value when there is a positive correlation, and a negative value for a negative one, and if it were zero when there's no correlation. It should have a rather special value when there is a perfect correlation, either positive or negative, and obviously it shouldn't depend on anything subjective such as the scale or units of measurement being used.

To illustrate the calculation of such a measurement, we will start off with some data which is rather simpler than that in the section on the sales manager's problem. The figures shown below represent a company's expenditure on advertising a certain product, and the sales revenue generated by that product, for five years:

| Year | Advertising expenditure (£000s) | Sales revenue (£000s) |
| --- | --- | --- |
| 1987 | 2 | 60 |
| 1988 | 5 | 100 |
| 1989 | 4 | 70 |
| 1990 | 6 | 90 |
| 1991 | 3 | 80 |

We would expect to find some degree of positive correlation here, since presumably the more one advertises a product, the more of it one will sell, at least within certain limits. This expectation is confirmed by the scattergraph of these figures (Fig. 12.6) – higher values of $x$, the advertising expenditure, correspond to higher values of $y$, the sales revenue. And it is this observation which suggests the form of our first measure of correlation: if the data were *ranked* in order, from say highest to lowest, we would expect the years with a high ranking for advertising expenditure to have a high sales ranking also.

The ranked data is as follows:

| Year | Advertising expenditure rank | Sales rank |
|------|:---:|:---:|
| 1987 | 5 | 5 |
| 1988 | 2 | 1 |
| 1989 | 3 | 4 |
| 1990 | 1 | 2 |
| 1991 | 4 | 3 |

Certainly the year with the lowest expenditure on advertising also had the lowest sales revenue, but for the other years the correspondence isn't exact. The greater the difference in the ranks of the two variables, the weaker the connection between them.

The measure of correlation based on this idea of the difference in ranks is called the *rank correlation coefficient*, or sometimes Spearman's coefficient after its inventor. To *prove* to you why it takes the precise form it does would involve a great deal of messy algebra, so for once I am going to present you with a formula like a rabbit out of a hat, and then try to demonstrate that the formula gives sensible results which comply with our requirements for a 'good' measure of correlation.

The coefficient is defined as follows:

rank correlation coefficient (usually written $r_{\text{rank}}$)

$$= \frac{6 \sum d^2}{n(n^2 - 1)}$$

where $d$ is the difference in ranks for each pair of variables, $n$ is the number of pairs altogether, and the $\sum$ sign means 'add together for all pairs in the data'. The 6, incidentally, is just 6 – it has nothing to do with the value of $n$, but always remains the same.

I imagine your reaction to this expression is a resounding 'So what?' – it certainly doesn't appear to mean very much. We can only begin to understand how the measurement works if we try calculating it for various sets of data. So to begin with, we will find the rank correlation coefficient for our advertising and sales data; we have already ranked this data, so all that remains is to calculate $d$ and $d^2$ for each pair of ranks and apply the formula:

| Advertising expenditure rank | Sales rank | Difference in ranks (d) | $d^2$ |
|:---:|:---:|:---:|:---:|
| 5 | 5 | 0 | 0 |
| 2 | 1 | 1 | 1 |
| 3 | 4 | 1 | 1 |
| 1 | 2 | 1 | 1 |
| 4 | 3 | 1 | 1 |
| | | | 4 |

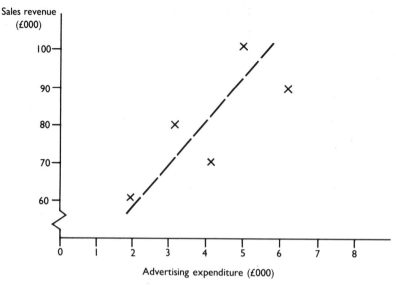

**Fig. 12.6** Scattergraph of advertising expenditure against sales revenue

$$r_{rank} = 1 - \frac{6 \times 4}{5(25 - 1)} = 1 - \frac{24}{5 \times 24} = 1 - \frac{1}{5} = 0.8.$$

## INTERPRETING THE RANK CORRELATION

As it stands, this figure still doesn't mean very much; we need some kind of scale with which to compare it. This can be obtained quite easily if we consider the two 'extreme' cases which might arise – that of perfect positive correlation on the one hand, and perfect negative correlation on the other. A perfect positive correlation would be represented, in terms of ranks, by the rankings of the two variables being exactly the same; thus the calculation of $r_{rank}$ would be:

| $X_{rank}$ | $Y_{rank}$ | $d$ | $d^2$ |
| --- | --- | --- | --- |
| 1 | 1 | 0 | 0 |
| 2 | 2 | 0 | 0 |
| 3 | 3 | 0 | 0 |
| 4 | 4 | 0 | 0 |
| 5 | 5 | 0 | 0 |

The sum of $d^2$ is clearly zero, so

$$r_{rank} = 1 - \frac{6 \times 0}{5(25 - 1)}$$

$$= 1.$$

Thus it appears that a perfect positive correlation gives a correlation coefficient of $+1$.

At the opposite extreme we have the case of perfect negative correlation, for which one set of ranks would be precisely the reverse of the other:

| $X_{rank}$ | $Y_{rank}$ | $d$ | $d^2$ |
|---|---|---|---|
| 1 | 5 | 4 | 16 |
| 2 | 4 | 2 | 4 |
| 3 | 3 | 0 | 0 |
| 4 | 2 | 2 | 4 |
| 5 | 1 | 4 | 16 |
| | | | 4 |

Thus

$$r_{\text{rank}} = 1 - \frac{6 \times 40}{5(25 - 1)} = 1 - \frac{240}{120} = 1 - 2 = -1.$$

So a perfect negative correlation yields a correlation coefficient of $-1$.

These two extremes provide the scale of comparison which we need in order to interpret other correlations; you can verify that you get the same values of $\pm 1$ if you use different numbers of points – there's nothing special about 5. One way of using the result is to draw a diagram like Fig. 12.7. The two perfect correlation extremes are at the two ends of the scale, and in the middle is zero correlation. The nearer a value of $r_{\text{rank}}$ is to either end of the scale, the closer the relationship it indicates; the nearer to 0, the weaker the relationship. The value of 0.8 which we obtained for the advertising and sales data thus indicated some degree of positive correlation.

However, by now I hope you are well enough educated to feel dissatisfied with a statement like 'close to 1' or 'close to zero' – how close *is* close? You should also be getting used to the idea that small sets of data are pretty unreliable, so you won't be surprised to learn that the interpretation placed on a calculated value of $r_{\text{rank}}$ depends on the number of data points we started with. It becomes clear why this is so if we consider the case where there are only two data points available; if these are plotted on a scattergraph, astonishingly they *always* show a perfect correlation, since we can always draw a straight line through them! In this case, of course, the 'perfect correlation' indicates nothing except that it's always possible to draw a straight line through two points.

This is an extreme case, but it does suggest that the size of correlation coefficient required to demonstrate fairly convincingly the existence of a relationship depends on the amount of data available. The greater the amount of data, the smaller the value of $r_{\text{rank}}$ we can afford to be satisfied with. But we've got involved in vague statements like 'the greater ... the smaller' again; a more definite statement about this aspect will have to wait until the next section.

We'll conclude our discussion of the rank correlation coefficient by calculating it for

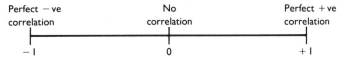

**Fig. 12.7** Scale for interpretation of $r_{\text{rank}}$

the data concerning the value of sales brought in by various salesmen, and the numbers of retail outlets they visited. The data is shown again below, together with the rankings (highest to lowest) and the remainder of the calculations needed to find $r_{rank}$.

| Salesman no. | Value of sales | No. of outlets visited | Sales rank | Outlets rank | d | $d^2$ |
|---|---|---|---|---|---|---|
| 1 | 2 | 63 | | | | |
| 2 | 5 | 42 | 1 | 1 | 0 | 0 |
| 3 | 9 | 47 | 2 | 2 | 0 | 0 |
| 4 | 11 | 51 | 3.5 | 3 | 0.5 | 0.25 |
| 5 | 11 | 56 | 3.5 | 4 | 0.5 | 0.25 |
| 6 | 12 | 64 | 5 | 6 | 1 | 1 |
| 7 | 14 | 60 | 6 | 5 | 1 | 1 |
| 8 | 15 | 68 | 7 | 7 | 0 | 0 |
| 9 | 17 | 75 | 8.5 | 8 | 0.5 | 0.25 |
| 10 | 17 | 81 | 8.5 | 9 | 0.5 | 0.25 |
| | | | | | | 3 |

Remember that we decided to omit the first salesman from our further consideration of the problem on the grounds that he is an outlier who for some reason or other doesn't conform to the pattern presented by the others. Notice, too, how the 'tied' values have been dealt with – for instance, there are two salesmen both producing sales of value £11,000. Had they had *different* values, these two would have been ranked as 3 and 4; because they in fact tie, they are each awarded the average of these two ranks – that's 3.5. The next person is then given rank 5, and so on.

We can therefore calculate $r_{rank}$ as follows:

$$r_{rank} = 1 - \frac{6 \times 3}{9(81 - 1)} = 1 - \frac{18}{720} = 1 - 0.025 = 0.975.$$

It thus appears that there is quite a marked positive relationship between the value of the sales which a salesman makes, and the number of outlets he visits regularly. (You might like to repeat the calculation *including* salesman number 1, and see what difference he makes.)

## MEASURING THE STRENGTH OF A RELATIONSHIP: PEARSON'S COEFFICIENT

The rank correlation coefficient is very easy to calculate and to interpret, but it is really rather an approximate method, since it involves, at least in the majority of cases, throwing away a certain amount of information about the variables being correlated. In each of the examples in the previous two sections of this chapter we began with a set of actual measurements, which were replaced in the course of the calculation by the undoubtedly simpler, but less precise, rankings.

This approximation may not be serious in many situations; and of course, in a case where all we have to start with is a set of rankings – if, for example, we were given the class positions of a group of schoolchildren in mathematics and English, and asked to investigate the existence of a correlation – the rank correlation will *have* to do. In a situation where the original measurements are available, however, using the ranked data instead could be quite misleading.

Suppose, for example, that we had values of x and y as shown (don't worry about what they might represent):

| $x$ | 1 | 2 | 4 | 5 | 7 |
|---|---|---|---|---|---|
| $y$ | 3 | 5 | 8 | 11 | 16 |

The rankings associated with these would be

| $rank_x$ | 1 | 2 | 3 | 4 | 5 |
|---|---|---|---|---|---|
| $rank_y$ | 1 | 2 | 3 | 4 | 5 |

which of course would produce a value of $+1$ for $r_{rank}$; yet if you plot the five points on a scattergraph you will see that they certainly don't all lie exactly on a straight line. In this case $r_{rank}$ has overestimated the degree of correlation and made it appear that there's a perfect correlation when there isn't.

If we want to overcome this problem, what is required is an alternative type of correlation coefficient which will make use of the actual measured values of the variables rather than replacing them by the less accurate rankings. This alternative correlation goes by the formidable title of Pearson's product moment correlation coefficient (invented, as you might expect, by Pearson), but the name is often shortened to 'correlation coefficient'. So if you hear someone talking about 'the' correlation coefficient this is the one they generally mean.

Once again, rather than building up the formula for the correlation coefficient, step-by-step, I will present you with a *fait accompli* and then try to establish how it works. Take a deep breath! The correlation coefficient, usually written as $r$, is defined by:

$$r = \frac{\text{Covariance of } x \text{ and } y}{\text{Standard deviation of } x \times \text{standard deviation of } y}$$

where covariance of $x$ and $y = \dfrac{\Sigma xy}{n} - \bar{x}\bar{y}$, $n$ being the number of data points and $\bar{x}, \bar{y}$ the means of $\bar{x}$ and $\bar{y}$. The standard deviations are calculated in the usual way, with s.d.

of $x = \sqrt{\dfrac{\Sigma x^2}{n} - \bar{x}^2}$, and similarly for $y$.

At first sight this is undoubtedly a fearsome looking object, but if you open your eyes and take another look at it, a certain pattern becomes apparent. Compare the covariance of $x$ and $y$ with the separate standard deviations of $x$ and $y$, and you will see that it's really a sort of combination of the two; it measures the variations in the combination of $x$s and $y$s, whereas the standard deviations measure the variations in either $x$ or $y$ alone. So the correlation coefficient is the ratio of the variations in $x$ and $y$ compared to those of $x$ and $y$ separately.

Calculating it isn't too bad, either. Inspection of the various bits which go to make it up indicates that the quantities involved are $\Sigma x$ (needed for $\bar{x}$), $\Sigma y$ (needed for $\bar{y}$), $\Sigma x^2, \Sigma y^2$, and $\Sigma xy$; so we set up columns for these items and then fill them in, not forgetting to make use of the memory in our calculators to do the summations as we go along. Reverting to the simple advertising/sales data which we used on p. 222 the calculation goes like this (we have advertising as $x$ and sales as $y$ simply because they occurred in that order, but the correlation coefficient would be exactly the same if they were taken the other way round).

If we take the components of the formula a bit at a time, then $\bar{x} = 20/5 = 4$, $\bar{y} = 400/5 = 80$, standard deviation of $x = \sqrt{90/5 - 4^2} = \sqrt{18 - 16} = \sqrt{2}$, standard deviation of $y = \sqrt{33,000/5 - 80^2} = \sqrt{6,600 - 6,400} = \sqrt{200}$, and covariance of $x$ and $y = 1,680/5 - (4 \times 80) = 336 - 320 = 16$. So, putting all the bits together:

$$r = \frac{16}{\sqrt{2 \times 200}} = \frac{16}{20} = 0.8.$$

| Advertising expenditure | Sales revenue | $x^2$ | $y^2$ | $xy$ |
|---|---|---|---|---|
| $x$ | $y$ | | | |
| 2 | 60 | 4 | 3,600 | 120 |
| 5 | 100 | 25 | 10,000 | 500 |
| 4 | 70 | 16 | 4,900 | 280 |
| 6 | 90 | 36 | 8,100 | 540 |
| 3 | 80 | 9 | 6,400 | 240 |
| 20 | 400 | 90 | 33,000 | 1,680 |

Like the mean and standard deviation the correlation coefficient is usually obtained from a computer package these days. So it is more important for you to be able to *interpret* it than merely grind through the calculation. We will see later how to calculate $r$ using MINITAB and LOTUS.

## INTERPRETING PEARSON'S COEFFICIENT

In this case, then, the values of $r$ and $r_{rank}$ coincide. This suggests that the manner of interpreting $r$ should be the same as that in which we interpreted $r_{rank}$ – by taking values close to $\pm 1$ as indicative of a close connection between the variables, and values near to zero as indicating little or no connection. You can verify that points which lie exactly on a straight line do indeed give the values $r = \pm 1$ (you might like to use the set of points $x = 2$, $y = 5$; $x = 3$, $y = 7$; $x = 4$, $y = 9$; $x = 5$, $y = 11$; $x = 7$, $y = 15$, which lie on the line $y = 2x + 1$, and should therefore give you $r = +1$).

We have one great advantage, however, when it comes to the interpretation of $r$ as against $r_{rank}$. Remember we noted earlier that this interpretation must depend to some extent on the number of points in our sample. With a bigger sample we can afford to be satisfied with a smaller value of $r$ as evidence of correlation. At that stage we went no further than this qualitative statement, but for Pearson's correlation coefficient we can do rather better. It happens that the sampling distribution followed by $r$ is not difficult to deduce, and with its help a table has been produced, which you will find in Appendix 8. This table tells us the value of $r$ which must be exceeded, for a given sample size, if we are to be able to deduce the existence of a correlation between $x$ and $y$ which is significant at the 5 per cent (or 1 per cent) level, in the same way in which we used this term in Chapter 11. In this table $v = n - 2$.

In the case just calculated, we found that $r = 0.8$, and there were 5 points in our sample of data. The table shows that, for such a sample, a value of at least 0.8783 or less than $-0.8783$ would be needed before we could conclude that there's a correlation between advertising expenditure and sales significant at the 5 per cent level. So we have failed to demonstrate the existence of a correlation between sales and advertising, at least at this level of significance. The value of $r$ obtained would occur quite often, even if sales and advertising are totally unconnected.

Incidentally, in cases which give a negative value of $r$, the minus sign is ignored when consulting the table. So, for example, a value of $-0.6$ would be significant at the 5 per cent level in a sample of 12 items.

We complete our practice in handling $r$ by calculating it for the sales/number of outlets data on p. 217. With the elimination of the 'outlying' salesman number one, the calculation is as follows:

| Salesman no. | Value of sales (y) | No. of outlets visited | $y^2$ | $x^2$ | xy |
|---|---|---|---|---|---|
| 2 | 5 | 42 | 25 | 1,764 | 210 |
| 3 | 9 | 47 | 81 | 2,209 | 423 |
| 4 | 11 | 51 | 121 | 2,601 | 561 |
| 5 | 11 | 56 | 121 | 3,136 | 616 |
| 6 | 12 | 64 | 144 | 4,096 | 768 |
| 7 | 14 | 60 | 196 | 3,600 | 840 |
| 8 | 15 | 68 | 225 | 4,624 | 1,020 |
| 9 | 17 | 75 | 289 | 5,625 | 1,275 |
| 10 | 17 | 81 | 289 | 6,561 | 1,377 |
| | 111 | 544 | 1,491 | 34,216 | 7,090 |

Then:

$$\bar{x} = 12.33, \bar{y} = 60.44,$$

$$\text{covariance} = \frac{7,090}{9} - 12.33 \times 60.44 = 42.30,$$

$$s_x = \sqrt{\frac{1,491}{9} - 12.33^2} = \sqrt{13.56} = 3.68,$$

$$s_y = \sqrt{\frac{34,216}{9} - 60.44^2} = \sqrt{148.78} = 12.20,$$

and finally,

$$r = \frac{\text{covariance}}{s_x \times s_y} = \frac{42.30}{3.68 \times 12.20} = 0.94.$$

Consultation of Appendix 8 shows that a value of 0.6664 would be significant at the 5 per cent level in a sample of 9 pairs such as we have here; so there is evidence of a significant correlation between sales value and number of outlets visited. In fact, inspection of the second column of the table shows that our value of $r$ is sufficiently large to be significant at the 1 per cent level. The value of $r_{\text{rank}}$ for the same data, calculated in the preceding section, was, you will recall, 0.975, so the loss of accuracy involved in ranking the data resulted, in this case, in $r_{\text{rank}}$ giving a slight overestimate of the amount of correlation. (The formula for $r_{rank}$, incidentally, is actually derived from that for $r$ by replacing $x$ and $y$ by the ranks $1, 2, 3, \ldots$).

## WHAT WE HAVE – AND HAVEN'T – PROVED

The cautionary note which we sounded at the end of our work on chi-squared needs repeating even more forcefully with regard to correlation: because so many problems boil down to the question 'Is $x$ connected with $y$?', and because the technique is relatively simple to apply (particularly now that computers and many scientific calculators give the correlation coefficient practically at the touch of a button), it is very much open to abuse. The main source of this abuse is, I think, a misunderstanding of the fundamental fact that *correlation does not mean causation* – in other words, just because $x$ correlates well with $y$, we can't necessarily deduce that $x$ *causes* $y$ – or vice versa.

The sillier examples of this fact – so-called 'spurious correlations' – are not hard to spot. Many totally unconnected quantities which show an increasing behaviour will produce quite respectable-looking correlation coefficients, and, of course, once the 'connection' has been 'proved' it is usually possible to find some kind of explanation for it. For example, students of mine produced a very high correlation between the numbers of divorces and the numbers of women in higher education in the UK over the past ten years: they then theorised that educated women don't make good wives, so their husbands divorce them! (Needless to say, these were male students.)

More difficult to detect are the correlations which are created by some 'hidden third factor'. If one were to correlate the numbers of deaths from, say, typhoid, over a few years towards the end of the nineteenth century with the numbers of children attending school over the same period, the resulting correlation coefficient would probably be quite high; but this would not prove that school attendance confers a degree of immunity to typhoid! Rather, both figures are indicative of an underlying trend of improvement in living standards from which hygiene and educational opportunities both benefited.

This problem in interpreting the correlation coefficient makes it very difficult, except in strictly controlled scientific experiments, to rule out the possibility that an apparent correlation is actually being caused by some unsuspected factor. To take a classic example: there is, as everyone knows by now, a very high correlation between the number of cigarettes a person smokes each day and his chance of dying of lung cancer. But opponents of the 'smoking causes cancer' theory could suggest that there is something which renders certain individuals more likely to smoke, and also more likely to contract lung cancer – perhaps, for instance, they are people who react to stress in a certain way. Although this particular case is now fairly conclusively sewn up, you can see how difficult such a suggestion might be, in general, to disprove.

If you really feel you have strong grounds for expecting a correlation to exist between two variables, yet find that $r$ does not appear significant when calculated in the usual way, there are two expedients open to you. One is, as we have indicated earlier, to try the elimination of dubious or outlying values. This has to be done with discretion, however. It is no good whittling down your data until there's so little of it left as to be meaningless; only those points which are genuinely outside the predominant pattern (preferably for some identifiable reason) should be discarded.

The other possibility only applies if you are correlating figures over a period of time. Suppose, for instance, that you have data referring to a large supermarket chain showing capital investment in opening new branches and total takings of all branches for a period of several years. Probably the effect of new premises on takings will not be apparent until some time, a year or maybe even two years, after the capital investment in those premises is made. Thus a direct correlation of capital investment with takings in the same year might not be very useful, whereas a correlation in which the investment figures were 'lagged' (displaced) by a year or two years to match up with the relevant takings might look very much more convincing.

We have taken a rather narrow-minded view in restricting our investigation to connections between *two* variables. We have already acknowledged, for example, that it is the factors neglected in our analysis which cause correlations to be less than perfect. The variations in sales revenue are not by any means solely related to the advertising budget; they are influenced by what competitors are doing, by the stage which the product's life-cycle has reached, by the rate of inflation, even perhaps by the weather if we are selling umbrellas or ice-cream. So it might be sensible, rather than investigating these connections one at a time, to try to evaluate the effect of all these things *simultaneously* on sales.

This can be done by means of measuring, not how close points on a graph are to a straight line, but how close points in umpteen-dimensional space are to the umpteen-dimensional equivalent of a straight line! Actually, although this sounds horrific, technically it's not much worse than the two-variable case we've looked at – at least with the aid of a computer. We will come across this idea again in the next chapter.

## ◧ CORRELATION WITH MINITAB AND LOTUS

If we have the two sets of data which we wish to correlate stored in columns C1 and C2 of a MINITAB worksheet, finding the correlation coefficient between them couldn't be simpler – the command is just CORRELATE C1 C2.

With LOTUS it's not so simple. The table for computing $r$ could, of course, easily be set up as a spreadsheet, but there is actually a more automated way of doing it. However, the method is closely tied to the calculation of the regression line, and so we defer a discussion of the details until the next chapter.

### Practical exercises

1 A rank correlation coefficient can be used as a measure of the consistency of judgment between two people. For example, a trainee wine-taster and a Master of Wine together try ten sample vintages, and then each ranks them in order of his opinion of their quality. The rankings are as follows:

| Sample | 1 | 2 | 3 | 4 | 5 | 6 | 7 | 8 | 9 | 10 |
|---|---|---|---|---|---|---|---|---|---|---|
| Master | 5 | 3 | 7 | 2 | 10 | 9 | 1 | 4 | 8 | 6 |
| Trainee | 4 | 1 | 7 | 3 | 8 | 9 | 2 | 5 | 10 | 6 |

How consistent does the trainee's judgment appear to be with the Master's?

**2** Eight samples of low-fat spread are ranked according to flavour by a panel of testers. Their consensus is:

| Sample | A | B | C | D | E | F | G | H |
|--------|---|---|---|---|---|---|---|---|
| Rank | 8 | 6 | 1 | 3 | 7 | 4 | 5 | 2 |

The measurements of a certain vegetable oil in the samples are known to be:

| Sample | A | B | C | D | E | F | G | H |
|----------|----|----|----|----|----|----|----|----|
| Per cent | 12 | 18 | 32 | 28 | 10 | 22 | 25 | 32 |

(a) By ranking the samples on oil content from highest to lowest, decide what you would say to the statement 'This oil imparts a better flavour'.

(b) Try ranking the samples the other way round, and see what difference it makes to your result.

**3** The manufacturers of Happihog pigfood have compiled the following table after studies at their test-farm:

| Age of pig (months) | Weight of Happihog consumed/week (kg) |
|:---:|:---:|
| 4 | 2 |
| 6 | 3 |
| 6 | 4 |
| 10 | 8 |
| 9 | 6 |
| 12 | 9 |
| 15 | 10 |
| 18 | 9 |
| 24 | 11 |

Calculate Pearson's correlation coefficient:

(a) for the first six pairs of data;

(b) for all the data, and explain using a scattergraph the difference between the two figures.

**4** Calculate $r$ for the following two sets of data:

| $x$ | 4 | 10 | 8 | 12 | 6 |
|-----|-----|-----|-----|-----|-----|
| $y$ | 180 | 300 | 210 | 270 | 240 |

Compare this with the correlation coefficient obtained for the advertising/sales figures on p. 222. What do you notice?

**5** Do the same with the data

| $x$ | 14 | 20 | 18 | 22 | 16 |
|-----|----|-----|-----|-----|-----|
| $y$ | 80 | 200 | 110 | 170 | 140 |

What can you deduce? By examining scattergraphs of the three sets of data, suggest why your deduction applies. How could this fact be used to simplify calculations?

**6** Look through the *Monthly Digest of Statistics* for two variables which you think may be correlated. If you enjoy economics you could try Retail Price Index/unemployment or inflation/money supply; if you're ecologically-minded, amount of carbon monoxide in the air/deaths from lung complaints; for something sociological, unemployment/ crime rate or numbers of divorces – the scope is endless. If the figures are complicated you may need either to use a rank correlation, or to round them off fairly drastically, before calculating *r*.

Try to interpret your result, bearing in mind the dangers of spurious correlation and seeking other factors which may be influencing your data. Remember, too, to look for outliers, and consider the possibility that you may need to 'lag' data – inflation may correlate with money supply a year earlier (or later). Nor does the data have to be for successive periods of time; you could use regional figures instead.

**7** ▣ Use the data in the MINITAB worksheet QUAL.MTW to compute the correlation coefficient between takings of branches and floorspace for (a) the entire group of stores, and (b) the shopping precinct and street branches separately. Plot the relevant scattergraphs, and comment on your results.

## Case study problem

Dear X,

Thanks for your help with the advertising experiment – I followed your advice, and discovered that the extra cost of the coloured advert wasn't really worthwhile in terms of effectiveness. So we have been running the black-and-white version several times a week for the last few months in the local morning and evening papers and the weekly free sheet. I've kept a note of the numbers of enquiries which come in after we run the ads, and I'm wondering whether the volume of enquiries increases with the number of times the ad. appears.

Here's what the figures look like (I've kept business and private customers separate, in case they are different).

| Number of appearances of ad. | Number of enquiries in same week | |
|---|---|---|
| | Business | Private |
| 1 | 19 | 14 |
| 2 | 11 | 17 |
| 4 | 23 | 21 |
| 6 | 20 | 25 |
| 7 | 24 | 27 |
| 8 | 16 | 28 |

Have you any comments to make as to what the relationships might be? I'd really value your ideas on this, as we don't want to pay for ineffective advertising.

I hope you enjoy the conference – I'll bet the catering isn't as good as ours!
Yours ever,

Jane

## Case study question

Draft your reply to this letter, using appropriate diagrams to illustrate your explanations.

# PART 4

# Numbers – a tool of planning

In this section we shall see how, by constructing a *mathematical model* of a practical problem, we can make decisions on a more sound and logical basis than if we were simply to rely on a subjective approach. You have in fact already encountered some mathematical models, though they were not specifically described as such. For instance, in Chapter 9 we used the theoretical probability distributions – binomial, normal and Poisson – as models for real-life situations which, while they might not fit the patterns of the theoretical distribution exactly, were adequately represented by them for many purposes. However, as the process of constructing a mathematical model will occur repeatedly in the following chapters, it is worthwhile to look briefly at the essential features of the process.

In most cases, the initial step will be the recognition that a problem exists – not always such an obvious step as it may sound. Even when the problem has been recognised, defining it precisely and deciding just what our objective should be in attempting to reach a solution can also be a lengthy process. To take an example which will be looked at in more detail in Chapter 16: if we are trying to decide what is the best level of stocks for a retailer to hold, we may have to keep records for many months before we have sufficient information about the demand for each product, how that demand varies in the course of time, how serious the effects of running out of a particular product may be, and so on – all of which information must be known before we can begin building our model. Then, when we come to specify the objective we are aiming to achieve, we are faced with several possibilities: do we want to find the policy which will minimise the total cost of stock-holding; do we want to minimise the risk of being out of stock; or do we perhaps want to cut down on administrative nuisance by placing standing orders for deliveries of stock which will only need to be changed at infrequent intervals?

Only after these questions have been answered can we proceed to build up a model for the problem, from which we hope to obtain a solution. The kinds of mathematical model we are going to use will take a variety of forms: algebraic equations, graphs, diagrams and charts, and so forth; but there is one major feature which will apply to some extent, no matter what kind of model we are using. That is, that some degree of simplification will be required before we can construct, and certainly before we can solve, our model. It is most important that we should be aware of the assumptions that we have had to make in simplifying the problem, as of course these will have a bearing on the validity of the solution we obtain, and the extent to which we can expect it to work in practice.

In many of the cases we are going to look at, actually obtaining the solution is a relatively simple matter once the model has been set up; but the process doesn't end there. The solution must be implemented – that is, applied in practice – and its validity checked against what happens in the real-life situation. Often at this stage it may become apparent that our problem was *too* simplified, or that circumstances have altered in the meantime and rendered some of our data obsolete, so that we then have to return to the stage of formulating the problem and repeat the whole process with the appropriate modifications. In other words, generally speaking the cycle is a dynamic, not a static one, because real-world situations are constantly altering. When mathematical methods are given a bad press by businessmen and other 'lay' people, quite often it is because this point has not been appreciated, so that solutions which are long out-of-date are still being blindly applied – which is naturally not a recipe for success!

We will try to emphasise these various stages of the modelling process in the ensuing chapters, and hopefully by doing so will avoid giving the impression that you are being armed with a mathematical 'box of tricks' for the solution to all the ills of British business. Before we proceed to examine specific techniques, however, one final word of warning may be in order.

You will encounter the term 'model' in all sorts of contexts, in many of which it is being applied much more loosely than we will be using it. It seems to have become one of those words – 'system' is another one – which can mean practically all things to all men! You should be careful to distinguish these looser usages from the more strict sense in which we shall be applying the term.

## CHAPTER 13

# Spotting the relationship: line fitting

## Objectives

Before starting work on this chapter, make sure you are happy with:

(a) the material on correlation in Chapter 12;
(b) the equation of a straight line (*see* Chapter 1, pp. 19–22);
(c) the basic ideas of graph plotting (*see* Chapter 1, pp. 19–22 and Chapter 5, pp. 76–9).

By the end of your work on this chapter you should be able to:

(a) calculate the equation of a regression line, say for what purposes it is the 'best' line through a set of points, and make sensible use of it to obtain forecasts;
(b) recognise situations in which a semi-logarithmic graph might be helpful, and plot and interpret such graphs.
(c) use suitable software to perform regression calculations, and interpret the output.

## MORE PROBLEMS FOR THE SALES MANAGER!

We have already encountered Tim Newton and his difficulties with salesmen in Chapter 12. But that was just a sample of the variety of headaches he encounters in trying to plan a rational sales policy. Many of these problems are connected with the fact that, if he is to get anywhere at all in planning sales targets and so on, he has to attempt to predict or forecast values of variables which are essentially out of his control. The more accurate his predictions, the better his planning can be.

We have seen one example of this in his need to determine the relationship between sales revenue brought in by the salesmen and the number of retail outlets they visit regularly. With a knowledge of this relationship he can decide what number of outlets salesmen should be aiming at. The existence of the relationship was demonstrated, with the aid of a correlation coefficient, in Chapter 12; as yet, however, we haven't tackled the second objective mentioned in Chapter 12 – the determination of the *form* of that relationship, so that it can be used to give estimates of sales if we know how many outlets a salesmen visits, or vice versa.

In the case of the sales/outlets data, we are seeking a relationship between two variables, both of which apply to all the salesmen, but a large number of Mr Newton's planning problems involve the rather special situation where one of the two variables we are trying to relate is *time*. This is what we usually understand by 'forecasting' or 'prediction' in its narrower sense. Although relationship problems of this kind *can* be treated just like questions of relationship between any two variables, there are a number of methods which are especially designed for the analysis of a series of figures over a period of time – a *time series*, as it's often called. We'll be looking at some of these methods later in this chapter, and in Chapter 14.

However, to begin with we return to the question of the relationship linking sales and number of outlets visited.

## WHAT IS A 'WELL-FITTING LINE'?

The scattergraph of the sales/number of outlets data is repeated in Fig. 13.1, which shows a straight line apparently fitting the set of points fairly well. But at this point we have to face the fact that, so far, we haven't really been precise about what a 'well-fitting' line is. I suppose the natural answer would be 'one which goes as near as possible to all the points', so let's begin from that idea.

Consider for a moment the question of the distance of one single point from the line. Figure 13.2 shows that, out of the infinite number of directions in which this distance might be measured, there are at least three which have some claim to consideration. Normally we understand 'the distance of a point from a line' to mean the perpendicular distance, but we could also choose to measure the distance parallel to the *x*-axis (which we could regard as the amount of error in the value of *x* between the line and the actual point) or parallel to the *y*-axis (which would give the corresponding error in the value of *y* as given by the line).

Which of these three ways of measuring the distance is most suitable? The answer depends very much on what we want to *use* the line for. The perpendicular distance can be disregarded, as it is never of much use; but if we want to use the line to predict *y* from a given *x*-value, then presumably we would like the 'error' in the estimate of *y* as given by the line to be as small as possible; so the appropriate procedure would be to choose the line in such a way that the *vertical* distances of the points from the line are minimised.

If, however, our objective was to estimate *x* given *y*, then we would wish to minimise the disagreement between the *x*-value as given by the line and the actual *x*-value of the points, so the horizontal measurement would be better. These two ways of measuring the

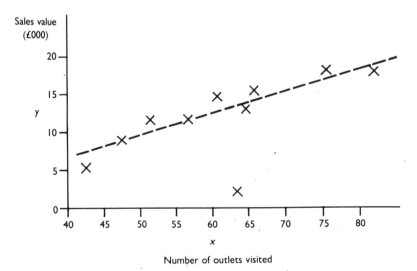

**Fig. 13.1** Scattergraph showing positive correlation

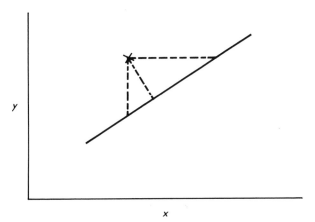

**Fig. 13.2** The distance of a point from a line

distance of points from the line give, in general, two completely different lines (the only exception being the case of perfect correlation when all the distances are zero), and it is very important that you choose the right line for the kind of estimation you want to do. You can, in fact, get away with always using the *same* line – the one which cuts down on the vertical, or *y*, errors – *if* you are careful always to make the 'given' quantity *x*, and the 'thing to be estimated' *y*. In the case of the sales outlets data, for example, if Mr Newton is interested in finding out how much revenue is likely to be brought in by a salesman who has, say 50 outlets on his regular 'beat', he should make the number of outlets his *x*-variable and the sales revenue his *y*. The straight-line equation which then needs to be determined is called the *regression equation of y on x*.

Even when we've decided how we are going to measure distance of points from the line, our problems are not at an end.

If we take 'as near as possible to all the points' to mean that the total of the vertical distances of all the points from the line chosen is smaller than it would be for any other line, we are immediately up against a difficulty. Do we take note of which side of the line the points are on, or not? If the answer is no, then we get the curious situation shown in Fig. 13.3(*a*) where line A is apparently a 'better' line than B, since the total distance of the three points from A is certainly smaller than that from B; most people, however, would feel that B fits the set of points better than A. So this attempted definition of 'best' gives results which run counter to our intuition.

If, on the other hand, we decide to say that points below the line are a negative distance from it, and those above a positive distance, then we get some very ambiguous cases. In Fig. 13.3(*b*), for instance, both lines give a total distance which is zero, yet they are completely different and even slope in opposite directions. So this definition of 'best', too, is a non-starter.

The next step may not come as too much of a surprise to you, after your experience with the standard deviation and $\chi^2$. We had difficulties with points above and below the mean in constructing the standard deviation, and difficulties with frequencies higher and lower than expected when constructing $\chi^2$. In both cases, the way out of our difficulty was to square the distances; and that's exactly what is done in this case, too. The 'line of best fit' is defined to be the one which makes the sum of the squares of the distance of the points from the line as small as possible.

This line is often called, for the obvious reasons, the 'least squares' regression line, and

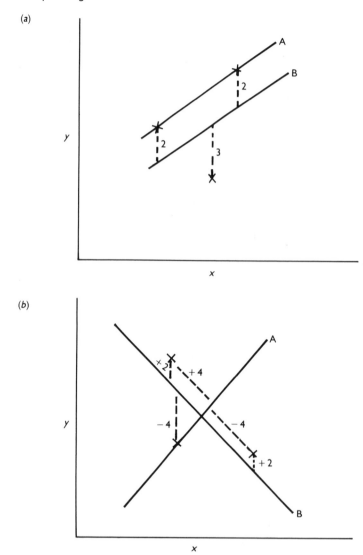

**Fig. 13.3** Lines of 'best' fit

the definition certainly gives one unambiguous line, which, as we'll see when we plot it, accords well with our ideas of what a 'well-fitting' line should look like. Working out just what the equation of such a best-fitting line will be for a given set of data is, however, by no means simple.

However, the determination of the values of slope and intercept, which, for a particular set of data, minimise the sum of squared deviations from the line, involves the use of calculus, and since many of you probably have not studied maths to that level, I will not give the general derivation of the regression equation. Instead I will simply present you with the relevant formulae, and then demonstrate how they work in practice. As with so many of the techniques we have studied, you are unlikely to need to use the formulae 'from scratch' very often, since many computer packages now perform regression calculations. We will have a look at the results of regression using MINITAB and LOTUS in the section, Regression with MINITAB and LOTUS, p. 245.

## CALCULATING THE REGRESSION LINE

The equation of the least-squares regression line of $y$ on $x$ is:

$$y - \bar{y} = \frac{r \times s_y}{s_x} (x - \bar{x}),$$

where as usual $\bar{x}$ and $\bar{y}$ denote the means of $x$ and $y$, the $s$s the standard deviations, and $r$ is the correlation coefficient. You should recognise this as the equation of a straight line, containing as it does just a single $x$ and a single $y$. It may look at first as if you're going to have to go yet again through the painful process of calculating the means and standard deviations, but if you think for a minute you will realise that you should already have done all the work in the process of finding the value of $r$ – because you shouldn't be going to the trouble of calculating a regression line unless first your scattergraph, then your value of $r$, suggest that the relationship between $x$ and $y$ is sufficiently close to make the calculation worthwhile. Of course, you can go through the motions of the calculation no matter *what* the amount of correlation, but the line you end up with won't tell you anything useful.

We'll use the formula to calculate two regression lines; first, the one for the simple set of advertising/sales data on page 222. In the process of calculating $r$ for this data we found that $\bar{x} = 4$, $\bar{y} = 80$, $s_x = \sqrt{2}$, $s_y = \sqrt{200}$, and $r$ itself was 0.8, so the equation of the regression line of $y$ on $x$ for this data is:

$$y - 80 = \frac{0.8 \times \sqrt{200}}{\sqrt{2}} (x - 4),$$

giving $y - 80 = 8(x - 4)$, that is, $y - 80 = 8x - 32$, $y = 8x - 32 + 80$, and finally $y = 8x + 48$.

This equation could now be used to give us an estimate of $y$ for any value of $x$ – at least, with certain reservations we will come to later. Remember, $x$ was the advertising expenditure and $y$ the sales revenue; the equation therefore shows that when the advertising expenditure is £7,000, so that $x = 7$, we have $y = 8 \times 7 + 48 = 104$, giving the predicted sales revenue as £104,000. What we could *not* do with this '$y$ on $x$' equation is answer the question 'How much would we need to spend on advertising to get sales of £110,000?' For that we would have to calculate a new equation with $x$ and $y$ interchanged, since the '$y$ on $x$' equation is only suited to finding $y$ given $x$.

The predictions obtained from this line can't be expected to be very reliable, since the correlation coefficient wasn't significant, so although the example has served to illustrate the method, in practice in this case one probably wouldn't bother calculating the equation. In the case of Mr Newton's sales/outlets data however, the correlation *was* significant, so a regression line can give us some useful information. Remember that the $x$ here was the number of outlets visited, while $y$ was the sales revenue generated by each salesman. Our '$y$ on $x$' regression line will therefore be suitable for estimating sales revenue given the number of outlets a salesman visits.

After the elimination of the 'outlying' salesman, number 1, we found (page 229):

$$\bar{x} = 60.44, \; \bar{y} = 12.33, \; s_x = 12.20, \; s_y = 3.68, \text{ and } r = 0.94$$

so the equation of the regression line required is:

$$y - 12.33 = \frac{0.94 \times 3.68}{12.20} (x - 60.44)$$

whence $y - 12.33 = 0.28(x - 60.44)$, $y - 12.33 = 0.28x - 16.92$, and finally $y = 0.28x - 16.92 + 12.33 = 0.28x - 4.59$.

If you feel that this method of calculating the regression equation is rather messy there is an alternative version which you may find easier, as long as you are comfortable with solving simultaneous equations. If we write the equation of the regression line as $y = a + bx$, so that $a$ is the intercept and $b$ the slope, then $a$ and $b$ can be found by solving the pair of equations:

$$\Sigma y = na \quad + b\Sigma x$$

$$\Sigma xy = a\Sigma x + b\Sigma x^2$$

where $n$ is the number of points for which we have data. For instance, with the sales/outlets data, substituting the values of $x$, $y$, etc. which we've already computed in the process of finding the correlation coefficient gives the equations:

$$111 = 9a \quad + \quad 544b$$

$$7090 = 544a + 34216.$$

You can verify that solving these equations leads to the same values of $a$ and $b$ as before; the numbers involved are large, but if you keep your head there are no real problems. So for hand calculation of regression lines, choose whichever of the two methods you prefer.

This line can easily be plotted on the scattergraph, using the point $x = 0$, $y = -4.59$ as one extreme, and perhaps $x = 80$, $y = 17.81$ as the other. A useful check on the accuracy of your plotting of the line is provided by the fact that, since it passes, as it were, through the 'middle' of the set of points, the means of the two sets of data should lie exactly on it. In this case, the point represented by the two means is $x = \bar{x} = 60.44$, $y = \bar{y} = 12.33$, and inspection of Fig. 13.4 shows that this point is indeed on the line.

Having plotted the line, we can use it to give predictions of the value of $y$ for a given value of $x$, simply by reading off the required values from the graph. However, there are important limitations to be borne in mind when doing this. We have fitted the line to the set of points, which in this case have $x$-values ranging from about 40 to 80, and certainly in this region the line fits the points very well; we are quite justified in using it to estimate

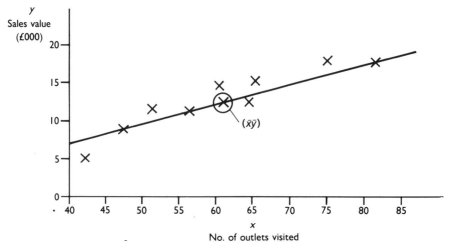

**Fig. 13.4** Regression line of sales value on number of outlets

*y* for, say an *x* of 50 or 70. But *outside* that region we cannot be sure that the line will continue to give us reliable estimates.

It could be, for example, that if we had data available for higher values of *x*, and plotted the corresponding points on the scattergraph, they would indicate that the straight-line relationship between *x* and *y* does not persist, but begins to level off as shown in Fig. 13.5. Indeed, this is what we might expect to happen in practice; after visiting a certain number of outlets, the salesman has saturated the market and so further increases in the number of outlets visited do not produce a corresponding increase in sales. In these circumstances, if we were to use the straight line to estimate sales when, say 100 outlets are visited, we would end up with a figure of about £23,400 – a serious overestimate, since Fig. 13.5 shows that the true figure is more likely to be in the region of £20,000.

This process of estimating *y* for values of *x* beyond the original range of the data is called *extrapolation*, and although it's sometimes necessary (and, for values of *x* fairly close to the original figures, won't give rise to too much inaccuracy), it should always be used with great caution. This becomes even clearer if we recognise that, as our regression line is based only on a sample of data, it is subject to sampling error, and therefore we should really consider where the 95 per cent confidence limits around the line might be.

Figure 13.6 shows roughly the shape of these confidence limits. Within the range of the original data, they are pretty well parallel to the line, so that the margin of error around estimates obtained from the line is reasonably narrow, at least if the correlation between *x* and *y* was significant to begin with.

As we go further and further away from the original data in either direction the confidence limits become further and further apart, showing that an estimate of *y* obtained from a value *x* = 100, such as we considered above, will be subject to a very wide margin of error, and could prove to be 'out', with respect to the true value of *y*, by more than 100 per cent.

Before leaving the subject of regression lines, there are one or two further points which are worth noting.

It is important not to go on using a regression line for prediction purposes after the circumstances in which it was constructed have altered. For example, in the case of the

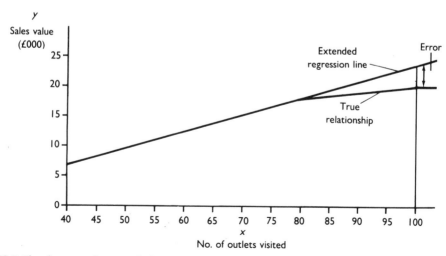

**Fig. 13.5** The dangers of extrapolation

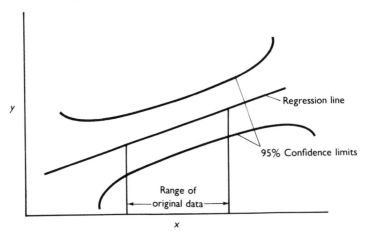

**Fig. 13.6** Confidence limits on a regression line

sales/outlets data above, a substantial change in marketing strategy, or a retraining course for the salesmen, would alter the situation considerably, and a new regression line would need to be computed (if a straight-line relationship still applied) using data collected subsequent to the change.

Both the examples we have looked at have involved positive correlations. If a negative correlation were involved then of course we would expect the number multiplying $x$ in the regression equation to be a negative one, since this number represents the slope of the line, which will be negative. The regression line in this case also provides a vivid illustration of the folly of unthinking extrapolation. Figure 13.7, for instance, shows the approximate position of the regression line representing the negative correlation between sales of umbrellas over twelve months and average hours of sunshine per day in the same twelve months. The more the sun shines, the less likely people are to buy umbrellas, which

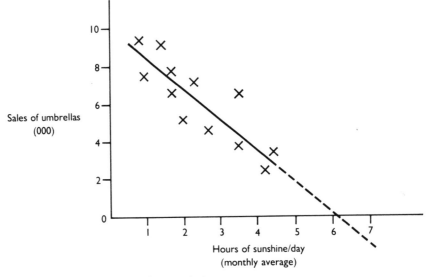

**Fig. 13.7** Extrapolation from a negative correlation

is perfectly reasonable. But if we continue the regression line and attempt to predict what umbrella sales will be in a month when there are 7 hours of sunshine a day, we find that the line has fallen below the horizontal axis – sales of umbrellas are negative, so presumably people are deciding that they have no further use for them and are selling them back to the manufacturer!

Finally, we return to the question of relationships between more than two variables which was mentioned briefly in the last chapter. It is, of course, very limiting to consider the effect of only one independent quantity on a dependent quantity; in most practical situations a whole host of variables may have an influence. The price of a house, for example, will depend on the number of bedrooms it has, whether it has a garden, where it is situated, what state of repair it is in . . . you can continue the list almost indefinitely.

It is possible to determine a linear relationship between a dependent quantity and many independent ones, in much the same way as we have fitted a regression line. The 'line' will be replaced by a plane if we are looking at the effect of 2 independent variables – in this case the 'scattergraph' could be drawn in 3-dimensional space. If there are more than 2 independent variables the equivalent of our line is a *hyperplane* – hard to visualise, but easy to express as an equation of the form $y = a_0 + a_1x_1 + a_2x_2 + \ldots$ The 'best' values for the $a$s in this equation can be determined, for a given set of data, by the same kind of least squares fitting we used to determine the best line in 2 dimensions. In this case, however, you would certainly need to use a computer package.

We will therefore be looking again at the ideas of multiple regression in the next section.

## ◩ REGRESSION WITH MINITAB AND LOTUS

### MINITAB

If you have the data which you wish to analyse stored as a MINITAB worksheet in which the $y$-values are in C2 and the $x$-values in C1, you can get the regression line (and, as we will see, a lot of other information) by typing the command

MTB⟩ REGRESS C2 ON 1 C1

The function of the 1 in this command is to indicate that you are only regressing $y$ on a single $x$-variable – that is, you're doing a *bivariate* (two variables) and not a multiple regression.

Below you will find the results of this command applied to the sales/outlets data. Number of outlets (the $x$-variable) has been stored in the column named 'OUT', and sales, the $y$-variable, in 'SALES'.

MTB ⟩ regr 'sales' on 1 'out'

The regression equation is
SALES = − 4.91 + 0.285 OUT

| Predictor | Coef | Stdev | t-ratio | p |
|---|---|---|---|---|
| Constant | − 4.912 | 2.335 | − 2.10 | 0.073 |
| OUT | 0.28531 | 0.03787 | 7.53 | 0.000 |

s = 1.383    R-sq = 89.0%    R-sq(adj) = 87.5%

Analysis of Variance

| SOURCE | DF | SS | MS | F | p |
|--------|----|----|----|----|----|
| Regression | 1 | 108.61 | 108.61 | 56.77 | 0.000 |
| Error | 7 | 13.39 | 1.91 | | |
| Total | 8 | 122.00 | | | |

MINITAB provides the regression equation in an easily understandable form, using the names of the variables. You can check that the coefficients in the equation are exactly the same as those we found by hand calculation. But we are also provided with a great deal more useful information, the interpretation of which is as follows.

1 Just below the equation is a table which, for the constant term in the equation and the coefficient of OUT, tells us the standard deviation of the coefficient, the associated $t$-value, and the corresponding probability level $p$. For example, the constant term is $-4.912$ as you know very well by now, but because this is only an estimate based on a sample of 9 values, it has, like any other sample statistic, a standard error. This is what is meant by the standard deviation 2.335.

Using this information we can test the hypothesis that the coefficient in question is in fact zero. Suppose that we want to test the hypothesis: constant term, $a = 0$, against the alternative $a \neq 0$. Then we calculate $t$ in the usual way, just as for our tests on means and proportions in Chapter 11: $t = $ (sample value – population value)/s.d.

$$= (-4.912 - 0)/2.333 = -2.10,$$

which MINITAB has in fact already done for us. Now we need to find whether this is significant or not; MINITAB computes the probability associated with this value of $t$ from a $t$-distribution (with $n - 2 = 7$ degrees of freedom in this case), and prints it as a $p$-value of 0.073. If we are testing at 5 per cent significance as usual, then this result is not significant, since it's greater than 0.05. So we've no reason to reject the null hypothesis: the constant term is not significantly different from zero.

What this means in practical terms is that the *true* line (the one for the whole population) could very well pass through the origin – which is quite reasonable when you think about it, implying 'no visits, no sales'. If you look at the $p$-value for the coefficient of OUT, on the other hand, you can see that it is zero, showing that the probability associated with this coefficient is so small that it doesn't even show up to three-figure accuracy. So it's certainly going to be much smaller than 0.05, suggesting that the coefficient of OUT is very significantly different from zero. This shouldn't come as any great surprise; it merely confirms in another form what we've already deduced from the correlation – that OUT is strongly associated with SALES.

2 The next thing to look at is the line giving values of $s$, R-sq and R-sq (adj). The $s$ is the standard deviation of the points around the regression line, so the bigger it is, the more scattered they are. However, we *can't* just use $s$ as it stands to get confidence limits around the line, for the reasons already explained in the previous section.

R-sq stands for R squared, and is nothing more than the square of the correlation coefficient (expressed as a percentage). You can check by taking the square root that it does indeed agree with the Pearson's coefficient we computed in Chapter 12. But R-sq has another useful interpretation – it tells us what percentage of the variation in our $y$-variable is explained by changes in $x$. Here we could say that 89 per cent of variations in sales are explained by differences in the numbers of outlets visited by salesmen. Clearly the nearer this figure is to 100 per cent, the better the fit of our regression equation – 100 per cent would represent a perfectly-fitting line.

R-sq (adj) means 'R-squared adjusted', and is a refined version of R-sq which allows for the fact that actually R itself has a small positive bias, so tends to overestimate the strength of the $x/y$ relationship. Technically it is therefore safer to use the adjusted value, though often there is little difference between the two figures.

3 Finally, you'll see a table headed 'Analysis of Variance'. We won't go into details on the interpretation of this table, since it requires knowledge of a new distribution called the F-distribution which we haven't covered. Suffice it to say that if the $p$-value at the end of this table is small, then again we have an indication that the relationship represented by our equation is a significant one.

MINITAB offers a further useful facility, namely the ability to obtain predicted $y$-values for given $x$s. This is done by including the subcommand

SUBC⟩PREDICT K.

in the regression command, K being the value of $x$ for which you want to predict $y$ (you can actually have lots of $x$s stored in a column if you wish – see MINITAB HELP or reference (15) in Suggestions for Further Reading in Appendix 1 for details). If I want to predict sales for a salesman who visits 53 outlets, I therefore type

MTB⟩ REGRESS 'SALES' ON 1 'OUT';
SUBC⟩ PREDICT 53.

In addition to all the information from the main REGRESS command, I now also get the output shown below.

| Fit | Stdev.Fit | 95% C.I. | 95% P.I. |
|---|---|---|---|
| 10.209 | 0.540 | ( 8.931, 11.488) | ( 6.697, 13.722) |

This tells us that the predicted sales for someone visiting 53 outlets are 10.209, with a standard deviation of 0.54. We also get a 95 per cent confidence interval (8.931 to 11.488), which tells us the range in which the *average* sales for someone visiting 53 outlets could be expected to lie; and a 95 per cent *prediction* interval (6.697 to 13.722), which is much wider since it indicates the range in which the sales of an *individual* person visiting 53 outlets might lie. These intervals aren't too wide, because we are interpolating here – 53 lies comfortably within the range of the original data. Contrast this with what we get if we try to predict for a salesman visiting 32 outlets – a much smaller number than anyone in the sample actually visited:

| Fit | Stdev.Fit | 95% C.I. | 95% P.I. |
|---|---|---|---|
| 4.218 | 1.172 | ( 1.447, 6.989) | ( −0.070, 8.505) X |

X denotes a row with X values away from the center

Not only is the standard deviation bigger, and the intervals correspondingly wider, but MINITAB actually warns us that the $x$-value we're trying to predict from is a long way from the centre of the data (or center, since it's an American program!). The changing size of the confidence and prediction intervals really explains the picture we drew in Fig. 13.6.

There is a great deal more information obtainable from MINITAB's regression procedures; if you want to know more, consult reference (15) or explore with the aid of the HELP function. One further feature worth mentioning is the ability to carry out multiple as well as bivariate regression. Suppose, for example, that we had information on salesmen's years of experience as well as the numbers of outlets they visited, and we suspected, quite reasonably, that both of these variables might influence their sales. Then if we put the experience data into a column called 'YEARS', the command

MTB 〉 REGRESS 'SALES' ON 2 'OUT' 'YEARS'

will get us an equation of the form

sales = $b0 + b1 \times$ out $+ b2 \times$ years

where $b0$, $b1$ and $b2$ are coefficients. We also get all the associated information discussed above. The only change is that we now need a 2 in the regression command line to indicate that there are 2 $x$-variables, not just one.

## LOTUS

Regression in LOTUS is much more primitive than in MINITAB, since it isn't a dedicated statistical package. The sequence of commands for obtaining a regression is quite simple: type / DATA REGRESSION, after which you will be prompted to specify the range of values for $x$ and for $y$, together with an output range. Make sure your output range is in a part of your worksheet well clear of any other figures, otherwise you may find you have overwritten something important!

The results from doing this with the sales/outlets data are shown below; as you can see, compared with MINITAB the regression equation is of a rather 'do-it-yourself' form, since you get the constant and (some distance below) the $x$-coefficient, but not the actual equation.

Regression Output:

| | |
|---|---:|
| Constant | − 4.91205 |
| Std Err of Y Est | 1.383167 |
| R Squared | 0.890228 |
| No. of Observations | 9 |
| Degrees of Freedom | 7 |

| | |
|---|---|
| X Coefficient(s) | 0.285309 |
| Std Err of Coef. | 0.037866 |

The coefficients are the ones which by now you are beginning to know by heart; you also get the standard error of the $x$-coefficient – but *not* the $t$- or $p$-values; if you want to do a $t$-test you have to carry out the computations yourself, and look up the $t$-tables. No standard error is given for the constant term; the 'standard error of $y$-est' is the standard deviation of the $y$s around the line, equivalent to MINITAB's $s$. R-squared is provided, though not as a percentage, and for good measure we are told that there were 9 observations and therefore the degrees of freedom are 7 ($n - 2$) – useful for looking up $t$-tables.

Where LOTUS has the edge is that it is very easy to plot a scattergraph of the data and the fitted regression line, using the GRAPH command. To fit the line, all you need do is enter the formula for the regression equation into a cell of the worksheet, addressing the first value in the $x$-column, and then copy this formula down the column to get a full set of predicted $y$s. You will find an example of this using the sales/outlets data, together with the graph which resulted, in the worksheet REG.WK1 on the diskette.

If you want to do a multiple regression with LOTUS, you need to have your $x$s in adjacent columns, so that when asked to specify the $x$-range you can highlight a whole set of $x$s instead of just one. In this case, too, the width of the output will be greater, so again you need to ensure you have room for it when you specify the output range.

Regression is an enormous subject − whole books have been written devoted to this single topic, and we have only been able to look at a small part of the theory. If you would like to read more, particularly about multiple regression, reference (7) in the Suggestions for Further Reading in Appendix 1 covers the topic very thoroughly.

## FORECASTING THE FUTURE: WHEN CAN WE DO IT?

At first sight, any attempt at forecasting sales − or for that matter, birth-rates, population figures or any other variable you care to think of − for future periods of time might seem to be a hopeless exercise. We cannot see into the future, so we have no way of anticipating social and economic changes which may drastically alter presently-established patterns. What can happen when forecasts *do* go wrong is shown rather dramatically in Fig. 13.8 which illustrates the official forecasts of numbers of births, together with the actual figures over a thirty-year period. The discrepancy between what was expected to happen and what actually did happen, explains among other things why we now have such a surplus of schoolteachers. The government planned the numbers of teachers to be trained on the assumption that there'd be far more children to be educated than has turned out to be the case.

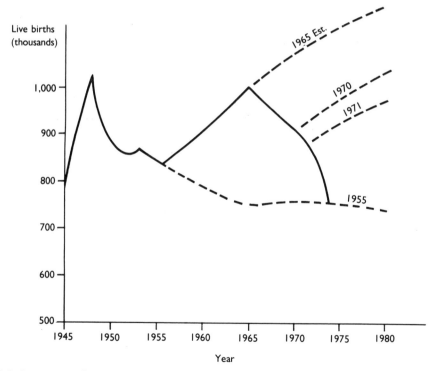

**Fig. 13.8** Government forecasts of live births in 1980

We shouldn't, however, be too quick to ridicule the government statisticians who produced these forecasts. After all, forecasting the value of a variable twenty-five years into the future is a pretty tall order, especially when the variable in question is one so susceptible to many influencing factors as the birth-rate. For most of their forecasts, they seem to have followed the fairly sensible course of assuming that the current trend would continue, at least for a while. Given that the government *must* have some data with which to plan, the estimates obtained in this way are at least slightly more soundly-based than would be figures arrived at by sticking a pin in a list of random numbers!

Certainly the forecasting of birth-rates must be a good deal easier in Third World countries where the 'natural rate of growth' of the population is not interfered with so much. In such cases we might expect a steady percentage rate of growth to be maintained – and this is an example of one forecasting situation where there is a method available which can give quite reliable forecasts fairly easily. Nor is its usefulness confined to questions of population; an expanding company, for instance, might show a steady percentage growth in turnover over a period of years, in which case we could make use of that fact in estimating future turnovers.

Many forecasting problems in business are a question of getting estimates for a few weeks or months, rather than years, ahead. In such cases there may be a discernible pattern to the figures for the *past* few weeks or months, which we might reasonably expect to persist, at least for a short time into the future. If such a pattern is observable, again there are well-established methods for making use of it to make predictions.

Finally, we should not forget that the method of fitting a regression line to data which shows a definite straight-line tendency can always be used even if one of the variables happens to be time. Figure 13.9, for example, shows the set of points obtained by plotting the numbers of employees taken on by a new company during its first five years of operation. There is a clear straight-line pattern here, and so fitting a regression line, using time as $x$ and numbers of employees as $y$, would give a good basis for forecasting labour requirements at least for a year or two. Do remember, though, that if the years of

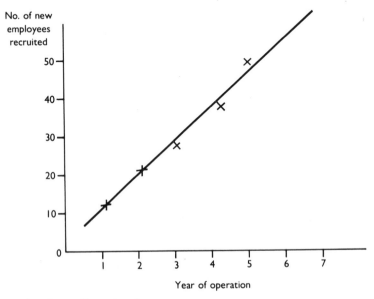

**Fig. 13.9** Forecasting from a linear trend

operation were given as 1983, 1984, ... there is no need to use these as your *x*-value — the calculation is greatly simplified by numbering them off as 1, 2, 3, ...

## FORECASTING A STEADY PERCENTAGE GROWTH

Imagine that inflation could be held by the government to a steady rate of ten per cent per annum; then if the price of an item which cost £1 in 1982 were followed up over the next five years, its subsequent prices would be:

|      |                            |
|------|----------------------------|
| 1987 | 100p                       |
| 1988 | 110p                       |
| 1989 | 121p                       |
| 1990 | 133.1p    = 133p approx.   |
| 1991 | 146.41p   = 146p approx.   |
| 1992 | 161.051p = 161p approx.    |

Although the *rate* of increase is a steady 10 per cent per year, the *amounts* of the increase are larger each year, and the same would apply no matter what the rate of increase we assume. (This, as we will see in Chapter 15, is the basic principle of compound interest.) So if the prices were plotted against time on a graph, the result would be a curve which climbs more and more steeply as time goes on, as you can see in Fig. 13.10.

It isn't easy to continue the line of this curve in order to obtain a forecast of the price of the item in 1993. Of course, in the present example that doesn't matter too much, since we know the percentage rate of increase is 10 per cent per year, and so we could go ahead and calculate the price in 1993 without reference to the graph. But now suppose we have a situation where we *suspect* a steady, or approximately steady, percentage rate of increase, but don't know exactly what that rate is. How, then, could we first confirm our suspicion and then obtain a reasonably accurate forecast?

As we've just seen, plotting the figures on an ordinary graph won't be much help, since

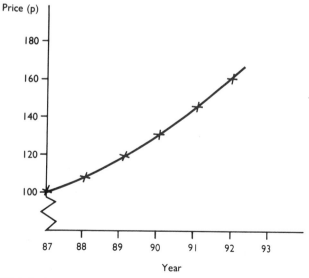

**Fig. 13.10** Steady 10% inflation

it's practically impossible to distinguish by eye a curve showing a steady percentage growth from any other type of curve. If, however, we could somehow arrange a type of graph in which steady growth, and no other kind of increase, gave a straight line, we would be in a much more hopeful position, straight lines being, as we know, really the only shape of graph which can be recognised with certainty.

At the mention of the word 'logarithm' you may blench; perhaps you thought that logarithms had been rendered obsolete by the advent of calculators. But don't worry – you don't need to remember anything about them to understand what follows, and even if you've never used them you shouldn't have any problem following the argument.

If, then, we take the logarithms of the prices of the item mentioned above, whose cost is going up by 10 per cent a year, the result is:

| Year | Price (p) | Logarithm of price | Increase in logarithm |
|------|-----------|--------------------|-----------------------|
| 1987 | 100 | 2.0000 | – |
| 1988 | 110 | 2.0414 | 0.0414 |
| 1989 | 121 | 2.0828 | 0.0414 |
| 1990 | 133 | 2.1239 | 0.0411 |
| 1991 | 146 | 2.1644 | 0.0405 |
| 1992 | 161 | 2.2068 | 0.0424 |

So apparently when the price increases by a constant *percentage* each year, the logarithm of the price increases by a constant *amount* (the slight variations above are caused by a rounding off of the prices). For those of you who remember something about logarithms, the reason for this is that a rate of increase of 10 per cent per year corresponds to multiplication of the previous year's price by 110 per cent, and as multiplication of numbers means addition of their logs, we are simply adding the log of 110/100 each year.

Thus, if the logs of the prices were to be plotted on a graph, the result would be a straight line, rising by equal amounts as it does each year. The prospect of plotting such a graph is not, however, very appealing, since it would involve first looking up the logs, then plotting nasty four-figure decimals, which would be difficult to do accurately.

Fortunately, it isn't necessary to go to such lengths. With the assistance of a special type of graph paper, straight-line graphs showing steady percentage rates of increase can be plotted quite easily without knowing anything about logs at all. The graph paper in question is usually known as semi-logarithmic (semi-log for short) paper, since it has a 'logarithmic' scale on one axis, and an ordinary 'linear' scale (where equal distances correspond to equal amounts of increase) on the other.

Figure 13.11 shows the data on the inflating price plotted on such a graph. As you can see, the vertical scale is not equally spaced, but has lines which are closer together towards the top of the graph. You can also see that there is a scale ready-printed on the vertical axis, and if you take a ruler and measure the distances, you can confirm that the distance from 2 to 4 is the same as that from 3 to 6 or 5 to 10 – in other words, the scale is such that equal *ratios* correspond to equal distances, which is just what we need to turn our steady rate of increase data into a straight line. This means, though, that we don't have as much flexibility in choosing the scale we will use as we would with an ordinary linear graph. If we choose to take an arbitrary scale on the vertical axis, we run the risk of spoiling this 'equal ratio/equal distances' property.

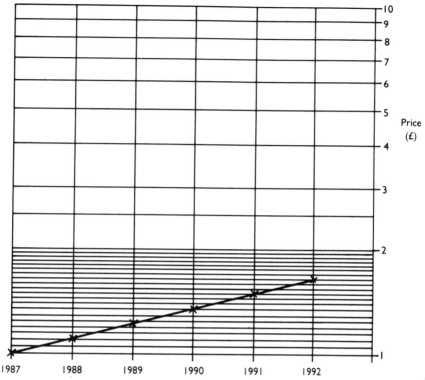

**Fig. 13.11** Semi-log graph showing 10% inflation

It's therefore safest if you remember that you are at liberty to multiply or divide the ready-printed figures by powers of ten, but not otherwise to alter them. For instance, in the case of our price data it is convenient to add two zeros to the scale, starting from 100. This involves wasting a certain amount of the space on the graph, but that can't be helped. Naturally we choose to plot time on the linear, or horizontal scale, since we are considering equal time intervals of one year.

When actually plotting the points, some careful counting of spaces is needed, but if this is done correctly the resulting graph is a straight line, as you can see. So a steady rate of increase is represented by a straight, upward sloping line on the semi-log graph. If a steady rate of *decrease* were in operation, the resulting line would, of course, still be straight but would slope downwards.

## MORE USES FOR SEMI-LOG GRAPHS

The great strength of this type of graph is that it enables us to recognise whether a time-series of figures exhibits an approximately steady rate of increase, simply by plotting the data on a semi-log graph and seeing if it is an approximate straight line. If it is, then, without working out just *what* the rate of increase may be, we can obtain a forecast by continuing the straight line with a ruler.

For example, suppose that our old acquaintance Mr Newton has the following data relating to sales of a new line of pork pies during the first few months on the market:

| Month | Sales volume (100s of pies) |
| --- | --- |
| May | 50 |
| June | 54 |
| July | 57 |
| August | 61 |
| September | 66 |
| October | 70 |

If he wants to check that sales are increasing at a steady rate, all he need do is plot them on a graph like that in Fig. 13.12 and see that a straight line fits them well. Then, to get a forecast of sales volume in December, he continues the line for two more time periods and reads off the figure of approximately 8,000 sold.

Of course, all the warnings about extrapolation sounded in the section on calculating the regression line also apply here. The sales of this product are not going to go on climbing at the same rate for ever. Sooner or later they will level off, and at that stage the semi-log graph will cease to be a straight line. Until that happens, however, it is very useful as a tool for planning.

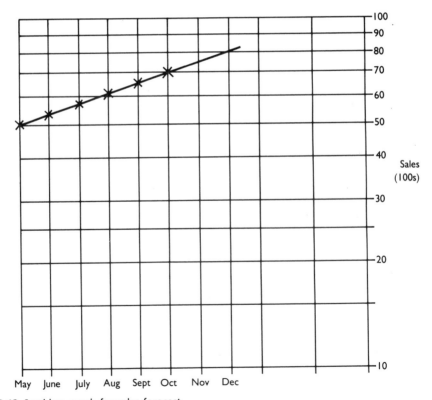

**Fig. 13.12** Semi-log graph for sales forecast

Semi-log graphs can also be used to compare two or more rates of change. This is particularly useful if the figures involved are of very different sizes. For example, suppose the turnovers of two competing firms, one large and one small, are as follows:

| Year | Megalithic (£ millions) | Minimal (£000s) |
|---|---|---|
| 1988 | 2.4 | 80 |
| 1989 | 2.7 | 92 |
| 1990 | 2.95 | 106 |
| 1991 | 3.28 | 122 |
| 1992 | 3.64 | 140 |

The fact that Megalithic's turnover is in millions of pounds, whereas Minimal's is only in thousands, makes direct comparison difficult, and plotting the two sets of figures on a single ordinary-scale graph would be awkward, since a scale which could accommodate Megalithic's figures would show Minimal's only in a very compressed form (*see* Fig. 13.13(*a*)). If, on the other hand, a semi-log graph like Fig. 13.13(*b*) is constructed, not only are the two sets of figures easy to accommodate but it becomes clear that, in spite of its smaller size, Minimal is actually expanding at a more rapid rate.

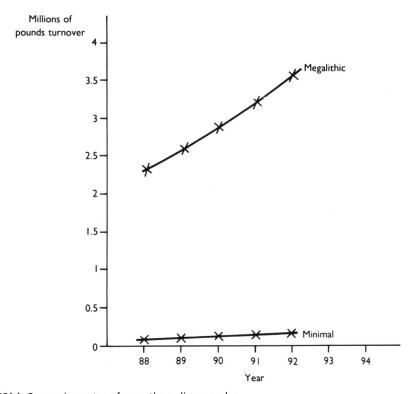

**Fig. 13.13(a)** Comparing rates of growth: ordinary scales

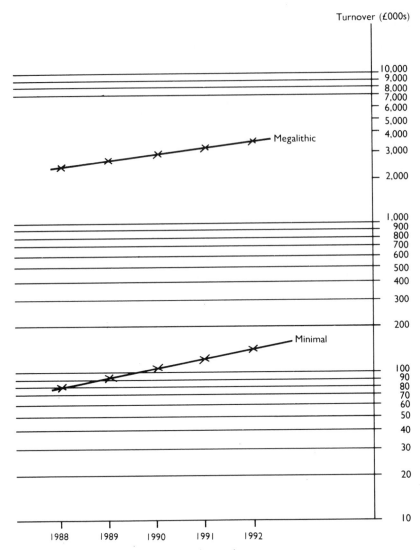

**Fig. 13.13(b)** Comparing rates of growth: semi-log scale

If we need to find the actual *rates* of expansion, the easiest way is simply to calculate the percentage change from year to year for each firm:

| Year | Megalithic | Minimal |
|------|-----------|---------|
| 1989 | $\dfrac{2.7}{2.4} \times 100 = 112.5\%$ | $\dfrac{92}{80} \times 100 = 115\%.$ |
| 1990 | $\dfrac{2.95}{2.7} \times 100 = 109.2\%$ | $\dfrac{106}{92} \times 100 = 115\%.$ |
| 1991 | 111% | 115%. |
| 1992 | 111% | 114.8%. |

a rate of expansion of about 11 per cent a year for Megalithic and 15 per cent a year for Minimal.

You've probably noticed that the graph in Fig. 13.13(*b*) shows several repetitions of the pattern of lines, whereas that in Fig. 13.12 shows only one. Semi-log paper is available in several different forms: that in Fig. 13.12 is called one-cycle paper, while that in Fig. 13.13(*b*) is three-cycle. The choice will depend on the range of the data which has to be accommodated on the graph, but however many cycles are used, the construction of the scale remains the same. In Fig. 13.13(*b*), for instance, since the first 'block' of the vertical axis has to represent 10,000 to 100,000 in order to cope with Minimal's earlier figures, the next must represent 100,000 to 1,000,000, so that the distance representing a factor of ten remains the same. Similarly, the top 'block' becomes 1,000,000 to 10,000,000.

You will find that logarithmic scales like the vertical scale of the semi-log paper are quite often used in government published statistics, not necessarily because a straight line graph results, but simply because a very wide range of figures have to be accommodated. Watch out for this kind of use, and don't fall into the trap of misinterpreting the graph because you haven't noticed the scale!

## ◘ LOGARITHMIC GRAPHS VIA LOTUS AND MINITAB

It's quite easy to plot semi-log graphs in either LOTUS or MINITAB. Suppose you want to plot the price inflation data discussed earlier:

| Year | Price |
|------|-------|
| 1987 | 100 |
| 1988 | 110 |
| 1989 | 121 |
| 1990 | 133 |
| 1991 | 146 |
| 1992 | 161 |

Whichever software we are using, we need to obtain the logs of the prices before plotting the graph. In MINITAB, this is done via the command:

MTB ⟩ LOG C2 C3

if the prices are stored in column C2. We can then plot C3, the log of the price, against C1, the year, and obtain a straight line.

Likewise in LOTUS, we can use the function @LN to find the logs of the cells containing the prices; once again plotting shows the straight-line relationship. The only problem is that, in either case, the scale shown on the vertical axis will be in logarithmic form, so if we read an approximate value off this scale to get a forecast, we then need to convert the resulting number back to an actual value by using the exponential function, which is the inverse of a log. This is obtained using the @EXP function in LOTUS, or EXP in MINITAB.

As an illustration, the graph obtained from LOTUS by this process is shown in Fig. 13.14.

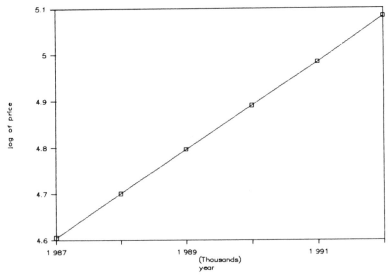

**Fig. 13.14** Log graph produced using LOTUS

## HOW FAR HAVE WE GOT?

The methods of this chapter have enabled us to find the equation of the 'best' straight line through a set of points, and such a line can then be used to obtain estimates, whether one of our variables is time (in which case the estimates are generally called forecasts) or some other quantity.

We've also looked at another way of obtaining straight line graphs – by plotting 'steady increase' data on semi-log paper. However, there are many situations in which we need to obtain forecasts, but where there is no possibility of using any kind of linear graph, because the data simply does not show that kind of pattern. It may exhibit a curved trend which is not of the 'steady rate of increase' type, or may show variations related to the time of year, or even vary in an apparently totally erratic way. We will be looking at two methods for dealing with these situations in the next chapter.

### Practical exercises

1. Refer to the data about age of pigs/consumption of Happihog in Chapter 12, Practical Exercise 3. From this data, obtain a regression equation suitable for predicting how much Happihog a 5 month old pig will eat in a week, and hence calculate the prediction.

2. A firm has costs and revenues as follows:

| Year | 1 | 2 | 3 | 4 | 5 | 6 | |
|------|----|----|----|-----|-----|-----|--------|
| Costs | 70 | 74 | 79 | 83 | 88 | 94 | (£000s) |
| Revenues | 90 | 94 | 97 | 101 | 105 | 109 | (£000s) |

Using semi-log graphs, confirm that, though both costs and revenues are increasing at an approximately steady rate, revenues will not keep pace with costs if the present trend continues, and find the year in which a loss will first be made. Do you think such a situation could arise in practice?

3 You receive the following memo from your sales manager:

'I got the quarterly figures of salesmen's performance through yesterday and I thought I'd see if there's any connection between how far they travel and how many sales they make, so I put them through our computer package that does correlations. While I was at it I thought I'd see if there's any evidence that they get better at making sales the longer they've been with us, so I tried that too. I must say I was pleased with that bit – apparently if they stay with us for six years they should be making about 51 sales a month! But I can't make sense of the other bits at all – could you interpret, please!'

The information enclosed with the memo is as follows:

| Salesman | Mileage month | No. of sales made | Time with company (months) |
|---|---|---|---|
| Smith | 256 | 27 | 32 |
| Adams | 462 | 8 | 6 |
| Williams | 322 | 34 | 36 |
| Green | 211 | 25 | 28 |
| Murphy | 153 | 18 | 8 |
| Evans | 186 | 23 | 12 |
| Newton | 372 | 38 | 50 |
| Halliday | 223 | 19 | 12 |

Correlation coefficient: time with company/no. of sales = 0.92. Regression equation for no. of sales on time with company is:

$$y = 11.35 + 0.55x.$$

Correlation coefficient: mileage/no. of sales = − 0.03. Regression equation for no. of sales on mileage is:

$$y = 24.72 − 0.003x.$$

Write notes to guide you in explaining to the sales manager what this information means, and how it should be interpreted in the light of the data.

4 Look up population figures for the last ten years or so for two developed countries (e.g. Britain and the USA) and two Third World countries (e.g. India and Brazil). Plot all the figures on a single semi-log graph, and hence compare the rates of growth of population in your four chosen countries. Suggest methods in each case for estimating the population of the country by the turn of the century.

5 Return to the data which you correlated in Chapter 12, Practical Exercise 6, and make use of your calculations from that problem to derive an appropriate regression equation. Use this equation to give a forecast which will be comparable with an actual published figure (one which wasn't used in your calculations). How much disagreement is there between the two, and what factors, neglected in your analysis, do you think might have caused the difference?

**6** ◪ Use the data in the file QUAL.MTW/QUAL.WK1/QUAL.DAT to examine the relationships between (*a*) gross takings and floor space (*b*) gross takings and number of sales staff (*c*) gross takings and both variables floor space and number of sales staff taken together. What can you conclude from your results? Can you think of a way to include the data about the location of the stores (street/precinct) in your analysis?

## Case study problem

Dear X,

Thanks for your prompt reply to last week's letter – I really should have given you a bit more background to my queries. What I want to know is, if I cut down my advertising to just the 5 issues of the evening paper on weekdays would it be a disaster? Or conversely, what if I went for every issue of both morning and evening papers – that's 12 altogether – but not the freesheet?

Quite a lot depends on getting this right, so fill me in on as much detail as possible – I think the figures I gave you last week give you all you need in the way of data.

In haste,

   Jane

## Case study question

Reply to this letter, paying particular attention to any assumptions or shortcomings which you think need mentioning.

## CHAPTER 14

# More about forecasting: time-series and exponential smoothing

## Objectives

Before starting work on this chapter, make sure you are happy with the basic ideas of graph plotting (Chapter 1, pp. 19–22 and Chapter 5, pp. 76–9. By the end of your work on this chapter, you should be able to:

(a) recognise and define components which may be present in a time-series;

(b) recognise a situation in which a moving average could be used to isolate the trend of a time-series, and calculate a moving average of suitable period;

(c) distinguish, by examining the graph of a time-series, when an additive or percentage-based approach to seasonal variations would be more suitable, and calculate the variations according to the method selected;

(d) make use of your analysis of a time series to obtain a forecast, and be aware of the considerations to be borne in mind when assessing the likely accuracy of such a forecast;

(e) recognise situations in which exponential smoothing would be a suitable forecasting method;

(f) carry out exponential smoothing calculations;

(g) suggest a suitable value of the smoothing constant for a given set of data;

(h) use the Mean Square Error as a measure of the quality of forecasts.

## THE AIRLINE MANAGER'S PROBLEM

In the last chapter we saw how a straight line graph could be fitted to a scatter of points, or to a set of values which increase at a steady percentage rate. However, there are many situations in which fitting a line will not tell us the whole story, and forecasting on the basis of such a fit might actually be downright misleading.

Consider, for example, the case of an airline which wishes to forecast demand for its flights over the four quarters of next year. If we have, say, four or five years' data on which to base our conclusions, we might well be able to see a linear trend in the figures, and we could fit a line by regression methods just as described in Chapter 13.

But what if the airline is expanding so rapidly that the trend is not a straight line, nor a 'steady rate of increase' curve, but some other kind of curve? What if the airline deals with many flights to holiday destinations, so that it is concerned not only to know the average amount by which demand for its flights is rising or falling in the long-term – which might be done by fitting a straight line – but also how much higher demand is in summer than in winter? What if there are other flights – perhaps to capital city destinations – for which demand does not show any particular seasonal behaviour, but moves up and down in a fairly haphazard sort of way?

None of these situations can be tackled by the methods of Chapter 13, and yet accurate forecasts will obviously be very important to a firm such as our airline. In this chapter we look at two further methods of forecasting which go some way towards coping with such problems.

## FORECASTING FROM A SHORT-TERM PATTERN

Although modern refrigerated storage and transport have made it perfectly safe for pork products to be eaten at any time of year, Mr Newton, our friend of the previous chapter, finds that many people still feel that it's not safe to eat pork pies in July. Accordingly, the sales of such products show quite a marked pattern of fluctuation from season to season. This pattern is particularly noticeable if the sales figures are plotted on a graph.

For one particular variety of pork pies, sales records broken down by quarters, are as shown:

| Year | Quarter | Number sold (00s) |
|------|---------|-------------------|
| 1990 | Spring | 142 |
| | Summer | 54 |
| | Autumn | 162 |
| | Winter | 206 |
| 1991 | Spring | 130 |
| | Summer | 50 |
| | Autumn | 174 |
| | Winter | 198 |
| 1992 | Spring | 126 |
| | Summer | 42 |
| | Autumn | 162 |
| | Winter | 186 |

We have already considered the graphs of such data briefly in Chapter 5, where we decided that the appropriate way to join the points of the graph is by straight lines, which bring out the pattern of the data. Figure 14.1 shows the graph of the time series above, and reveals the pattern we might have expected to find given the information about low summer sales.

But a closer examination of the graph tells us more than this. The most obvious feature is that, although the ups and downs from one quarter to the next tend to obscure the fact to some extent, there is a definite downwards movement apparent when the figures are considered overall. This general downward – or upward, or steady – behaviour of the figures is called their *trend*.

Superimposed on the trend is, of course, the seasonal behaviour already noted, which repeats itself in a regular way from year to year. Variations of this kind in a time series, which repeal themselves regularly over a fairly short term – less than a year, generally speaking – are called *seasonal variations*, though the name is perhaps unfortunate, as the pattern may repeat itself over a period much shorter than a year. The takings of a supermarket, for example will probably show a 'seasonal' pattern which repeats from one

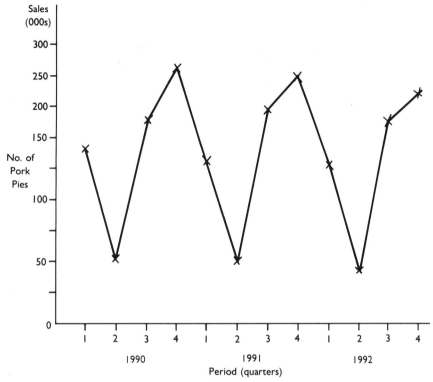

**Fig. 14.1** Time series graph for pork pie sales

week to the next – higher on Friday and Saturday, lower perhaps on Monday and Wednesday, average on the remaining two days. It is the repeating and predictable pattern which is important in deciding what we may call a 'seasonal' variation.

The seasonal pattern in Fig. 14.1 does *not*, however, continue entirely undisturbed; sales for the autumn quarter of 1990 do not pick up to the same extent as those for 1991 and 1992. This variation of the pattern is probably due to some *random* effect, such as sudden competition from a rival product, or exceptionally warm autumn weather causing housewives to continue feeling uneasy about the safety of buying pork pies well into this quarter. Other sources of random variation, in general, might be government intervention in an industry, a strike by workers, or a shortage of raw materials. Such variations are, of their very nature, unpredictable and may completely upset a carefully calculated forecast.

Conventionally, a fourth type of variation, called *cyclical*, is believed to influence many time series. This is a tendency, only apparent when the figures for quite a long period of time are examined, for an alternation of upward and downward movements to appear, roughly connected with periods of expansion and contraction in the economy. Although these cycles are a well-established fact in certain industries, in most circumstances it is not easy to establish their existence, let alone allow for them in forecasts. In any case, as they are a long-term phenomenon and we are only going to be making short-term forecasts, neglecting them should not lead to any serious errors. So we will simply regard them, if they exist at all in a particular case, as being included with the random variations. The term 'residual variations' is often used to refer to the combination of cyclical and random variations.

## EXTRACTING THE TREND

The two components of the time series which we can hope to identify and predict for the future are, then, the trend and the seasonal variation. We'll look at the trend first and will begin with a slightly smaller set of figures than the sales data above, and one which does not have the added complication of the large random variation noticed in the sales figure for the autumn quarter of 1986.

If you were simply presented with the data we are going to use as follows:

$$170, 140, 230, 176, 152, 233, 182, 161, 242$$

with no explanation as to what it represents or what the time periods involved are, your first step might well be to plot the figures on a graph (labelling the horizontal axis 'Period 1', 'Period 2', etc.) which would bring out clearly the fact you may already have noticed when examining the figures, that there is a marked pattern which repeats itself every three periods. The data may be taken to refer to the takings in some suitable units of a filling station during the three periods 8–12 noon, 12–4 p.m. and 4–8 p.m. over three days, with a tendency for higher takings during the morning and evening rush-hours than in the quieter mid-day period.

If we wish to start by extracting the trend of the figures, there are several ways we might go about it. If the trend on the graph appears to be reasonably close to a straight line, we could try fitting a regression line to the points. If it seems to be some sort of recognisable curve, then we could do worse than sketch it in by eye. But there is one well-established method for extracting the trend from a set of data like this with a strong repeating pattern, based on the following idea. One period of the data tends to be somewhat higher than average – in this case, the evening period. The afternoon period is lower than average, and the morning period is somewhere in between. If we take an average over three periods at a time, then the higher-than-average and lower-than-average figures should, roughly speaking, cancel each other, leaving an average for the three periods which is somewhere in between. This smoothing out of the 'seasonal' ups and downs is, of course, just what we require of a trend.

We *could* just take one average for each day's takings, which would give us the figures shown below:

|       |           |     | Average |
|-------|-----------|-----|---------|
| Day 1 | Morning   | 170 |         |
|       | Afternoon | 140 | 540/3 = 180 |
|       | Evening   | 230 |         |
| Day 2 | Morning   | 176 |         |
|       | Afternoon | 152 | 561/3 = 187 |
|       | Evening   | 233 |         |
| Day 3 | Morning   | 182 |         |
|       | Afternoon | 161 | 585/3 = 195 |
|       | Evening   | 242 |         |

Notice that the average for each day has been placed opposite the mid-point of that day – this is, the afternoon period.

This is all very well, but ideally we need a trend figure for *every* period, not just the afternoons, so that we have a basis for comparison from which we can say things like 'The morning of day 2 was so many units higher than average'. We can fill in the gaps in the set of averages above if we use, not just one average for each day, but what's called a *moving average*. The idea is very simple: we begin by working out the first average as shown in the calculation above – that's the average for the morning, afternoon and evening of day 1. But as soon as the figure for the morning of day 2 becomes available, we work out a *new* average which is obtained from the afternoon and evening of day 1 and the morning of day 2: $(140 + 230 + 176)/3 = 546/3 = 182$. And we continue in this way through the set of figures, so the next average would be $(230 + 176 + 152)/3 = 186$, and so on, always using the three most up-to-date figures.

Thus at each stage we are taking the average of a morning, an afternoon and an evening figure, but not always in that order. There's a quick way of doing this which may already have struck you, too. The first average was 180. To get the next one we dropped the 170 from the morning of day 2. The total will therefore go up by 6, and the average (when we divide by 3) by 2; so the next average should be 182, as indeed it is. (The only trouble with this method is that, if you make a mistake near the beginning of the column, it will affect all the subsequent figures, so it's as well to check at least the last average by straightforward addition and division.)

When this process is completed we have the set of moving averages shown below, which will provide our estimate of the trend of the data. Notice the gaps opposite the first and last figures of the actual data; these are inevitable; for unless we have data for day 0 and day 4, there is no way of calculating the averages at those points in time.

|       |   | Actual | Moving average = Trend |
|-------|---|--------|------------------------|
| Day 1 | M | 170    |                        |
|       | A | 140    | 180                    |
|       | E | 230    | 182                    |
| Day 2 | M | 176    | 186                    |
|       | A | 152    | 187                    |
|       | E | 233    | 189                    |
| Day 3 | M | 182    | 192                    |
|       | A | 161    | 195                    |
|       | E | 242    |                        |

If you look at Fig. 14.2 you can see how well this method of calculating the trend smooths out the peaks and troughs in the original data. The trend line is reasonably straight, too, certainly towards the later periods, so that continuing it to obtain some kind of forecast for the next few periods would not be too risky a process.

But the trend alone will not give us a very good forecast, since we have already seen that individual periods vary considerably around it. We need, therefore, to analyse the 'seasonal' fluctuations as well, in order to make allowance for them in our forecasts.

## ANALYSING THE SEASONAL VARIATIONS

As a preliminary step towards finding the seasonal variation for each of our three daily periods, we find out how much each period differs from the trend. In other words, we

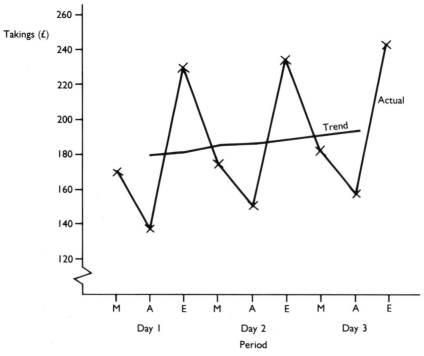

**Fig. 14.2** Trend of the filling station data

calculate Actual minus Trend for each period (except, of course, the first and last where we don't have a trend figure). The resulting figures are as follows:

|        |   | Actual – Trend |
|--------|---|----------------|
| Day 1  | M | –              |
|        | A | – 40           |
|        | E | 48             |
| Day 2  | M | – 10           |
|        | A | – 35           |
|        | E | 44             |
| Day 3  | M | – 10           |
|        | A | – 34           |
|        | E | –              |

If the process were not subject to any random influences, then we would expect the Actual – Trend figures for, say, all the afternoon periods to be the same. But because there *are* random effects at work, they are not quite the same, though they *are* similar in size and sign (– 40, – 35 and – 34). The same applies to the evening figures of 48 and 44; as it happens, in this case the morning figures actually are the same, both being – 10. Although of course we only have a small set of data here, and in practice one would need to use far more, you can already see the beginning of a regular pattern of signs in these Actual – Trend figures (morning and afternoon negative, evening positive). This reflects the pattern we observed in the original data, and if when you reach this stage in the analysis of a time series you find that more than a couple of figures fail to conform to this sign pattern you should rethink your calculations carefully – it may be that you have made an arithmetical error, or perhaps you have picked the wrong number of periods over which to average in the first place.

In order to eliminate as far as possible the random effects, what we do next is collect together the Actual – Trend figures corresponding to each period of the day and thus find out what the average variation is for each period:

|         | M     | A      | E   |
|---------|-------|--------|-----|
| Day 1   | –     | – 40   | 48  |
| Day 2   | – 10  | – 35   | 44  |
| Day 3   | – 10  | – 34   | –   |
| Total   | – 20  | – 109  | 92  |
| Average | – 10  | – 36   | 46  |

In the averaging, we had to divide the middle total by three, since three afternoon figures were available, but the morning and afternoon totals are for only two figures, so need only be divided by two. Notice, too, that the middle average should really be 36.33, but to avoid fractions it has been rounded to 36. This makes the total of the average variations $-10 - 36 + 46 = 0$, which is what we would expect if the trend really does pass 'through the middle' of the figures: variations above and below the trend cancel out. If by any chance this total differs slightly from zero, judicious rounding of the averages will usually adjust it sufficiently, as it has here. If the total is *very* different from zero, however, it may be another warning sign of faulty arithmetic or a bad choice of moving average.

We call the figures $-10$, $-36$ and 46 the *seasonal variations* for the morning, afternoon and evening periods. So we have now achieved our objective of isolating the trend and seasonal effects present in the time series. A knowledge of these seasonal effects is useful not only in forecasting, but in removing strong seasonal effects which may obscure other important movements in a set of data; see, for example, the government's 'de-seasonalised' unemployment figures.

Although a knowledge of the random variations is of no use in forecasting, these variations being essentially unpredictable, it is useful as a guide to the reliability of a forecast; a process on which, in the past, the random influences have been very small is likely to produce a reasonably reliable forecast. If, however, the time series is habitually subject to large random fluctuations, then our carefully calculated forecast may be completely upset by such a fluctuation.

So our final step in analysing the series, prior to obtaining a forecast, is to extract the random variations from the figures. Now a random variation is anything which isn't accounted for either by trend or by seasonal effects. So we start by working out what the figures would have been, if the trend and seasonal effects had operated in the absence of random influences. For the afternoon of day 1, we had a trend figure of 180; afternoons tend however to be 36 lower, on the whole, than the trend, which would reduce our figure to 144. What *actually* occurred was a value of 140, so some random effect reduced what we might have expected to occur by 4 units. We therefore say that the random variation in this period was $-4$.

Proceeding in a similar way with the rest of the figures, we find the following:

| | | | | | | | |
|---|---|---|---|---|---|---|---|
| Actual | 140 | 230 | 176 | 152 | 233 | 182 | 161 |
| Expected (trend + seasonal) | 144 | 228 | 176 | 151 | 235 | 182 | 159 |
| Random (actual – expected) | –4 | 2 | 0 | 1 | –2 | 0 | 2 |

So the random variations here are very small, the largest, –4, being only 4/180 or about 2 per cent of the corresponding trend figure. In other words, any forecast obtained from this analysis may be expected to be reasonably reliable. The data fits the 'pattern' of trend + seasonal variation pretty well.

## GETTING A FORECAST

You may have lost sight in all this arithmetic of what we originally set out to do – obtain a forecast for a few periods into the future. Suppose we specifically require a forecast of the figure for the afternoon of day 4. It will consist of two parts:

Forecast = trend for afternoon of day 4 + 'seasonal' adjustment for afternoon period.

How we extend the trend for a day beyond our original data depends very much on what it looks like when plotted on a graph. Had it shown a pronounced curve, we might do better by continuing the curve approximately and simply reading off the figure for the afternoon of day 4 from the graph; this would then have to be reduced by 36, the typical amount by which the afternoon period falls below the trend.

In the present case, however, inspection of the trend figures shows that, at least over the past few periods, it has risen by steps of 3 per period; so we may assume without too much inaccuracy that it will continue to do so for a few more periods. This would give 198 as the trend figure for the evening of day 3, 201 for the morning of day 4, and 204 for the afternoon of day 4. When adjusted downwards by the seasonal variation of 36, this produces a final forecast of 168, and inspection of the actual data shows that at least this is a credible figure, fitting in as it does with the general pattern.

Naturally, the further ahead we are forecasting, the less reliable will our forecasts be, based as they are upon the assumption that present trends will continue. But for a few periods ahead this assumption should be reasonably safe. As a rough rule of thumb, this method could be used to give figures for about one seasonal cycle ahead – for example, three periods in the case of the above data – with reasonable confidence.

## OTHER PATTERNS OF VARIATION

The seasonal variations in the example given in the previous section were analysed by regarding them simply as a constant amount added to or subtracted from the trend. Inspection of the graph of the original data (Fig. 14.2) shows that this is a reasonable assumption, since the seasonal peaks and troughs are indeed of roughly constant size.

It is quite conceivable, however – in fact, in many ways it is more likely in practice – that seasonal variations will *not* be constant, but will themselves vary as the trend increases or decreases, the seasonal peak above a high trend value being greater than that above a low one. Such a situation is illustrated in Fig. 14.3, where it is clear that the peaks and troughs are becoming less pronounced as the value of the trend declines. In this case it is probable that, rather than the seasonal variations being constant *amounts added* to the trend, they are constant *percentages multiplying* the trend. For this reason, the type of situation shown in Fig. 14.3 is often referred to as a *multiplicative model* time series, that in Fig. 14.2 and the corresponding analysis being known as an *additive model series*.

The only way to decide to which, if either, of these patterns a set of real-life data conforms, is to plot it on a graph and examine the seasonal variations. If this appears to be inconclusive, analysing the series by both methods and inspecting the resulting random variations may help. Remember that the smaller the random variations, the more closely does the series conform to the chosen pattern.

The actual analysis of a multiplicative model series does not differ greatly from that of the additive model discussed in the earlier section on analysing the seasonal variations, except that the seasonal variations are expressed as percentages of the trend figure for the period rather than as simple *differences* between actual and trend. Rather than go into the details of the analysis here I will guide those who need it through the process in Practical Exercise I at the end of the chapter.

Another problem which may have occurred to you is how we might decide what moving average to use in a case which was less cut-and-dried than the ones we have looked at – as most real-life examples would tend to be. One possibility is to try calculating several different moving averages, using perhaps three, four and five periods at a time, and choose the one which appears to 'smooth' the ups and downs of the data best. However, if it is really so difficult to decide what you should be doing because of the absence of any noticeable pattern in the data, it may be that the moving average method is not the

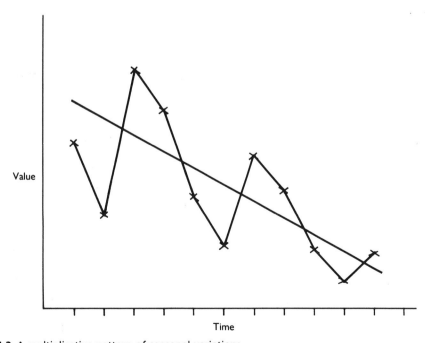

**Fig. 14.3** A multiplicative pattern of seasonal variations

best way of trying to get a forecast, and you should have resort either to a freehand graph or another technique, such as *exponential smoothing*, described later in this chapter.

## FORECASTING THE PORK PIE SALES FIGURES

Now that we have set up all the machinery for analysing a time series with a definite repeating seasonal pattern, let's go back to the data on pork pie sales mentioned earlier in this chapter and carry out a complete analysis and forecast, using the additive model.

Figure 14.1 shows the series to be of the additive pattern, since the summer 'low' and winter 'high' are roughly constant deviations from the trend, even though the trend itself is declining. The appropriate number of periods for the moving average is clearly four, and so the first moving average figure would be calculated as

$$\frac{142 + 54 + 162 + 206}{4} = 141.$$

When we come to write this figure down, however, we have a slight problem. It obviously belongs in the middle of the first year – but the middle of the first year comes half-way in between the summer and autumn quarters; the same thing will occur with all the other moving averages too. This means that are not directly comparable with the original figures, which is a nuisance when it comes to calculating the seasonal variations. So we have to insert an additional step, called *centring* the moving averages. Since the moving average 141 applies to a point half-way between the summer and autumn quarters of 1990, while the figure 138 applies midway between the autumn and winter quarters, we can obtain a moving average directly comparable with the autumn quarter by taking the mean of 141 and 138 – that is, 139.5. It is these *centred moving averages* which will represent the trend in this case and, of course, a similar procedure will be needed whenever we average over an even number of periods.

The calculation is then as shown:

| Actual | Moving average | Centred moving average (trend) | Actual minus trend | Trend plus seasonal | Random |
|---|---|---|---|---|---|
| 142 | | | | | |
| 54 | | | | | |
| | 141 | | | | |
| 162 | | 139.5 | 22.5 | 169.5 | 7.5 |
| | 138 | | | | |
| 206 | | 137.5 | 68.5 | 197.5 | 8.5 |
| | 137 | | | | |
| 130 | | 138.5 | −8.5 | 130.5 | −0.5 |
| | 140 | | | | |
| 50 | | 139.0 | −89.0 | 51.0 | −1.0 |
| | 138 | | | | |
| 174 | | 137.5 | 36.5 | 167.5 | 6.5 |
| | 137 | | | | |
| 198 | | 136.0 | 62.0 | 196.0 | 2.0 |
| | 135 | | | | |
| 126 | | 133.5 | 7.5 | 125.5 | 0.5 |
| | 132 | | | | |
| 42 | | 130.5 | −88.5 | 42.5 | −0.5 |
| | 129 | | | | |
| 162 | | | | | |
| 186 | | | | | |

|            | Spring | Summer  | Autumn | Winter |
|------------|--------|---------|--------|--------|
| 1990       | –      | –       | 22.5   | 68.5   |
| 1991       | – 8.5  | – 89.0  | 36.5   | 62.0   |
| 1992       | – 7.5  | – 88.5  | –      | –      |
| Total      | – 16   | – 177.5 | 59     | 130.5  |
| Average    | – 8    | – 88.25 | 29.5   | 65.25  |
| Rounded so as to add to zero | – 8 | 88 | 30 | 66 |

The greatest random variation is thus 8.5, which is only about 6 per cent of the corresponding trend value of 137.5, so the data fits our model pretty well, and would in fact be an even better fit if it were not slightly distorted by the presence of the exceptionally low figure of 162 for autumn 1990.

This 'odd' figure has caused the slight ups and downs apparent when the trend is plotted on Fig. 14.4. From summer, 1991 however, there has been a steady downward trend. In making a forecast from this trend, we adopt a slightly different approach to that used in the earlier section on analysing the seasonal variations, since there is no steady decrease evident from one period to another. We say that over the time from summer 1991 to the latest trend figure available – summer 1992 – the trend declined from 139 to 130.5; that is, over 4 quarters or one year its decrease was 8.5. Now in spring 1992 the trend value was 133.8, so if we assume that the annual decrease of 8.5 is going to persist at least for a while then we would expect the trend in spring 1993 to be 133.5 – 8.5, or 125. We must adjust this to allow for the fact that the spring quarter is, on average, 8 below trend, giving a final forecast of 125 – 8 = 117 for spring 1993.

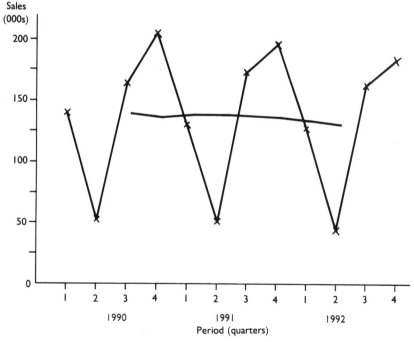

**Fig. 14.4** Trend of the pork pie data

How reliable is this figure likely to be? The method we have used to obtain it is based on the assumption that the trend and the seasonal pattern will persist – an assumption which clearly becomes less likely to be valid the further ahead we forecast. However, the small random variations evident here suggest that in the short-term the forecasts should be quite close to what actually occurs.

You may feel that all this is a great deal of work to arrive at a figure which, when all is said and done, can be little more than a hopeful approximation to what will actually happen. But the forecasts are not the only use of our analysis. The knowledge of seasonal variations in particular can be a very useful tool of control for the sales manager. In the absence of such knowledge, he might feel suicidal when the sales figure drops from 142 in spring 1990 to only 54 in summer 1990, not realising that this is a well-established yearly event. Equally, he might feel he could rest on his laurels when the figure leaps up to 206 in winter of that year, in blissful ignorance of the fact that this is only a temporary, seasonal reversal of a dangerous downward trend in the sales of his product which, to project our trend to its ultimate point, will become negative by about 2008. Perhaps by then we shall all be vegetarian!

## FORECASTING IN AN UNPREDICTABLE SITUATION

The two methods we have looked at so far for obtaining short-term forecasts have both depended on certain features being evident in the recent data on which our forecast is to be based. In the case of semi-log graphs, we needed to have a roughly steady rate of increase in the data, while to use time-series analysis, there had to be a repeating pattern of seasonal variations so that we could decide what moving average to use.

There are, however, many cases which do not conform to either of these patterns. Consider, for example, the following sales figures for another of our meat-producer's products, a high-quality beef sausage, which are given weekly over an 8-week period:

| Week no. | Sales (hundreds of pounds weight) |
|---|---|
| 1 | 45 |
| 2 | 40 |
| 3 | 38 |
| 4 | 46 |
| 5 | 46 |
| 6 | 42 |
| 7 | 36 |
| 8 | 41 |

You can see that here there is no obvious trend, no short-term pattern – in fact the best we can say is that the sales hover around the 4,200 mark, making unpredictable excursions to either side of this figure but not by very large amounts. Either of our previous methods is useless, and yet it is perfectly reasonable to ask how one might try to get a useful forecast of week 9's sales in week 8.

The method developed for use in such circumstances is very much in accordance with what you might do faced with this situation and armed only with your intuition. Suppose you, in the position of the sales manager of this company, were trying to make a forecast of week 2's sales at the point in time where all you know is that the week 1 sales were 4,500. In the absence of any other information, your best guess would have to be that the sales will stay the same; so your week 2 forecast would be 4,500 also. The position so far is therefore —

| Week no. | Actual sales | Forecast |
|---|---|---|
| 1 | 4500 | – |
| 23 | 4000 | 4500 |

You now wait until the actual sales figures for week 2 come in. These were, as we know from the table above, only 4,000, so your forecast of 4,500 has turned out to be 500 too high. Now most people's reaction to this would be to say, 'Ah, I overestimated last week, so this time I will compensate for that overestimate in making my forecast, and therefore reduce it somewhat from last week's level of 400'.

However, to compensate by the entire error you made last time — 500 in this case — is a little drastic; if you do that, you will end up with every week's forecast being merely the previous week's actual sales. Instead, what we do is allow for a *proportion* of the error we made last time. Expressed formally what we are saying is that

$$\text{new forecast} = \text{old forecast} + \text{proportion of error}$$

or

$$\text{new forecast} = \text{old forecast} + \alpha \times (\text{old actual} - \text{old forecast}),$$

where the Greek letter $\alpha$ (alpha) is used to represent the proportion of error we allow for. Of course, the choice of a value of $\alpha$ to use is very important, and we will look later at criteria for making this choice. For the time being, we choose fairly arbitrarily to use $\alpha = 0.3$; that is, we are allowing for 30 per cent of the error. Our week 3 forecast will then be

$$4,500 \text{ (week 2 forecast)} + 0.3 \times (4,000 - 4,500)$$
$$= 4,500 - 0.3 \times 500 = 4,350.$$

So the effect of this method of reaching the forecast is that, having overestimated on our last forecast by 500, we reduce the next one somewhat, but not by the full 500 — only by 30 per cent of it.

As usual there is no need to go into this detail once you have the idea of the method. The best way to lay out the calculation is in a table, as follows:

| Week no. | Actual | Forecast | Error (actual – forecast) | $\alpha \times$ error |
|---|---|---|---|---|
| 1 | 4,500 | – | – | – |
| 2 | 4,000 | 4,500 | – 500 | – 150 |
| 3 | 3,800 | 4,350 | – 550 | – 165 |
| 4 | 4,600 | 4,185 | 415 | 124.5 |
| 5 | 4,600 | 4,309.5 | 290.5 | 87.2 |
| 6 | 4,200 | 4,396.7 | – 196.7 | – 59 |
| 7 | 3,600 | 4,337.7 | – 737.7 | – 221.3 |
| 8 | 4,100 | 4,116.4 | – 16.4 | – 4.92 |
| 9 | – | 4,111.4 | | |

There are a number of points to note here. Whenever our last forecast was too high, the next one should be lower; whenever it was too low, the next one should be higher.

Remembering this should make sure you get the signs the right way around – the error is always Actual – Forecast. Another point on which newcomers to the technique are often confused is that the correction - the '$\alpha \times$ error' term – is always added to the last forecast, not to the actual figure. Finally, as you will discover when you try to follow through the steps of the construction of this table for yourself, decimal places proliferate at an alarming rate in this type of calculation, and you should round off to just a couple more figures than were in the original data to keep things under control.

The method of forecasting we have developed here is known as *exponential smoothing*, and the constant $\alpha$ is called the *smoothing constant*. The 'smoothing' part of this name is easy to understand, as a glance at the forecasts above will show – they are smoother than the actual figures, in the sense that they do not fluctuate by such large amounts. The 'exponential' bit is not quite so obvious; I will explain it here for those who are interested, but do not worry if you do not follow all the details of the argument.

We write $A_t$ to denote the Actual figure in period $t$, and similarly $F_t, E_t$, for that period's Forecast and Error. We then use $A_{t-1}, A_{t-2}$, and so on to denote the figures from one period back, two periods back, etc. Thus we can express the rule for obtaining a forecast in the form $F_t = F_{t-1} + \alpha (A_{t-1} - F_{t-1}) = \alpha A_{t-1} + (1 - \alpha)F_{t-1}$. However, since $F_{t-1} = \alpha A_{t-2} + (1 - \alpha)F_{t-2}$, we can substitute this to get

$$F_t = \alpha A_{t-1} + (1 - \alpha)[\alpha A_{t-2} + (1 - \alpha)F_{t-2}]$$
$$= \alpha [A_{t-1} + (1 - \alpha)A_{t-2}] + (1 - \alpha)^2 F_{t-2}.$$

You may like to do the next step, replacing $F_{t-2}$ by $A_{t-3} + (1 - \alpha)F_{t-3}$ and rearranging to get

$$F_t = \alpha [A_{t-1} + (1 - \alpha)A_{t-2} + (1 - \alpha)^2 A_{t-3}] + (1 - \alpha)F_{t-3}.$$

If we carry on like this, we find that all previous Actual values of the data are included in the forecast for time period $t$, but multiplied by higher powers of $(1 - \alpha)$ the further back we go. Since we are using an $\alpha$ between 0 and 1, $1 - \alpha$ will also be between 0 and 1, and so its powers get smaller and smaller (for example, with $\alpha = 0.3$, $\alpha^2 = 0.09$, $\alpha^3 = 0.027$, and so on).

The upshot of all this (and this is the part you should remember even if the previous discussion has left you behind) is that the importance, or *weight*, given to old Actual data gets smaller and smaller the older the data is. This, of course, is entirely sensible – up-to-date figures are surely more relevant, and should be given a bigger importance, than more out-of-date ones. The weights actually get exponentially smaller (they behave like powers of $(1 - \alpha)$), and it is from this that the technique gets the other half of its name. You can also see from this that the smaller the value of $\alpha$, the greater the weight given to older data, since the weights decrease like powers of $(1 - \alpha)$. We will be coming back to this point later.

You will also find this method referred to in some books as *exponentially weighted moving averages*, which ties it in with the last method we looked at. In the 'ordinary' moving average over, say, 4 quarters, each of the last four quarters' data is given a 'weight' of 1/4, while anything before then is completely ignored. So in some respects the present method is an improvement.

We still have to consider under what circumstances this method would be a suitable one to use, but before we address that question in the next section, you should try working through the exponential smoothing process described above using a value of $\alpha$ equal to 0.1, to make sure you have the basic idea clear.

## FEATURES OF EXPONENTIAL SMOOTHING

We began our discussion of this method with a set of data which varied apparently in a random way around a steady value – there was no trend and no apparent 'seasonal' pattern to the variations. The forecasts obtained by exponential smoothing with $\alpha = 0.3$ were certainly smoother than the actual data, and this smoothness is often a desirable feature in a set of forecasts. In the present case, by passing more or less through the 'middle' of the data, the forecasts ensure that over-estimates in one week will be compensated by under-estimates in another (though this is, perhaps, not very reassuring in the case of a highly perishable product where stocks not needed in one week cannot be carried forward to the next).

If you have performed the calculations with $\alpha = 0.1$ you will notice that the forecasts are even smoother. But we do not always want forecasts to exhibit this kind of smoothness. Suppose, for example, that due to a health scare about food poisoning from sausages, there is a sudden drop in the market for our product, so that sales are reduced to exactly 2,000 in each of weeks 9,10 and 11.

If you continue the series of forecasts started above, you should find that the forecasts for these three weeks would be, using our two values of 0.3 and 0.1, as shown:

| Week no. | Actual | $\alpha = 0.3$ | $\alpha = 0.1$ |
|---|---|---|---|
| 9 | 2,000 | 4,111.1 | 4,300.6 |
| 10 | 2,000 | 3,478.0 | 4,070.6 |
| 11 | 2,000 | 3,034.6 | 3,863.5 |
| 12 | – | 2,724.2 | 3,677.2 |

You can see that at this rate it will take the $\alpha = 0.1$ a lot longer to catch up with the drop in sales than the $\alpha = 0.3$ forecast – though even that is not brilliant. This is because with a higher value of $\alpha$, as explained in the last section, old data is given less weight, and therefore the new, changed situation carries proportionately more importance. The two extremes are, of course, $\alpha = 1$ where the next forecast is simply the last period's Actual figure, and $\alpha = 0$ where our initial forecast will never change at all. It seems, therefore that in a situation where sudden changes of this kind are the norm, a higher value of $\alpha$ might be preferable.

Now imagine that later in the year, sales pick up again in such a way that a steady trend appears – say the sales for weeks 22–26 are 2,200, 2,400, 2,600, 2,800, 3,000. How will each of our $\alpha$ values respond to this new factor? For simplicity we will assume that in each case we start with a totally accurate forecast.

Again, you should verify for yourself that the position will be:

| Week no. | Actual | $\alpha = 0.3$ | $\alpha = 0.1$ |
|---|---|---|---|
| 22 | 2,200 | 2,200 | 2,200 |
| 23 | 2,400 | 2,200 | 2,200 |
| 24 | 2,600 | 2,260 | 2,220 |
| 25 | 2,800 | 2,362 | 2,258 |
| 26 | 3,000 | 2,943.4 | 2,312.2 |

It is easy to see here that in both cases the forecasts are falling further and further behind the actual figures. It looks as if exponential smoothing, at least in this form, is not a suitable method to use when there is evidence of a trend in the actual figures.

You may be feeling that we are taking a rather piecemeal approach to the connected questions (*a*) what kind of situations can exponential smoothing cope with and (*b*) what are 'good' values of $\alpha$ to use in given circumstances? Would it not be better to establish a definite criterion for deciding when an $\alpha$ value is 'good'?

This criterion is provided by the *mean square error* (MSE), which is calculated in a way which may remind you of the standard deviation. We have already defined the error at any point in our forecasting exercise as Actual – Forecast. We find the mean square error at that point by squaring all the errors up to and including the present one, and dividing by the number of periods we have included in the adding-up process. For example, using weeks 22–26 and the $\alpha = 0.3$ forecasts worked out above:

| Week | Actual | Forecast | Error | $0.3 \times$ error | Error$^2$ | MSE |
|------|--------|----------|-------|-------------|-----------|-----|
| 22 | 2,200 | 2,200 | 0 | 0 | 0 | 0 |
| 23 | 2,400 | 2,200 | 200 | 60 | 4,000 | 2,000 |
| 24 | 2,600 | 2,260 | 340 | 102 | 115,600 | 39,866.67 |
| 25 | 2,800 | 2,362 | 438 | 131.4 | 191,844 | 77,861 |
| 26 | 3,000 | 2,493.4 | 506.6 | 152.0 | 256,643.56 | 113,617.51 |

Here the week 24 MSE is arrived at by taking $(0 + 4{,}000 + 115{,}600)/3$, and similarly for the others. You can see how the MSE confirms what, in this case, we had already noted – that the forecasts get worse as time goes on. The sign of good forecasts would be an MSE that stabilises as the forecasting proceeds. Roughly speaking it has been found that $\alpha$ values of between 0.1 and 0.3 generally perform best.

One final point: when starting our forecasting process in the present example, we chose to wait for a week and then use the first week's sales as the forecast for week 2. An alternative method of getting started is to use some ad hoc method to get a forecast for week 1 – perhaps by looking at advance orders, or by asking salesmen to give estimates based on their experience – and begin the forecasting process in the first week instead.

## ◧ SOFTWARE FOR FORECASTING

People who are seriously interested in forecasting tend to use software which is specifically designed for that purpose, but general-purpose packages such as LOTUS can also help. In fact both the decomposition method and exponential smoothing are well suited to spreadsheet implementation, since both involve repetitive calculations which can easily be carried out by copying suitable formulae down the necessary number of rows of the spreadsheet. Moreover, in exponential smoothing different value of alpha can be tried very quickly simply by changing the contents of one cell.

As an example, you will find a spreadsheet for the analysis of the pork-pie sales data stored under the name TS.WK1 on the diskette, and another which analyses the beef-sausage sales via exponential smoothing stored as ES.WK1. Explanatory notes about the contents of the cells are given with each spreadsheet; you should examine the various formulae carefully and ensure you follow what is going on. You can then modify the spreadsheets to tackle the Practical Exercises below.

If you are interested in learning more about forecasting using a spreadsheet, you might find reference (19) in Suggestions for Further Reading in Appendix 1 useful; it includes a diskette with forecasting software which, being based on LOTUS, is particularly easy for LOTUS-users to get used to.

Typing HELP COMMANDS while in MINITAB gives, as you probably know, a list of topics on which help is available. Among these is a whole section under the title of Time Series; however, the methods included under that heading are not those we have been discussing. MINITAB is not in fact particularly helpful for carrying out simple decomposition and smoothing.

## THE STORY CONTINUES...

You will have realised by now that exponential smoothing requires a good deal of tedious arithmetic – not difficult to carry out, but perhaps difficult to carry out accurately. It is, of course, an ideal candidate for computer implementation, and indeed there are many packages available which not only do the basic forecasting and enable the user to try different $\alpha$ values, but give the MSE and often incorporate more sophisticated versions of the method. Forecasting is a very large subject, and the simple methods we have looked at are merely a selection from an extensive range. However, if you have cause to use a package based on more advanced techniques, the work of this and the previous chapter should enable you to do so in an informed way.

## Practical exercises

1  Plot the following figures on a graph and confirm that they appear to fit the 'multiplicative' model of a time series:

$$22, 70, 40, 121, 196, 85, 220, 322, 130.$$

Calculate a three-period moving average in the usual way, and complete the analysis of the series by filling in columns under the following headings:

| Moving average (trend) | Actual minus trend | (Actual minus trend) as % of trend |
|---|---|---|

Hence confirm that the seasonal variations for the three periods are roughly 3 per cent above trend, S0 per cent above trend and 49 per cent below trend.

Also confirm by carrying out the ordinary 'additive' analysis that the additive model is *not* a good fit to the data, as it leads to very large random variations.

2  More published statistics! Lots of the data in the *Monthly Digest* is given quarterly, and some of these sets of data are suitable for analysis by moving average methods (for example, domestic gas or electricity consumption, production of home-grown cereals, passenger movements into the UK). Choose such a set of data and analyse it by the moving average method, rounding the figures if necessary to simplify calculations. Try to compare a forecast given by your analysis with what happened to the real figure at the same period. (You may be surprised to find that numbers of live births have a strongly seasonal behaviour, at least for England and Wales. Try them and see!)

## Case study problem

Dear X,

I take your point that the numbers of business enquiries which come in each week aren't likely to be closely related to advertising in local papers. But given that I can't think what else can be influencing them, and that they are hovering around the 20 a week mark, can you suggest any way we might try to forecast them? And if there is such a method, how would we spot if and when they start increasing steadily – as I hope they will during the Autumn? I remember what you said to me once about the dangers of continuing to use an out-of-date method of analysis!

Life is not quite so frantic now the children are back at school – we must meet for lunch when you are up here.

Best wishes,

Jane

## Cast study question

Draft your reply to this letter, using the data of the case study in Chapter 12.

## CHAPTER 15

# Allowing for interest: financial mathematics

## Objectives

Before starting work on this chapter, make sure you are happy with the following topics:

(a) the meaning of the notations $x^n$ and $x^{-n}$ (*see* Chapter 1, pp. 12–13);
(b) the method of working out powers of numbers on your calculator (refer to the instruction booklet if necessary);
(c) calculation of percentages (*see* Chapter 1, p. 11).

By the end of your work on this chapter you should be able to

(a) apply the compound interest method to problems such as the establishment of sinking funds;
(b) use discounting tables to solve problems involving annuities, hire purchase and mortgage repayments, etc.;
(c) compare and choose between different capital investment projects using discounting methods.

## THE MANAGEMENT ACCOUNTANT'S PROBLEM

The Paramount Manufacturing Company last year achieved a very satisfactory level of profits, and the Board has decided to retain part of these in order to finance the purchase of new machinery. There are two alternative machines, only one of which is to be purchased; one costs £3,900 and the other £4,000. At first sight, it would seem clear that they should, all other things being equal, buy the cheaper of the two – but *are* all other things equal? For instance, do the two machines operate at the same rate, and if not, what difference is there in the revenues which they may be expected to generate? To enable them to make a more informed decision, Paramount's Board has asked the firm's management accountant to carry out a detailed analysis of the results to be expected from the two machines.

His first step is to obtain an estimate of the amounts of saleable goods which will be produced by each of the machines – let's for convenience refer to them as Machine A, the dearer of the two, and Machine B. He then decides how much revenue is likely to be generated by the sale of these goods, and also, by talking to the firm's production engineers and others who have experience of the performance of similar machines, finds out what the running costs and the likely lifetimes of the two will be. Finally, he investigates the market for second-hand models of each machine.

His analysis is simplified by the discovery that both machines will only be used by the firm for three years. However, Machine A could then be resold for £500, whereas Machine B would simply be scrapped at no return to the company.

When running costs are taken into account, he finds that the revenues generated by the two are as follows:

|  | Machine A | Machine B |
|---|---|---|
| Year 1 | 2,000 | 1,500 |
| Year 2 | 2,500 | 2,500 |
| Year 3 | 1,000 | 2,000 |

So if we include the £500 resale value of Machine A, then the returns for the two machines are exactly the same, both being equal to £6,000. Surely the management accountant should therefore recommend the purchase of the cheaper machine?

This conclusion would be quite reasonable if he knew that the purchase price of the machine would simply be taken out of an old tin trunk under the managing director's bed, to which the profits would in due course be returned. But this is most unlikely to be the case. Much of the capital required to finance the purchase of the machine may need to be borrowed, in which case interest will certainly be charged on the loan by the lender. Even if the firm can finance the purchase from existing capital such as retained profits, it must consider the possibility that the money could be put to better use elsewhere – for example, left to earn interest in a bank deposit or other investment account, rather than used to buy either of the machines.

It therefore becomes clear that to make a fair comparison of two capital projects such as these at a less than superficial level, a knowledge of the workings of interest is required. So, leaving Paramount Manufacturing's problems to be re-examined later in the Chapter, we will begin with the basics.

## THE FUNDAMENTALS OF COMPOUND INTEREST

Many readers will already be familiar with the difference between simple and compound interest, but for those who are not we will give a brief definition of the two. Interest is said to be *simple* if it is withdrawn at the end of each interest period – that is, monthly, annually or whatever – so that the value of the investment remains the same no matter how long the period for which it is invested. With *compound* interest, on the other hand, the interest is added to the investment at the end of each period – that is, is *compounded* – so that the value of the investment increases steadily. Suppose, for example, that £100 is invested at a rate of 10 per cent per annum for five years. By the end of the first year it will have attracted £10 in interest, so that the initial investment for year 2 is £110. The interest for the second year will therefore be 10 per cent of £110, which is £11, giving a balance of £121 at the start of year 3. If you continue the process you will find that by the end of year 3 the amount will be £133.10, increasing to £146.41 by the end of year 4 and £161.05 by the end of year 5.

The actual amounts by which the total increases are, of course, getting larger as time goes on. In fact, those of you who have read Chapter 13 will probably recognise this as a situation in which year-end totals, if plotted against time on a semi-logarithmic graph, would give a straight line. But although it was easy enough to work year-by-year in this particular case, because the percentage chosen was an easy one, in general the year-by-year approach will be very inefficient. Imagine, for instance, trying to work in this way if we wanted to find how much an investment of £2,427 would amount to if invested for 25 years at an annual rate of $17\frac{1}{2}$ per cent! As we aren't interested in the intermediate figures for each year, but only in the final amount, and as $17\frac{1}{2}$ per cent isn't a particularly nice quantity to calculate 25 times over, what we need is a way of going direct to the final figure without having to do the calculations for all the in-between years.

To discover what this direct route to the answer is, let's return to our easy problem of £100 invested at 10 per cent per annum for 5 years and re-do it in what will undoubtedly seem a very long-winded manner, for which, however, a reason will become apparent. By the end of the first year our original £100 has increased to:

£100 + 10% of £100

or £100 + 0.1 × £100, since 10% as a decimal is 0.1,

or £100 (1 + 0.1), taking out the £100 as a common factor.

This is the amount with which we start the second year of the investment, so by the end of that year we have:

£100 (1 + 0.1) + 10% of £100 (1 + 0.1)

or £100 (1 + 0.1) + 0.1 × £100 (1 + 0.1)

or £100 (1 + 0.1)(1 + 0.1), taking out £100 (1 + 0.1) as a common factor

or £100 $(1 + 0.1)^2$.

Similarly, by the end of year 3 we will have:

£100 $(1 + 0.1)^2$ + 10% of £100 $(1 + 0.1)^2$

or £100 $(1 + 0.1)^2$ + 0.1 × £100 $(1 + 0.1)^2$

or £100 $(1 + 0.1)^2(1 + 0.1)$

or £100 $(1 + 0.1)^3$.

You should now be able to see a pattern emerging. Every year the starting amount gets multiplied by another factor of (1 + 0.1), the 1 corresponding to the fact that the initial amount is still there at the end of the year, and the 0.1 to the 10 per cent interest which has been added during the year. So by the time our money has been invested for 5 years, the original £100 will have been multiplied by this factor 5 times, and the final amount in the account will therefore be £100 $(1 + 0.1)^5$. It isn't too difficult to work this out with a calculator, making use of the 'constant multiplier' facility to save putting the factor (1 + 0.1) in via the keyboard 5 times, or using the $x^n$ key if your calculator has one. The final amount at the end of the five years is £161.05, just as we already found using step-by-step methods.

We can generalise this to apply to any starting amount, invested for any number of years at any rate of interest, if we introduce a bit of notation. The usual name for the starting sum is the *principal*, written P; we will call the percentage rate $r$ per time period (month, half-year, etc.), and suppose that the investment is left for $n$ time periods. Then, the final sum in the investment is called the *amount*, written A, and since the initial amount will be multiplied by a factor of $(1 + r/100)$ for each time period which elapses, the final value of the investment will be:

$$A = P(1 + r/100)^n.$$

This is the basic compound interest formula, which enables us to calculate the value of an investment at any time in the future if we know the rate of interest earned; I would advise you to commit it to memory. (You will sometimes find it written on the assumption that the rate is already expressed as a decimal R, in the form $A = P(1 + R)^n$.)

## APPLICATIONS OF THE COMPOUND INTEREST FORMULA

We will now examine some of the uses to which the basic result derived in the previous section can be put. You may encounter in other textbooks a variety of formulae obtained from that fundamental result, for applications such as sinking funds, regular savings, and so on; but as the 'formula' approach means that you not only have to commit the various formulae themselves to memory, but also to remember in what context each is applicable, I would recommend just learning the basic result, and then applying that from first principles in each case, as will be illustrated in the following examples.

(*a*)   Your parents invest £200 in your name on your 18th birthday, to be paid to you on your 21st birthday, together with interest earned at $12\frac{1}{2}$ per cent per annum. How much will you receive?

In the notation of the previous section, P = £200, $r = 12.5$, and $n = 3$, so the amount at the end of the three years will be:

$$A = 200(1 + 12.5/100)^3 = 200(1 + 0.125)^3$$
$$= 200 \times 1.125^3 = £284.77.$$

(*b*)   You decide not to withdraw the money from the account described in (*a*), but to leave it there and to add £50 per year to the investment, making the first payment on your 21st birthday. How much will there be in the account by the eve of your 25th birthday, assuming that the rate of interest remains the same?

There are two ways we could proceed with this calculation, and not a great deal to choose between them. We could operate on a year-by-year basis, saying:

| | |
|---|---|
| Amount invested on 21st birthday | = £284.77 + £50 |
| | = £334.77 |
| Interest for year 21–22 | = £  41.85($12\frac{1}{2}$% of £334.77) |
| Payment on 22nd birthday | = £  50.00 |
| Amount invested on 22nd birthday | = £426.62 |
| Interest for year 22–23 | = £  53.33 |
| Payment on 23rd birthday | = £  50.00 |
| Amount invested on 23rd birthday | = £529.94 |
| Interest for year 23–24 | = £  66.24 |
| Payment on 24th birthday | = £  50.00 |
| Amount invested on 24th birthday | = £646.19 |
| Interest for year 24–25 | = £  80.77 |
| Amount invested on eve of 25th birthday | = £726.96 |

Alternatively, we could deal with each year's investment separately, and make use of the formula again, thus:

From 21st to 25th birthday is 4 years, so the £284.77 already in the account will be there for another 4 years, together with the £50 you put in on your 21st birthday. That is, we have a principal of £334.77 invested for 4 years at $12\frac{1}{2}$ per cent per annum giving:

$$\begin{aligned} \text{Amount} &= £334.77(1 + 12.5/100)^4 \\ &= £334.77 \times 1.125^4 \\ &= £536.24. \end{aligned}$$

The £50 you invest on your 22nd birthday will only be invested for 3 years, so that will amount to:

$$£50 \times 1.125^3 = £71.19.$$

Similarly for the payment made on your 23rd birthday we have:

$$\text{Amount after 2 years} = £50 \times 1.125^2 = £63.28$$

and for the last payment, made on your 24th birthday, which will only be invested for one year, we have:

$$\begin{aligned} \text{Amount after 1 year} &= £50 \times 1.125 \\ &= £56.25. \end{aligned}$$

Altogether, then, there will be the sum of these four amounts, which is £726.96 to the nearest penny, as before.

Of course many of these steps would not need to be written down in practice, especially if you are using a calculator with a memory; the total could then be calculated as you go along by adding each separate amount into the memory as soon as it is calculated.

(c) The term *sinking fund* is usually understood as describing the situation which arises when a firm wishes to purchase some piece of capital equipment at a future date, and decides to make regular savings to finance the purchase. Nearly always, these savings will be in the form of equal instalments, invested annually, monthly or whatever. So the problem, given the price of the piece of equipment, is to determine what the instalments should be. Suppose, for example, that it has been estimated that a certain machine costing £3,000 will have to be purchased in 3 years time, and that provision for this purchase is to be made by three equal investments, the first to be made now, the second in one year's time and the third in two years – that is, one year before the purchase. If no interest were going to be earned by the investment, then obviously the annual amount to be saved would be £1,000, but if, as is much more likely, the investments *will* earn interest – let's say, for simplicity, at 10 per cent per annum – then part of the £3,000 will be provided by that interest, so that the actual amount put away each year will be somewhat less than £3,000.

To find out just how much less, call the annual instalment £$x$. Then, using our compound interest formula, we can see that the first payment of £$x$, which will be in the account for the full 3 years before it is withdrawn to pay for the machine, will by then amount to £$x(1 + 0.1)^3$. The second payment, being in the account for only two years, will have increased to £$x(1 + 0.1)^2$, and the third, which is only invested for a year, will by the time it's withdrawn amount to £$x(1 + 0.1)$. Altogether, then, there will be £$x(1 + 0.1)^3 + £x(1 + 0.1)^2 + £x(1 + 0.1)$ in the account, which can be written more simply as £$x(1.1^3 + 1.1^2 + 1.1)$.

But this has to be just sufficient to pay for the £3,000 machine. So we have an equation:

$$x(1.1^3 + 1.1^2 + 1.1) = 3{,}000,$$

from which we can determine $x$:

$$x = \frac{3,000}{1.1^3 + 1.1^2 + 1.1} = £823.95.$$

(*See* the computational note at the end of the chapter for a note on calculating this.)

This confirms what we have already stated on common-sense grounds – that the amount to be saved is less than the £1,000 a year we would need if no interest were being earned.

It is instructive, though not something one would want to do in every such problem, to work through the calculation 'backwards', as it were, to follow the progress of the account as it would accumulate in practice.

| | |
|---|---|
| 1st instalment | 823.95 |
| 1st year's interest | 82.40 |
| 2nd instalment | 823,95 |
| Amount in a/c at start year 2 | 1,730.30 |
| 2nd year's interest | 173.03 |
| 3rd instalment | 823.95 |
| Amount in a/c at start year 3 | 2,727.28 |
| 3rd year's interest | 272.73 |
| Total by end of year 3 | 3,000.01 |

Thus the amount saved by the end of the third year will just cover the purchase of the new machine, as required. (The 1p discrepancy is due to rounding off of figures.)

Be careful, when tackling problems of this kind, about the date of the final instalment: sometimes, as here, it is invested one year before the purchase, but alternatively it may be paid in immediately before the purchase is made.

## THE IDEA OF PRESENT VALUE

One of the characteristics which is said to distinguish adults from small children (and animals) is that adults will frequently defer gratifications – for instance, save half of a bar of chocolate until tomorrow – whereas your average baby will almost certainly eat the lot now, even if it doesn't *really* want it. There are circumstances, though, in which the baby's 'grab it now' instinct is actually sounder than the adult's willingness to wait – though not for reasons that the baby could appreciate!

Consider, for example, the decision you would have to make if offered the choice of £100 now or £100 in a year's time. Setting aside the possibility that you might want to spend the money, we'll suppose that you are going to invest it, whenever you get it. Now, if you have it in your hand today, you can have it in your Post Office account, or wherever you keep your savings, by tomorrow, and in a year's time it will have increased, if the going rate of interest is, say 13 per cent, to £113 – considerably more than the alternative of £100 in a year's time. We say that the *present value* of the £100 which you are going to get in a year's time is less than the value to you of £100 now.

That's pretty easy to see. It isn't quite so obvious if the choice is between £100 in a year's time or £90 now; but again, if the interest rate stays at 13 per cent, we can expect our £90 to have increased to £101.70 in a year, so it still has the edge over the £100 received a year hence. (It's important here, and in what follows, to realise that we are concentrating on the effects of *interest* – nowhere are we considering the effects of *inflation*, which of course might well have chewed away at the value of money in the interim. Try, if you can, to forget inflation for the rest of this chapter!)

An alternative way of making the comparison between £100 now and £100 in a year's time, rather than looking at the increased value of the 'now' amount in a year, is to ask 'How much would we need to be given now in order to have the £100 a year from now?' In other words what amount must be invested – let's stick with our rate of 13 per cent for the moment – in order to accumulate to £100 in one year? This is the reverse of the question we were answering in the section on the fundamentals of compound interest, where we *knew* the initial sum invested and wanted to know what it would amount to in the future. Now we know the final amount, and want to find out what we should have started with.

However, we can still make use of the basic formula derived in that earlier section, setting $n = 1$ (since we are only interested at present in a single year), $r = 13$ per cent, and $A = 100$. If we put these into the formula we have:

$$100 = P(1 + 13/100)^1$$

where P is the unknown starting investment.

Solving for P we find:

$$P = \frac{100}{(1 + 13/100)^1}$$

$$\text{or } P = 100(1 + 13/100)^{-1} \tag{$a$}$$

recalling the definition of a negative power which we made in the section 'Powers and roots' in Chapter 1.

We define this value of P as the *present value* of £100 payable one year from now at 13 per cent per annum interest. It's the amount we would need to invest for 1 year at 13 per cent interest in order to get £100 at the end of the year.

Similarly we could say that the present value of £600 in 4 years' time at 10 per cent per annum will be P, where P is given by:

$$600 = P(1 + 10/100)^4,$$

$$\text{so } P = \frac{600}{(1 + 10/100)^4} \text{ or } 600(1 + 10/100)^{-4} \tag{$b$}$$

We can generalise this to get an expression for the present value of an amount A payable in $n$ interest periods from now at a rate of $r$ per cent per period, simply by inverting the formula on p. 282.

$$P = A(1 + r/100)^{-n}.$$

This is the *present value* formula (from now on we will often write PV for present value), which as you can see involves a negative power. Of course, we know that this simply means that we have to *divide* A by $(1 + r/100)^n$, but that still leaves us with some quite messy calculations to do. So it has become the standard practice, particularly among actuaries and other people who are doing such calculations all the time, not to do them from first principles, but to use tables of the quantities $(1 + r/100)^{-n}$ which someone has obligingly worked out for a whole range of different values of $r$ and $n$ – with the aid of a computer, of course!

The sets of tables which professionals in the field use are arranged with the rate increasing in steps of $\frac{1}{2}$ per cent, or even $\frac{1}{4}$ per cent at a time, and run up to times of 25 years or longer, as they must if they are to be used for calculations connected with, for instance, mortgage repayments, which rarely run for less than ten years. However, we will use a much simpler table, which you will find in Fig. 15.1. Just four rates – 5, 10, 15 and 20 per cent – are shown, and the table runs for only ten years. The numbers in the body of the table are simply the values of $(1 + r/100)^{-n}$ worked out for the various combinations of $r$ and $n$.

Using the table is therefore very easy. To find the present value of any given amount at a known rate, payable a known number of years from now, all we have to do is to look up the figure for the appropriate combination of $r$ and $n$ in the table, and multiply the amount by that figure. It's really the same sort of calculation as in equations (*a*) and (*b*) above, except that the hard part of the calculations has already been done for us by the compiler of the tables – in this case, me!

For instance, to work out the example of equation (*b*) using the tables, we look up the figure in the 10 per cent column and the 4-year row, which is 0.683. What this is telling us is the value of the $(1 + 10/100)^{-4}$ part of equation (*b*). So all we need do is multiply that by the 600 to get the present value of £600 in 4 years' time at 10 per cent per annum as £409.81. You can check by working forwards, if you like, that £409.81 invested at 10 per cent for 4 years really does come to £600, give or take a penny.

Tables such as Fig. 15.1 are called *discount tables*, the numbers in the body of the table are called *discount factors*, and the process of finding present values is called *discounting*. The whole area of problem-solving using these ideas is often referred to as *discounted cash flow*, or DCF for short.

Before we go on to look at applications of present values and discounting, let's quickly recap on the differences between the two processes we've looked at so far in this chapter. They might be summarised as follows:

Compound interest: moves *forward* in time;
values are *increasing*;
Discounting: moves *backward* in time;
values are *decreasing*.

If you get confused as to which process you should be using in a particular situation, going back to these two basics should help you to decide.

| $n$ | 5 | 10 | 15 | 20 |
|---|---|---|---|---|
| 1 | 0.952 | 0.909 | 0.870 | 0.833 |
| 2 | 0.907 | 0.826 | 0.756 | 0.694 |
| 3 | 0.864 | 0.751 | 0.658 | 0.579 |
| 4 | 0.823 | 0.683 | 0.572 | 0.482 |
| 5 | 0.784 | 0.621 | 0.497 | 0.402 |
| 6 | 0.746 | 0.564 | 0.432 | 0.335 |
| 7 | 0.711 | 0.513 | 0.376 | 0.279 |
| 8 | 0.677 | 0.467 | 0.327 | 0.233 |
| 9 | 9.645 | 0.424 | 0.284 | 0.194 |
| 10 | 0.614 | 0.386 | 0.247 | 0.162 |

**Fig. 15.1** Table of discount factors

# APPLICATIONS OF DISCOUNTING

Again, there is a variety of more complicated results derived from the fundamental discounting formula, and corresponding sets of tables to simplify the calculation of such things as mortgage or hire-purchase repayments. However, the fairly straightforward applications which we shall examine can all be tackled merely with the aid of Fig. 15.1.

## Calculating annuities

People who are self-employed, or for some other reason will have no pension over and above the state retirement pension, often purchase an *annuity* to provide them with additional income when they are no longer working. What happens is that the purchaser pays, to an insurance company or similar organisation, a lump sum, in return for which he receives a guaranteed income of a fixed amount per year for a fixed number of years. Imagine, for instance, that you wish to purchase an annuity which will pay you £1,000 per year for five years. How much would you expect to have to pay for it, assuming that investments earn interest at 10 per cent per annum?

Clearly, if no interest were being paid, you would have to pay £5,000. The process then would simply be that someone would hold the money on your behalf and return it to you in five payments of £1,000 each. But what will happen in practice is that the organiser of the annuity won't just, as it were, keep the money in his piggy-bank; he will invest it on your behalf. So you would expect to pay *less* than £5,000 for it, since some of each year's payment will be provided for by the interest which the money has been earning.

Although you would really only make *one* payment at the start of the period the calculation is simplified if you think of that payment as made up of five separate bits: the amount which will give you £1,000 in one year's time, the amount which will give you £1,000 in two years' time, and so on. From what we have said in the previous section about present values, you should recognise 'the amount that will give you £1,000 in one year's time' as being the present value of £1,000 payable in a year's time at 10 per cent. Altogether, then, we will have:

$$
\begin{aligned}
\text{PV of £1,000 in 1 year from now} &= 1,000 \times 0.909 \\
\text{PV of £1,000 in 2 years from now} &= 1,000 \times 0.826 \\
\text{PV of £1,000 in 3 years from now} &= 1,000 \times 0.751 \\
\text{PV of £1,000 in 4 years from now} &= 1,000 \times 0.683 \\
\text{PV of £1,000 in 5 years from now} &= 1,000 \times \underline{0.621} \\
&\phantom{= 1,000 \times {}} 3.970
\end{aligned}
$$

So total PV of the five payments, which
  is the minimum you could expect
  to pay for the annuity $\qquad = 1,000 \times 3.970$
$\qquad\qquad\qquad\qquad\qquad\qquad\qquad = £3,790$

It is much more efficient, of course, to add up the discount factors and then multiply the total by 1,000, rather than to do the multiplications first and then the addition. This would be all the more true if the annual payment were not a nice tidy amount like £1,000 but something more complicated. The total amount to be paid is considerably less than £5,000, just as we expected. We have said that £3,970 is the *minimum* you could expect to pay, because the insurance company organising the annuity will presumably want to make some profit out of the whole operation.

Once again, we can check by working through the five years step-by-step that this solution gives just enough for five payments of £1,000, with nothing left over at the end, though you would not wish to do the check every time. At the start, the £3,790 is paid into the account:

| | |
|---|---:|
| Amount in account at start yr 1 | 3,790.00 |
| Interest earned during yr 1 | 379.00 |
| Amount in account at end yr 1 | 4,169.00 |
| First payment made | 1,000.00 |
| Amount in account at start yr 2 | 3,169.00 |
| Interest earned during yr 2 | 316.90 |
| Amount in account at end yr 2 | 3,485.90 |
| Second payment made | 1,000.00 |
| Amount in account at start yr 3 | 2,485.90 |
| Interest earned during yr 3 | 248.59 |
| Amount in account at end yr 3 | 2,734.49 |
| Third payment made | 1,000.00 |
| Amount in account at start yr 4 | 1,734.49 |
| Interest earned during yr 4 | 173.45 |
| Amount in account at end yr 4 | 1,907.94 |
| Fourth payment made | 1,000.00 |
| Amount in account at start yr 5 | 907.94 |
| Interest earned during yr 5 | 90.97 |
| Amount in account at end yr 5 | 998.73 |

The slight shortfall on the final payment is due to the fact that we are using discount tables which only give three decimal places, so that by the time the discount factors are multiplied by 1,000 there is some doubt as to the last digit. However, this is easily overcome by using more accurate tables, and in fact insurance professionals use tables which give seven or more decimal places.

One can also pose a slightly different annuity problem by asking how much annual income could be generated by a given initial investment over a fixed period of time. For example, if you have a lump sum of £4,000 to invest, and would like to receive your return in the form of ten equal annual payments, how much will you get each year?

Denoting the annual payment by £$x$, what we are saying is that the present value of the ten annual payments together must be equal to the £4,000 which is being invested. So, assuming as before that the rate of interest is 10 per cent per annum and that the first payment is to be made one year after the initial investment, we have:

PV of £$x$ in one year's time + PV of £$x$ in two years' time
$\cdots$ + PV of £$x$ in ten years' time = £4,000.

Using the discount table in Fig. 14.1 then gives:

$$0.909x + 0.826x + 0.751x + 0.683x + 0.621x$$
$$+ 0.564x + 0.513x + 0.467x + 0.424x$$
$$+ 0.386x = 4000, \text{ whence } 6.144x = 4,000,$$
$$\text{so that } x = 4,000/6.144 = £651.04.$$

Again, this is a good deal more than the £400 per year which is all we could expect to get if no interest were being earned. You might like to do the 'check' calculation here, and convince yourself that, apart from small errors due to rounding-off of figures, the £4,000 plus its interest will just provide the ten annual payments of £651.04.

## Calculating mortgage and hire purchase repayments

We can make use of the discount table to work out what the annual or monthly repayments on a mortgage or hire purchase will be. If you buy, say, a three piece suite costing £800 under a hire-purchase agreement which requires you to pay a deposit of 20 per cent now and the balance in six equal monthly payments, how much can you expect to pay each month if you are being charged interest at the rate of 5 per cent per month?

If we call the monthly repayment £$x$, and assume that you are required to make the first repayment one month after purchase, then the balance after the deposit has been paid – that's 80 per cent of £800, or £640 – must be equal to the present value of £$x$ paid in one month's time, plus the present value of £$x$ paid in two months' time ... and so on up to six months. Referring again to Fig. 15.1, but now using the 5 per cent column, we have:

$$640 = 0.952x + 0.907x + 0.864x$$
$$+ 0.823x + 0.784x + 0.746x,$$
$$\text{so } 640 = 5.076x, \text{ which means } x = £126.08.$$

You will therefore actually pay the deposit of £160, plus £126.08 × 6, for the furniture – that's £916.51, a good deal more than the cash price of £800. The additional cost, of course, is really the price you are being charged for the convenience of deferring part of the payment, which effectively gives you the use of someone else's money – or of the furniture, whichever way you like to look at it – for six months.

You will see, if you compare this with the second annuity example above, that this is essentially the same calculation. It is interesting to carry out the check calculation for the first few months at least, because this demonstrates a fact of which anyone who is buying a house with a mortgage will be only too well aware; at the start of your repayments you are paying off only a very small amount of the capital each month – by far the greater part of each month's repayment is interest. However, as time goes on the ratio capital : interest in each month's payment increases, until by the time the mortgage is paid off, only a very small element of each month's payment is taken up by interest. The working goes as follows:

| | |
|---|---:|
| Amount borrowed initially (after paying deposit) | 640.00 |
| Interest incurred during month 1 | 32.00 |
| Total owed by end of month 1 | 672.00 |
| First payment made at end of month 1 | 126.08 |
| Total owed at start of month 2 | 545.92 |
| Interest incurred during month 2 | 27.30 |
| Total owed by end of month 2 | 573.22 |
| Second payment made at end of month 2 | 126.08 |
| Total owed at start of month 3 | 447.14 |

and so on. You can finish the checking if you like, but the point we are making is that, out of the first repayment of £126.08, £32.00 consists of the first month's interest, and only the remaining £94.08 is paid off the capital. In the second repayment however, the balance has altered to £27.30 of interest and £98.78 of capital, and if you complete the calculation you will find that in the remaining four repayments, a larger and larger proportion is taken up by capital. With a house-purchase mortgage, which typically would run for some 20–30 years, and would involve a much larger amount borrowed, the effect is far more noticeable, so that at the start of the repayments one sometimes wonders if one is *ever* going to pay off all the capital!

## SOME FURTHER POINTS

In all the problems we have looked at so far, whether of compound interest or discounting type, we have assumed that the interest rate was known. There are situations where this isn't the case, and where one perhaps needs to work out the interest rate, given other information. For example, if you were offered a loan of £60, to be paid back in three monthly instalments each of £22, the first to be paid one month after the money was borrowed, then you might ask what interest rate per month this offer represents.

But solving problems of this kind is much more difficult than dealing with those where the interest rate is known. To solve this particular one exactly we would need to look at the equation which tells us that the present value of the three instalments of £22 is equal to £60, when discounted at the applicable rate of interest.

If we call the interest rate per month $r$ per cent then this can be written as:

$$22(1 + r/100)^{-1} + 22(1 + r/100)^{-2} \\ + 22(1 + r/100)^{-3} = 60$$

which is a pretty nasty equation to have to solve for $r$. One way to go about solving it is to try putting in different values for $r$ and see how close the two sides of the equation are to being equal. With a sufficiently detailed set of discount tables, this can lead to a reasonably accurate answer, but you can see that, particularly for a problem which involves not just three but twenty or twenty-five years, the process is going to be a slow one, and the assistance of a computer would probably be called for.

One point which *shouldn't* need mentioning after our work on index numbers and semi-logarithmic graphs, but which often causes confusion, is that you can't say '3 per cent interest per month – that means 36 per cent per year'. If you want to translate an interest rate of 3 per cent per month into an annual rate, then you must use the compound interest formula to tell you how large a year's increase would be. This gives an annual increase factor of $(1 + 0.03)^{12}$, which works out at about 1.42 – an increase of 42 per cent per year. The consequence of this is that you need to be very careful when comparing rates of interest which are quoted for different periods. What looks like a nice low monthly rate may well turn out, when calculated annually, to be quite astronomical. There are now legal requirements for loan companies and so on to quote their Annual Percentage Rate (APR) – you may have seen this mentioned in advertisements.

## COMPARING INVESTMENTS

We now have the techniques at our disposal for making a comparison of the Paramount Manufacturing Company's two investment projects introduced in the first section of this chapter. You will recall that, including scrap value of Machine A, the costs and revenues for the two machines under consideration are as follows:

|  | Machine A | Machine B |
|---|---|---|
| Cost | 4,000 | 3,900 |
| Year 1 revenue | 2,000 | 1,500 |
| Year 2 revenue | 2,500 | 2,500 |
| Year 3 revenue | 1,500 | 2,000 |

The units here are pounds.

We have seen that we cannot justifiably add together, say, the revenue of £2,000 which Machine A earns in year 1 and that of £2,500 which it earns in year 2, because the value of money payable in the future is not the same as that of money now. If we want to combine the revenues for the different years so that we can compare the two projects, then we must first find the present value of each year's revenue. We will then make our comparison on the basis of the total present value of the surplus (if any) produced by the projects, and will also be able to see whether we might do better not to invest in either of the projects, but to leave the money in the bank.

To find present values, of course, we need to know the appropriate discount rate to use. Let us suppose, without worrying too much about where the figure comes from for the moment, the firm knows that the rate to be used with investments of this kind is generally 15 per cent per year. If we assume that all the revenues are received at the *end* of the relevant year, and that the initial costs are incurred at the *start* of year 1, then we have the calculations below (once again expressed in pounds):

|  | Machine A | | Machine B | |
|---|---|---|---|---|
| Cost |  | (4,000) |  | (3,900) |
| Year 1 revenue | $2,000 \times 0.870 =$ | 1,740 | $1,500 \times 0.870 =$ | 1,305 |
| Year 2 revenue | $2,500 \times 0.756 =$ | 1,890 | $2,500 \times 0.756 =$ | 1,890 |
| Year 3 revenue | $1,500 \times 0.658 =$ | 987 | $2,000 \times 0.658 =$ | 1,316 |
| Total PV of surplus |  | 617 |  | 666 |

So both projects will produce a surplus, when the returns are discounted at 15 per cent. But what exactly does this mean? There are two useful ways of interpreting the fact. We can say that, since we have used a rate of 15 per cent in discounting, the surplus shows that both projects actually give a return *better* than 15 per cent – better, that is, than we would get by leaving the money in the bank or wherever at 15 per cent interest. Or we can say that, to achieve these returns from an investment giving 15 per cent interest, we would need to invest, in the case of Machine A, £4,617, and for Machine B, £4,511 – the cost of each machine plus the surplus it produces. This second way of looking at the result is perhaps the easier to grasp, since we can actually demonstrate what is happening.

Take Machine A as an example. We are claiming to have proved that, to get returns of £2,000 in year 1, £2,500 in year 2, and £1,500 in year 3, an investment of £4,617 would be required. How would that work? Well, we can follow the course of the investment over the three years for which it runs:

| | |
|---|---:|
| Start of year 1 | 4,617.00 |
| Year 1 interest | 692.55 |
| End of year 1 | 5,309.55 |
| Less year 1 revenue | 2,000.00 |
| Start of year 2 | 3,309.55 |
| Year 2 interest | 496.43 |
| End of year 2 | 3,085.98 |
| Less year 2 revenue | 2,500.00 |
| Start of year 3 | 1,305.98 |
| Year 3 interest | 195.90 |
| End of year 3 | 1,501.88 |

Thus, apart from the slight discrepancy due to rounding, there is just sufficient at the end of year 3 to provide that year's revenue of £1,500. This confirms that £4,617 would have to be invested at 15 per cent to give these returns, so that we are doing rather better by buying Machine A, which gives us the same returns from an investment of only £4,000, than we would by simply investing our money at 15 per cent. You might like to perform the same calculation for Machine B.

We now certainly have evidence that either machine is worth buying, but we don't as yet have enough information to enable us to make a choice between them. There's no doubt that A gives a slightly bigger profit than B, but then so it should – after all, it's costing more to begin with. What we need to look at is not the actual *size* of the surplus produced by each machine, but what kind of return this represents on the purchase price. For Machine A we have:

$$\frac{617}{4,000} \times 100 = 15.43\%$$

while for B the calculation is:

$$\frac{611}{3,900} \times 100 = 15.66\%$$

So, viewing the surplus as a percentage of the initial cost, Machine B does very slightly better than Machine A, and would be the one recommended by Paramount's accountant – *if* he chose to adopt this method of *investment appraisal*, as it's called.

For it would be misleading to give the impression that this is the only method in use; there are a number of assumptions which we have made in the course of the analysis, which render the whole process open to criticism. First, we assumed that all the revenues were received tidily at the ends of the years, whereas in practice they are much more likely to come in during the year, maybe not even at a steady rate. We *could* work on a monthly rather than a yearly basis, or use even smaller time units, but then of course the amount of work involved would increase substantially.

Secondly, how do we *know* before either project has even started that the costs and revenues are going to be as stated? Our calculations could be totally invalidated if the machine purchased turns out to be the one-in-a-thousand which has serious running problems during its first year of operation, thus drastically raising overall costs and cutting away at our revenues.

Finally, and perhaps most seriously, how do we know that 15 per cent is the right discounting rate to use – and why, in any case, should we use the same rate over the whole lifetime of the projects? Again, an error in selecting the discounting rate could easily lead to a wrong decision.

One alternative approach to the problem would be, rather than using some definite rate, to ask just *what* rate of return is represented by the revenue from each project. We went some way towards answering this question when we said earlier in this section that the existence of a surplus on a project when discounted at 15 per cent means that the rate of return from the project is better than 15 per cent, but finding out how much better is an example of one of those 'find the rate' problems we mentioned in the previous section as being somewhat awkward to solve. Generally a trial-and-error strategy is adopted discounting the returns at various rates until the one is found which gives perfect balance between discounted revenues and costs, with neither a surplus nor a deficit. The rate which produces this effect is known as the *internal rate of return* of the project, but clearly for the trial-and-error method to be successful we would need to have tables of discount factors for rates increasing by steps of 1 per cent or even less.

Another criterion which we haven't looked at so far is how quickly each project will give us our money back – an important consideration, particularly if the money had to be borrowed in the first place. In determining the so-called *pay-back* period we are really just finding out when the projects break even – a topic we've already discussed in Chapter 1. In the particular case of Paramount Manufacturing, you may like to verify that Machine A comes off slightly better, having paid for itself after 1.8 years, while Machine B doesn't do so until 1.95 years have elapsed (what has been assumed in reaching these figures?). In these calculations, of course, we have used the *non*-discounted revenues.

Perhaps the existence of so many methods, which can lead to quite different decisions, is an indication of the complexity of the problem. Ultimately, there is no 'right' method which will lead us inevitably to the best decision; there are too many imponderable factors in the problem for that. What the methods of this section *can* do, however, is to provide a spectrum of approaches from which the most suitable can be chosen as a back-up to sound judgment and experience.

## COMPUTATIONAL NOTE

In calculations connected with sinking funds, etc., one often has to deal with expressions such as

$$1.1^4 + 1.1^3 + 1.1^2 + 1.1$$

There is no need to do each multiplication separately and then do the addition. The whole calculation can be done without writing down any intermediate steps on a calculator with memory and automatic constant multiplier as follows.

Think of the expression in the reverse order:

$$1.1 + 1.1^2 + 1.1^3 + 1.1^4$$

Enter 1.1, and add this into memory (M +).

Now enter $\times 1.1$ (on some calculators you have to press the $\times$ sign twice to get the automatic constant to operate).

Press $=$ followed by M$+$ (adds 1.21 into memory).
Press $=$ again, then M$+$ (adds 1.331 into memory).
Press $=$ again, then M$+$ (adds 1.4641 into memory).

Now your 'memory recall' button should produce 5.1051, the total of the four terms. (On some calculators, the $=$ before M$+$ is not needed.)

If you do not have discounting tables available, you can easily generate them with the aid of your calculator. Suppose, for example, that you want to find $1.1^{-1}$, $1.1^{-2}$ and $1.1^{-3}$. Enter 1.1, followed by $\div$ and $=$ (again, you may find you have to press $\div$ twice to get the automatic constant divisor). This gives you the *reciprocal* of $1.1$ – that's $1.1^{-1}$, or 0.909090 ... Now press $=$ again to get $1.1^{-2}$ or 0.8264462, and a further $=$ for $1.1^{-3}$ which is 0.7513147. You can carry on like this to get the discount factors for any number of years.

◧ Compound interest and discounting calculations are also well suited to the use of a spreadsheet. You will find sample spreadsheets for annuity and sinking fund calculations stored as ANN.WK1 and SINK.WK1 on the diskette, together with full explanations of the way they are constructed and used.

## Practical exercises

**1** On January 1st 1987 you invested £1,000 in a building society. Assuming a constant interest rate of 15 per cent per year, how much will be in the account by January 1st 1992?

**2** You now decide to withdraw £200 a year from the account mentioned in 1, making the first withdrawal on January 1st 1992. Will this reduce the total investment if interest remains at 15 per cent?

**3** A machine which currently costs £600 will increase in price by 20 per cent per year as a result of inflation.

    (a)   What will it cost in 3 years' time?
    (b)   How much should be invested each year in a sinking fund earning interest at 15 per cent per annum to cover this purchase? (The first investment is to be made at once.)

**4** Fred borrows £500 from Bill, and promises to pay it back in instalments of £100 monthly. If Bill charges interest at 5 per cent a month, how long will it take Fred to pay back the loan, and how much will the last payment be? The first payment is made one month after the money is borrowed.

**5** 'Brackleycard' credit cards charge 4 per cent per month interest on debts; 'Excess' charge 25 per cent half-year. Which represents the better value to the borrower?

**6** When employees retire from a certain firm, they are given a lump sum of £5,000 in lieu of pension. If the firm has worked its employees so hard that their life expectancy on retirement is only 5 years, how much per year will they have to live on if they invest the lump sum at 15 per cent? (Assume that the first withdrawal from the account is made one year after retirement.)

**7** A man has an annuity which will pay him £500 a year for four years, the first payment to be made three years from now. However, he is short of cash and proposes to sell the annuity. What is the most he can expect to get for it? Use a discounting rate of 10 per cent.

**8** The cost of an Eskimo deep freeze is £150. It will last four years, and I estimate that the cost of servicing and repairs, including insurance, will be £20 for the first two years, £25 for the third year, and £40 for the fourth (assumed payable at the end of the year). At the end of the fourth year I expect to be able to sell the machine for £50.

   The rival brand, Polar Bear, costs £140, but I can get a discount of 10 per cent on this because my brother works for the firm. However, the cost of servicing, repairs and insurance for this model will be £25 per year for each of the four years that it lasts (again paid at the year-end), and I will have to pay the dustmen £5 to take it away.

   Assuming a discount rate of 15 per cent, which deep-freeze would you recommend me to buy?

**9** A firm is considering the purchase of one of two machines. The first, costing £1,700, is expected to bring in revenues of £1,000, £800 and £500 respectively in the three years for which it will be operative, while the second, which costs £2,000, produces revenues of £1,200, £900, and £600, and has the same lifetime. Neither machine will have any appreciable scrap value at end of its life. A discount rate of 20 per cent has been suggested as appropriate.

   Advise the firm as to the financial wisdom of purchasing one or the other of these machines.

## Case study problem

Dear X,

We're on the move! The business has grown so much that working from home is getting really impossible, and I've heard of an old church hall which is for sale very cheaply – only £30,000. Of course it will need a lot doing to it to make it suit my purposes – a good kitchen installing, plus decorating the main room as a function room. I'm considering how to finance the operation, and though my accountant assures me he has it all under control, I hope you may be able to explain things a bit more clearly than he does.

I can put down half the price immediately, and then arrange to borrow the rest and pay it back in eight annual instalments. If the interest rate I'm charged stays at 11 per cent, how much will each payment be? (The first one will be due a year after the purchase.)

I can't start on the conversion straight away, but I should be able to get going in six months' time, and meanwhile I'd like to set aside some cash each month towards the conversion costs. I reckon £20,000 should cover the major works; if I start a savings account immediately, paying me 0.5 per cent per month interest, how much do I need to save each month? Or would an alternative account, offering a quarterly rate of 1 per cent plus a bonus of 1 per cent on withdrawal, be better value?

If all these plans come off, my family will be glad to get our kitchen back!
All the best,

Jane

## Case study question

Answer the queries raised in this letter, giving as much detail of working as you think necessary to a clear understanding of the processes involved.

## CHAPTER 16

# Planning an inventory policy: stock control

## Objectives

Before starting work on this chapter, make sure you are happy with the following topics:

(a)   construction of equations (*see* Chapter 1, p. 16);
(b)   plotting graphs from algebraic expressions (*see* Chapter 1, pp. 19–26);
(c)   the basic ideas of modelling (*see* pp. 235–6).

By the end of your work on this chapter you should be able to:

(a)   construct an algebraic model for a simple inventory system involving replenishment costs and stock-holding costs.
(b)   determine the cost-minimising solution graphically.
(c)   state the simplifying assumptions involved in constructing your model;
(d)   compare specific inventory policies involving stock-outs;
(e)   examine the effect on our solution of small changes in the quantities involved.

## THE SMALL BUSINESSMAN'S PROBLEM

John and Mary Williams have just set up a two-person picture framing business. They offer three basic styles of frame – a plastic and a metal frame, both of which they purchase ready-made in various standard sizes, and a wooden frame which they make themselves from lengths of wooden framing supplied by a wholesaler. They have plenty of customers, and there are no cash-flow problems so far, but they are finding it very difficult to manage the ordering of the ready-made frames and the lengths of wooden framing. Because their premises only have a very limited amount of storage space, they don't want to have too much stock at any one time, but several times in recent weeks they have lost a customer because they did not have the required type of frame in stock.

Up to now they have been reordering on a rather haphazard basis, simply taking a look at the stocks of the various types of frame on Monday morning and ringing the supplier to order items which seem to be getting low. However, they now feel that this *ad hoc* approach isn't very successful and may be costing them money, so they are hoping to establish a reordering policy on a more rational basis.

## THE INFORMATION NEEDED

John and Mary's problem reflects, on a small scale, a situation faced by every enterprise which has to obtain and store in some quantity items which are used in its operations. This clearly applies to all manufacturing concerns, which use raw materials and components purchased from other manufacturers in the production of their own goods, but it also holds in other types of enterprise. For example, firms of accountants and solicitors need large stocks of stationery; banks require supplies of paying-in slips and cheque books; and so on.

Obviously one major requirement in any such situation is that the firm should be able to satisfy demand as it arises. This suggests that a knowledge of the likely demand, with any regular patterns of variation therein, is a prerequisite for further progress with the problem. It also suggests that one should try to keep as large stocks as one can, so as to be able to satisfy any unusually high demands which may arise. Failure to do this may result in delays to production due to lack of raw materials, or, as the picture-framers have found, in loss of business and customer goodwill.

There are other reasons, too, why it might be a good idea to keep stocks as high as possible. If we order large quantities at a time, we may well be entitled to bulk discounts from suppliers. And there will probably be charges associated with obtaining further supplies from outside the business – at least the cost of the telephone call or letter by which we place the order, and very likely a charge for delivering the goods or going to collect them. In a large organisation, the overheads associated with running a purchasing department will probably also be apportioned as cost associated with ordering. Order costs are thus in the nature of a 'fixed cost' – they do not vary significantly with the size of orders. If we order large stocks at a time, then, to satisfy a given level of demand we will need to re-order less frequently than we would if we ordered only a few items at once, thus cutting costs. We will need to know exactly what the ordering costs, discounts, and so on are in order to be more precise about this.

But there is another side to the coin. Even given unlimited amounts of storage space, it can be very expensive to hold large quantities of stock at a time. Capital will be tied up in the stock, which could otherwise be earning interest; it will need to be insured in case anything happens to it before we have time to use it up; and we will probably have to employ someone to spend at least part of his time looking after stocks, perhaps carrying out maintenance if items are held for a very long time. If our stocks are perishables like foodstuffs we may even find that if they are held for too long they become unusable and have to be wastefully discarded. So now it's beginning to look as if it might be cheaper in the long run to hold only a small amount of stock. Indeed, many firms today operate on the so-called 'just in time' principle, holding no stocks at all, but having raw materials delivered 'just in time' for manufacture. Even if we *do* decide to hold stock, we'd want to know what the various costs associated with holding items in stock – the *stock-holding costs* – are before deciding on a policy. Notice that, as the major contribution to these costs is the loss of interest on tied-up capital, they will vary with the amount of stock ordered.

As with many of the problems we've looked at earlier in the book, what we are trying to do here is arrange a compromise. *Large* orders mean infrequent orders, therefore low ordering costs but high holding costs. *Small* orders mean frequent orders, increasing ordering costs but cutting down on stock-holding costs. So we can now be much more precise and say that the objective of a good stock-holding policy (or *inventory* policy, as it's often called) is to determine the size of order which will give us the best trade-off between these two extremes, and result in *minimum total cost*. We have also identified the information that we will need to gather in order to try to determine this best policy – we need to know the demand, the ordering costs,[*] and the stock-holding costs.

---

[*] Ordering costs are sometimes alternatively referred to as replenishment costs. This is perhaps a slightly better name, as it covers also the situation where we are replenishing stocks from within the firm, rather than ordering them from outside.

## SIMPLIFYING THE PROBLEM

The graph in Fig. 16.1 shows what our picture-framers might discover if they keep a count of their stocks of one item over a period of several months. The graph shows stocks held on the vertical axis against time on the horizontal axis, and as you can see it has a markedly 'stepped' appearance. This is the appropriate way to draw it, because on some days, when there is a demand for several of the items, stocks will drop suddenly; then perhaps for several days no-one will want that particular item, so the stock will remain steady. When a delivery of the items is received, the stock level will increase sharply — this happens at A and B on the graph, though the deliveries are of different amounts. At C there is a period when the items are out-of-stock, and a backlog of orders is building up, and so on.

At first sight the graph looks so irregular as to be very difficult to analyse, and certainly we would expect all stock control problems to have this element of irregularity to a greater or lesser extent, since demand for an item is bound to be subject to some unpredictable fluctuations. However, a second look at Fig. 16.1 shows that there are discernible patterns among the irregularities, notably a repeating pattern of sudden increases in stock followed by gradual drops. We call this pattern the *stock cycle*.

In order to make the problem simpler, we are going to take this essential element from the realistic stock cycle and idealise it somewhat by assuming five things. First, we will assume that demand is *steady*, so that we can replace the irregular 'steps' in Fig. 16.1 with a smoothly-declining line, as shown in Fig. 16.2. This, in many cases, isn't such a sweeping assumption as it seems. If the items are used in very large numbers and at frequent intervals, the 'steps' in the first graph would be so small that they almost lie on a straight line.

Second, we will assume that all deliveries are of the same size — in other words, all the upward 'steps' are of the same height. This again is moderately realistic, at least in many situations. For example, the proprietor of a retail newsagency is not going to telephone his wholesaler every night and say 'I think I'll take 40 *Telegraphs* tomorrow'; he will put

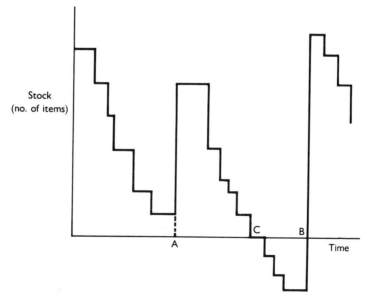

**Fig. 16.1** A realistic stock graph

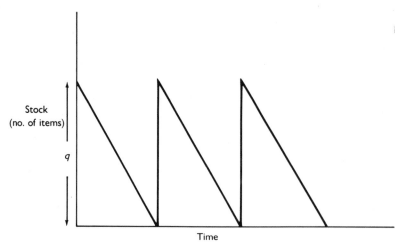

**Fig. 16.2** An idealised stock graph

in an order for a fixed number of each paper to be delivered daily, at least for a month or two ahead.

Third, we will assume that the suppliers can deliver the goods immediately we order them, and that therefore we can afford to let stocks run right down to zero before ordering more, secure in the knowledge that as soon as we sell the last item, further supplies will be rushed round! This is obviously a less realistic assumption, but as we'll see later it's one which is quite easy to eliminate.

Our last two assumptions will be that we refuse to allow stock-outs (i.e. what happened at C in Fig. 16.1) and that the situation has already arrived at a steady state – that is, we are not looking at the initial period when word of the new business or product might be getting around to potential customers, so creating a rising demand, but at the time when the business is established and has a regular pattern of demand.

There is in fact one more assumption which we will have to make in the course of our analysis of the problem, but these five are sufficient to enable us to draw the version of the stock cycle shown in Fig. 16.2.

## SOLVING THE SIMPLIFIED PROBLEM

As stated earlier, our objective is to determine what size of order will minimise the total cost of our stock policy. Let us call this order size $q$ (as indicated in Fig. 16.2). Then with our simplified version of the problem, the contributions to the total cost will come from just two sources – the ordering costs and the stock-holding costs. We will look at each of these separately.

Taking the ordering costs first, suppose that our picture-framing friends have kept a record of the demand for ready-made metal frames over the past six months, and have discovered that they sold 1,200 of them over that period. That means, on our assumption that demand is steady, that there is a demand for 200 per month. So if they were to order 50 at a time, they would have to put in 4 orders a month; if they ordered only 25 at a time, they would need 8 orders. In other words, to find out how many orders are placed in a month we divide the size of each order into the total quantity demanded during the month. Thus if they order some unknown amount $q$ at a time, then they will need to place $200/q$ orders per month. To find out how much this will cost, they will need information as to the costs involved in placing an order – and this is where our last assumption comes in. We are going to assume that each order placed costs £2, *irrespective* of the size of the order. As mentioned earlier in the chapter, this is a reasonably sensible assumption, since the major part of this cost probably arises from administrative charges. If we accept this assumption, then the ordering costs will be $(200/q) \times$ £2, which comes to £$400/q$ per month.

Now for the stock-holding costs. If a quantity $q$ is delivered and used up at a steady rate until none remains, then the average amount in stock will be $\frac{1}{2}q$; this, of course, would not be the case if the demand were erratic, which is why we needed our 'steady demand' assumption. If this *is* so, then supposing that the overall cost of holding stock has been found to work out at $\frac{1}{2}$p per item for each month the item is held, we can say that the total stock-holding cost per month will be equal to the average stock held during the month multiplied by the cost of holding one item for a month – that is $\frac{1}{2}q \times \frac{1}{2}$ pence.

We can now write down what the total cost per month is going to be, but we have to be rather careful about units here. Our ordering cost was $400/q$ *pounds* per month, our stock-holding cost $\frac{1}{4}q$ *pence* per month, so before we can add them together to give the total cost, we need to express them in the same units. Let's take pence as the unit, and write the ordering cost as $40,000/q$ pence per month; then the total cost will be T, where

$$T = \frac{40,000}{q} + \frac{q}{4} \text{ pence per month.}$$

Our objective, you recall, was to find what value of $q$ will give T its minimum value, and we are going to determine this by plotting the relationship between T and $q$ on a graph. As a preliminary step we draw up the following table:

| Order size, $q$ | No. of orders per month | Order cost | Average stock | SH cost | Total cost, T |
|---|---|---|---|---|---|
| 50 | 4 | 800 | 25 | 12.5 | 812.5 |
| 100 | 2 | 400 | 50 | 25 | 425 |
| 200 | 1 | 200 | 100 | 50 | 250 |
| 400 | 0.5 | 100 | 200 | 100 | 200 |
| 500 | 0.4 | 80 | 250 | 125 | 205 |

In the table all the costs are in pence. We chose to start at $q = 50$ fairly arbitrarily, simply because it's pretty clear that if something is being used up at a rate of 200 a month, we are hardly likely to be ordering it in quantities of one or two at a time. Having found that at $q = 50$ the order cost far exceeds the stock-holding cost, we need to consider larger (and less frequent) orders; the actual numbers used are chosen for convenience in arithmetic. There is no need to go beyond $q = 500$ because you can see that the total cost, having decreased to $q = 400$, has started to increase again, so we must already have passed its minimum.

Before plotting these figures on a graph, it's as well to check that they fit in with common sense. We expected big orders to give lower ordering costs, because we won't need to order as often, but higher stock-holding costs because there will be more stock to be held. This is what the figures seem to confirm, which, while it doesn't *prove* our analysis correct, is certainly encouraging.

Figure 16.3 shows the costs graphed against $q$. We have put in not just the total cost, but also the two components, order cost and stock-holding cost, which go to make it up. As you can see, the total cost reaches its minimum precisely where the two contributory costs are equal – at $q = 400$, as you may check from the table above.

Roughly speaking, total cost is minimised where the increasing stock-holding cost and the decreasing order cost 'balance out'.

Now, this is a very useful fact to know, because it gives us the key to a method of finding the best stock policy without having to plot a graph. Of course, we haven't actually proved that the minimum total cost will *always* occur where order cost is equal to stock-holding cost, but this *can* be proved mathematically. If we accept this as fact, then we can say that the value of $q$ which minimises total cost will be given by the equation:

$$\text{Order cost} = \text{SH cost, or } \frac{40,000}{q} = \frac{q}{4}.$$

Solving this equation (some of the intermediate steps are left out, but you can check the algebra for yourself) we get $q^2 = 160,000$, or $q = 400$, which agrees with our graphical solution. So the best policy will be to order 400 frames at a time. From this we can calculate other useful things, such as the time between orders – two months – or the fact that there will be six orders placed every year.

We could repeat this argument using letters to represent arbitrary values of the various contributory costs, instead of the specific values 200 items demanded per month, order cost £2, and so on. This in fact gives a well-known formula which is often referred to as the Economic Batch Quantity (EBQ) or Economic Order Quantity (EOQ) formula. By this stage in the book you are probably well aware of the author's attitude to formulae, and certainly I would say that the present case is no exception to the rule that it is a good

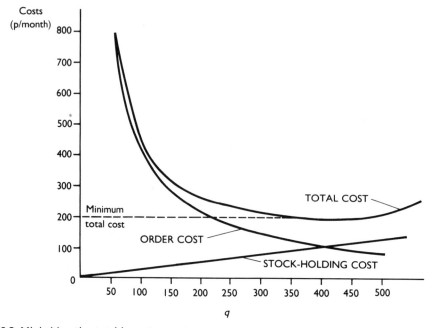

**Fig. 16.3** Minimising the total inventory cost

deal safer to work from scratch using the figures concerned than substitute blindly – and possibly wrongly! – into a formula. However, as this one *is* very widely used, it is interesting to see how it is obtained.

Suppose there is a demand for a quantity D of some commodity per month (or week, or year – the time-periods involved need not concern us). Suppose also that the cost of placing an order for the items is C, and that the cost of holding one item in stock for a month is H, both C and H being expressed in the same units. Then there will be $D/q$ orders placed per month, at a cost of $C \times D/q$ or $CD/q$ per month altogether, while the stock-holding cost will be the average stock, $\frac{1}{2}q$, multiplied by H, giving $\frac{1}{2}qH$. Using the fact demonstrated above, that total cost will be a minimum when order cost is equal to stock-holding cost, we may say that the best value of $q$ will be the solution of the equation:

$$\frac{CD}{q} = \frac{qH}{2}$$

which can be solved (again, you should supply the intermediate steps) to give:

$$q = \sqrt{\frac{2CD}{H}}$$

and this, with various alternative notations, is the EBQ formula. It is easy to see from this result that increases in holding costs will result in a smaller quantity being the most economical, while increases in ordering costs will mean that it is preferable to order larger quantities at a time – all of which accords with common sense.

It is worth noting that if you know some calculus, the EBQ formula can also be arrived at by minimising the total inventory cost $T = \frac{CD}{q} + \frac{qH}{2}$ with respect to $q$.

◧ The table of ordering, stock-holding and total costs drawn up above is very well suited to computation using a spreadsheet. You will find a LOTUS worksheet for the table, together with the associated graph, stored as INV.WKl on the diskette. The figures in this worksheet can be overwritten for solution of other inventory problems.

## ELIMINATING SOME ASSUMPTIONS

The easiest of our six simplifying assumptions to get rid of is the one concerning instant replenishment of stocks. If instead of obtaining immediate delivery when they re-order, our picture-framers have discovered that they generally have to wait a week for the supplier to send the goods, then if they wish to avoid running out of stock they will have to allow for this in their re-ordering policy. In one week they will need 50 frames (if we take it that there are four weeks in a month) and so they should allow for the *lead time*, as it is known, of one week on deliveries by re-ordering when their stock falls, not to zero but to 50 items. This sort of policy is easily implemented in practice by for instance, inserting a re-order reminder into a stack of goods on top of the 50th item from the bottom of the stack, so that on reaching that item the person in charge of issuing stock is alerted to the need to place an order.

Another popular method is the three-bin system where most of the stock is in a first 'bin', the 50 items needed during the lead time are in a second, and a certain amount of 'buffer stock' for emergency use in a third. When the first bin is empty, it is time to re-order. Of course, this requires careful attention to stock rotation.

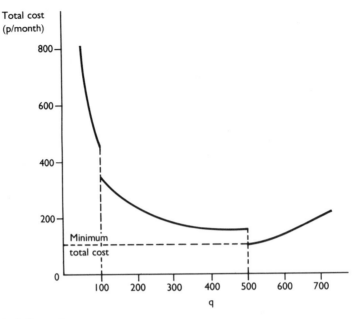

**Fig. 16.4** Effect of discounts

It is also fairly easy to see the effect on our 'best' solution of discounts offered by a supplier for larger orders. If the supplier of picture-frames offers say, a certain discount on orders for more than 100 items, and an even large discount for orders for 500 items or more, it could be more economical to order 500 at a time, as can be seen by looking at Fig. 16.4. In such a situation the best policy is most easily seen from a graph, and to apply the EBQ formula blindly could result in quite the wrong policy being chosen.

## MAKING AND USING

You may recall from the information given in the first section of this chapter that the wooden picture frames used by the Williams' business are not purchased ready-made from the supplier, but are made-to-measure from lengths of framing. The control of stocks of this type of frame, therefore, constitutes a rather different problem from the one we have just looked at. If we imagine that John wants to spend a few days from time to time making these frames down to the finishing stage, rather than making them one at a time when the demand arises, then we have a situation where, instead of the stocks suddenly increasing sharply when a delivery is received, they will build up gradually over the period when he is making them. At the same time, some of the ones he has just made may be sold immediately, so that he will never actually have the entire quantity that he has made in stock at one time. All this results in a stock-cycle graph which looks like Fig. 16.5.

To find out what effect this modification to the stock-cycle has on the solution, we need some figures to work with. Let us suppose that John can produce frames at a rate of 15 per day, and that a demand for them exists at the rate of 5 per day. The costs associated with producing a batch of frames (equivalent to the ordering costs in the previous case) have been calculated at £3, and because the frames are more fragile than the metal ones the cost of storing them is much greater – say, 5p per frame per day.

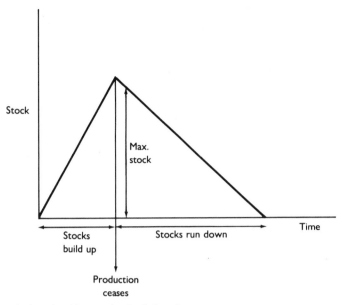

**Fig. 16.5** Stock cycle in a 'making and using' situation

If we take the stock-holding cost first, then in order to find the average stock held we need to know what is the maximum amount ever held in stock at one time. If John decides to produce a batch of $q$ frames at once, it will take him $q/15$ days to make them (for example, 45 frames would take 3 days). But during those $q/15$ days, there would also be a demand for 5 frames per day, so altogether during this 'producing' part of the cycle $5 \times q/15$, or $q/3$, frames would be used up; so the most that will ever be in stock will be $2q/3$. Thus the average stock held is a half of this, which is $q/3$. The stock-holding cost will therefore be $5 \times q/3$ pence per day.

As for the production costs, the batch of $q$ frames will last $q/5$ days, so if we average out the £3 cost associated with producing a batch of frames over this period we have a cost per day of £3$/(q/5) = 300/(q/5)$ pence $= 1,500/q$ pence per day.

From here on the solution proceeds in exactly the same way as for our earlier problem with the minimum total cost again being reached when ordering cost (or, in this case, the cost of setting up production of a batch) is equal to stock-holding cost. At this point, $\dfrac{1,500}{q} = \dfrac{5q}{3}$, which gives $q^2 = \dfrac{1,500 \times 3}{5} = 900$, so $q = 30$. This means that John should produce a batch of 30 frames at a time, taking two days to do so. These 30 frames will be used up in six days, so that he will wait four days before producing another batch.

## ALLOWING STOCK-OUTS

Up to now we have been assuming that the Williams' have unlimited space in which to store the frames they receive from the supplier, but of course in practice this may not be the case. What happens if, when we recommend the 'best' policy worked out earlier of ordering 400 ready-made frames at a time, they reply 'But we only have room for 350'?

In such a situation, it may actually be worthwhile deliberately allowing stock to run out, thus causing a stock-cycle which looks like Fig. 16.6. Of course, there will be some costs associated with the part of the cycle where they are out of stock – due to loss of goodwill when customers' orders are held up and other such factors – but whether or not the policy is worthwhile will depend on how these *stock-out costs* relate to the other costs involved in the problem. What is happening is that while there is no stock, orders are building up, so that when new stocks eventually arrive some of them – the amount $q_2$ in Fig. 16.6 – are sent out immediately to fulfil this backlog of orders. Thus the greatest quantity which actually has to be stored at one time is only $q_1$ and not the entire batch $q$.

To examine this problem in complete generality is complicated, firstly because we no longer have only two contributions to the total cost – the stock-out cost now also contributes – and so we do not get the simple result order cost = stock-holding cost for minimum total cost. Second, and a more serious blow to our previous method of solution, there are now not two but *three* variable quantities in the problem – the total cost T is related both to $q_1$ and to $q_2$. So we certainly can't resort to drawing a graph any more – unless a 3-dimensional one!

What we will do here, rather than solve the general problem, is compare certain specific policies involving stock-outs. As we have been told that only 350 frames can be stored, we will take as our *Policy 1* the case where the batch size ordered is reduced to 350 frames, and no stock-outs arise. In this case with a demand, as before, for 200 frames per month, we will need to order rather more often than every two months – in fact, there will be 200/350 orders per month, at a cost of £2 an order as already stated. The ordering cost will therefore be $\frac{200}{350} \times 200$, or $\frac{4,000}{35}$ pence per month.

The maximum stock now held at one time is 350, so that the average stock will be half of this, costing $\frac{1}{2}$p per month each to store; thus the stock-holding cost is $(350/2) \times \frac{1}{2}$, or

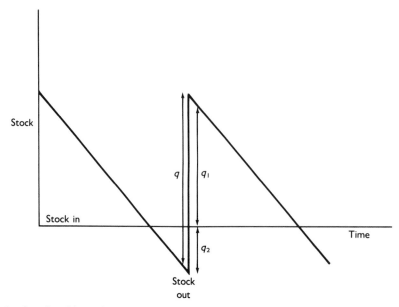

**Fig. 16.6** Stock cycle with stock-outs

$87\frac{1}{2}$ p a month. To find the total cost of operating Policy 1, we add this to the order cost already worked out:

$$\text{Total cost of Policy 1} = \frac{4,000}{35} + 87.5$$

$$= 202\text{p per month approximately.}$$

*Policy 2* attempts to overcome the limited amount of storage space in a different way. Rather than reduce the size of the orders to the amount which can be stored, we advise continuing to order 400 frames at a time, but allow stock-outs in such a way as to ensure that no more than 350 frames ever need to be stored at one time. What will occur is easily seen by referring to Fig. 16.6. During the 'out-of-stock' part of the cycle, orders to the amount of 50 frames are allowed to accumulate, so that when the new delivery of 400 frames eventually arrives, 50 of them will be needed straight away to satisfy this accumulated demand, and only the remaining 350 will need to be stored.

What effect will this have on our total cost? The order cost will, of course, decrease, since we are now placing larger orders at less frequent intervals, it will in fact be $\frac{200}{400}$ $\times$ 200 or 100 pence per month. Stock-holding costs will also be reduced, since although our maximum stock held is still 350 frames, as it was under Policy l, there is now a period of the cycle when we don't *have* any stocks, and so don't incur any stock-holding costs (that is, if we ignore things such as rent and rates on warehouses which have to be paid whether they are full or empty). We take this into account by saying that the average stock held is $350 \times \frac{1}{2}$ or 175 frames, at a cost of $\frac{1}{2}$p per frame per month, but held for only 7/8 of the cycle. You can see why the fraction is 7/8 by looking at Fig. 16.6. We therefore have a stock-holding cost of $175 \times \frac{1}{2} \times \frac{7}{8} = 76.5$ pence per month approximately.

Finally, there is a third contribution to the total cost from the costs of being out-of-stock. If we suppose that John Williams has estimated the cost of being out-of-stock at 5p per frame per month, then we can work out what this will contribute to the total cost in much the same way as we have found the stock-holding cost. The average amount by which stocks run out is half of the maximum stock-out, which means $\frac{1}{2} \times 50$ or 25 frames; each costs 5p per month, but the out-of-stock situation only actually arises for 1/8 of the cycle, so that the stock-out cost altogether will be $25 \times 5 \times \frac{1}{8}$ or about $15\frac{1}{2}$ pence.

Policy 2 therefore has a total cost of $15.5 + 76.5 + 100 = 192$ pence per month, as opposed to the 202 pence per month for Policy 1; so in this case it would be slightly cheaper to run out of stock by 50 frames, rather than reduce the size of orders. In another case, where the balance between the various components of the total cost was different, we might come to a different conclusion. There is no easy way of deciding in advance which policy would be best, other than to work out the total cost of each.

## THE EFFECT OF ERRORS IN ESTIMATES

You may have noticed that a good deal of 'supposing' has gone on in the preceding sections. We 'supposed' that the stock-holding costs had been worked out to be $\frac{1}{2}$p per frame per month, we 'supposed' that the charge for placing an order was £3, and so on. Now, in practice, some of these suppositions may well turn out to be wide of the mark. Certainly if we are planning a stock policy for the whole of next year, it's quite likely that the order cost *won't* stay put at £3, but will increase during the year. Similarly, the demand, which we need to know in order to solve the problem, will certainly vary, and the same could well apply to all the other quantities required in the solution of the problem.

So a point which might justifiably worry John Williams when we present him with our recommendations as to his 'best' stock policy is: 'What happens if some of these figures change? Will just a small error in one of my cost estimates result in your so-called 'best' policy being wildly wrong, giving me a lot of unnecessary expense? Or can I be fairly confident that, even if I do go somewhat astray in my estimates, the solution you've come up with will still be pretty close to the cheapest?'

From a practical point of view, we might agree with John that a *good* solution is one which is *stable* – that is, it stays near to the real 'best' solution even in the face of minor errors in some of the data which has gone into its calculation. Another way of putting this would be to say that the solution mustn't be too *sensitive* to minor errors in the data, and we will come across this idea of *sensitivity analysis*, as it's called, again in later chapters. In any problem where solution relies heavily on data which may not be completely accurate, it's vital that we should have some idea whether such inaccuracies are going to be disastrous to our solution, or just have minor effects.

In this particular case, the easiest way of examining the results of an error in, say, one of the cost figures which appear in the solution, is to use the EBQ result found at p. 303. We have already seen that if all the demands and cost estimates for the problem on pp. 300–2 are accepted, then the total cost will be at a minimum if 400 frames are ordered at a time. But now imagine that in fact the estimated cost of placing an order, £2, turns out to be an underestimate – that the cost in practice is £2.50. This is really, in percentage terms, quite a serious error; our original figure has been increased by 25 per cent. What will be the effect on the total cost?

To find out what the correct EBQ should have been, we will, for once, make use of the formula. We have C = 250 pence, and if we take it that all the other quantities were estimated correctly, then D = 200 and H = 0.5 pence. So

$$q = \sqrt{\frac{2 \times 250 \times 200}{0.5}}$$

which comes to about 447 frames, instead of our previous value of 400. This is certainly quite a difference, but the crucial question is: if we persist in ordering 400 at a time, not realising that in fact the 'best' policy in the changed circumstances would be to order 447, how serious an effect will our error have on our total costs?

To answer this question, we need to work out the costs of the two policies. If we carry on ordering 400 at a time, the order cost will be (200/400) × 250 = 125 pence per month, while the stock-holding cost will still be 100 pence per month, as we worked out earlier. So the total cost will be 225 pence per month.

If we were, as we should be, now ordering 447 in a batch, then the ordering cost would only be (200/447) × 250 = 112 pence per month, but the stock-holding cost would increase to $\frac{1}{2} \times 447 \times \frac{1}{2} = 112$ pence per month also – the two amounts are of course equal, because this is our 'best' solution now. So the minimum total cost would be 112 + 112 = 224 pence per month. In other words, even though we have made a 25 per cent error in the estimate of the ordering cost, the error in the total cost – that is, the unnecessary extra cost we are incurring by sticking to our original 'best' policy – is only 1p per month, which percentage-wise over the total cost is less than 0.5 per cent.

You can check that this is not just a cooked-up example by trying out the effect of errors in the other quantities – the demand, for instance, or the stock-holding cost – on the solution. In all cases, you will find that the solution is not very *sensitive* at all. This relates to the fact that the total cost graph is pretty flat near to its minimum, as you can see by looking back at Fig. 16.3. So we can reassure John Williams that even if he is slightly askew in his estimates of the data needed to get a solution, he can be fairly confident that he isn't going to be paying out much more than he needs to pay.

## FURTHER POSSIBILITIES

All the analysis we have done in this chapter has been completely deterministic – that is, we haven't attempted to take into account any of the unpredictable elements which actually affect stock-control, such as erratic variations in demand, or variable delivery-times from suppliers. There *are* situations in which these factors (which, although they may follow a discernible pattern, are basically unpredictable), must be taken into consideration. Recourse is then often had to *simulating* the entire problem by the methods we will be looking at in Chapter 19.

Nevertheless, the techniques of this chapter, with some modifications, form the basis of the real-life stock-control systems adopted by many large companies.

### Practical exercises

1 Complete the 'stock in hand' column of the following extract from the stock book of a do-it-yourself supplier, and use the information in the table to calculate the average weekly demand for the item concerned over the two weeks March 4th–16th:

**Item – wood screws ref. S101/3**

| Date | No. of boxes received from suppliers | No. of boxes sold to customers | Stock in hand (no. of boxes) |
|---|---|---|---|
| March 1 | – | – | 35 |
| March 4 | 20 | 8 | 47 |
| March 5 | – | 6 | |
| March 6 | – | 7 | |
| March 7 | – | 3 | |
| March 8 | – | 9 | |
| March 9 | – | 11 | |
| March 11 | 40 | 5 | |
| March 12 | – | 7 | |
| March 13 | – | 7 | |
| March 14 | – | 5 | |
| March 15 | – | 10 | |
| March 16 | 25 | 12 | |

2 Plot a graph to show the stock position of the firm in Problem 1 over the period shown.

3 If the cost to this firm of raising an order is 50p, and the stock-holding cost is reckoned to be 5p per box per week, advise the firm as to its most economic order policy.

4 Should the storage space available for the boxes of screws become limited to 20 boxes, would the firm do better to reduce the size of its orders to 20 boxes also, or continue to order 30 and allow stock-outs? Assume the cost of being out-of-stock is 5p per box per week.

## Case study problem

Dear X,

Until the church conversion is completed, I am going to be very pushed for storage space, so I need to use it effectively. But I don't want to cut down too drastically on the items I keep in stock, as they aren't always easy to replace economically if I suddenly run out.

For example, I use a lot of flour, which I buy direct from the mill in 10-kilo sacks costing about £6.50. I get through 4 sacks a month, in round figures, and it takes a week to get a delivery through from the mill. The sacks are quite bulky, so I would rather not store too many – we can't get the car into the garage as it is! – but I daren't risk running out of such a basic item. Now the miller has complicated things by offering me a 5 per cent discount if I buy at least 5 sacks at a time – presumably to make up for the flat charge of £2 makes for delivery, regardless of how many sacks I buy.

Have you any useful ideas? Let me know if you need any more information to fill out the picture.

Thanks,

Jane

## Case study question

Reply to this letter, where necessary estimating the figures you would need in order to carry out calculations.

## CHAPTER 17

# Planning production levels: linear programming

## Objectives

Before starting work on this chapter, make sure you are happy with the following topics:

(a) construction of equations and inequalities (*see* Chapter 1, p. 16);
(b) plotting graphs from equations and inequalities (*see* Chapter 1, pp. 19–26);
(c) slopes of straight-line graphs (*see* Chapter 1, p. 19);
(d) solution of simultaneous equations (*see* Chapter 1, p. 17);
(e) the basic ideas of modelling (*see* pp. 235–6).

By the end of your work on this chapter you should be able to:

(a) recognise, and formulate an algebraic model of, a problem involving maximisation or minimisation of an objective function subject to a set of linear constraints;
(b) in cases where the problem involves only two variables, plot the graph representing the problem, and hence determine the feasible and optimal solutions;
(c) state which variables are slack in the optimal solution;
(d) determine the scarcity values of the tight constraints, and the ranges over which they apply;
(e) determine the range of profits or costs over which the solution remains valid.

## THE PRODUCTION MANAGER'S PROBLEM

Jim Brown is the production manager of Apex Tools, a small firm which specialises in the manufacture of high quality tools for the amateur gardening market. The firm produces quite a wide range of items, but has a flexible work-force which can easily be switched from one production line to another. Much of the machinery is also used in the production of more than one type of tool, as are many of the raw materials – sheet and tubular metal, wood, paint, and so on. The profits gained by Apex from the sale of different types of tool naturally vary widely – a wheelbarrow will generate a lot more profit than a trowel – as do the times taken to produce them, and the potential markets for them.

Jim Brown's problem is to decide how Apex ought to divide up its production among the various types of tool it manufactures in order to obtain the maximum possible profit, taking into account all the factors mentioned above. In other words, it isn't sufficient for him simply to say 'Produce as many as you can of everything' – there will be many limitations or *constraints* within which the production must operate, such as limited quantities of raw materials available, limited amounts of machine time, a fixed number of man-hours per week for each type of worker ... the list could be continued almost indefinitely. Moreover, because the profits generated by each type of tool vary, perhaps it would be better not to produce *any* of a less profitable line, but to concentrate all resources on producing the more profitable ones. But then again, maybe we won't be able to sell them because of limitations to the market ....

You can see from this brief outline of the problem that the chances of arriving at the 'best' solution – the one giving maximum possible profits – by simply thinking about it are minimal. Mr Brown is more likely to obtain a nervous breakdown than an optimal solution! What he needs is a *systematic* way of tackling the problem – preferably a way which *guarantees* that he will end up with the most profitable solution, at the same time ensuring that the firm operates within all its limitations of materials, manpower, etc.

Such a method is provided, for a wide class of problems of this kind, by the techniques of *linear programming* which form the subject of this chapter.

## SETTING UP THE MODEL

As usual, we need a rather simplified problem in order to illustrate the basics of the technique. Real-life problems like the one in the previous section tend to involve a great many products and a great many limitations, with consequent complications in getting a solution. So, let's suppose that Apex has drastically rationalised its range of products, and decided to concentrate on producing just two: a single-wheeled barrow called the 'Workhorse', and a two-wheeled model called the 'Donkey'. We will find in the next section that this reduction to only two products means that the problem can be solved in a particularly simple way.

Let's cut down, too, on the number of limitations or constraints, and assume that there are just four which need to be allowed for: only 40 wheels (purchased ready-made from a supplier) can be obtained per week; not more than 24 barrows per week can be sold to wholesalers; the 'Workhorse' needs a rubber tyre, of which only 16 per week are available; and the skilled metalwork for the barrows, which takes 3 hours for a 'Workhorse' and 2 hours for a 'Donkey', has to be done by one of two men, each of whom only works a 30-hour week.

Our first step is to define some *variables*: what are the quantities which can be varied at will by the company? Obviously not the amounts of wheels, tyres, and so on; they are all fixed by external circumstances beyond the company's control. The only things which it *can* determine at will – subject, of course, to the various constraints – are the numbers of each type of barrow which it chooses to make. It is those numbers which Mr Brown hopes to determine in such a way as to get the maximum possible profit. So, our variables are going to be:

$w$, the number of 'Workhorse' barrows made per week, and
$d$, the number of 'Donkey' barrows made per week.

Having defined these two variables, we can now translate the four constraints into inequalities involving the variables.

Consider the wheels constraint first. Each 'Workhorse' has one wheel, so producing, say, 4 'Workhorses' would need 4 wheels, and more generally producing $w$ of them will need $w$ wheels. On top of that, we need 2 wheels for each 'Donkey' produced; thus 6 'Donkeys' would need 12 wheels, 8 would need 16 wheels, and in general $d$ of them will need $d \times 2$ or $2d$ wheels. The total number of wheels used in making both $w$ 'Workhorses' and $d$ 'Donkeys', then, will be $w + 2d$. But we know this can't be more than 40, because that's all the wheels available in one week. So we arrive at the inequality:

$$w + 2d \leqslant 40 \qquad (a)$$

representing the wheels constraint.

We can now obtain the other inequalities in a slightly less long-winded way. The total number of barrows made in a week is $w + d$, and it's no good letting this be more than 24 because that's the most the wholesalers will take. So:

$$w + d \leqslant 24 \qquad (b)$$

is the wholesaler constraint.

Three hours metalworking time for a 'Workhorse' means that $w$ of them will take $w \times 3$ or $3w$ hours; we also need $2d$ hours to make $d$ 'Donkeys' at 2 hours each. So the total time needed is $3w + 2d$, and as the two men who can do the work only have 60 hours a week available between them, we have:

$$3w + 2d \leqslant 60 \qquad (c)$$

as the metalwork constraint.

Finally, since each 'Workhorse' has one tyre, and there are at most 16 available per week, we have:

$$w \leqslant 16 \qquad (d)$$

as the tyre constraint – this inequality only involves one of the variables, because clearly any limitation on the numbers of tyres available won't have any effect at all on how many 'Donkeys' we can produce, since they don't need tyres!

We haven't yet introduced the question of profits, so let's now assume that we know each 'Workhorse' will give £4 profit when sold, and each 'Donkey' £3. Our objective is to maximise the total profit, and so we can write down the *objective function* to be maximised as:

$$\text{Profit} = 4w + 3d.$$

The problem has now been reduced to the set of four inequalities $(a)$–$(d)$[*] plus the objective function. What is more, you should recognise that it involves only *linear* expressions – there are no $w^2$ or $1/d$ terms, for example – so that, if plotted on a graph, all would give straight lines. This explains why the technique is called *linear* programming – and it also gives the clue as to how we should proceed with trying to find the solution.

## GRAPHING THE MODEL

Because we have only two variables in this problem we are able to plot the constraints on a two-dimensional graph. There will be four lines on the graph, one for each constraint, and it is most important that you concentrate on plotting one at a time, without worrying about the effect of the others. To start trying to think about more than one constraint at a time is a recipe for disaster, and is in any case unnecessary since the graph itself is going to show us *how* they interact with each other.

Consider then, inequality $(a)$, representing the wheels constraint. The easiest way of deciding where it should be plotted is to concentrate on the two extreme cases,

[*] Strictly speaking we should include the two 'non-negativity constraints' $w \geqslant 0$ and $d \geqslant 0$, expressing the fact that one can't make a negative number of wheelbarrows!

supposing first that the entire supply of wheels is to be used up on making 'Workhorses', and no 'Donkeys' are to be made at all. Clearly this would mean that 40 'Workhorses' could be produced. So one point on the line bounding this constraint will be $w = 40$, $d = 0$. At the other extreme, we have the possibility of making 20 'Donkeys' if no 'Workhorses' are made, giving a second point at $w = 0$, $d = 20$. Thus the line bounding the constraint will run from 40 on the $w$-axis to 20 on the $d$-axis, and all combinations of $w$ and $d$ using *less* than or equal to 40 wheels will fall in the region below this line, as indicated in Fig. 17.1. Of course, in practice we couldn't actually make 40 'Workhorses' because we wouldn't have enough tyres for them, but at the moment we aren't considering that constraint. This is what was meant earlier by 'Concentrate on one constraint at a time'.

If we go on to inequality (*b*), and repeat the 'extremes' argument, you should be able to see that the line for this constraint will run from $w = 0$, $d = 24$, to $w = 24$, $d = 0$. Once again, all points below this line are possible as far as the wholesaler constraint is concerned. For inequality (*c*), the same process gives the two extremes of the line as $w = 0$, $d = 30$ and $w = 20$, $d = 0$. In other words, if the metalworkers spent all their time on making 'Workhorses', which take 3 hours apiece, and didn't make any 'Donkeys' at all, they could in their 60 hours produce 20 'Workhorses'; or, alternatively, they could concentrate on 'Donkeys' and make 30, since they only take 2 hours each.

You can see these three constraints plotted and labelled in Fig. 17.2. It is customary, as shown there, to shade the 'forbidden' side of the line – the side on which the constraint would be violated – as this avoids having lots of criss-crossing shading where the constraints interact. You can also see in the figure the slightly different sort of line which results from inequality (*d*). This told us that, regardless of how many 'Donkeys' are made, the number of 'Workhorses' can never exceed 16, and so is represented by a line which, however big $d$ becomes, will restrict $w$ to below 16 – in other words, a line parallel to the $d$-axis at $w = 16$. Incidentally, the choice of $w$ as the horizontal and $d$ as the vertical axis is quite arbitrary – there is no reason why you should not take them the other way round.

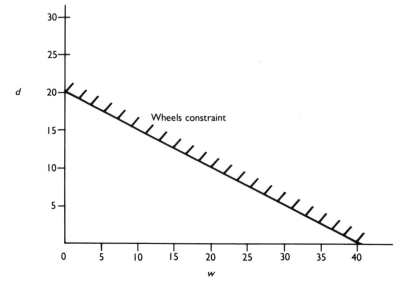

**Fig. 17.1** Beginning the linear programming graph

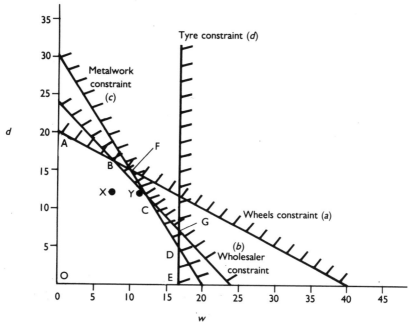

**Fig. 17.2** The completed linear programming graph

Having drawn all the constraints on the graph, we can now see the effect of their interaction: the possible combinations of 'Workhorses' and 'Donkeys' which can be made will be represented by the points inside the region ABCDEO which correspond to whole-number values of $w$ and $d$, because only within that region are all the constraints satisfied. We call these points the *feasible solutions*, and the region ABCDEO is called the *feasible region*. The reason for the restriction to whole-number values of $w$ and $d$ is, of course, that we are not interested in manufacturing fractions of a wheelbarrow!

## FINDING THE BEST SOLUTION

Now that, in theory at least, we know what all the possible solutions are, we *could* go about trying to find which of them is the 'best' — in the sense of yielding maximum possible profit — by finding out what profit each of the possible solutions would give, and then choosing as our 'best' combination the one for which the profit is greatest. But even in such a simple problem as this, there are a great many possible solution points within the feasible region; even to write them all down would be a time-consuming process — and also an unnecessary one, as can easily be seen.

Consider, for example, the point X, at which 13 'Donkeys' and 8 'Workhorses' are being produced. This will yield a profit of $13 \times 3 + 8 \times 4 = £63$. But clearly we will get more profit from point Y, where the same number of 'Donkeys' but 3 more 'Workhorses' are being produced, or from point B, where the number of 'Workhorses' is the same as at X but 3 more 'Donkeys' are being made. This argument suggests that the 'best' solution is going to be a point on the edge of the feasible region rather than in the middle of it.

That still leaves us with quite a few points to look at. But fortunately there is a way we can narrow down the candidates for the 'best' solution still further. Imagine for a moment that we are interested, not in gaining the maximum possible profit, but simply in achieving a profit of, say £60. We could do that in a variety of ways: by making no 'Donkeys' at all and just 15 'Workhorses', or by making no 'Workhorses' and 20 'Donkeys', or by producing and selling 6 'Workhorses' and 12 'Donkeys' . . . and so on. But there is one important fact about all these combinations giving us our £60 profit: they all lie on the line AQ, as shown in Fig. 17.3.

This line is called a *profit line*. The particular one we have drawn represents combinations giving a profit of £60. Bigger profits will be shown by lines further away from the origin, smaller profits by lines closer to the origin, but all the profit lines will have one thing in common: they will have the same *slope*, since that is determined by the ratio of the profits on the two products. You can check this by working out another profit line, perhaps the one for profit of £48. So what we are doing, as we try to increase the possible profit, is simply sliding the profit line outwards from O, while keeping it always parallel to AQ.

Now, as we do this, there will come a point at which, if we were to move the profit line out any further, it would cease to intersect the feasible region, and therefore profits any larger cannot be achieved in practice because of the constraints. In the present case that will happen, as you should test for yourself, when the profit line is just passing through C. So the point C will give us the 'best' combination of the two items to produce.

This probably seems rather a complicated process, and you may well be wondering if it mightn't have been quicker to examine all the whole-number points around the edge of the feasible region. But, in fact, it isn't necessary to go through the whole process of drawing profit lines every time, for the following reason. The 'best' point we finally found, C, is at a corner of the feasible region, and if you try using profit lines of different slopes you will find that, in general, the furthest extreme to which the profit line can be

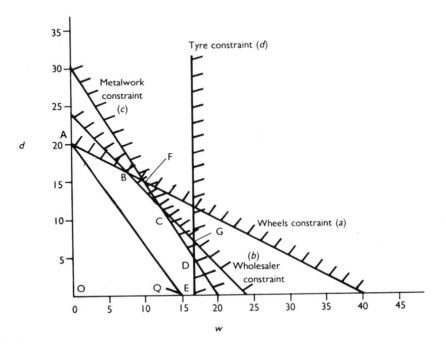

**Fig. 17.3**

moved – the point giving maximum possible profit – is *always at a corner* of the feasible region. (The only exception to this would be if the profit line happened to be parallel to one of the edges of the feasible region, in which case we would not get just one, but a whole set of 'best' solutions.)

Having once demonstrated this fact, we may quote it without proof in future, which gives us a very simple rule for finding the 'best' solution in any such problem: having drawn the graph, we now know that the maximum profit will occur at one of the corners of the feasible region. So, all we need do is work out the profit at each of those corners – there won't usually be too many of them – and pick the one where the profit is greatest. It's easiest to do this systematically in the form of a table:

| Corner | w | d | Profit (£) |
|--------|-----|-----|------------|
| A | 0 | 20 | 60 |
| B | 8 | 16 | 80 |
| C | 12 | 12 | 84 |
| D | 16 | 6 | 82 |
| E | 16 | 0 | 64 |

This confirms what we already know from our study of the profit line in this case – that the maximum possible profit is obtained by producing 12 of each type of barrow. Notice that although strictly speaking O is also a corner of the feasible region, we didn't bother to include it in the table because it obviously represents the point where zero profit is made. Actually we really didn't need to put in E either. D is bound to give a bigger profit than E since it involves making the same number of 'Workhorses' as at E, and 6 'Donkeys' as well.

We have now solved the problem posed in the earlier section on setting up the model, using a process which could be summarised in the four steps:

(a)  write down the algebraic model for the problem;
(b)  plot the graph representing this model;
(c)  identify the feasible region and its corners;
(d)  find the profit at each corner, and select the one for which this is greatest.

But, as you will have learned to expect by now, we have had to make quite a lot of assumptions to simplify the problem enough to solve it in this way. So we now need to ask just what those hidden assumptions were, and how disastrous an effect it will have on our 'best' solution if one or more of them turns out to be wrong. If you have read Chapter 16 you will recognise that what we are going to do is carry out a *sensitivity analysis* on the solution.

## VARYING THE CONSTRAINTS

In setting up the model for our problem, we had to assume that we had adequate information about two sets of things: first of all the amounts of the various resources by which the production is constrained, and secondly the profits which would be generated by the sale of the products. In practice, of course, these can be quite difficult to estimate, particularly if we are trying to plan production not just for a week or two, but for a whole year or more ahead. We may expect to receive deliveries of 4,000 tons of raw materials from our suppliers, and plan our production accordingly, only to find that shortages cut down our deliveries to 3,000 tons. We may expect to be able to use a certain machine for 50 hours a week, and then find that, due to breakdowns, the figure is closer to 40 hours. Or we may hope to be able to sell a product at a price which will give us a profit of £6 per item, and then discover that a competitor has put a cheap new alternative product on the market and we must cut our profit margins if we are to maintain our market share.

All of these circumstances will result in our so-called 'best' solution, worked out for a set of assumptions which are no longer valid, failing to be the 'best' any more. However, to avoid being *too* pessimistic we will not assume that everything goes wrong at once! We will begin by supposing that the profits of £3 and £4 on our two products can actually be realised, but that some of our estimates as to the constraints are in doubt.

You will see if you refer again to Fig. 17.2 that only two of the constraint lines actually pass through the solution point, C; these two are the metalwork constraint and the wholesaler constraint. We say that these two constraints are *tight* at C – in other words, *all* the available metalwork time, and *all* the wholesaler's purchasing capacity, are being used up when we produce the optimum quantities of 12 'Donkeys' and 12 'Workhorses'. The wheels constraint and the tyres constraint, however, are said to be *slack*, because there is some spare capacity in these two resources. Making 12 of each type of barrow will use up 36 wheels, and there were 40 available, so 4 will be spare per week. As for the tyres, although we could have had up to 16 a week, we will only in fact be using 12, so again there will be 4 left unused.

It's clear from this that as far as the slack constraints go, we could make a small error in estimating the amounts available without affecting the solution at all. For example, if we had *hoped* to get 16 tyres a week but in fact only 14 materialised next week, we would still be able to make our chosen quantities of 12 of each kind of barrow, and our profits would be unaffected. Equally, if our wheel supplier suddenly rang up and said 'You can have 50 wheels next week if you want', we'd be rather silly to accept, because we wouldn't be able to use them – there wouldn't be enough metalworking time to make more barrows than our present 12 of each kind, nor would the wholesaler take them if we did make them.

It follows that we need only worry about the effect of errors in the *tight* constraints on our solution. And again, we will be optimistic and suppose that *one* of the tight constraints is definitely all right – let's say the metalwork constraint. We can then narrow down the problem to the question: what effect will an increase of 1 barrow in the number that the wholesaler is prepared to take have on our profits? (We could, of course, equally well have looked at the effect of a *decrease*, but that's rather depressing, and we get the same result in the end!)

An increase of 1 in the number of barrows the wholesaler will take means that inequality (b) of section 2 changes to:

$$w + d \leqslant 25$$

while the other tight constraint remains the same (inequality (c)):

$$3w + 2d \leqslant 60.$$

We *could* try to find the new position of our 'best' point C by moving the line (b) on the graph out by one unit, and watching what happens to C. This, however, is not easily done unless one has drawn the graph on a very big scale, so we choose instead to use an alternative method. You will recall from Chapter 1 in the section on making use of graphs, that the point of intersection of two lines on a graph represents the simultaneous solution of the equations of those lines. Now C is the point where the two lines (*b*) and (*c*) intersect, so if we solve the equations:

$$w + d = 25 \qquad \text{and} \qquad 3w + 2d = 60$$

simultaneously, we will find what the new value of C should be. If we multiply the first equation by 2, we get

$$2w + 2d = 50$$
$$3w + 2d = 60$$

and on subtracting the top equation from the bottom one, *d* will be eliminated:

$$w = 10.$$

Replacing this value of *w* in the first equation $w + d = 25$ gives us $10 + d = 25$, whence $d = 15$. So our new profit-maximising solution is to make 10 'Workhorses' and 15 'Donkeys'. What effect will this change have on the profit?

Well, the old maximum profit was £84, as we calculated in the previous section. We will now be making 10 'Workhorses' with a profit of £4 each – that's £40 – and 15 'Donkeys' with a profit of £3 on each – that's £45 – giving a total of £85 altogether. So the fact that the wholesaler is willing to take one more barrow enables us to obtain £1 more profit. We call this the *scarcity value* of the resource 'wholesaler's capacity', because it tells us how valuable, in terms of its effect on profits, this *scarce* resource is. By the same token, of course, every 1 barrow *reduction* in the number that he is willing to take will cut down our profits by £1.

However, useful though this information is, it does not represent the whole story. We would be quite mistaken, for instance, if we proceeded to say 'Right – if we can persuade the wholesaler to take 60 more barrows a week, that'll give us another £60 profit' – because there is no way in which we can produce a further 60 barrows per week – there wouldn't be enough wheels for them, to name just one problem! The scarcity value only applies over a limited range of wholesaler capacities, and we need to know what that range is in order to have a complete picture of the situation.

To find the range, we need to return to Fig. 17.2, and look at what happens to the solution point, C, as the wholesaler constraint is varied. When we move the constraint outwards, C will move *up* the metalwork line (you can easily see this by putting a ruler along the wholesaler line and then sliding it out), but it can only move as far as the point labelled F, since beyond that we would be violating the wheels limitation. So the greatest number of barrows which it would be useful to us to persuade the wholesaler to take is represented by point F, at which 10 'Workhorses' and 15 'Donkeys' – a total of 25 barrows – are being made. Conversely, when the wholesaler line is moved inwards, C will move *down* the metalwork line, until its progress is halted at D by the tyres constraint. In other words, the smallest number of barrows which the wholesaler can accept, without making our choice of C as the 'best' solution wrong, is represented by point D, at which 16 'Workhorses' and 6 'Donkeys' are being made – 22 barrows in total.

Thus the complete statement regarding alterations to the wholesaler constraint is that every extra barrow which the wholesaler is prepared to take will generate £1 extra profit, but only within the limits 22 to 25 barrows. Outside these limits, the problem is changed by the operation of the other constraints, and one can no longer rely on point C – the intersection of constraints (*b*) and (*c*) – to give the most profitable solution.

We must now repeat this process to see what will happen if it should turn out that our estimate of the wholesaler's capacity was correct, but the metalwork hours were wrong.

In that case, inequality (b) would stay the same:

$$w + d \leqslant 24$$

but if (c) were in fact an underestimate by 1 hour, then we would have

$$3w + 2d \leqslant 61.$$

Solving these simultaneously as before to find the new position of C, we find that $w = 13$ and $d = 11$ are the new 'best' production levels. You can check that this solution, with $w$ bigger than before and $d$ smaller, is reasonable, by watching how C moves as the line (c) is moved out on the graph. The new profit will therefore be $4 \times 13 + 3 \times 11 = £85$, so once again we are gaining an extra £1 profit by increasing the metalwork hours by one hour.

To find the range over which this applies, we must move line (c) on the graph outwards and inwards, watching what happens to C when we do so. As the metalwork line is moved out, C slides down until it reaches G, where the tyres constraint prevents any further increase. At G, 16 'Workhorses' and 8 'Donkeys' are being made, which will use up $3 \times 16 + 2 \times 8 = 64$ hours of metalwork time; more hours than that won't be any use to us because there will be insufficient tyres. When we move the metalwork line inwards, C slides up until, at B, it comes up against the wheels constraint. So the minimum number of metalwork hours for which C represents the best solution will be the number used at B, where 8 'Workhorses' and 16 'Donkeys' are being produced. The metalwork hours requirement for these is $3 \times 8 + 2 \times 16 = 56$ hours.

We can therefore state that for every extra hour of metalworking time which can be gained, an extra profit of £1 will be made, but this only applies between 56 and 64 hours. Outside that range the problem becomes a completely different one for which C may no longer be the best solution. Using the terminology introduced earlier, we say that the scarcity value of metalwork hours is £1 per hour. Of course, the larger the scarcity value of a resource, the more serious will be the effect on our profits of an error in estimating the amount of that resource we're going to be able to use.

## CHANGES IN THE PROFITS

The other kind of error in estimation which we might make is a wrong assessment of the profit resulting from the sale of each product. Suppose we were in fact only able to sell the 'Donkey' at a price which gave a profit of £2 per item, would our so-called 'best' policy of making 12 of each type of barrow still gives us the biggest possible profit, or should we perhaps be operating at totally different production levels under these changed circumstances?

To answer this question we need to go back to the profit line which we drew on Fig. 17.3. The point C turned out to be the most profitable in this case because it was the furthest limit to which the profit line could be moved without going outside the feasible region. But this will only be the case as long as the slope of the profit line lies between the slopes of the metalwork constraint and the wholesaler constraint. If the profits are such that the slope of the profit line becomes steeper than that of the metalwork line, then point D will be the furthest it can be moved, while if the profit line should become flatter than the wholesaler line, it can be moved up to B before going outside the feasible region. You can verify these statements by sliding rulers around the graph again.

So our best solution at C only remains valid as long as the profits are such that the slope of the profit line is between those of the two constraints passing through C. Now the slope of the wholesaler line is $24/24 = 1$ (actually, according to the definition we had in Chapter 1, it is $-1$, since it's going downhill, but as the same applies to *all* the lines on the graph we will omit the $-$ signs). Similarly, the slope of the metalwork line is $30/20 = 1.5$. Thus the slope of the profit line has to be between 1 and 1.5 if C is to be the best solution. But what *is* the slope of the profit line?

Well, recalling that we saw in the previous section in this chapter on finding the best solution, that all the profit lines are going to be parallel and therefore have the same slope, it doesn't matter which of them we look at to work out the slope, so we might as well use the one plotted on Fig. 17.3. The slope of that one is $20/15$ or $4/3$, and if you remember that the profit on a 'Workhorse' is £4 and that on a 'Donkey' is £3, you will realise that the slope of the profit line is just Profit on $w$/Profit on $d$. This may be the opposite way up from what you might have expected, if you are used to thinking of slope as vertical/horizontal. So, if you feel you are likely to get confused, it's always safer to draw in a typical profit line on the graph.

The result of all this is that we have shown that as long as the profits on the two products are such that

$$1 < \frac{\text{Profit on } w}{\text{Profit on } d} < 1.5$$

we are safe in using C as our best production level. But, to go back to the hypothetical case quoted at the start of this section, if the profits on each 'Donkey' fell to £2, we certainly couldn't use C any more to get the maximum profit, since the profit ratio would now be $4/2 = 2$, which is outside the allowable range we've just calculated. On the other hand, in the problem as originally posed, the ratio is $4/3$ which certainly lies inside the range we've calculated, just as it should. This in fact provides a useful check as to whether you have the profit ratio the right way up: if you have, the profit ratio as it exists in the original problem should lie within the calculated range.

## A DIFFERENT TYPE OF PROBLEM

The problem we have been looking at so far has involved the maximising of a profit subject to various linear constraints. But the same approach can also be used to minimise costs, in a situation where that is a more appropriate objective. We will illustrate this by the following example.

Suppose that our garden tool manufacturer produces, in addition to wheelbarrows, spades and forks. Both of these are made by the same workman, who takes one hour to make a spade but two to make a fork, and has been promised at least 48 hours of work a week. A wholesaler has a standing order for ten forks per week, so at least that number of forks must be made, while a productivity agreement with the unions specifies a minimum production of 32 items per week altogether (forks and spades).

If we let $s$ represent the number of spades made each week, and $f$ represent the number of forks, then we can set up the algebraic model for the problem in the form of three inequalities. First, the workman's hours constraint: the time he takes to make $s$ spades will be $s$ hours, on top of which he takes $2f$ hours for the forks, so his total working time is $s + 2f$ hours per week. This must be at least 48 hours; so we have:

$$s = 2f \geqslant 48 \qquad\qquad (a)$$

The wholesaler's constraint is easily written as:

$$f \geqslant 10 \qquad\qquad (b)$$

while the total number of items made per week will be $s + f$, giving the union agreement constraint the form

$$s + f \geqslant 32. \qquad\qquad (c)$$

By looking at the extremes for each constraint – that is, the cases in which all the resource in question is used up on one type of product and none of the other is made – we can find where the 'ends' of the constraint lines must be plotted. The line for ($a$) will run from $s = 48$ to $f = 24$; that for ($b$) will, of course, simply be plotted at $f = 10$, parallel to the $s$-axis; and that for ($c$) will join $s = 32$ to $f = 32$. The resulting graph is shown in Fig. 17.4, where as before the 'forbidden' side of each constraint – the side on which it is violated – has been shaded.

One difference between this graph and Fig. 17.3 should strike you immediately – the fact that the feasible region in Fig. 17.4, instead of being an enclosed area as it was in Fig. 17.3, now consists of the whole unbounded area above the three constraint lines. However, we can still identify the three corners of the region, which have been labelled as A, B and C on the graph.

We haven't yet got an objective function, so let us now suppose that we are interested in determining the combination of forks and spades which will incur the least total costs, and that we have already found out the costs associated with producing one spade and one fork, which are £4 and £6 respectively. We could now plot a cost line just as we plotted the profit line in the earlier section on graphing the model, but of course, we are now interested in moving it *in* as close to the origin as possible, rather than out. Naturally

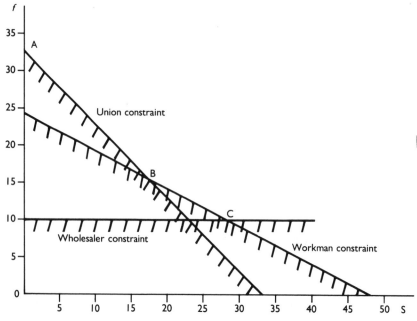

**Fig. 17.4** Linear programming graph for a cost-minimisation problem

there is no limit to how far *out* it could be moved – we can incur costs as large as we choose, though to do so wouldn't be very good business sense!

When it comes to moving the cost line *in*, however, the same arguments as used for the profit line will show that the smallest costs must arise at one of the three corners A, B or C. If we tabulate the costs at each of these points, we have:

| Point | f | s | Cost (£) |
|-------|-----|-----|----------|
| A | 32 | 0 | 192 |
| B | 16 | 16 | 160 |
| C | 10 | 28 | 172 |

So the objective (cost) function $6f + 4s$ is minimised when 16 forks and 16 spades are produced.

We could now proceed to a sensitivity analysis of this solution, asking what extra cost would be incurred if the workman wanted to work 49 hours a week instead of 48, or if the union raised its minimum production requirement to 33 items per week (the other 'wholesaler' constraint is slack by 6 forks per week at the solution point). However, we will leave it to you to verify, by the methods given in the previous two sections, that the extra cost of increasing the workman's hours by 1 would be £2 and that this would apply so long as his hours per week were between 42 and 64. As for the union's requirement, every extra item per week which they demand will increase costs by £2 also, and this statement holds true for numbers of items from 24 to 38 per week. The solution we have found will remain the best so long as the ratio Cost of spade/Cost of fork falls between 0.5 and 1.

## RESERVATIONS AND CONCLUSIONS

You will probably realise by now that linear programming, at least at this simple level, is a technique which can be carried out in a fairly 'handle-turning' manner, once you have got the basic ideas sorted out. This perhaps accounts for its strong 'student appeal' in examination questions! But the apparent simplicity of the technique should not be allowed to conceal its many limitations in practice, so it will be salutary to have a look at some of these.

The most obvious, if you glance back at the original problem of Apex Tools as posed at the beginning of this chapter, is that the method as we have studied it is restricted, by the graphical nature of the solution, to problems in which only two variables are involved. Had we had three products to consider in the section on setting up the model rather than two, we would have needed a 3-dimensional graph, which is just about imaginable; but for a company with, say 160 different lines, a 160-dimensional graph might be required, which certainly defies *my* imagination!

Fortunately there are other ways of arriving at the best solution without having recourse to graphs, though for very large numbers of variables these would certainly require the use of a computer. The method has such wide practical application that there are many computer packages on the market which will produce the solution once the model has been properly specified, together with all the information obtained from a sensitivity analysis. However, even setting up the model can be quite complicated if there are many variables and/or constraints, as you will see if you attempt Practical Exercise 7 at the end of this chapter.

Once the solution has been found, by whatever means, more difficulties may arise when attempts are made to implement it. For instance, the theory may tell you that you should concentrate all your efforts on producing just one very profitable item, but if abandonment of other products would lead to redundancies among your workforce, then you may have difficulty convincing your union representatives that this really is the best solution! Moreover, the 'maximum profit' solution which we found earlier was based on the assumption that all the items made could be sold at the same profit; but in practice laws of supply and demand, economies of scale for higher production levels, and so on, might render this assumption very dubious.

So linear programming isn't, after all, a cure for every industrial ill, but it *is* a very powerful technique with many applications in a much wider range of problems than we have been able to examine in this chapter. Other areas in which the method can be applied include transportation problems, where items have to be distributed according to demand from suppliers to customers and the objective is to determine the most economical way of achieving this; determination of minimum manning levels needed to operate a factory or production line; and blending problems, where raw materials have to be mixed in specified proportions to produce a variety of products, and we seek the best usage for the materials available.

You will find illustrations of some of these, together with further examples of a more elementary kind for you to practise on, in the questions below. If you want to read more about the topic, try reference (9) in the Suggestions for Further Reading in Appendix 1.

## Practical exercises

1 An amateur gardener wants to use part of his allotment to grow cabbages and cauliflowers. Each cabbage takes an average of 2 minutes to plant (including preparing the soil, etc.) and each cauliflower takes 3 minutes, and he's only got 2 hours to spare for planting them. He would have room for 72 cabbages if he did not grow any cauliflowers, but a cauliflower needs twice as much space as a cabbage. Moreover, his wife, who doesn't like cabbage, says she won't cook more than three dozen of them, whereas she insists that he grow at least 10 cauliflowers.

   (a) If a cabbage, on average, gives 4 helpings and a cauliflower 3, how many of each vegetable should the gardener plant to get the maximum number of helpings?

   (b) If the cauliflowers turn out to be very large, so that they give 4 helpings rather than the 3 he had reckoned on, would the solution you have recommended in (a) still give the most helpings?

   (c) What will be the effect on the number of helpings in part (a) if the gardener finds he only has an hour and three quarters to spend on the planting?

2 You have been asked to help your managing director, Mr Green, to plan the transport for his daughter's forthcoming wedding. He has already decided to hire Silver Shadow and/or Princess cars; a Silver Shadow will hold 6 guests but a Princess only 4. At present 36 guests must be accommodated. He insists that there must be at least two Silver Shadows, since the Joneses next door had two for *their* daughter's wedding last year. He has also promised the owner of the car-hire firm, in a rash

moment while playing golf with him, that he will be hiring at least seven cars altogether. On the other hand, the church carpark cannot hold more than 12 vehicles.

(a)  If the hire charges are £10 an hour for a Silver Shadow and £9 an hour for a Princess, how would you advise Mr Green to minimise his costs?
(b)  Mrs Green keeps inviting extra guests. By how much does the total cost increase for each extra guest, and over what range of numbers of guests will this apply?
(c)  Between what limits must the ratio of the costs of the two types of car fall, if the solution you have found is to remain valid?

3  What would happen to the optimum solution you found in Practical Exercise 2 if both types of car cost £10 an hour to hire?

4  Why do the constraints need to be linear in form if this chapter's method is to work? (Try drawing a feasible region with non-linear edges and see what happens when you push a profit line around in it.)

5  Find out if there is a package for solving linear programming problems on your college's computer, and if there is, find out how it works and use it to solve Practical Exercises 1 and 2 above.

6  The Foo-Ti Tea Company produces two grades of packaged tea, Puce Label and Olive Label, and teabags in a single grade. All three products are made by blending China, Indian and Ceylon teas in varying proportions: in Puce Label the ratio is $2:4:3$, in Olive Label, $1:6:2$, and in tea bags, $1:5:4$. Puce Label sells at 36p a quarter-pound packet, Olive Label at 30p a quarter, and tea bags at 32p a quarter, while the costs of the ingredients are £1.20 a pound for China tea, 80p a pound for Indian and £1 a pound for Ceylon. The company wishes to spend at most £480 a week on the ingredients, and wants to determine how much of each kind of product it should make each week in order to attain maximum possible profits within the constraints outlined.

Formulate the set of equations and inequalities describing this problem, and write down the objective function (you will not, of course, be able to solve the problem by hand, since it involves more than two variables. If, however, you have done Practical Exercise 5 then you *may* be able to use your package to solve the problem once you have formulated the mathematical model).

7  Make up, and then solve, a linear programming problem involving two variables and three or four linear constraints. Try to draw on an area that you know something about (don't invent a problem about making two sorts of cakes if you never set foot in the kitchen!) and make the problem as realistic as possible. Think about the ways in which it can't be completely realistic.

This problem will give you more insight into whether you really understand the technique than solving a dozen exercises set by someone else – and perhaps it will also give you a bit of sympathy for people who have to invent such problems all the time!

## Case study problem

Dear X,

You may remember that some time ago I bought a lot of integrated business software for our computer system. This included a program to do Linear Programming calculations, and I think I have a problem which it could help me to solve. It's related to the catering I do for afternoon teas – for cricket matches and so on – for which I make cakes among other things. I can either produce large sandwich cakes, which take longer to mix and bake but are quicker to decorate, or little fancy cakes which can be mixed and baked quickly but are very fiddly to decorate. I can mix up a large cake in 5 minutes and a batch of a dozen small ones in 3 minutes with my food processor; I can get 5 large cakes or two trays of a dozen small ones in my oven, and the time required is 20 minutes for the small ones and 40 minutes for the large (regardless of the number I'm baking at a time). But a dozen small ones take 10 minutes to decorate, whereas the big ones only take 4 minutes each.

With other things to be fitted in, I've decided I don't want to spend more than two hours on mixing the cakes and the same on decorating them, and the oven needs to be used for other things so only four hours oven time are available.

Of course, small cakes only serve one person each, but I can get 8 slices out of the large ones. What I wanted to know was how many of each I should make, within these time constraints, to get the maximum number of helpings possible (a large cake gives 8 helpings, and I regarded a small one as one helping).

The difficulty I have is in getting the problem into a shape that the computer program will accept! The questions it asks are:

Number of variables?
Number of constraints?
Next constraint? (enter coefficients, sign, RHS; to terminate constraints enter 99999)

(it keeps on asking this until I put in 99999 to keep it happy, then it goes on to – )

Objective function? (enter coefficients)
Maximise or minimise?

Do you think you could give me an idea what I should be answering to all these questions? I realise you aren't familiar with the package, but perhaps knowing about linear programming will enable you to make an educated guess at what it wants!

Could I actually solve this problem without using the package? I know I've paid for it, but this seems a great deal of hassle for what looks a very simple problem. There are actually some other things I'd like to know, apart from the numbers of each cake I should make – like if I can get someone to help with the decorating, so that the time goes up to 3 hours, what difference would that make? And what if I was mean and cut the large cakes into 10 slices instead of 8?

I'll be glad of your advice on this – it seems a simple problem, but as we expand there are going to be similar but more complex problems cropping up all over the place. Thanks for recommending my service to the Greenfield Rugby Club for their annual dinner, by the way – it looks as if that will be a lucrative contact.

All the best,

Jane

## Case study question

Indicate how you would respond to the queries raised in this letter.

## CHAPTER 18

# Planning a project: network analysis

## Objectives

Before starting work on this chapter, make sure you are happy with the general principles of modelling (*see* pp. 235–6). By the end of your work on this chapter you should be able to:

(a) draw up a dependence table for a set of activities;
(b) construct a network from the dependence table;
(c) find the earliest and latest starting and finishing times for the activities in your network, and hence determine the critical path and the shortest time in which the job can be completed;
(d) draw up a Gantt chart from the network;
(e) where appropriate, adjust the sequence of activities to make the best use of available manpower.

## THE OFFICE SUPERVISOR'S PROBLEM

Mrs Holmes is in charge of the general office in a large firm of chartered surveyors, and it is her responsibility to divide the workload among the three typists who work in the office. On this particular morning she is in something of a state; an important report *must* be delivered to clients as early in the day as possible, but its preparation is as yet far from complete. Her problem is to organise the tasks which remain to be done to complete the report in such a way as to have it ready at the earliest possible time.

She has made a start by drawing up a list of all the jobs which must be done before the report is ready, together with the number of typists needed to do each job and the time it may be expected to take (rounded off to the nearest 15 minutes). The list looks like this:

A   Dictation to be taken from senior partner – 1 typist – $\frac{1}{2}$ hour.
B   Dictated notes to be typed – 1 typist – $\frac{1}{2}$ hour.
C   Notes already dictated yesterday to be typed – 1 typist – 45 minutes.
D   All typed notes to be combined and arranged in order – 2 typists – $\frac{1}{4}$ hour.
E   Results of typing to be checked through with senior partner – 1 typist – $\frac{1}{4}$ hour.
F   Plans, for inclusion in report, to be collected from drawing office – 1 typist – $\frac{1}{2}$ hour.
G   All typed material and plans to be photocopied – 1 typist – $\frac{1}{2}$ hour.
H   Report to be collated and stapled together – 2 typists – 45 minutes.
I   Report to be delivered by hand to client's head office – 1 typist – $\frac{1}{2}$ hour.
J   Copy of report to be delivered personally to client's managing director's home – 1 typist – 45 minutes.

After a little thought she adds three further activities:

K   Make and serve senior partner's morning coffee – 1 typist – $\frac{1}{4}$ hour.
L   Allow 15 minutes for senior partner to drink coffee.
M   Collect and wash coffee cup – 1 typist – $\frac{1}{4}$ hour.

It is immediately clear to Mrs Holmes that, although she has written down the various tasks in the order in which they occurred to her, they don't necessarily have to be carried out in this order. In fact, many of them can go on side by side so long as there are enough people available. So her next step is to try to differentiate between those jobs which can go on simultaneously, and those which have to be completed before another task can begin. She can do this by means of a *precedence table*.

## DRAWING UP A PRECEDENCE TABLE

The idea of a precedence table is to help identify which jobs precede others, so that the logical sequence of the process becomes clearer. Two columns are drawn up, under the headings, 'Activity' and 'Preceding Activity'. Under 'Activity' the entire list of jobs noted in the previous section is written down, while under 'Preceding Activity' are written the activities (there may be just one or more than one) which *immediately* precede each of the jobs in the first column. By 'immediately' here we mean that the 'preceding' job or jobs lead directly into the following activity with nothing intervening, and that they must all be completed before the following activity can start. So, for example, we would say that activity L is the preceding activity for M. Although, of course, K – serving the coffee – also precedes M, it doesn't 'immediately' precede it in this sense.

Of course, there's a lot of scope for opinion in deciding what precedes what, even in such a simple problem as the one we are dealing with. In real-life project planning, this may be one of the major headaches. However, for the present we will abide by Mrs Holmes' experience and judgment in deciding precedence. Some are obvious: activity B (typing notes from this morning's dictation) can't start until the notes have actually *been* dictated, so A must precede B. On the other hand, typing the notes from yesterday's dictation can start straight away, so that has *no* essential preceding activity. Some activities have two jobs immediately preceding them; for instance, the photocopying (activity G) can't be done until the plans have been collected (activity F) *and* the typing checked (activity E).

When all these considerations are combined the following table results:

| Activity | Preceding |
|----------|-----------|
| A | – |
| B | A |
| C | – |
| D | B, C |
| E | D |
| F | – |
| G | E, F |
| H | G |
| I | H |
| J | H |
| K | E |
| L | K |
| M | L |

You can see from this that Mrs Holmes has apparently decided that the senior partner will not get his coffee until after the checking of typing (activity E) has been done. This is a fairly arbitrary decision, but if you go through the precedence table you will find that most of the other precedences are a matter of common sense. Notice that although the typing must be done before the photocopying, we don't show B or C as preceding E – only D, which comes *immediately* before E. B and C have already been done before D. This is what was meant by 'immediately preceding'.

The precedence table is certainly a step towards sorting out a sequence of jobs to be done – for example, it indicates to Mrs Holmes that it's no good telling one of the typists to do the photocopying unless the plans have already been brought from the drawing office – but it doesn't make clear which activities are going on simultaneously. To do that we need to construct a *network* from the table.

## CONSTRUCTING THE NETWORK

The basic principle behind the construction of a network is very simple: each activity will be represented by a line; the starting point of each line, marked by a circle, represents the stage of the process at which all preceding activities have been completed and the activity represented by that line can begin. The end-point of a line, similarly marked, represents the stage of the process at which that activity has been completed. The lines are linked together in such a way as to follow the logical dependencies established in the precedence table.

Thus we express the dependence of activity B on A as shown:

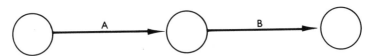

If we have *two* activities immediately preceding another, as is the case with E and F both preceding G, we show this as follows:

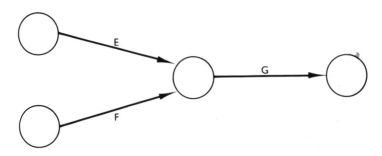

The circle where the E and F lines meet then represents the stage at which both E and F have been completed, so that G may be started.

Note that the *length* of the lines in the network has absolutely no significance. It cannot, for example, be interpreted in terms of the duration of the activities, as newcomers to the technique often imagine. Note, too, the use of arrows to clarify the direction of flow through the network; the general convention is that it is read from left to right.

The major difficulty in actually drawing the network is the connecting together of all its component parts in such a way that the logic of the precedence table is followed, without accidentally introducing any further, unnecessary dependencies. To start off, we identify the initial activities by looking for those which have no preceding activity – in this case, A, C and F. We might then attempt to represent the beginning of the network as below:

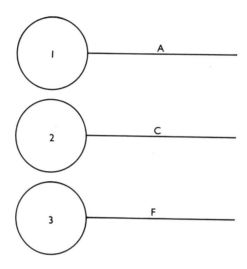

However, this would lead to a certain amount of ambiguity when we look for the point at which the whole process may be started. Is that point represented by the point marked 1 above, or by 2 or 3? Clearly we must avoid this ambiguity by having just one starting point for all three initial activities, as shown:

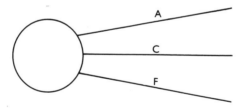

The same will apply at the end of the whole process: there must be a single point terminating all the final activities, to represent the point in time at which the whole process has been completed.

A similar situation arises when we have more than one preceding activity, as for example with B and C which both precede D. The only way this can be shown is by having B and C end at the same place, which is also the point at which D may start:

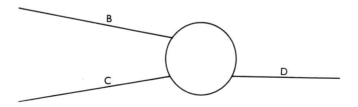

After this it isn't too hard to build up the network for all the activities except K, L and M – though it *is* a good idea to start off drawing it in pencil, since you will undoubtedly have to rub bits out! There's no one 'right' version either; there could be several equally correct networks looking quite different at first glance, though of course all would be logically equivalent. Anyway, my version for the network excluding K, L and M is as shown:

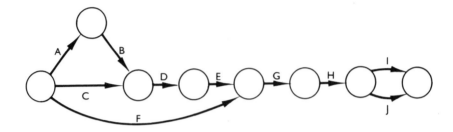

However, problems arise when we try to put in activity K. It follows E, certainly, but if we put it in starting at the endpoint of E, where F also terminates, that would suggest that F is a necessary prerequisite for K, which it isn't. But what else can we do? F *has* to end on the beginning of G, so we can't get round the difficulty that way.

In fact, the only way we *can* show the logic of this bit of the network is by making use of what's called a *logical dummy* – an activity which has no duration, occupies no people, and exists simply as a device to render the logic of the network correct. If, instead of attaching E directly to G, we introduce one of these dummy activities to connect E to G, then we can have K starting from the endpoint of E without implying any dependence of K and F. The dummy activity is generally indicated by a dotted line, thus:

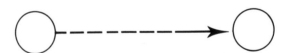

A dummy of this kind will be needed whenever the same activity appears in more than one place in the 'preceding' column in combination with different activities – here E and F precede G, but E alone precedes K.

We can now complete the network without difficulty, to obtain the final version shown in Fig. 18.1.

You can now see how the network helps to clarify which activities are going on simultaneously. For instance, there appears to be no reason why A, C and F should not

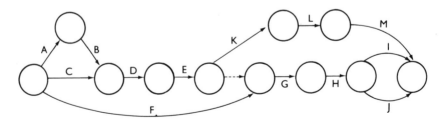

**Fig. 18.1** The completed network

be going on at once, and the same is true of I and J, among others. Of course there may not be enough people to do these jobs all together; we haven't yet bothered about that aspect of the problem.

## NUMBERING THE NETWORK

When we were discussing where to introduce activity K, we had to keep referring to 'the endpoint of activity E' and 'the beginning of activity G'. This is really rather long-winded; what we need is a shorthand way of mentioning the beginnings and ends of the activities, and this shorthand is provided by *numbering* the starting/finishing points of the activity lines. There are lots of different ways this could be done, as long as two simple rules are borne in mind.

First, in line with common sense, the start of an activity should be given a lower number than the end of that activity – we don't, as it were, go 'backwards' with the numbering. Second, no two activities should have the same pair of numbers at start and finish. This again is based on common sense; if we *did* have two activities starting at the point labelled 3 and ending at 4, how would we know which one was meant if someone referred to activity 3–4? There would be an ambiguity.

This point is particularly pertinent when networks of a more complex character are being analysed by computer, since many computer packages for network analysis *do* identify activities by their starting and ending numbers in just this way.

Armed with these rules, let's return to Fig. 18.1 and attempt to put some numbers in the circles. There's no real problem until we arrive at activities I and J, right at the end of the network, both of which start and end in the same place. How can we arrange a numbering which won't result in ambiguity? Once again, the dummy idea comes to the rescue. This time, by introducing a dummy activity after I (it could equally well be put after J) we can ensure that every activity has a *unique* pair of numbers associated with it. One possible numbering of the network is shown in Fig. 18.2.

## AN ALTERNATIVE WAY OF DRAWING THE NETWORK

In the section on constructing the network, we drew our network diagram according to what is called the 'activity on arrow' method – that is, the lines or arrows of the network were used to represent the activities, and their beginning and end points represented the points in time when an activity was begun or completed.

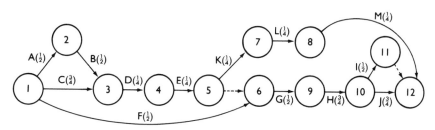

**Fig. 18.2** Numbering the network

There is an alternative method of constructing the network, known as 'activity on node', in which the nodes or points (in practice drawn as circles) of the network represent the activities, and these are connected by arrows to show the logical flow of activities. In this method the arrows themselves have no real significance. It is easiest to see how the method works by looking at the diagram above, which shows the network for the office supervisor's problem drawn in the 'activity on node' format.

There are a few points worth noticing here. First, note how we use a 'dummy' starting and ending activity so as to get a single beginning and ending node for the network. If we allowed the network to have several starts and/or finishes it would be difficult to identify the shortest finishing time for the project, and to identify where the zero time point should be.

Second, you will probably have spotted that, unlike the 'activity on arrow' version of the network, this one does not require the use of any logical dummy activities – the fact that both E and F precede G whereas E alone precedes K can be quite easily shown simply by organising the connecting lines correctly. This is what many people would regard as one of the great strengths of the 'activity on node' method.

Both methods are widely used, and I would not particularly recommend the use of one rather than another. What I would advise, however, is that you do not try to use both interchangeably – that can become very confusing. Choose one and stick to it. Most of what follows in this chapter applies equally whichever method you are using; where there is any difference, I will point it out.

## THE SHORTEST TIME FOR THE JOB

You'll notice that the time each activity takes (in hours) has been put into the network in Fig. 18.2 because one of the main objectives in drawing it was to try to find a way of organising the job to get the report completed in the shortest possible time. Now that we have the network to help us decide which activities may go on simultaneously, we are in a position to find this shortest possible time for the whole process.

If you examine Fig. 18.2 or Fig. 18.3, you will see that there are several ways of getting from the start of the network to the finish – that is, several different sequences of activities which must be completed. Identifying these 'routes' through the network by

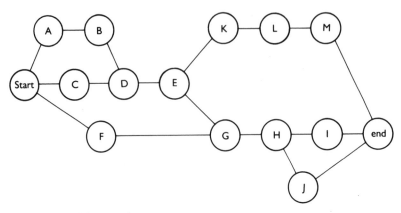

**Fig. 18.3** 'Activity-on-node' network

their numbers, we have eight possibilities:

$$1-2-3-4-5-7-8-12 \qquad 1-2-3-4-5-6-9-10-11-12$$
$$1-3-4-5-7-8-12 \qquad\qquad 1-3-4-5-6-9-10-11-12$$
$$1-2-3-4-5-6-9-10-12 \qquad 1-6-9-10-11-12$$
$$1-3-4-5-6-9-10-12 \qquad\quad 1-6-9-10-12$$

Each of these eight sequences of activities must be completed before the whole job is finished, and each will take a different time to complete. If you add up the times encountered along each route you will find that, for the eight routes in order as listed above, the times required are $2\frac{1}{4}$, 2, 3, $3\frac{1}{2}$, $3\frac{1}{4}$, 3, $2\frac{1}{4}$ and $2\frac{1}{2}$ hours respectively.

Now comes the crucial point: the *shortest* time in which the whole job can be completed will be determined by the *longest* of these routes. It is easiest to see why this must be so if we examine a bit of the network at a time. Between 1 and 3, for instance, we have two possible routes, 1–2–3 or 1–3. Now, although 1–3 (activity C) can be accomplished in three-quarters of an hour, the next activity, D, can't be started until route 1–2–3 (activities A and B) are also finished – and they will take an hour. So that will determine the earliest time at which D can begin; and the same will apply throughout the network. At each stage, it is the *slowest* activities which are going to determine how long the whole job takes.

So, looking back at the list of total times above, you can see that the shortest time in which the report can be completed is $3\frac{1}{2}$ hours. The route which gives this time (1–2–3–4–6–5–9–10–12, or activities A, B, D, E, G, H, J) is called the *critical path*, and the activities on this route are said to be *critical*. This term expresses the fact that, if any of these activities in practice turns out to take longer than had been estimated, the whole job will also take longer; if any of them can be speeded up, the job can be completed more quickly. So the time taken by those activities is critical to the completion of the job on schedule.

The remaining, non-critical activities, on the other hand, can be subject to a certain amount of variation in time without affecting the overall project duration. For example, if activity C took 50 minutes instead of 45, the start of the next activity, D, wouldn't be affected because it would still have to wait on the completion of A and B, which together take an hour. Equally, it would be pointless trying to speed up activity F; it only takes half an hour anyway, whereas A, B, D and E, which are going on at the same time, take an hour and a half altogether, and until they are finished the next activity, G, can't begin. We say that there is some leeway or *float* on the non-critical activities, and it's by playing around with this float that we can try to make best use of the available manpower.

However, it is by no means obvious from the network at present just how much float there is on any given activity. For that matter, the way we arrived at the critical path in the first place was rather hit-and-miss; even in this relatively simple case, there were eight possible routes to be considered, and it's easy to imagine that in a more complex network, listing all the possible routes would be a very slow process, in which some routes might well be overlooked. So we are going to develop an alternative, and more systematic way of finding the critical path, based on the fact that critical activities have no float.

## FINDING THE FLOATS

We begin by working through the network from start to finish, finding the earliest times at which activities can be begun and completed. For example, if we call the start of the

C AND F

whole process time 0, then that's the earliest activities A, ~~B and C~~ can start. Now A takes half an hour, so the earliest it can finish is time $\frac{1}{2}$. This determines the earliest starting time for B, which therefore finishes, at the earliest, at time 1 hour. Meanwhile C, having also started at its earliest time of 0, can be finished by time $\frac{3}{4}$. Now comes the slightly tricky part. D follows on from both B and C, so both of these must be completed before it can start. This means that the earliest starting time for D is 1 hour; although C is finished by $\frac{3}{4}$ there's no way B can be finished before 1 hour.

All this is really just common sense, and takes much longer to explain than to do. There are two ways of setting out the results of the arguments – on the network, as shown in Fig. 18.4, or in a table such as Table XI. You should follow through the calculation of all the earliest starting and finishing times either on the network or in the table; if you are using 'activity-on-node', the table may be easier to follow.

To determine the latest starting and finishing times for activities we begin at the *end* of the network, since the whole process has to be finished by time $3\frac{1}{2}$ hours. That means that the latest time by which activities I, J and M (the final activities in the network) must be completed is $3\frac{1}{2}$, otherwise the job will last longer than it need do. We then proceed

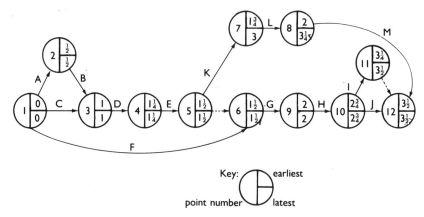

**Fig. 18.4** Earliest and latest times

**Table XI.  Starting and finishing times**

| Activity | Duration (hours) | Earliest start | Latest start | Earliest finish | Latest finish | Total float |
|---|---|---|---|---|---|---|
| A | $\frac{1}{2}$ | 0 | 0 | $\frac{1}{2}$ | $\frac{1}{2}$ | 0 |
| B | $\frac{1}{2}$ | $\frac{1}{2}$ | $\frac{1}{2}$ | 1 | 1 | 0 |
| C | $\frac{3}{4}$ | 0 | $\frac{1}{4}$ | $\frac{3}{4}$ | 1 | $\frac{1}{4}$ |
| D | $\frac{1}{4}$ | 1 | 1 | $1\frac{1}{4}$ | $1\frac{1}{4}$ | 0 |
| E | $\frac{1}{4}$ | $1\frac{1}{4}$ | $1\frac{1}{4}$ | $1\frac{1}{2}$ | $1\frac{1}{2}$ | 0 |
| F | $\frac{1}{2}$ | 0 | 1 | $\frac{1}{2}$ | $1\frac{1}{2}$ | 1 |
| G | $\frac{1}{2}$ | $1\frac{1}{2}$ | $1\frac{1}{2}$ | 2 | 2 | 0 |
| H | $\frac{3}{4}$ | 2 | 2 | $2\frac{3}{4}$ | $2\frac{3}{4}$ | 0 |
| I | $\frac{1}{2}$ | $2\frac{3}{4}$ | 3 | $3\frac{1}{4}$ | $3\frac{1}{2}$ | $\frac{1}{4}$ |
| J | $\frac{3}{4}$ | $2\frac{3}{4}$ | $2\frac{3}{4}$ | $3\frac{1}{2}$ | $3\frac{1}{2}$ | 0 |
| K | $\frac{1}{4}$ | $1\frac{1}{2}$ | $2\frac{3}{4}$ | $1\frac{3}{4}$ | 3 | $1\frac{1}{4}$ |
| L | $\frac{1}{4}$ | $1\frac{3}{4}$ | 3 | 2 | $3\frac{1}{4}$ | $1\frac{1}{4}$ |
| M | $\frac{1}{4}$ | 2 | $3\frac{1}{4}$ | $2\frac{1}{4}$ | $3\frac{1}{2}$ | $1\frac{1}{4}$ |

backwards through the network, using the same kind of logic as we did in obtaining the earliest times. For example, M has to finish by time $3\frac{1}{2}$, so it must begin by time $3\frac{3}{4}$, since it takes a quarter of an hour. That means that L, its preceding activity, must be finished by $3\frac{1}{4}$ at the latest and so on.

Just as with the earliest times, the places to be careful are those where two or more activities are preceded by or precede a single one. H, for instance, precedes both I and J. I can be started as late as 3 hours without holding the job up, but J has to be under way by $2\frac{3}{4}$ hours to be completed at $3\frac{1}{2}$. Thus H needs to be completed by $2\frac{3}{4}$ at the latest.

Again, you should follow through the calculation of these latest times in Table XI or on the network.

Once the earliest and latest times have been calculated, it is a simple matter to find the float on each activity. Those activities which have no float, and are therefore critical, are the ones for which the earliest and latest starting times (and, of course, the finishing times also) are identical. If you compare the zero float activities in Table XI with the critical activities we discovered in the earlier section on numbering the network, you will find that they are the same. On the remaining activities, the float is the difference between the earliest and latest starting (or finishing) times. Thus deferring the beginning of activity K, for example, by anything up to an hour and a quarter won't alter the overall time taken by the project – though it *will* affect some of the following activities. We will be returning to this point later.

## MAKING THE BEST OF IT

We still haven't considered the possibility that three typists may not be enough to carry out the job in the fashion represented by the network. Even if they are sufficient, we want them to make the best use of their time; it is more satisfactory to have a long spell at a job than to be doing it for a short time, go off and start something else, and then be called back to the original task. Perhaps by juggling around with the spare float time, we can free one of the typists entirely to get on with other jobs. But it's not easy to see from the network whether this is the case, so we introduce a further diagram known a *Gantt chart*, after its inventor.

Probably the best way to get to grips with the idea of a Gantt chart is to look at Fig. 18.5. Each of the vertical columns in the chart represents a fifteen minute period (if you are drawing such a chart on lined writing paper the easiest way to do it is to turn the paper sideways), and a horizontal line is drawn to represent each activity in the network, the number of columns occupied by the line corresponding to the duration of the activity. Conventionally the critical activities are put at the top of the chart. All activities are shown starting at their earliest possible starting times. while for the non-critical activities, the float is indicated by the dotted portion of the line. For example activity F could finish any time up to $1\frac{3}{4}$, although at its earliest it will be completed by $\frac{1}{2}$.

You will notice that the beginnings and ends of the activities have been marked with their numbers as on the original network. This is particularly useful when we start pushing the non-critical activities around, as it helps us to distinguish between those activities which can be moved freely up to the full extent of their float, and those for which the full amount of float can be taken up only if some of the following activities are also moved.

This distinction becomes clear if we contrast activity F with K. Both have some float, but whereas F could be carried out between 1 and $1\frac{3}{4}$ hours without altering anything else, any postponement of K will immediately mean a corresponding postponement of L and

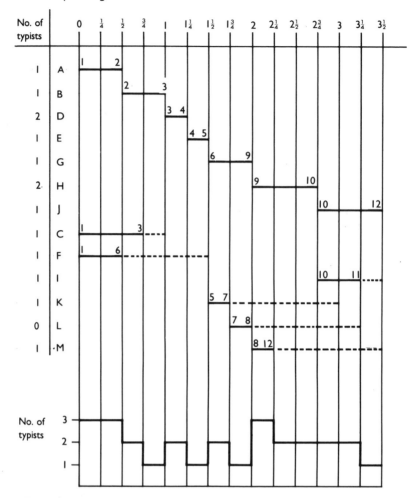

**Fig. 18.5** A Gantt chart

M also. This is made evident by the numbering, the end of K being number 7, which is also the start of L, so that these two activities cannot overlap. The technical name for float which can be taken up without altering any following activities is *free float*; thus F has 1 hour of free float while none of the float on K is free. It is possible although it does not happen in this particular network, to have an activity some, but not all, of whose float is free.

The advantage of the Gantt chart is that, by glancing down a column of the chart, we can see at once what activities are going on during that period. This in turn helps us to find out how many people are going to be occupied at any point in the process. To this end, the number of typists required for each task has been noted at the side of the table, and at the bottom of each column is shown the number of typists occupied during that period. To make the ups and downs in these totals even more obvious, they have also been translated into a histogram.

You can now appreciate how inconvenient the process as it stands is going to be from the point of view of Mrs Holmes, who is trying to organise the typists' time. There are several slack times during the three-and-a-half hour duration of the job, when only one typist is needed; but then the demand suddenly jumps up to three again, just for fifteen minutes. This could be quite simply avoided if activity M – washing the senior partner's coffee cup – were deferred until the last fifteen-minute period.

The other irregularities are not so easy to get rid of. Even if it is permissible to split some activities into bits – for example to do the first half-hour of C, then go away and do something else for fifteen minutes before finishing C off – it does not appear possible to avoid the need for all three typists at some stage. This could only be achieved by splitting F, which clearly can't be done – F, you will recall, is the job of fetching the plans from the drawing office, which can hardly be done in two halves. So it looks as if Mrs Holmes could be in trouble if one of her typists is off work on this of all mornings!

## LIMITATIONS OF THE METHOD

By now you will probably agree that the construction and use of networks is as much of an art as a science. This is particularly true of the juggling around – or *smoothing*, to give it the technical name – of the profile of workers occupied. There is no guaranteed way of arriving at the 'best' use of manpower; it's merely a question of trial and error.

There are also a number of difficulties which we've quietly swept under the carpet in arriving at the network in the first place. The scope for differences of opinion about what precedes what was mentioned in the earlier section on drawing up a precedence table, but argument can arise at an even earlier stage, when the process is being broken down into individual activities. The durations of the activities were only estimates, too. What happens if one of the wordprocessors in the office goes wrong, and using an ordinary

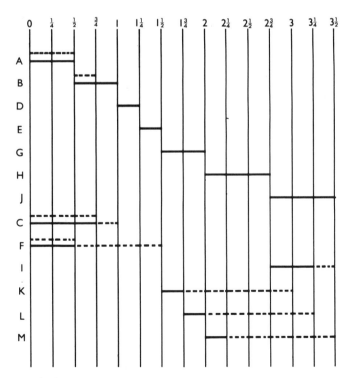

**Fig. 18.6** A progress chart

typewriter takes twice as long? The effect on the overall project duration could be serious. And the same could be said of the estimated labour requirements; the final stages of the project would look quite different if the typist assigned to deliver the report to the managing director's home insists on being accompanied by a colleague. We've also assumed that the typists are interchangeable, but suppose the photocopier jams and only one of them knows how to unjam it? And we have not considered any questions of cost – for example, it would be possible to complete the project more quickly by hiring extra staff, but this would have to be offset against the penalty cost of being late, in order to decide whether it is worthwhile.

To allow for the fact that what happens in practice may not be quite the same as what was planned for in theory, the Gantt chart is often converted, once the project gets under way, into a progress chart. Such a chart for the project under consideration can be seen in Fig. 18.6; it represents the situation at 10.15, the process having been started at 9 a.m. The dotted lines above each activity represent the portion of that activity which has been completed; in practice they would probably be coloured so as to stand out clearly. It seems that activity B hasn't finished yet, so D has been unable to start – which doesn't bode well for the completion of the project by 12.30 as scheduled, unless something else can be speeded up.

In spite of these difficulties, network analysis remains a very powerful tool for project planning and control. Of course, if the project is something such as designing, building and marketing a new model of car, the resulting network will be highly complex, and the analysis will require the help of a computer package. Such packages can often deal with some of the complications mentioned above, such as variable durations for activities.

## Practical exercises

(The first two exercises refer to the situation discussed in this chapter.)

1 What would be the shortest time in which the report could be ready if only two typists were available that morning?

2 Would the time for the project be extended if the senior partner insisted on having his coffee before checking the typing (activity E)?

3 If the use of an automatic collator reduces the time for activity H to 15 minutes, what effect, if any, will this have on the critical path?

4 Consider the following report from a (purely imaginary!) newspaper:

> Three Mudport housewives claim to be operating Britain's fastest freshly-cooked take-away pizza service. When our reporter visited *Casa Mudport* yesterday, it was the work of a minute for blond, petite Mrs Carole Smith (37) to take his order. The team leapt into action immediately. Strapping mother-of-two Julie Jones had the dough out of the fridge, kneaded, rolled and into the tin in four minutes flat. Meanwhile, glamorous 56-year-old granny Iris Brown took only half a minute to get the frying pan on. At the same time, onions were being chopped for 1 minute, then they went into the pan while tomatoes and herbs were prepared; when the onions had fried for 2 minutes, in went the remaining ingredients, and the whole lot was simmered and stirred for 3 minutes. Then this filling was tipped on to the dough ready in its tin, and the pizza went into the microwave oven for 5 minutes, while Carole took five minutes to make out a bill and collect the payment. After the cooked pizza had been whizzed into a paper bag in under a minute, our reporter was able take his first bite less than ten minutes after placing his order. Ugh!

(a) Draw up a network for this process, on the assumption that all members of the team can carry out any of the tasks, and hence show that the claim to service in 'less than ten minutes' is not consistent with the information given in the article.

(b) If one of the team is ill and cannot work, what will be the shortest time in which the remaining two can complete the process as described?

5 Pat, Mike and Tim have a lucrative business distilling and selling spirits. They are interviewed about this on TV chat show:

*Pat*: Well, we don't start operations until we've spent about three days going round our customers to check that they're ready to buy.

*Mike*: If they are, then I've to dig up the still – we keep it buried just to be on the safe side. That's a full day's work.

*Pat*: Then we need to get going straight away on the brewing – it takes all of seven days to make a batch.

*Tim*: Ah, but first we have to collect the potatoes, and you know we can never get them here in less than five days.

*Mike*: That's right; we have to collect enough empty bottles for the stuff, too, but that only takes a couple of days, and we can do it any time as long as we've got them by the time the brew's finished.

*Tim*: While the bottling's being done, which is half a day's job, someone has to take a day to go and fetch the hired van we use for distribution.

*Pat*: Yes – and then we get the stuff out to the customers in the next four days.

*Tim*: Of course, one of us has to keep watch for Customs and Excise men all the time the brewing and bottling's going on.

(a) Draw a network to show this process, and hence find the shortest time, if the process is started immediately after the show, in which the interviewer could be drinking a glass of the product.

(b) If Pat is arrested by the Customs and Excise officers, what effect, if any, will this have on the job?

6 Two motorway approach roads have to be constructed. The construction of each involves three separate stages: excavation, which takes three weeks; laying of the hard-core, which takes a fortnight; and laying and rolling of the top surface, which takes a week. Each job is done by a separate gang of workers, and each gang can work on only one road at a time.

(a) Draw a network to represent the task of constructing the two roads.

(b) Union agreements make it imperative that all three gangs should be on-site during the entire time the two construction jobs take. If each gang costs £400 a week when idle, and £800 a week when occupied, what will be the total cost of labour for the project?

## Case study problem

Dear X,

The purchase of the church has at last gone through, and we have got the planning permission we needed – it took much longer than we expected, so we are now in a financial position to go straight ahead with the building works. It's hard to know just how long it will all take, but we've worked out that the tasks to be carried out are the following.

The first priority is the roof – this needs to be done before anything else gets started, and will take about four weeks. Then there are structural alterations to the interior (three weeks), new plumbing (two weeks), and the installation of a gas supply (one week) – these could all go on at once, if necessary. Once the structural changes are finished, the decorations to the function room can be started, and should be done in a fortnight if there are no hitches. The cloakrooms, however, can't be decorated until the plumbing is all finished – though once the job's started it will only last a week – and the fitting of the kitchen, which is going to take a good six weeks to complete, depends on having both gas and plumbing finished.

We want to have the outside landscaped (to provide nice surroundings for wedding photographs etc.), which will be a slow job – the contractor reckons eight weeks, but of course that can be started as soon as the roof works are out of the way. When everything else is over we will need a fortnight to shift all the equipment from home to the new location, and then we can start operations!

However, there are a number of complications. We'd like to be ready in time for a big job we have booked in twelve weeks' time. The Gas Board is being difficult at present and refusing to install the pipe until after the plumbers have finished their digging; and there's a chance that the people who are doing the decorating of the function room won't be able to start until eight weeks from now, as they have another job on which they may overrun.

Taking all this into account, when would you estimate we could be operational? And where are the bottlenecks likely to be – should we lean on the Gas Board to be more co-operative, for example?

Can you ring me to talk about the problems – it is a fairly urgent matter for us? Monday is a good day to catch me. Thanks,

Jane

## Case study question

Make notes to assist you in discussing Jane's problems with her.

## CHAPTER 19

# Cutting down on queues: simulation

## Objectives

Before starting work on this chapter make sure you are happy with:

(a) the general principles of modelling (*see* pp. 235–6);
(b) the idea of a probability distribution (Chapter 9).

By the end of your work on this chapter you should be able to:

(a) construct a random number distribution which models the behaviour of a given experimental distribution;
(b) use random number tables in conjunction with your distribution to simulate a given process;
(c) set out the simulation in a meaningful way;
(d) draw conclusions from the results of your simulation.

## THE COMPUTER MANAGER'S PROBLEM

Dick Owen manages the computer section of a medium-sized manufacturing firm, and is responsible, among other things, for advising senior management on the purchase of new computing equipment. All the major departments within the firm – the warehouse, the accounting office, and so on – are equipped with their own computer terminals, but there is also a 'terminal room' which any authorised person may use. This room is used mainly by personnel of the Research and Development unit within the company, and at present it contains only one terminal. But the Research and Development unit's director has received complaints that the provision is inadequate and so he has asked Mr Owen to look into the possibility of purchasing more terminals for the terminal room.

However, terminals are not particularly cheap, and Mr Owen wants to convince himself that another one really is needed before he goes ahead and buys it. Of course, he could try hiring an extra terminal for a month or so and see what effect that has, but even that will cost money, as well as causing a certain amount of disruption in terms of rewiring and so on. He would also like to find out, while he is about it, whether a second terminal will produce enough improvement, or whether a third might be needed.

What he needs is a way of imitating or reflecting the main features of the pattern of terminal usage, so that he can look at the current pressure on the system and try out the effect of providing an extra terminal quickly, cheaply, and without disrupting current operations. But this problem differs from others which we have modelled in previous chapters, in that it contains a random or unpredictable element – in fact two such elements: the time for which each user occupies a terminal and the frequency with which users arrive. It is true that there have been unpredictable elements in some of our previous problems – for example, unpredictable demands for stocks in the inventory problems of Chapter 16 – but in those cases we could get somewhere near to a useful solution by smoothing out the random effects and treating the problems as if they were completely predictable. In the present case, the unpredictability *is* the problem; if users arrived at regular intervals and occupied a terminal for a standard length of time, it would be possible to work out whether or not there is time in the working day to fit everyone on two terminals, and the problem would be easy.

Technically, we say that the problems we've looked at so far have been *deterministic* – once we know all the necessary data about the problem, the solution is fixed. What we have in the current problem is a *probabilistic* problem, in which the effects of chance variations must be taken into consideration to get a useful answer. The way round this difficulty is to use some simpler sort of random process to imitate another more complex one; the method is called *simulation*.

## BUILDING UP THE PICTURE

However much this problem may differ from our other modelling situations, it resembles them in one essential respect: before any progress can be made towards modelling the problem, data has to be collected about the behaviour of the process as it stands. In the present case, if we are to imitate in some way the pattern of demand for the terminals, we have to know what that pattern is. This may seem a bit contradictory at first sight; here we are talking about the *pattern* of demand, when we've just been saying that it is random and unpredictable. But of course there is no real contradiction; although we can't predict exactly for any individual user who walks into the terminal room just how long he's going to be occupying a terminal, we *can* describe the overall picture of demand in terms of the average length of time users require, the longest and shortest times required, and so on. It's rather the same kind of situation as arises when you toss a fair dice; you know that the chance of throwing a 6 on any one throw is 1/6, even though you cannot predict whether the next throw will produce a 6. The pattern – 1/6 of the throws are 6s – is clear, but the individual cases are unpredictable.

With all this in mind, Mr Owen has been monitoring the usage of the terminal room for the past few weeks, and has gathered his findings into two tables. The first shows the length of time for which users are actually occupy a terminal:

| Time terminal occupied (mins.) | Percentage of users |
|---|---|
| 10 | 4 |
| 11 | 11 |
| 12 | 15 |
| 13 | 18 |
| 14 | 22 |
| 15 | 16 |
| 16 | 8 |
| 17 | 6 |

The second shows the interval which elapses between the arrival of one user and the next:

| Time between arrivals (mins.) | Percentages of occurrences |
|:---:|:---:|
| 5 | 6 |
| 6 | 14 |
| 7 | 17 |
| 8 | 19 |
| 9 | 14 |
| 10 | 12 |
| 11 | 10 |
| 12 | 8 |

His first step has been to work out the average length of time for which each user occupies a terminal, which, using an arithmetic mean, turns out to be 13.53 minutes. The mean interval between arrivals of users, on the other hand, is only 8.37 minutes, so it certainly seems clear that the one terminal at present in use is not sufficient and that queues *will* sometimes build up.

However, it is the random variations in arrivals and users' times on the terminals which are likely to cause delays and possible build-up of queues. So it is necessary to construct a process which will imitate the essential features of these two distributions in a simpler way. Such a process can be devised with the aid of random number tables and can help us to discover whether the provision of a second terminal will remedy the situation.

## IMITATING NATURE

We have already had a brief encounter with random number tables in our Chapter 3 discussion of sampling methods. A page from a set of these tables is reproduced as Appendix 3. You can see, if you refer to that page, that the numbers are arranged in two-digit pairs, and although this is only done for ease of reading, it is very convenient for our present purposes. There are one hundred possible two-digit pairs of this kind, running $01, 02, 03, \ldots$, and so on up to $98, 99, 00$. We want to distribute these pairs in such a way that they mirror the behaviour of, first of all, the 'time terminal occupied' distribution.

Now there are eight possible times in this distribution, so we could assign the numbers 01 to 12 to represent the first of these times, 13 to 24 to represent the second, and so on down to 85 to 96 representing the last; we would agree to ignore the leftover four numbers $97, 98, 99, 00$. Then, if we chose a figure from the random number tables which turned out to be 16, we would say that this would correspond to a user who occupies the terminal for 11 minutes.

But there's a defect in this system. We have assigned equal numbers of figures to each class, and since all the figures occur with equal frequency in the random number tables, overall we will end up with an equal number of users arising for each time – which is very far from being the case in practice. Our system of assigning the numbers to represent the times has failed to reflect the *frequency* with which each time occurs.

So what we need to do, rather than dividing up the numbers equally among the times, is to divide them up in proportion to the percentage of occasions on which each time occurs. We therefore assign the numbers $01, 02, 03, 04$ – four per cent of the total set of numbers – to represent the occasions when a user occupies a terminal for ten minutes, 05 to 15 to represent the eleven-minute users, and so on. With this arrangement, we have a four per cent chance, when we select a number from the random number tables, of obtaining one corresponding to a user time of 10 minutes, an eleven per cent chance of selecting one which represents a user time of 11 minutes, etc. – exactly as in the real-life situation.

Working in this way, we arrive at the complete distribution of the two-digit numbers as shown:

| Time terminal occupied (mins.) | Corresponding numbers |
|---|---|
| 10 | 01–04 |
| 11 | 05–15 |
| 12 | 16–30 |
| 13 | 31–48 |
| 14 | 49–70 |
| 15 | 71–86 |
| 16 | 87–94 |
| 17 | 95–00 |

We can do the same sort of thing with the distribution of inter-arrival times

| Time between arrivals (mins.) | Corresponding numbers |
|---|---|
| 5 | 01–06 |
| 6 | 07–20 |
| 7 | 21–37 |
| 8 | 38–56 |
| 9 | 57–70 |
| 10 | 71–82 |
| 11 | 83–92 |
| 12 | 93–00 |

A check on the accuracy with which we have apportioned the numbers between the times is provided by the fact that, all being well, we should end up at 00 – as indeed we do in both cases here.

Of course, had we had percentages for each time which, rather than being given to the nearest whole number, were given accurate to one decimal place, then we would need three-digit numbers to reflect them. For instance, if a more accurate figure for the 10-minute class of the 'time occupied' distribution were 4.3 per cent, then the numbers representing this group would be 001 to 043, chosen out of a complete set running 001, 002, . . . , and so on up to 998, 999, 000. Selecting random numbers of this form from the table, arranged as it is in pairs, is not quite so easy, but the method to be discussed in the next section would be exactly the same in this situation.

## CARRYING OUT THE SIMULATION

You may wonder how translating the two distributions into sets of numbers has helped us with the problem. After all, the numbers are really just another way of expressing the percentages, aren't they? This of course is true, but it is when we make use of the random number distributions we've constructed *in association with the table of random numbers* that we really start to get somewhere. For, by using the tables to give us the inter-arrival times and the 'terminal occupied' times, we can be sure that individual times will be as unpredictable as they are in real life, and yet the overall pattern of times will follow that established by observation of the real-life situation.

The way we choose to lay out the simulation is very much a matter of personal taste – there is no 'right' way. What is required is a layout which gives us space to record all the necessary data in a meaningful and fairly self-explanatory way. I have chosen to record the simulation under the following headings:

|  |  | *Terminal 1* | *Terminal 2* | *Queue* |
|---|---|---|---|---|
| Minute no. | 1 |  |  |  |
|  | 2 |  |  |  |
|  | etc. |  |  |  |

We will place a 1, 2, etc., in the appropriate column when a terminal is occupied during that minute by user number 1, 2, etc., and will also keep track of how many people (if any) are waiting for a terminal to become free.

If we decide to simulate a one-hour period, then we need to generate a number of inter-arrival times and 'terminal occupied' times. Taking the first of these, we will make use of the section of the random number tables beginning with 38 at the left-hand end of the third main block of the tables, and will read across the table by rows. There is, of course, no need to jump about in the tables; since the numbers are already occurring randomly, we won't make them any more so by taking them from here and there in the tables.

The first random number, 38, corresponds, on reference to the inter-arrival time distribution, to a time of 8 minutes elapsing between arrivals. The next, 41, gives an inter-arrival time of 8 minutes also, while the following figure, 14, gives the time as 6 minutes. Continuing like this, we find the first eight random digits in this row give inter-arrival times as follows:

| *Random no.* | *Corresponding inter-arrival time* |
|---|---|
| 38 | 8 |
| 41 | 8 |
| 14 | 6 |
| 59 | 9 |
| 53 | 8 |
| 03 | 5 |
| 52 | 8 |
| 85 | 11 |

For the 'terminal occupied' times, we will use the fifth block of the tables, beginning with 46, and will again read across to obtain the times:

| Random no. | Corresponding 'terminal occupied' time |
|:---:|:---:|
| 46 | 13 |
| 69 | 14 |
| 28 | 12 |
| 64 | 14 |
| 81 | 15 |
| 02 | 10 |
| 41 | 13 |
| 89 | 16 |

We are now in a position to write down the results of the simulation, but we need to make some sort of assumption about the initial state of the terminals. We will suppose that a user, the first in our simulation, has just arrived at time zero. Referring to the 'terminal occupied' times, we see that he will occupy a terminal – let's say it's terminal 1 – for 13 minutes. The inter-arrival times tell us that it will be 8 minutes until another user arrives, so the start of our simulation looks like this:

| | | Terminal 1 | Terminal 2 | Queue |
|:---|:---:|:---:|:---:|:---:|
| Minute no. | 1 | 1 | | |
| | 2 | 1 | | |
| | 3 | 1 | | |
| | 4 | 1 | | |
| | 5 | 1 | | |
| | 6 | 1 | | |
| | 7 | 1 | | |
| | 8 | 1 | 2 | |

The second user will occupy *his* terminal for 14 minutes, according to the times we've generated, and it will be another 8 minutes before anyone else arrives. Meanwhile the first user will free his terminal after 13 minutes. So we now have, continuing from above:

| | Terminal 1 | Terminal 2 | Queue |
|:---:|:---:|:---:|:---:|
| 9 | 1 | 2 | |
| 10 | 1 | 2 | |
| 11 | 1 | 2 | |
| 12 | 1 | 2 | |
| 13 | 1 | 2 | |
| 14 | | 2 | |
| 15 | | 2 | |
| 16 | 3 | 2 | |

User number three, who arrived after 16 minutes, will, it seems, occupy his terminal for only 12 minutes, and the next user will arrive after a further 6 minutes. If we carry on in this fashion we obtain the results below for the first 60 minutes of operation.

The simulation so far certainly confirms the computer manager's suspicion that a third terminal isn't necessary; only one user in the hour had to wait to get on to a terminal, and *he* only had to wait for two minutes.

Of course, an hour is a very short time, and in practice one would want to simulate a much longer period of time. This would get very tedious by hand, but with the aid of a computer many hours, even days or weeks, of operation could be simulated very quickly. This is the great strength of the method: the average length of time users have to queue to get on a terminal, the time that one or other terminal is unoccupied, the effect of introducing a third terminal, or of removing one of the existing ones — all can be determined quickly, cheaply and with no disruption to the real-life situation.

| Minute no. | Terminal 1 | Terminal 2 | Queue |
|---|---|---|---|
| 1 | 1 | | |
| 2 | 1 | | |
| 3 | 1 | | |
| 4 | 1 | | |
| 5 | 1 | | |
| 6 | 1 | | |
| 7 | 1 | | |
| 8 | 1 | 2 | |
| 9 | 1 | 2 | |
| 10 | 1 | 2 | |
| 11 | 1 | 2 | |
| 12 | 1 | 2 | |
| 13 | 1 | 2 | |
| 14 | | 2 | |
| 15 | | 2 | |
| 16 | | 2 | |
| 17 | 3 | 2 | |
| 18 | 3 | 2 | |
| 19 | 3 | 2 | |
| 20 | 3 | 2 | |
| 21 | 3 | 2 | |
| 22 | 3 | | |
| 23 | 3 | 4 | |
| 24 | 3 | 4 | |
| 25 | 3 | 4 | |
| 26 | 3 | 4 | |
| 27 | 3 | 4 | |
| 28 | 3 | 4 | |
| 29 | | 4 | |
| 30 | | 4 | |

| Minute no. | Terminal 1 | Terminal 2 | Queue |
|---|---|---|---|
| 31 | | 4 | |
| 32 | 5 | 4 | |
| 33 | 5 | 4 | |
| 34 | 5 | 4 | |
| 35 | 5 | 4 | |
| 36 | 5 | 4 | |
| 37 | 5 | | |
| 38 | 5 | – | |
| 39 | 5 | | |
| 40 | 5 | 6 | |
| 41 | 5 | 6 | |
| 42 | 5 | 6 | |
| 43 | 5 | 6 | |
| 44 | 5 | 6 | |
| 45 | 5 | 6 | 7 |
| 46 | 5 | 6 | 7 |
| 47 | 7 | 6 | |
| 48 | 7 | 6 | |
| 49 | 7 | 6 | |
| 50 | 7 | | |
| 51 | 7 | | |
| 52 | 7 | | |
| 53 | 7 | 8 | |
| 54 | 7 | 8 | |
| 55 | 7 | 8 | |
| 56 | 7 | 8 | |
| 57 | 7 | 8 | |
| 58 | 7 | 8 | |
| 59 | 7 | 8 | |
| 60 | | 8 | |
| | | ↓ | |

## WHAT CAN WE SIMULATE?

The sort of problem examined in the preceding sections is a very common candidate for solution by simulation. The terminal problem is what is known as a 'single queue, multiple server' problem. Presumably if the users are well-behaved they wait their turn in the order in which they arrived, then take the first terminal to become free. You may have come across a similar system in operation in some banks and post-offices: customers form a single queue, then go to whichever cashier happens to become free first.

But one can also use simulation to examine the alternative kind of queuing problem in which there are as many queues as there are servers – the situation which arises, for example, at most supermarket checkouts, where one has to make a decision as to which queue one will join. This further complication means that additional assumptions have to be made, in setting up the simulation, about which queue arrivals will join. The simplest such assumption is that a new arrival joins the shortest queue. This is perhaps a little unrealistic since most people, in such a situation, make some attempt to assess which queue is moving most rapidly – or which one contains the customers with fewest items in their baskets! So more complex assumptions have to be devised to fit the practicalities of each case.

These are all examples of queuing problems; but it is important to understand the word 'queueing' in a rather wider sense than that in which it is used colloquially. For example, patients under the National Health Service often 'queue' for a hospital bed – they wait according to some disciplined rule, then occupy the bed for a certain length of time, even though they do not actually queue in the hospital corridors!

Nor should we think of queuing as a process confined to humans. Planes arriving at a busy airport queue to land (the technical term used here is 'stacking' rather than queuing); items coming off a production line may 'queue' for the attention of the Quality Inspector; cars queue at traffic lights, intersections and petrol stations – the list could be continued almost indefinitely. So, the approach outlined in this chapter is actually of very wide applicability, though clearly it needs much refinement to be able to cope with the complexities of a realistic problem.

A rather different class of simulations involves problems where timetabling of interviews, appointments, and so on is concerned. For example, a market researcher conducting an in-depth enquiry might want to know how long to allow for each interview to be carried out, taking into account the way in which the exact lengths of such interviews tend to vary and the fact that some interviewees will arrive early and some late. You will find an example of this kind of simulation in Practical Exercise 2 at the end of the chapter.

Yet again, simulation could be used to help render our solution of the inventory problem of Chapter 16 more realistic. We assumed that there was no variability in demand, and no unpredictable element in the arrival – or non-arrival – of ordered goods. But with a knowledge of how the demand actually varied in practice, and of the times orders take to be delivered, we could build these unpredictable elements into our solution by means of simulation.

In fact, as you will begin to see, almost any problem in which a random or chance element is a significant feature which cannot justifiably be ignored lends itself to the methods of simulation – usually with the aid of a computer. However, don't get too carried away by the method – it is *not* going to iron out all the difficulties caused by the unpredictable nature of business conditions. It will help you to imitate a situation whose pattern of random behaviour is already known. It will make it easier for you to play around with that situation with a view to improving it. What it will *not* do is give you a guaranteed 'best' strategy in a given situation. The methods of simulation provide the evidence – a great deal of it, if you wish, very quickly, very cheaply; what you choose to *do* with that evidence is up to you.

## ◧ SOFTWARE FOR SIMULATION

As we have already noted, carrying out a simulation by hand becomes very tedious, so for realistic amounts of simulation some kind of software will certainly be required. This is often in the form of a special simulation language – rather like a computer programming language – in which *models* of the situation we wish to simulate can be written. There are quite a number of these languages on the market, many now enabling the user to carry out visual interactive simulation: to see a pictorial representation of the situation on the screen (queues containing little ikons of people, for example), and to intervene in the simulation, by altering distributions, changing the queuing systems, and so on, in order to explore the behaviour of the process.

MINITAB can be used in a limited way in conjunction with simulation, since its RANDOM command allows us to generate random samples from a number of useful distributions. If, for example, we want a sample of 50 'terminal occupied' times from the distribution given in the section, 'Building up the picture', p. 344 we first need to store the information about the distribution in two columns of the worksheet. Suppose we write

```
MTB) READ C1 C2
DATA)10 4
DATA)11 1
DATA)12 15
DATA)13 18
DATA)14 22
DATA)15 16
DATA)16 8
DATA)17 6
DATA)END
```

which has the effect of putting the times into C1, and the corresponding probabilities into C2. Then the command

```
RAND 50 C3;
DISCRETE C1 C2.
```

will generate 50 values into C3 from the discrete distribution in C1 and C2. We could do the same for the inter-arrival times – but we would still need to keep track of the simulation by hand.

LOTUS enables us to do something a bit more sophisticated, with the aid of its conditional (@IF) functions. You will find a worksheet for carrying out the simulation described in this chapter stored as SIM.WK1 on the diskette, together with notes describing the function of the various cell entries. Playing around with this – altering the distributions and seeing how the queue builds up, for example – will help you develop more of a feel for how simulation can actually help in decision-making.

## Practical exercises

1 Construct the distribution of two-digit numbers corresponding to the following:

| Queueing time (mins.) | Percentage of customers |
|:---:|:---:|
| 0 | 6 |
| 1 | 11 |
| 2 | 18 |
| 3 | 25 |
| 4 | 21 |
| 5 | 14 |
| 6 | 5 |

2 A sociological investigator wishes to interview a large number of unemployed persons, and is wondering how best to schedule the interviews. By keeping careful records over the first few days of interviewing, he finds that the times occupied by interviews are distributed as follows:

| 8 minutes | 8 per cent of interviews |
|:---|:---|
| 9 minutes | 14 per cent of interviews |
| 10 minutes | 23 per cent of interviews |
| 11 minutes | 30 per cent of interviews |
| 12 minutes | 18 per cent of interviews |
| 13 minutes | 7 per cent of interviews |

He schedules interviews at 10-minute intervals, but finds that only 40 per cent of interviewees arrive on time. Twenty per cent are one minute early and 12 per cent are two minutes early, while 16 per cent are one minute late and 12 per cent are two minutes late. Simulate a three-hour interviewing session, and suggest whether the 10-minute schedule will be adequate.

You may find it helpful to arrange your simulation as below:

| Interview due to start | Interviewee arrives | Interview starts | Interview lasts | Interview ends |
|:---:|:---:|:---:|:---:|:---:|

3 A small electrical repair business at present employs just one skilled repair worker, who is having difficulty coping with the volume of work. The length of time taken by repairs is distributed as follows (rounded to the nearest 15 minutes):

| Time for repair | Percentage of repairs |
|:---:|:---:|
| 15 mins. | 10 |
| 30 mins. | 27 |
| 1 hour | 35 |
| 2 hours | 17 |
| 3 hours | 11 |

The intervals between the arrivals of repair jobs are as shown:

| Interval between arrival of jobs (hrs) | Percentage of occasions |
|---|---|
| $\frac{1}{4}$ | 25 |
| $\frac{1}{2}$ | 30 |
| 1 | 20 |
| 2 | 15 |
| 3 | 10 |

By simulating an eight-hour working day, examine the effect of employing one additional repair worker, finding how much time, if any, each worker would spend unoccupied, and how long on average repair jobs would be kept waiting before work on them was started.

## Case study problem

Dear X,

I'm sorry not to have been in touch for such a long time – a lot has been happening! We got the church alterations finished eventually (your advice helped a great deal in deciding where to concentrate our efforts) and the new location has been a great success. So much so, in fact, that I have hired a full-time manager to run that side of the business, and I am now diversifying into contract catering for local private schools, small factories, and so on.

However, I've discovered one big problem in these situations, where we tend to use self-service with payment at a series of checkouts – that is, the checkouts are a bottleneck in the system. The trouble is that people arrive in a very haphazard way, and some take longer to pay than others. It's obviously a waste to have too many checkouts, but we've had complaints at several places that the food is cold by the time people have actually paid and start eating it.

Rather than come down here to look at our situation, perhaps you could see how things work in your own canteen and make some general recommendations based on your observations?

I'm very grateful for all your advice and help in the past – I hope I will not be bothering you quite so much from now on.

With all good wishes,

Jane

## Case study question

Take a queuing situation which you can study easily (e.g. your college canteen, a local petrol station, supermarket or Post Office, etc.) and collect sufficient information to enable you to carry out a simulation of the chosen situation, either by hand or using a computer package. Then draft a short report outlining your conclusions and recommendations.

# APPENDICES

# Suggestions for further reading

If you have read conscientiously through much of this book, you will realise that in many places it offers only an introductory treatment of topics which would repay much deeper study. One of the problems with statistics, especially for the newcomer to the subject, is that it is possible to treat many topics at a great range of levels, from school-standard to postgraduate. This makes it difficult to judge whether a book will be useful to you merely by looking at its title: something called 'An Introduction to Multiple Regression Methods' may be an introduction written for people who have already learned a lot of advanced mathematics.

I am therefore giving here a selective list of books which you may find helpful if you want to pursue in more detail some of the areas which I have covered at an introductory level or mentioned only briefly. You may want to do this either because your course requires it, or simply out of interest. In any case, I should point out that there are probably hundreds of books with titles such as 'Statistics for Business' or 'Statistical Decision-making for Managers'; those listed below are there because I and/or my students happen to have found them helpful. Some of them have been around for quite a long time, but that doesn't mean they are out of date – simply that they have stood the test of time.

## Revision of basic mathematics

1  *Essential Mathematics*: a *Refresher Course for Business and Social Studies*, Morris and Thanassoulis (Macmillan, 1993) – covers all the mathematical skills needed by someone embarking on a quantitative methods course as part of a business studies or social science qualification.

## Introductory or background level texts

2  *Statistics without Tears*, Rowntree (Penguin, 1991) – an excellent book which manages to cover quite a lot of theory using hardly any mathematical formulae at all. Good for self-study.

3  *How to Lie with Statistics*, Huff (Penguin, 1991; first published 1954) – the fact that this little book has been around for such a long time indicates that it has never been bettered as a guide to some of the peculiar ways in which statistics can be misused.

6  *Invitation to Statistics*, Kennedy (Martin Robertson, 1983) – a stimulating book which introduces some fundamental ideas in a readable and discursive way. Will appeal to those who like a rather philosophical approach.

## More thorough and mathematical treatments of so-called elementary statistics

7  *Introductory Statistics for Business and Economics*, Wonnacott and Wonnacott (4th edition, Wiley, 1990) – one of the best of the many large American volumes with similar titles; a very thorough and thought-provoking coverage of all the statistical topics included in this book, plus much more. Particularly strong on multiple regression and hypothesis testing.

8  *A Basic Course in Statistics*, Clarke and Cooke (Arnold, 3rd revised edition, 1992) – this excellent book modestly describes itself as a text for A-level; however, it gives fully worked out mathematical treatments of many topics which this book has covered without proofs. The reader needs to have a good grasp of calculus and algebra. Lots of nice exercises.

## Further reading on particular topics

9   *Decision Analysis*, Gregory (Pitman, 1988) – clear and easy-to-read coverage of operational research topics in much greater depth than in this book; includes simulation, investment appraisal, linear programming as well as decision theory.

10   *Making Decisions*, Lindley (2nd edition, Wiley, 1985) – a classic volume which covers decision-making and its ramifications with depth, clarity and conciseness.

11   *Decision Analysis for Management Judgement*, Goodwin and Wright (Wiley, 1991) – integrates the statistical treatment of decision making with other aspects such as psychology.

12   *Survey Methods in Social Investigation*, Moser and Kalton (Gower, 1985; first published 1971) – essential reading for anyone designing a survey or questionnaire.

13   *Plain Figures*, Chapman (HMSO, 1986) – a small book which manages to convey a great deal of sensible advice on presenting data via tables and diagrams; first written for civil servants to help them in writing Government reports.

14   *Statistical Process Control and Continuous Improvement*, Owen (IFS, 1989) – a very clear and readable introduction to the application of statistical ideas to quality and process control.

## Books making extensive reference to computers/packages

15   *MINITAB Student Handbook*, Ryan, Joiner and Ryan (2nd edition, Duxbury, 1985) – much more than just a handbook to MINITAB, this is a complete introductory statistics course illustrated by MINITAB material, and many interesting sets of real-life data (not all business-related).

16   *Statistics with LOTUS 1-2-3*, Lee and Soper (Chartwell-Bratt, 2nd revised edition, 1990) – a guide to using LOTUS for statistical work.

17   *Mastering Statistics with your Microcomputer*, Boyle (Macmillan, 1986) – a little book which gets through a lot of material in an entertaining way; particularly good on Exploratory Data Analysis (i.e. picking the bones out of a set of data without too much heavy work!).

18   *Exploring Operations Research and Statistics in the Micro Lab*, Kalvelagen and Tijms (Prentice-Hall, 1990) – very good value, providing plenty of interesting suggestions for experiments using the two diskettes of OR and statistical software which come with the book.

19   *Business Forecasting in a LOTUS 1-2-3 Environment*, Lewis (Wiley, 1989) – covers numerous forecasting models using specially-written spreadsheet routines which are provided on the accompanying diskette.

# Solutions to selected practical exercises

## Chapter one

**Answers to test of basic mathematical skills**

1. $(+)1$
2. $-2.5$ or $-2\frac{1}{2}$

$\left.\right\}$ If you got any of these wrong, read pp. 5–7.

3. $47/40$ or $1\dfrac{7}{40}$

4. $\dfrac{21}{40}$

5. $4$

$\left.\right\}$ Problems with any of these? *See* pp. 7–8.

6. $0.125$
7. $40$
8. $0.41666...$
9. $28/100$ or $7/25$

$\left.\right\}$ If you got any of these wrong, read pp. 9–10.

10. $67.5$      *See* p. 10 if you got this wrong.

11. $1.28$
12. $28.125\%$
13. £30

$\left.\right\}$ These three are covered on p. 11.

14. $x^6$
15. $x^8$

$\left.\right\}$ *See* pp. 12–13 if either of these is wrong.

16. $5a + 4b$      *See* pp. 13–14 if you got this wrong.

17. £$\dfrac{24}{k}$

18. £$m/12$

$\left.\right\}$ *See* pp. 16–17 if either of these is wrong.

19. $f + m < 150$      This is covered on p. 17.

20. $x = 5$
21. $y = 32/7$

$\left.\right\}$ *See* pp. 14–16 if these caused problems.

22. $p = 4$, $q = -1.5$      *See* pp. 17–18 if you couldn't do this.
23. At $t = -5/3$ or $-1\frac{2}{3}$      *See* pp. 19–21 if you got this wrong.

24. $(c)$
25. Below and to the right

$\left.\right\}$ Pp. 21–4 if you got these wrong.

## Exercise 1

1. $-16$  2. $0$  3. $2$  4. $32$  5. $14$  6. $-3$
7. $-12$  8. $-6$  9. $(+)24$  10. $-9$  11. $(+)2$  12. $25$

## Exercise 2

1. $\dfrac{7}{48}$  2. $-\dfrac{1}{12}$  3. $\dfrac{3}{22}$  4. $\dfrac{1}{8}$  5. $\dfrac{18}{7}$ or $2\dfrac{4}{7}$

6. $\frac{14}{20}$ or $\frac{7}{10}$  7. $20$  8. $\frac{15}{64}$  9. $-\frac{9}{32}$  10. $\frac{1}{6}$

## Exercise 3

1. $0.444$  2. $70$  3. $14.4$  4. $120$  5. $17{,}000$
6. $\frac{85}{100}$ or $\frac{17}{20}$  7. $4.2$  8. $0.1$  9. $1$

## Exercise 4

1. $3.2$  2. $0.17$  3. $42\%$ to the nearest whole number
4. £15  5. £16

## Exercise 5

1. $y^2$  2. $x^{-\frac{1}{3}}$  3. $x^2$  4. $p^3 q^3$  5. $n^{-3}$

6. $\dfrac{b}{a}$ or $a^{-1}b$  7. $1$  8. $\dfrac{x}{3}$ or $\dfrac{1}{3}x$  9. $x^{\frac{11}{2}}$

## Exercise 6

1. $6x^2 - 18x$  2. $a^2 + a - 2$  3. $3xy + xz$
4. $32{,}256$  5. $-33.75$  6. $2x^3 - 2xy^2 - x^2 + y^2$

## Exercise 7

1. $x = -5$  2. $x = \frac{1}{2}$  3. $x = 3$ or $-3$  4. $x = 1$

5. $f = \dfrac{v - u}{t}$ or $\dfrac{1}{t}(v - u)$  6. $x = -2.5$  7. $V = \dfrac{R - P - F}{n}$

8. $a = \pm 4\sqrt{c - b}$  9. $y = \dfrac{27z^3}{x^2}$

## Exercise 8

1. Cost $= (50 + 5m)$ pence  2. $1.5h + 1.25s \leqslant 12$
3. £1.60  4. $25 + (y - 12) \times 3$ pence

## Exercise 9

1. $x = 3$, $y = -3$  2. $x = 1$, $y = 2$  3. Equations are the same
4. $x = 1.5$, $y = -2$  5. $x = 3$, $y = 0$

**Exercise 10**

    1.  $(a)$, $(c)$, $(d)$        2.  $(a)$ slope $= 2$; $(c)$ slope $= 6$; $(d)$ slope $= 5/2$

3.

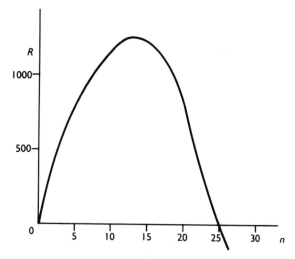

4.

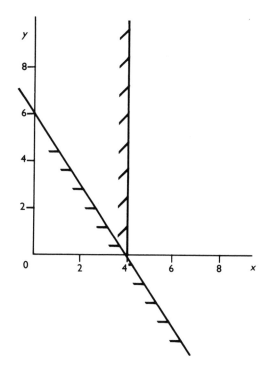

**Exercise 11**

    1.  Break-even at 1,677 items approximately

    2.  $x = 1$ and $x = 5$

    3.  500 items

**Exercise 12**

| | | | |
|---|---|---|---|
| 1. | 1394 | 2. | 1096 |
| 3. | − 10 | 4. | 11.45 |
| 5. | 20.608 | 6. | 239 |
| 7. | 3.93 | 8. | 869 |
| 9. | 9.9 | 10. | 11.3 |
| 11. | £8.84 | 12. | 3.15, 10.63, 12.99, 19.29, 28.35 |
| 13. | 82.5 | 14. | 29, 46, 55, 74, 91 |
| 15. | £297 | 16. | £19.98 |
| 17. | 1.48 | 18. | 0.64 |
| 19. | 5.11 | 20. | 6.2 |
| 21. | 3.68 | 22. | 0.18 |
| 23. | − 16 | 24. | £431.52 |

# Chapter two

1. (a) Systematic − every tenth person arriving to collect payment.
   (b) Stratified by grade of employee, using payroll as sampling frame.
   (c) A difficult one − perhaps a quota subdivided by time of day and day of week.
   (d) Random − using randomly generated account numbers.
2. Continuous − (a) and (d) (unless (d) is measured as 'numbers of sacks'). Discrete − (b) and (c).
3. (a) Leading question.
   (b) Too vague.
   (c) Two questions in one.
   (d) Hypothetical − under what circumstances?

# Chapter five

1.

**Breakdown of customers**

| | Home | Overseas | Total |
|---|---|---|---|
| Regular | 6,270 | 1,650 | 7,920 |
| Occasional | 2,860 | 1,100 | 3,960 |
| Dormant | 770 | 550 | 1,320 |
| Total | 9,900 | 3,300 | 13,200 |

(Last year's total: 11,000)
(*Source:* Company report.)

2. A compound bar chart, with major bars representing 'home/overseas' and subdivisions for 'regular/occasional/dormant' is probably best, though there are other possibilities.
3. A bar chart with bars arranged horizontally and axis in the middle, is perhaps best, so that positive and negative errors can be shown to left and right respectively.
4. 

| *Distance travelled* | *Number of visitors* |
|---|---|
| Under 5 miles | 0 |
| 5 but under 15 miles | 12 |
| 15 but under 25 miles | 10 |
| 25 but under 35 miles | 12 |
| 35 but under 45 miles | 4 |
| 45 miles and more | 2 |

This is only one possible version.
5. This should be a stepped graph.

# Chapter six

1.
|  | *Barsetshire* | *Cokeshire* |
|---|---|---|
| mean | £90,792 | £84,750 |
| median | £85,500 | £78,947 |
| mode | £80–90,000 class | £75–80,000 class |
| s.d. | £18,272 | £17,787 |
| quartiles | £77,083 and £98,571 | £75,000 and £87,333 |
|  | approximately | approximately |
| range | indeterminate | indeterminate |

(To obtain the mean and s.d., the top classes have been closed at £200,000; other closing points will give slightly different answers.)

   Both distributions have a longer right-hand tail, rendering the median perhaps more 'typical' than the means. Prices in Cokeshire are lower on average, and tend to be less variable (smaller s.d. and inter-quartile range).

2. 2.72 in each case; adding a constant to a set of data does not alter its s.d.
3. 2.72 and 8.18 ($= 3 \times 2.72$); multiplying a set of data by a constant multiplies its s.d. by the same constant.

# Chapter seven

1. Base-weighted 110; current-weighted 111.
2. £16 m, £16.70 m, £18.65 m
3. From 245 to 265 is a rise of only $20/245 =$ about 8%.

# Chapter eight

1. $\frac{2}{3} \times \frac{3}{5}$ or $\frac{2}{5}$

2. (a) $\frac{1}{2}$; (o) $\frac{1}{5}$; (c) $\frac{1}{10}$

3. (a) $\frac{4}{5} \times \frac{95}{100}$ or 0.76; (b) $\left(\frac{1}{5} \times \frac{95}{100}\right) + \left(\frac{4}{5} \times \frac{5}{100}\right)$ or 0.23

4. (a) $\frac{4}{5} + \left(\frac{1}{5} \times \frac{3}{5}\right) + \left(\frac{1}{5} \times \frac{2}{5} \times \frac{1}{2}\right)$ or 0.96;

   (b) No – he weeds out the easy ones.

5. $\frac{4}{12} \times \frac{8}{11} \times \frac{7}{10} \times 3$ or 0.51

6. Move – expected cost £220, as against £260 for staying.
7. No – expected cost of not paying is £2.50.
8. Sell now – expected result of keeping it is only £58.50.
11. It is *always* worth carrying on, even if $p$(series) $= 0$.
12. 2/250; standard charge would need to be $\geqslant$ £2.50.
13. (b) (i) go ahead even if results are negative – EMV is £2,400; (ii) Full launch is still the best option.

## Chapter nine

1. (a) 0.5940 (b) 0.1353 (Poisson, mean = 2)
2. 0.1298 (Binomial, $n = 10$, $p = 0.15$)
3. (a) 0.0668; (b) 0.8413; (c) 0.91045
4. 0.8965; once (Binomial, $n = 5$, $p = 0.25$; 'most likely' = having greatest probability)
5. 3 minutes approx.
6. 0.328 (Binomial, $n = 5$, use $p$(no order) = 0.1)
7. 0.0014 (Poisson, mean = 4.8)
8. (a) 2.66 g; (b) 1005.45 g
9. (a) 0.3770; (b) 0.3745
10. (a) 0.4013; (b) 0.3935
11. 0.1788 (using all values below 30.5)

## Chapter ten

1. Probability of vote greater than 50% is 0.7881
2. (a) Between about 22.2% and 52.8%;
   (b) between about 17.8% and 57.2%.
3. Probability of a sample with this percentage or more who can distinguish is only 0.0418, so claim is open to doubt.
4. Between about 5.5 and 5.7 minutes.
5. Approximately 16,640!

## Chapter eleven

1. Yes (STEM = 75 pence)   2. No (STEP = 5.5%)
3. There is an association between sex and unionisation ($x^2$ with Yates' correction is 4.69).
4. No ($x^2 = 0.55$, 2 degrees of freedom)
5. Yes ($x^2 = 2.56$, 2 degrees of freedom)

## Chapter twelve

1. $r_{rank} = 0.90$ − quite consistent.
2. (a) $r_{rank} = 0.95$, (b) The sign of $r_{rank}$ changes.
3. (a) 0.99; (b) 0.90

## Chapter thirteen

1. $y = 0.92x - 1.87$; 2.73 kg (use first 6 points only).
2. Year 15

## Chapter fifteen

1. £2,011.36   2. No   3. (a) £1,036.80; (b) £259.63
4. 6 months; £89.86   5. 'Excess'
6. £1,491.20   7. £1,309.50

## Chapter sixteen

1. Average weekly demand 45 boxes.
3. Order 30 boxes at a time.
4. Continue to order 30 (cost of this policy is £1.17 per week as against £1.62$\frac{1}{2}$ per week if orders are reduced to 20).

## Chapter seventeen

1. (a) 36 cabbages and 16 cauliflowers for 192 helpings. (b) Yes. (c) Only 177 helpings.
2. (a) 4 Shadows and 3 Princesses costing £67.
   (b) 50p; between 32 and 42 guests.
   (c) $\dfrac{2}{3} \leqslant \dfrac{\text{Cost of Princess}}{\text{Cost of Shadow}} \leqslant 1$
3. There will be a whole set of solutions instead of one unique solution.

## Chapter eighteen

1. No increase in duration of job.
2. No increase required.
3. Yes – the critical activities remain the same but the time for the job is reduced to 3 hours.

## Chapter nineteen

1. 01–06, 07–17, 18–35, 36–60, 61–81, 82–95, 96–00.

# Random sampling numbers

| | | | | | | | | |
|---|---|---|---|---|---|---|---|---|
| 78 41 | 11 62 | 72 18 | 66 69 | 58 71 | 31 90 | 51 36 | 78 09 | 41 00 |
| 70 50 | 58 19 | 68 26 | 75 69 | 04 00 | 25 29 | 16 72 | 35 73 | 55 85 |
| 32 78 | 14 47 | 01 55 | 10 91 | 83 21 | 13 32 | 59 53 | 03 38 | 79 32 |
| 71 60 | 20 53 | 86 78 | 50 57 | 42 30 | 73 48 | 68 09 | 16 35 | 21 87 |
| 35 30 | 15 57 | 99 96 | 33 25 | 56 43 | 65 67 | 51 45 | 37 99 | 54 89 |
| | | | | | | | | |
| 09 08 | 05 41 | 66 54 | 01 49 | 97 34 | 38 85 | 85 23 | 34 62 | 60 58 |
| 02 59 | 34 51 | 98 71 | 31 54 | 28 85 | 23 84 | 49 07 | 33 71 | 17 88 |
| 20 13 | 44 15 | 22 95 | 98 97 | 60 02 | 85 07 | 17 57 | 20 51 | 01 67 |
| 36 26 | 70 11 | 63 81 | 27 31 | 79 71 | 08 11 | 87 74 | 85 53 | 86 78 |
| 00 30 | 62 19 | 81 68 | 86 10 | 65 61 | 62 22 | 17 22 | 96 83 | 56 37 |
| | | | | | | | | |
| 38 41 | 14 59 | 53 03 | 52 86 | 21 88 | 55 87 | 85 59 | 14 90 | 74 87 |
| 18 89 | 40 84 | 71 04 | 09 82 | 54 44 | 94 23 | 83 89 | 04 59 | 38 29 |
| 34 38 | 85 56 | 80 74 | 22 31 | 26 39 | 65 63 | 12 38 | 45 75 | 30 35 |
| 55 90 | 21 71 | 17 88 | 20 08 | 57 64 | 17 93 | 22 34 | 00 55 | 09 78 |
| 81 43 | 53 96 | 96 88 | 36 86 | 04 33 | 31 40 | 18 71 | 06 00 | 51 45 |
| | | | | | | | | |
| 59 69 | 13 03 | 38 31 | 77 08 | 71 20 | 23 28 | 92 43 | 92 63 | 21 74 |
| 60 24 | 47 44 | 73 93 | 64 37 | 64 97 | 19 82 | 27 59 | 24 20 | 00 04 |
| 17 04 | 93 46 | 05 70 | 20 95 | 42 25 | 33 95 | 78 80 | 07 57 | 86 58 |
| 09 55 | 42 30 | 27 05 | 27 93 | 78 10 | 69 11 | 29 56 | 29 79 | 28 66 |
| | | | | | | | | |
| 46 69 | 28 64 | 81 02 | 41 89 | 12 03 | 31 20 | 25 16 | 79 93 | 28 22 |
| 28 94 | 00 91 | 16 15 | 35 12 | 68 93 | 23 71 | 11 55 | 64 56 | 76 95 |
| 59 10 | 0€ 29 | 83 84 | 03 68 | 97 65 | 59 21 | 58 54 | 61 59 | 30 54 |
| 41 04 | 70 71 | 05 56 | 76 66 | 57 86 | 29 30 | 11 31 | 56 76 | 24 13 |
| 09 81 | 81 80 | 73 10 | 10 23 | 26 29 | 61 15 | 50 00 | 76 37 | 60 16 |
| | | | | | | | | |
| 91 55 | 76 68 | 06 82 | 05 33 | 06 75 | 92 35 | 82 21 | 78 15 | 19 43 |
| 82 69 | 36 73 | 58 69 | 10 92 | 31 14 | 21 08 | 13 78 | 56 53 | 97 77 |
| 03 59 | 65 34 | 32 06 | 63 43 | 38 04 | 65 30 | 32 82 | 57 05 | 33 95 |
| 03 96 | 30 87 | 81 54 | 69 39 | 95 69 | 95 69 | 89 33 | 78 90 | 30 07 |
| 39 91 | 27 38 | 20 90 | 41 10 | 10 80 | 59 68 | 93 10 | 85 25 | 59 25 |
| | | | | | | | | |
| 89 93 | 92 10 | 59 40 | 26 14 | 27 47 | 39 51 | 46 70 | 86 85 | 76 02 |
| 99 16 | 73 21 | 39 05 | 03 36 | 87 58 | 18 52 | 61 61 | 02 92 | 07 24 |
| 93 13 | 20 70 | 42 59 | 77 69 | 35 59 | 71 80 | 61 95 | 82 96 | 48 84 |
| 47 32 | 87 68 | 97 86 | 28 51 | 61 21 | 33 02 | 79 65 | 55 49 | 89 93 |
| 09 75 | 58 00 | 72 49 | 36 58 | 19 45 | 30 61 | 87 74 | 43 01 | 93 91 |
| | | | | | | | | |
| 63 24 | 15 65 | 02 05 | 32 92 | 45 61 | 35 43 | 67 64 | 94 45 | 95 66 |
| 33 58 | 69 42 | 25 71 | 74 31 | 88 80 | 04 50 | 22 60 | 72 01 | 27 88 |
| 23 25 | 22 78 | 24 88 | 68 48 | 83 60 | 53 59 | 73 73 | 82 43 | 82 66 |
| 07 17 | 77 20 | 79 37 | 50 08 | 29 79 | 55 13 | 51 90 | 36 77 | 68 69 |
| 16 07 | 31 84 | 57 22 | 29 54 | 35 14 | 22 22 | 22 60 | 72 15 | 40 90 |
| | | | | | | | | |
| 67 90 | 79 28 | 62 83 | 44 96 | 87 70 | 40 64 | 27 22 | 60 19 | 52 54 |
| 79 52 | 74 68 | 69 74 | 31 75 | 80 59 | 29 28 | 21 69 | 15 97 | 35 88 |
| 69 44 | 31 09 | 16 38 | 92 82 | 12 25 | 10 57 | 81 32 | 76 71 | 31 61 |
| 09 47 | 57 04 | 54 00 | 78 75 | 91 99 | 26 20 | 36 19 | 53 29 | 11 55 |
| 74 78 | 09 25 | 95 80 | 25 72 | 88 85 | 76 02 | 29 89 | 70 78 | 93 84 |

# Cumulative binomial probabilities*

The table gives the probability of *r or more* successes in *n* trials, with the probability *p* of success in one trial.

| n | r | p = 0.05 | 0.1 | 0.15 | 0.2 | 0.25 | 0.3 | 0.35 | 0.4 | 0.45 | 0.5 |
|---|---|---|---|---|---|---|---|---|---|---|---|
| 1 | 0 | 1.0000 | 1.0000 | 1.0000 | 1.0000 | 1.0000 | 1.0000 | 1.0000 | 1.0000 | 1.0000 | 1.0000 |
|   | 1 | 0.0500 | 0.1000 | 0.1500 | 0.2000 | 0.2500 | 0.3000 | 0.3500 | 0.4000 | 0.4500 | 0.5000 |
| 2 | 0 | 1.0000 | 1.0000 | 1.0000 | 1.0000 | 1.0000 | 1.0000 | 1.0000 | 1.0000 | 1.0000 | 1.0000 |
|   | 1 | 0.0975 | 0.1900 | 0.2775 | 0.3600 | 0.4375 | 0.5100 | 0.5775 | 0.6400 | 0.6975 | 0.7500 |
|   | 2 | 0.0025 | 0.0100 | 0.0225 | 0.0400 | 0.0625 | 0.0900 | 0.1225 | 0.1600 | 0.2025 | 0.2500 |
| 3 | 0 | 1.0000 | 1.0000 | 1.0000 | 1.0000 | 1.0000 | 1.0000 | 1.0000 | 1.0000 | 1.0000 | 1.0000 |
|   | 1 | 0.1426 | 0.2710 | 0.3859 | 0.4880 | 0.5781 | 0.6570 | 0.7254 | 0.7840 | 0.8336 | 0.8750 |
|   | 2 | 0.0072 | 0.0280 | 0.0608 | 0.1040 | 0.1562 | 0.2160 | 0.2818 | 0.3520 | 0.4252 | 0.5000 |
|   | 3 | 0.0001 | 0.0010 | 0.0034 | 0.0080 | 0.0156 | 0.0270 | 0.0429 | 0.0640 | 0.0911 | 0.1250 |
| 4 | 0 | 1.0000 | 1.0000 | 1.0000 | 1.0000 | 1.0000 | 1.0000 | 1.0000 | 1.0000 | 1.0000 | 1.0000 |
|   | 1 | 0.1855 | 0.3439 | 0.4780 | 0.5904 | 0.6836 | 0.7599 | 0.8215 | 0.8704 | 0.9085 | 0.9375 |
|   | 2 | 0.0140 | 0.0523 | 0.1095 | 0.1808 | 0.2617 | 0.3483 | 0.4370 | 0.5248 | 0.6090 | 0.6875 |
|   | 3 | 0.0005 | 0.0037 | 0.0120 | 0.0272 | 0.2148 | 0.0837 | 0.1265 | 0.1792 | 0.2415 | 0.3125 |
|   | 4 |  | 0.0001 | 0.0005 | 0.0016 | 0.0039 | 0.0081 | 0.0150 | 0.0256 | 0.0410 | 0.0625 |
| 5 | 0 | 1.0000 | 1.0000 | 1.0000 | 1.0000 | 1.0000 | 1.0000 | 1.0000 | 1.0000 | 1.0000 | 1.0000 |
|   | 1 | 0.2261 | 0.4094 | 0.5564 | 0.6723 | 0.7627 | 0.8320 | 0.8840 | 0.9222 | 0.9498 | 0.9686 |
|   | 2 | 0.0225 | 0.0814 | 0.1649 | 0.2627 | 0.3672 | 0.4718 | 0.5716 | 0.6630 | 0.7439 | 0.8124 |
|   | 3 | 0.0011 | 0.0085 | 0.0267 | 0.0579 | 0.1035 | 0.1631 | 0.2352 | 0.3174 | 0.4070 | 0.4999 |
|   | 4 |  | 0.0004 | 0.0023 | 0.0067 | 0.0156 | 0.0308 | 0.0541 | 0.0870 | 0.1313 | 0.1874 |
|   | 5 |  |  | 0.0001 | 0.0003 | 0.0010 | 0.0024 | 0.0053 | 0.0102 | 0.0185 | 0.0312 |
| 6 | 0 | 1.0000 | 1.0000 | 1.0000 | 1.0000 | 1.0000 | 1.0000 | 1.0000 | 1.0000 | 1.0000 | 1.0000 |
|   | 1 | 0.2648 | 0.4686 | 0.6229 | 0.7379 | 0.8220 | 0.8822 | 0.9246 | 0.9533 | 0.9724 | 0.9845 |
|   | 2 | 0.0327 | 0.1143 | 0.2236 | 0.3447 | 0.4660 | 0.5797 | 0.6809 | 0.7667 | 0.8365 | 0.8907 |
|   | 3 | 0.0022 | 0.0159 | 0.0474 | 0.0989 | 0.1694 | 0.2556 | 0.3529 | 0.4557 | 0.5585 | 0.6563 |
|   | 4 | 0.0001 | 0.0013 | 0.0059 | 0.0170 | 0.0376 | 0.0704 | 0.1174 | 0.1792 | 0.2553 | 0.3438 |
|   | 5 |  | 0.0001 | 0.0004 | 0.0016 | 0.0046 | 0.0109 | 0.0223 | 0.0410 | 0.0692 | 0.1094 |
|   | 6 |  |  |  | 0.0001 | 0.0002 | 0.0007 | 0.0018 | 0.0041 | 0.0083 | 0.0156 |
| 7 | 0 | 1.0000 | 1.0000 | 1.0000 | 1.0000 | 1.0000 | 1.0000 | 1.0000 | 1.0000 | 1.0000 | 1.0000 |
|   | 1 | 0.3017 | 0.5218 | 0.6796 | 0.7904 | 0.8666 | 0.9177 | 0.0510 | 0.9713 | 0.9847 | 0.9922 |
|   | 2 | 0.0444 | 0.1498 | 0.2836 | 0.4234 | 0.5551 | 0.6706 | 0.7662 | 0.8413 | 0.8975 | 0.9375 |
|   | 3 | 0.0038 | 0.0258 | 0.0799 | 0.1481 | 0.2436 | 0.3529 | 0.4677 | 0.5800 | 0.6835 | 0.7734 |
|   | 4 | 0.0002 | 0.0028 | 0.0122 | 0.0334 | 0.0706 | 0.1260 | 0.1998 | 0.2897 | 0.3917 | 0.5000 |
|   | 5 |  | 0.0002 | 0.0013 | 0.0047 | 0.0129 | 0.0288 | 0.0556 | 0.0962 | 0.1529 | 0.2266 |
|   | 6 |  |  | 0.0001 | 0.0004 | 0.0014 | 0.0038 | 0.0090 | 0.0188 | 0.0357 | 0.0625 |
|   | 7 |  |  |  |  | 0.0001 | 0.0002 | 0.0006 | 0.0016 | 0.0037 | 0.0078 |
| 8 | 0 | 1.0000 | 1.0000 | 1.0000 | 1.0000 | 1.0000 | 1.0000 | 1.0000 | 1.0000 | 1.0000 | 1.0000 |
|   | 1 | 0.3366 | 0.5695 | 0.7275 | 0.8322 | 0.8999 | 0.9424 | 0.9681 | 0.0933 | 0.9915 | 0.9961 |
|   | 2 | 0.0573 | 0.1869 | 0.3428 | 0.4967 | 0.6329 | 0.7447 | 0.8308 | 0.8937 | 0.9367 | 0.9649 |
|   | 3 | 0.0058 | 0.0381 | 0.1052 | 0.2031 | 0.3214 | 0.4482 | 0.5721 | 0.6847 | 0.7798 | 0.8555 |
|   | 4 | 0.0004 | 0.0050 | 0.0213 | 0.0563 | 0.1138 | 0.1941 | 0.2935 | 0.4060 | 0.5230 | 0.6367 |
|   | 5 |  | 0.0044 | 0.0028 | 0.0104 | 0.0273 | 0.0580 | 0.1060 | 0.1738 | 0.2603 | 0.3633 |
|   | 6 |  |  | 0.0002 | 0.0012 | 0.0042 | 0.0113 | 0.0252 | 0.0499 | 0.0884 | 0.1445 |
|   | 7 |  |  |  | 0.0001 | 0.0004 | 0.0013 | 0.0035 | 0.0086 | 0.0181 | 0.0351 |
|   | 8 |  |  |  |  |  | 0.0001 | 0.0002 | 0.0007 | 0.0017 | 0.0039 |

| n | r | p = 0.05 | 0.1 | 0.15 | 0.2 | 0.25 | 0.3 | 0.35 | 0.4 | 0.45 | 0.5 |
|---|---|---|---|---|---|---|---|---|---|---|---|
| 9 | 0 | 1.0000 | 1.0000 | 1.0000 | 1.0000 | 1.0000 | 1.0000 | 1.0000 | 1.0000 | 1.0000 | 1.0000 |
|   | 1 | 0.3697 | 0.6125 | 0.7684 | 0.8659 | 0.9249 | 0.9595 | 0.9793 | 0.9898 | 0.9954 | 0.9982 |
|   | 2 | 0.0712 | 0.2251 | 0.4005 | 0.5639 | 0.6996 | 0.8039 | 0.8789 | 0.9293 | 0.9615 | 0.9806 |
|   | 3 | 0.0083 | 0.0529 | 0.1408 | 0.2619 | 0.3993 | 0.5371 | 0.6627 | 0.7681 | 0.8505 | 0.9103 |
|   | 4 | 0.0006 | 0.0083 | 0.0339 | 0.0857 | 0.1657 | 0.2703 | 0.3911 | 0.5173 | 0.6386 | 0.7642 |
|   | 5 |        | 0.0009 | 0.0056 | 0.0196 | 0.0489 | 0.0988 | 0.1717 | 0.2665 | 0.3786 | 0.5001 |
|   | 6 |        | 0.0001 | 0.0006 | 0.0031 | 0.0100 | 0.0253 | 0.0536 | 0.0993 | 0.1658 | 0.2540 |
|   | 7 |        |        |        | 0.0003 | 0.0013 | 0.0043 | 0.0112 | 0.0250 | 0.0498 | 0.0899 |
|   | 8 |        |        |        |        | 0.0001 | 0.0004 | 0.0014 | 0.0038 | 0.0091 | 0.0196 |
|   | 9 |        |        |        |        |        |        | 0.0001 | 0.0003 | 0.0008 | 0.0020 |
| 10 | 0 | 1.0000 | 1.0000 | 1.0000 | 1.0000 | 1.0000 | 1.0000 | 1.0000 | 1.0000 | 1.0000 | 1.0000 |
|   | 1 | 0.4013 | 0.6513 | 0.8030 | 0.8926 | 0.9437 | 0.9717 | 0.9866 | 0.9940 | 0.9975 | 0.9991 |
|   | 2 | 0.0862 | 0.2639 | 0.4556 | 0.6242 | 0.7560 | 0.8506 | 0.9141 | 0.9537 | 0.9768 | 0.9893 |
|   | 3 | 0.0116 | 0.0702 | 0.1797 | 0.3222 | 0.4744 | 0.6171 | 0.7384 | 0.8328 | 0.9005 | 0.9454 |
|   | 4 | 0.0011 | 0.0128 | 0.0499 | 0.1209 | 0.2241 | 0.3503 | 0.4862 | 0.6178 | 0.7340 | 0.8282 |
|   | 5 | 0.0001 | 0.0016 | 0.0098 | 0.0328 | 0.0781 | 0.1502 | 0.2485 | 0.3670 | 0.4956 | 0.6231 |
|   | 6 |        | 0.0001 | 0.0013 | 0.0064 | 0.0197 | 0.0473 | 0.0949 | 0.1663 | 0.2616 | 0.3770 |
|   | 7 |        |        | 0.0001 | 0.0009 | 0.0035 | 0.0105 | 0.0260 | 0.0548 | 0.1020 | 0.1719 |
|   | 8 |        |        |        | 0.0001 | 0.0004 | 0.0015 | 0.0048 | 0.0123 | 0.0274 | 0.0547 |
|   | 9 |        |        |        |        |        | 0.0001 | 0.0005 | 0.0017 | 0.0045 | 0.0108 |
|   | 10 |       |        |        |        |        |        |        | 0.0001 | 0.0003 | 0.0010 |

\* This table is taken in part from Table 1 of *Statistical Tables for Science, Engineering, Management and Business Studies* by J. Murdoch and J. A. Barnes published by Macmillan, London and Basingstoke, and by permission of the authors and publishers.

# APPENDIX 5

# Cumulative Poisson probabilities*

The table gives the probability that *r or more* random events are contained in an interval when the average number of events per interval is *m*.

| m = | 0.1 | 0.2 | 0.3 | 0.4 | 0.5 | 0.6 | 0.7 | 0.8 | 0.9 | 1.0 |
|---|---|---|---|---|---|---|---|---|---|---|
| r = 0 | 1.0000 | 1.0000 | 1.0000 | 1.0000 | 1.0000 | 1.0000 | 1.0000 | 1.0000 | 1.0000 | 1.0000 |
| 1 | 0.0952 | 0.1813 | 0.2592 | 0.3297 | 0.3935 | 0.4512 | 0.5034 | 0.5507 | 0.5934 | 0.6321 |
| 2 | 0.0047 | 0.0175 | 0.0369 | 0.0616 | 0.0902 | 0.1219 | 0.1558 | 0.1912 | 0.2275 | 0.2642 |
| 3 | 0.0002 | 0.0011 | 0.0036 | 0.0079 | 0.0144 | 0.0231 | 0.0341 | 0.0474 | 0.0629 | 0.0803 |
| 4 | | 0.0001 | 0.0003 | 0.0008 | 0.0018 | 0.0034 | 0.0058 | 0.0091 | 0.0135 | 0.0190 |
| 5 | | | | 0.0001 | 0.0002 | 0.0004 | 0.0008 | 0.0014 | 0.0023 | 0.0037 |
| 6 | | | | | | | 0.0001 | 0.0002 | 0.0003 | 0.0006 |
| 7 | | | | | | | | | | 0.0001 |

| m = | 1.1 | 1.2 | 1.3 | 1.4 | 1.5 | 1.6 | 1.7 | 1.8 | 1.9 | 2.0 |
|---|---|---|---|---|---|---|---|---|---|---|
| r = 0 | 1.0000 | 1.0000 | 1.0000 | 1.0000 | 1.0000 | 1.0000 | 1.0000 | 1.0000 | 1.0000 | 1.0000 |
| 1 | 0.6671 | 0.6988 | 0.7275 | 0.7534 | 0.7769 | 0.7981 | 0.8173 | 0.8347 | 0.8504 | 0.8647 |
| 2 | 0.3010 | 0.3374 | 0.3732 | 0.4082 | 0.4422 | 0.4751 | 0.5068 | 0.5372 | 0.5663 | 0.5940 |
| 3 | 0.0996 | 0.1205 | 0.1429 | 0.1665 | 0.1912 | 0.2166 | 0.2428 | 0.2694 | 0.2963 | 0.3233 |
| 4 | 0.0257 | 0.0338 | 0.0431 | 0.0537 | 0.0656 | 0.0788 | 0.0932 | 0.1087 | 0.1253 | 0.1429 |
| 5 | 0.0054 | 0.0077 | 0.0107 | 0.0143 | 0.0186 | 0.0237 | 0.0296 | 0.0364 | 0.0441 | 0.0527 |
| 6 | 0.0010 | 0.0015 | 0.0022 | 0.0032 | 0.0045 | 0.0060 | 0.0080 | 0.0104 | 0.0132 | 0.0166 |
| 7 | 0.0001 | 0.0003 | 0.0004 | 0.0006 | 0.0009 | 0.0013 | 0.0019 | 0.0026 | 0.0034 | 0.0045 |
| 8 | | | 0.0001 | 0.0001 | 0.0002 | 0.0003 | 0.0004 | 0.0006 | 0.0008 | 0.0011 |
| 9 | | | | | | | 0.0001 | 0.0001 | 0.0002 | 0.0002 |

| m = | 2.1 | 2.2 | 2.3 | 2.4 | 2.5 | 2.6 | 2.7 | 2.8 | 2.9 | 3.0 |
|---|---|---|---|---|---|---|---|---|---|---|
| r = 0 | 1.0000 | 1.0000 | 1.0000 | 1.0000 | 1.0000 | 1.0000 | 1.0000 | 1.0000 | 1.0000 | 1.0000 |
| 1 | 0.8775 | 0.8892 | 0.8997 | 0.9093 | 0.9179 | 0.9257 | 0.9328 | 0.9392 | 0.940 | 0.9502 |
| 2 | 0.6204 | 0.6454 | 0.6691 | 0.6916 | 0.7127 | 0.7326 | 0.7513 | 0.7689 | 0.7854 | 0.8009 |
| 3 | 0.3504 | 0.3773 | 0.4040 | 0.4303 | 0.4562 | 0.4816 | 0.5064 | 0.5305 | 0.550 | 0.5768 |
| 4 | 0.1614 | 0.1806 | 0.2007 | 0.2213 | 0.2424 | 0.2640 | 0.2859 | 0.3081 | 0.3304 | 0.3528 |
| 5 | 0.0621 | 0.0725 | 0.0838 | 0.0959 | 0.1088 | 0.1226 | 0.1371 | 0.1523 | 0.182 | 0.1847 |
| 6 | 0.0204 | 0.0249 | 0.0300 | 0.0357 | 0.0420 | 0.0490 | 0.0567 | 0.0651 | 0.0742 | 0.0839 |
| 7 | 0.0059 | 0.0075 | 0.0094 | 0.0116 | 0.0142 | 0.0172 | 0.0206 | 0.0244 | 0.0287 | 0.0335 |
| 8 | 0.0015 | 0.0020 | 0.0026 | 0.0033 | 0.0042 | 0.0053 | 0.0066 | 0.0081 | 0.0099 | 0.0119 |
| 9 | 0.0003 | 0.0005 | 0.0006 | 0.0009 | 0.0011 | 0.0015 | 0.0019 | 0.0024 | 0.0031 | 0.0038 |
| 10 | 0.0001 | 0.0001 | 0.0001 | 0.0002 | 0.0003 | 0.0004 | 0.0005 | 0.0007 | 0.0009 | 0.0011 |
| 11 | | | | | 0.0001 | 0.0001 | 0.0001 | 0.0002 | 0.0002 | 0.0003 |
| 12 | | | | | | | | | 0.0001 | 0.0001 |

| $m =$ | 3.1 | 3.2 | 3.3 | 3.4 | 3.5 | 3.6 | 3.7 | 3.8 | 3.9 | 4.0 |
|---|---|---|---|---|---|---|---|---|---|---|
| $r =$ 0 | 1.0000 | 1.0000 | 1.0000 | 1.0000 | 1.0000 | 1.0000 | 1.0000 | 1.0000 | 1.0000 | 1.0000 |
| 1 | 0.9550 | 0.9592 | 0.9631 | 0.9666 | 0.9698 | 0.9727 | 0.9753 | 0.9776 | 0.9798 | 0.9817 |
| 2 | 0.8153 | 0.8288 | 0.8414 | 0.8532 | 0.8641 | 0.8743 | 0.8838 | 0.8926 | 0.9008 | 0.9084 |
| 3 | 0.5998 | 0.6201 | 0.6406 | 0.6603 | 0.6792 | 0.6973 | 0.7146 | 0.7311 | 0.7469 | 0.7619 |
| 4 | 0.3752 | 0.3975 | 0.4197 | 0.4416 | 0.4634 | 0.4848 | 0.5058 | 0.5265 | 0.5468 | 0.5665 |
| 5 | 0.2018 | 0.2194 | 0.2374 | 0.2558 | 0.2746 | 0.2936 | 0.3128 | 0.3322 | 0.3516 | 0.3712 |
| 6 | 0.0943 | 0.1054 | 0.1171 | 0.1295 | 0.1424 | 0.1559 | 0.1699 | 0.1844 | 0.1994 | 0.2149 |
| 7 | 0.0388 | 0.0446 | 0.0510 | 0.0579 | 0.0653 | 0.0733 | 0.0818 | 0.0909 | 0.1005 | 0.1107 |
| 8 | 0.0142 | 0.0168 | 0.0198 | 0.0231 | 0.0267 | 0.0308 | 0.0352 | 0.0401 | 0.0454 | 0.0511 |
| 9 | 0.0047 | 0.0057 | 0.0069 | 0.0083 | 0.0099 | 0.0117 | 0.0137 | 0.0160 | 0.0185 | 0.0214 |
| 10 | 0.0014 | 0.0018 | 0.0022 | 0.0027 | 0.0033 | 0.0040 | 0.0048 | 0.0058 | 0.0069 | 0.0081 |
| 11 | 0.0004 | 0.0005 | 0.0006 | 0.0008 | 0.0010 | 0.0013 | 0.0016 | 0.0019 | 0.0023 | 0.0028 |
| 12 | 0.0001 | 0.0001 | 0.0002 | 0.0002 | 0.0003 | 0.0004 | 0.0005 | 0.0006 | 0.0007 | 0.0009 |
| 13 | | | | 0.0001 | 0.0001 | 0.0001 | 0.0001 | 0.0002 | 0.0002 | 0.0003 |
| 14 | | | | | | | | | 0.0001 | 0.0001 |

| $m =$ | 4.1 | 4.2 | 4.3 | 4.4 | 4.5 | 4.6 | 4.7 | 4.8 | 4.9 | 5.0 |
|---|---|---|---|---|---|---|---|---|---|---|
| $r =$ 0 | 1.0000 | 1.0000 | 1.0000 | 1.0000 | 1.0000 | 1.0000 | 1.0000 | 1.0000 | 1.0000 | 1.0000 |
| 1 | 0.9834 | 0.9850 | 0.9864 | 0.9877 | 0.9889 | 0.9899 | 0.9909 | 0.9918 | 0.9926 | 0.9933 |
| 2 | 0.9155 | 0.9220 | 0.9281 | 0.9337 | 0.9389 | 0.9437 | 0.9482 | 0.9523 | 0.9561 | 0.9596 |
| 3 | 0.7762 | 0.7898 | 0.8026 | 0.8149 | 0.8264 | 0.8374 | 0.8477 | 0.8575 | 0.8667 | 0.8753 |
| 4 | 0.5858 | 0.6046 | 0.6228 | 0.6406 | 0.6577 | 0.6743 | 0.6903 | 0.7058 | 0.7207 | 0.7350 |
| 5 | 0.3907 | 0.4102 | 0.4296 | 0.4488 | 0.4679 | 0.4868 | 0.5054 | 0.5237 | 0.5418 | 0.5595 |
| 6 | 0.2307 | 0.2469 | 0.2633 | 0.2801 | 0.2971 | 0.3142 | 0.3316 | 0.3490 | 0.3665 | 0.3840 |
| 7 | 0.1214 | 0.1325 | 0.1442 | 0.1564 | 0.1689 | 0.1820 | 0.1954 | 0.2092 | 0.2233 | 0.2378 |
| 8 | 0.0573 | 0.0639 | 0.0710 | 0.0786 | 0.0866 | 0.0951 | 0.1040 | 0.1133 | 0.1231 | 0.1334 |
| 9 | 0.0245 | 0.0279 | 0.0317 | 0.0358 | 0.0403 | 0.0451 | 0.0503 | 0.0558 | 0.0618 | 0.0681 |
| 10 | 0.0095 | 0.0111 | 0.0129 | 0.0149 | 0.0171 | 0.0195 | 0.0222 | 0.0251 | 0.0283 | 0.0318 |
| 11 | 0.0034 | 0.0041 | 0.0048 | 0.0057 | 0.0067 | 0.0078 | 0.0090 | 0.0104 | 0.0120 | 0.0137 |
| 12 | 0.0011 | 0.0014 | 0.0017 | 0.0020 | 0.0024 | 0.0029 | 0.0034 | 0.0040 | 0.0047 | 0.0055 |
| 13 | 0.0003 | 0.0004 | 0.0005 | 0.0007 | 0.0008 | 0.0010 | 0.0012 | 0.0014 | 0.0017 | 0.0020 |
| 14 | 0.0001 | 0.0001 | 0.0002 | 0.0002 | 0.0003 | 0.0003 | 0.0004 | 0.0005 | 0.0006 | 0.0007 |
| 15 | | | | 0.0001 | 0.0001 | 0.0001 | 0.0001 | 0.0001 | 0.0002 | 0.0002 |
| 16 | | | | | | | | | 0.0001 | 0.0001 |

| $m =$ | 5.2 | 5.4 | 5.6 | 5.8 | 6.0 | 6.2 | 6.4 | 6.6 | 6.8 | 7.0 |
|---|---|---|---|---|---|---|---|---|---|---|
| $r =$ 0 | 1.0000 | 1.0000 | 1.0000 | 1.0000 | 1.0000 | 1.0000 | 1.0000 | 1.0000 | 1.0000 | 1.0000 |
| 1 | 0.9945 | 0.9955 | 0.9963 | 0.9970 | 0.9975 | 0.9980 | 0.9983 | 0.9986 | 0.9989 | 0.9991 |
| 2 | 0.9658 | 0.9711 | 0.9756 | 0.9794 | 0.9826 | 0.9854 | 0.9877 | 0.9897 | 0.9913 | 0.9927 |
| 3 | 0.8912 | 0.9052 | 0.9176 | 0.9285 | 0.9380 | 0.9464 | 0.9537 | 0.9600 | 0.9656 | 0.9704 |
| 4 | 0.7619 | 0.7867 | 0.8094 | 0.8300 | 0.8488 | 0.8658 | 0.8811 | 0.8948 | 0.9072 | 0.9182 |
| 5 | 0.5939 | 0.6267 | 0.6579 | 0.6873 | 0.7149 | 0.7408 | 0.7649 | 0.7873 | 0.8080 | 0.8270 |
| 6 | 0.4191 | 0.4539 | 0.4881 | 0.5217 | 0.5543 | 0.5859 | 0.6163 | 0.6453 | 0.6730 | 0.6993 |
| 7 | 0.2676 | 0.2983 | 0.3297 | 0.3616 | 0.3937 | 0.4258 | 0.4577 | 0.4892 | 0.5201 | 0.5503 |
| 8 | 0.1551 | 0.1783 | 0.2030 | 0.2290 | 0.2560 | 0.2840 | 0.3127 | 0.3419 | 0.3715 | 0.4013 |
| 9 | 0.0819 | 0.0974 | 0.1143 | 0.1328 | 0.1528 | 0.1741 | 0.1967 | 0.2204 | 0.2452 | 0.2709 |
| 10 | 0.0397 | 0.0488 | 0.0591 | 0.0708 | 0.0839 | 0.0984 | 0.1142 | 0.1314 | 0.1498 | 0.1695 |
| 11 | 0.0177 | 0.0225 | 0.0282 | 0.0349 | 0.0426 | 0.0514 | 0.0614 | 0.0726 | 0.0849 | 0.0985 |
| 12 | 0.0073 | 0.0096 | 0.0125 | 0.0160 | 0.0201 | 0.0250 | 0.0307 | 0.0373 | 0.0448 | 0.0534 |
| 13 | 0.0028 | 0.0038 | 0.0051 | 0.0068 | 0.0088 | 0.0113 | 0.0143 | 0.0179 | 0.0221 | 0.0270 |
| 14 | 0.0010 | 0.0014 | 0.0020 | 0.0027 | 0.0036 | 0.0048 | 0.0063 | 0.0080 | 0.0102 | 0.0128 |
| 15 | 0.0003 | 0.0005 | 0.0007 | 0.0010 | 0014 | 0.0019 | 0.0026 | 0.0034 | 0.0044 | 0.0057 |
| 16 | 0.0001 | 0.0002 | 0.0002 | 0.0004 | 0.0005 | 0.0007 | 0.0010 | 0.0014 | 0.0018 | 0.0024 |
| 17 | | 0.0001 | 0.0001 | 0.0001 | 0.0002 | 0.0003 | 0.0004 | 0.0005 | 0.0007 | 0.0010 |
| 18 | | | | | 0.0001 | 0.0001 | 0.0001 | 0.0002 | 0.0003 | 0.0004 |
| 19 | | | | | | | | 0.0001 | 0.0001 | 0.0001 |

* This table is taken from part of Table 2 of *Statistical Tables for Science, Engineering, Management and Business Studies* by J. Murdoch and J. A. Barnes published by Macmillan, London and Basingstoke, and by permission of the authors and publishers.

# Areas under the standard normal curve*

The tables give the area A under one tail:

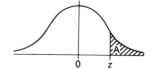

| z | 0.00 | 0.01 | 0.02 | 0.03 | 0.04 | 0.05 | 0.06 | 0.07 | 0.08 | 0.09 |
|---|------|------|------|------|------|------|------|------|------|------|
| 0.0 | 0.5000 | 0.4960 | 0.4920 | 0.4880 | 0.4840 | 0.4801 | 0.4761 | 0.4721 | 0.4681 | 0.4641 |
| 0.1 | 0.4602 | 0.4562 | 0.4522 | 0.4483 | 0.4443 | 0.4404 | 0.4364 | 0.4325 | 0.4286 | 0.4247 |
| 0.2 | 0.4207 | 0.4168 | 0.4129 | 0.4090 | 0.4052 | 0.4013 | 0.3974 | 0.3936 | 0.3897 | 0.3859 |
| 0.3 | 0.3821 | 0.3783 | 0.3745 | 0.3707 | 0.3669 | 0.3632 | 0.3594 | 0.3557 | 0.3520 | 0.3483 |
| 0.4 | 0.3446 | 0.3409 | 0.3372 | 0.3336 | 0.3300 | 0.3264 | 0.3228 | 0.3192 | 0.3156 | 0.3121 |
| 0.5 | 0.3085 | 0.3050 | 0.3015 | 0.2981 | 0.2946 | 0.2912 | 0.2877 | 0.2843 | 0.2810 | 0.2776 |
| 0.6 | 0.2743 | 0.2709 | 0.2676 | 0.2643 | 0.2611 | 0.2578 | 0.2546 | 0.2514 | 0.2483 | 0.2451 |
| 0.7 | 0.2420 | 0.2389 | 0.2358 | 0.2327 | 0.2296 | 0.2266 | 0.2236 | 0.2206 | 0.2177 | 0.2148 |
| 0.8 | 0.2119 | 0.2090 | 0.2061 | 0.2033 | 0.2005 | 0.1977 | 0.1949 | 0.1922 | 0.1894 | 0.1867 |
| 0.9 | 0.1841 | 0.1814 | 0.1788 | 0.1762 | 0.1736 | 0.1711 | 0.1685 | 0.1660 | 0.1635 | 0.1611 |
| 1.0 | 0.1587 | 0.1562 | 0.1539 | 0.1515 | 0.1492 | 0.1469 | 0.1446 | 0.1423 | 0.1401 | 0.1379 |
| 1.1 | 0.1357 | 0.1335 | 0.1314 | 0.1292 | 0.1271 | 0.1251 | 0.1230 | 0.1210 | 0.1190 | 0.1170 |
| 1.2 | 0.1151 | 0.1131 | 0.1112 | 0.1093 | 0.1075 | 0.1056 | 0.1038 | 0.1020 | 0.1003 | 0.0985 |
| 1.3 | 0.0968 | 0.0951 | 0.0934 | 0.0918 | 0.0901 | 0.0885 | 0.0869 | 0.0853 | 0.0838 | 0.0823 |
| 1.4 | 0.0808 | 0.0793 | 0.0778 | 0.0764 | 0.0749 | 0.0735 | 0.0721 | 0.0708 | 0.0694 | 0.0681 |
| 1.5 | 0.0668 | 0.0655 | 0.0643 | 0.0630 | 0.0618 | 0.0606 | 0.0594 | 0.0582 | 0.0571 | 0.0559 |
| 1.6 | 0.0548 | 0.0537 | 0.0526 | 0.0516 | 0.0505 | 0.0495 | 0.0485 | 0.0475 | 0.0465 | 0.0455 |
| 1.7 | 0.0446 | 0.0436 | 0.0427 | 0.0418 | 0.0409 | 0.0401 | 0.0392 | 0.0384 | 0.0375 | 0.0367 |
| 1.8 | 0.0359 | 0.0351 | 0.0344 | 0.0336 | 0.0329 | 0.0322 | 0.0314 | 0.0307 | 0.0301 | 0.0294 |
| 1.9 | 0.0287 | 0.0281 | 0.0274 | 0.0268 | 0.0262 | 0.0256 | 0.0250 | 0.0244 | 0.0239 | 0.0233 |
| 2.0 | 0.02275 | 0.02222 | 0.02169 | 0.02118 | 0.02068 | 0.02018 | 0.01970 | 0.01923 | 0.01876 | 0.01831 |
| 2.1 | 0.01786 | 0.01743 | 0.01700 | 0.01659 | 0.01618 | 0.01578 | 0.01539 | 0.01500 | 0.01463 | 0.01426 |
| 2.2 | 0.01390 | 0.01355 | 0.01321 | 0.01287 | 0.01255 | 0.01222 | 0.01191 | 0.01160 | 0.01130 | 0.01101 |
| 2.3 | 0.01072 | 0.01044 | 0.01017 | 0.00990 | 0.00964 | 0.00939 | 0.00914 | 0.00889 | 0.00866 | 0.00842 |
| 2.4 | 0.00820 | 0.00798 | 0.00776 | 0.00755 | 0.00734 | 0.00714 | 0.00695 | 0.00676 | 0.00657 | 0.00639 |
| 2.5 | 0.00621 | 0.00604 | 0.00587 | 0.00570 | 0.00554 | 0.00539 | 0.00523 | 0.00508 | 0.00494 | 0.00480 |
| 2.6 | 0.00466 | 0.00453 | 0.00440 | 0.00427 | 0.00415 | 0.00402 | 0.00391 | 0.00379 | 0.00368 | 0.00357 |
| 2.7 | 0.00347 | 0.00336 | 0.00326 | 0.00317 | 0.00307 | 0.00298 | 0.00289 | 0.00280 | 0.00272 | 0.00264 |
| 2.8 | 0.00256 | 0.00248 | 0.00240 | 0.00233 | 0.00226 | 0.00219 | 0.00212 | 0.00205 | 0.00199 | 0.00193 |
| 2.9 | 0.00187 | 0.00181 | 0.00175 | 0.00169 | 0.00164 | 0.00159 | 0.00154 | 0.00149 | 0.00144 | 0.00139 |
| 3.0 | 0.00135 | | | | | | | | | |
| 3.1 | 0.00097 | | | | | | | | | |
| 3.2 | 0.00069 | | | | | | | | | |
| 3.3 | 0.00048 | | | | | | | | | |
| 3.4 | 0.00034 | | | | | | | | | |
| 3.5 | 0.00023 | | | | | | | | | |
| 3.6 | 0.00016 | | | | | | | | | |
| 3.7 | 0.00011 | | | | | | | | | |
| 3.8 | 0.00007 | | | | | | | | | |
| 3.9 | 0.00005 | | | | | | | | | |
| 4.0 | 0.00003 | | | | | | | | | |

* This table is based on Table 3 of *Statistical Tables for Science, Engineering, Management and Business Studies* by J. Murdoch and J. A. Barnes published by Macmillan, London and Basingstoke, and by permission of the authors and publishers.

# Percentage points of the $\chi^2$ distribution*

The tables give the area $\alpha$ under one tail:

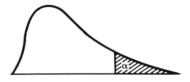

| $\alpha =$ | 0.995 | 0.99 | 0.98 | 0.975 | 0.95 | 0.90 |
|---|---|---|---|---|---|---|
| $v =$ 1 | $0.0^4393$ | $0.0^3157$ | $0.0^3628$ | $0.0^3982$ | 0.00393 | 0.0158 |
| 2 | 0.0100 | 0.0201 | 0.0404 | 0.0506 | 0.103 | 0.211 |
| 3 | 0.0717 | 0.115 | 0.185 | 0.216 | 0.352 | 0.584 |
| 4 | 0.207 | 0.297 | 0.429 | 0.484 | 0.711 | 1.064 |
| 5 | 0.412 | 0.554 | 0.752 | 0.831 | 1.145 | 1.610 |
| 6 | 0.676 | 0.872 | 1.134 | 1.237 | 1.635 | 2.204 |
| 7 | 0.989 | 1.239 | 1.564 | 1.690 | 2.167 | 2.833 |
| 8 | 1.344 | 1.646 | 2.032 | 2.180 | 2.733 | 3.490 |
| 9 | 1.735 | 2.088 | 2.532 | 2.700 | 3.325 | 4.168 |
| 10 | 2.156 | 2.558 | 3.059 | 3.247 | 3.940 | 4.865 |
| 11 | 2.603 | 3.053 | 3.609 | 3.816 | 4.575 | 5.578 |
| 12 | 3.074 | 3.571 | 4.178 | 4.404 | 5.226 | 6.304 |
| 13 | 3.565 | 4.107 | 4.765 | 5.009 | 5.892 | 7.042 |
| 14 | 0.075 | 4.660 | 5.368 | 5.629 | 6.571 | 7.790 |
| 15 | 4.601 | 5.229 | 5.985 | 6.262 | 7.261 | 8.547 |
| 16 | 5.142 | 5.812 | 6.614 | 6.908 | 7.962 | 9.312 |
| 17 | 5.697 | 6.408 | 7.255 | 7.564 | 8.672 | 10.085 |
| 18 | 6.265 | 7.015 | 7.906 | 8.231 | 9.390 | 10.865 |
| 19 | 6.844 | 7.633 | 8.567 | 8.907 | 10.117 | 11.651 |
| 20 | 7.434 | 8.260 | 9.237 | 9.591 | 10.851 | 12.443 |
| 21 | 8.034 | 8.897 | 9.915 | 10.283 | 11.591 | 13.240 |
| 22 | 8.643 | 9.542 | 10.600 | 10.982 | 12.338 | 14.041 |
| 23 | 9.260 | 10.196 | 11.293 | 11.688 | 13.091 | 14.848 |
| 24 | 9.886 | 10.856 | 11.992 | 12.401 | 13.838 | 15.659 |
| 25 | 10.520 | 11.524 | 12.697 | 13.120 | 14.611 | 16.473 |
| 26 | 11.160 | 12.198 | 13.409 | 13.844 | 15.379 | 17.292 |
| 27 | 11.808 | 12.879 | 14.125 | 14.573 | 16.151 | 18.114 |
| 28 | 12.461 | 13.565 | 14.847 | 15.308 | 16.928 | 18.939 |
| 29 | 13.121 | 14.256 | 15.574 | 16.047 | 17.707 | 19.768 |
| 30 | 13.787 | 14.953 | 16.306 | 16.791 | 18.493 | 20.599 |
| 40 | 20.706 | 22.164 | 23.838 | 24.433 | 26.509 | 29.051 |
| 50 | 27.991 | 29.707 | 31.664 | 32.357 | 34.764 | 37.689 |
| 60 | 35.535 | 37.485 | 39.699 | 40.482 | 43.188 | 46.459 |
| 70 | 43.275 | 45.442 | 47.893 | 48.758 | 51.739 | 55.329 |
| 80 | 51.171 | 53.539 | 56.213 | 57.153 | 60.391 | 64.278 |
| 90 | 59.196 | 61.754 | 64.634 | 65.646 | 69.126 | 73.291 |
| 100 | 67.327 | 70.065 | 73.142 | 74.222 | 77.929 | 82.358 |

| $\alpha =$ | | 0.80 | 0.75 | 0.70 | 0.50 | 0.30 | 0.25 | 0.20 | 0.10 |
|---|---|---|---|---|---|---|---|---|---|
| $v =$ | 1 | 0.0642 | 0.102 | 0.148 | 0.455 | 1.074 | 1.323 | 1.642 | 2.706 |
| | 2 | 0.446 | 0.575 | 0.713 | 1.386 | 2.408 | 2.773 | 3.219 | 4.605 |
| | 3 | 1.005 | 1.213 | 1.424 | 2.366 | 3.665 | 4.108 | 4.642 | 6.251 |
| | 4 | 1.649 | 1.923 | 2.195 | 3.357 | 4.878 | 5.385 | 5.989 | 7.779 |
| | 5 | 2.343 | 2.675 | 3.000 | 4.351 | 6.064 | 6.626 | 7.289 | 9.236 |
| | 6 | 3.070 | 3.455 | 3.828 | 5.348 | 7.231 | 7.841 | 8.558 | 10.645 |
| | 7 | 3.822 | 455 | 4.671 | 6.346 | 8.383 | 9.037 | 9.903 | 12.017 |
| | 8 | 4.594 | 5.071 | 5.527 | 7.344 | 9.524 | 10.219 | 11.030 | 13.362 |
| | 9 | 5.380 | 5.899 | 6.393 | 8.343 | 10.656 | 11.389 | 12.242 | 14.684 |
| | 10 | 6.179 | 6.737 | 7.267 | 9.342 | 11.781 | 12.549 | 13.442 | 15.987 |
| | 11 | 6.989 | 7.584 | 8.148 | 10.341 | 12.899 | 13.701 | 14.631 | 17.275 |
| | 12 | 7.807 | 8.438 | 9.034 | 11.340 | 14.011 | 14.845 | 15.812 | 18.549 |
| | 13 | 8.634 | 9.299 | 9.926 | 12.340 | 15.119 | 15.984 | 16.985 | 19.812 |
| | 14 | 9.467 | 10.165 | 10.821 | 13.339 | 16.222 | 17.117 | 18.151 | 21.064 |
| | 15 | 10.307 | 11.036 | 11.721 | 14.339 | 17.322 | 18.245 | 19.311 | 22.307 |
| | 16 | 11.152 | 11.912 | 12.624 | 15.338 | 18.418 | 19.369 | 20.465 | 23.542 |
| | 17 | 12.002 | 12.792 | 13.531 | 16.338 | 19.511 | 20.489 | 21.615 | 24.769 |
| | 18 | 12.857 | 13.675 | 14.440 | 17.338 | 20.601 | 21.605 | 22.760 | 25.989 |
| | 19 | 13.716 | 14.562 | 15.352 | 18.338 | 21.689 | 22.718 | 23.900 | 27.204 |
| | 20 | 14.578 | 15.452 | 16.266 | 19.337 | 22.775 | 23.828 | 25.038 | 28.412 |
| | 21 | 15.445 | 16.344 | 17.182 | 20.337 | 23.858 | 24.935 | 26.171 | 29.615 |
| | 22 | 16.314 | 17.240 | 18.101 | 21.337 | 24.939 | 26.039 | 27.301 | 30.813 |
| | 23 | 17.187 | 18.137 | 19.021 | 22.337 | 26.018 | 27.141 | 28.429 | 32.007 |
| | 24 | 18.062 | 19.037 | 19.943 | 23.337 | 27.096 | 28.241 | 29.553 | 33.196 |
| | 25 | 18.940 | 19.939 | 20.867 | 24.337 | 28.172 | 29.339 | 30.675 | 34.382 |
| | 26 | 19.820 | 20.843 | 21.792 | 25.336 | 29.246 | 30.434 | 31.795 | 35.563 |
| | 27 | 20.703 | 21.749 | 22.719 | 26.336 | 30.319 | 31.528 | 32.912 | 36.741 |
| | 28 | 21.588 | 22.657 | 23.647 | 27.336 | 31.391 | 32.620 | 34.027 | 37.916 |
| | 29 | 22.475 | 23.567 | 24.577 | 28.336 | 32.461 | 33.711 | 35.139 | 39.087 |
| | 30 | 23.364 | 24.478 | 25.508 | 29.336 | 33.530 | 34.800 | 36.250 | 40.256 |
| | 40 | 32.345 | 33.660 | 34.872 | 39.335 | 44.165 | 45.616 | 47.269 | 51.805 |
| | 50 | 41.449 | 42.942 | 44.313 | 49.335 | 54.723 | 56.334 | 58.164 | 63.167 |
| | 60 | 50.641 | 52.294 | 53.809 | 59.335 | 65.227 | 66.981 | 68.972 | 74.397 |
| | 70 | 59.898 | 61.698 | 63.346 | 69.334 | 75.689 | 77.577 | 79.715 | 85.527 |
| | 80 | 69.207 | 71.145 | 72.915 | 79.334 | 86.120 | 88.130 | 90.405 | 96.578 |
| | 90 | 78.558 | 80.625 | 82.511 | 89.334 | 96.524 | 98.650 | 101.054 | 107.565 |
| | 100 | 87.945 | 90.133 | 92.129 | 99.334 | 106.906 | 109.141 | 111.667 | 118.498 |

| 0.05 | 0.025 | 0.02 | 0.01 | 0.005 | 0.001 | $= \alpha$ |
|---|---|---|---|---|---|---|
| 3.841 | 5.024 | 5.412 | 6.635 | 7.879 | 10.827 | $v =$ 1 |
| 5.991 | 7.378 | 7.824 | 9.210 | 10.597 | 13.815 | 2 |
| 7.815 | 9.348 | 9.837 | 11.345 | 12.838 | 16.268 | 3 |
| 9.488 | 11.143 | 11.668 | 13.277 | 14.860 | 18.465 | 4 |
| 11.070 | 12.832 | 13.388 | 15.086 | 16.750 | 20.517 | 5 |
| 12.592 | 14.449 | 15.033 | 16.812 | 18.548 | 22.457 | 6 |
| 14.067 | 16.013 | 16.622 | 18.475 | 20.278 | 24.322 | 7 |
| 15.507 | 17.535 | 18.168 | 20.090 | 21.955 | 26.125 | 8 |
| 16.919 | 19.023 | 19.679 | 21.666 | 23.589 | 27.977 | 9 |
| 18.307 | 20.483 | 21.161 | 23.209 | 25.188 | 29.588 | 10 |
| 19.675 | 21.920 | 22.618 | 24.725 | 26.757 | 31.264 | 11 |
| 21.026 | 23.337 | 24.054 | 26.217 | 28.300 | 32.909 | 12 |
| 22.362 | 24.736 | 25.472 | 27.688 | 29.819 | 34.528 | 13 |
| 23.685 | 26.119 | 26.873 | 29.141 | 31.319 | 36.123 | 14 |
| 24.996 | 27.488 | 28.259 | 30.578 | 32.801 | 37.697 | 15 |
| 26.296 | 28.845 | 29.633 | 32.000 | 34.267 | 39.252 | 16 |
| 27.587 | 30.191 | 30.995 | 33.409 | 35.718 | 40.790 | 17 |
| 28.869 | 31.526 | 32.346 | 34.805 | 37.156 | 42.312 | 18 |
| 30.144 | 32.852 | 33.687 | 36.191 | 38.582 | 43.820 | 19 |
| 31.410 | 34.170 | 35.020 | 37.566 | 39.997 | 45.315 | 20 |
| 32.671 | 35.479 | 36.343 | 38.932 | 41.401 | 46.797 | 21 |
| 33.924 | 36.781 | 37.659 | 40.289 | 42.796 | 48.268 | 22 |
| 35.172 | 38.076 | 38.968 | 41.638 | 44.181 | 49.728 | 23 |
| 36.415 | 39.364 | 40.270 | 42.980 | 45.558 | 51.179 | 24 |
| 37.652 | 40.646 | 41.566 | 44.314 | 46.928 | 52.620 | 25 |
| 38.885 | 41.923 | 42.856 | 45.642 | 48.290 | 54.052 | 26 |
| 40.113 | 43.194 | 44.140 | 46.963 | 49.645 | 55.476 | 27 |
| 41.337 | 44.461 | 45.419 | 48.278 | 60.993 | 56.893 | 28 |
| 42.557 | 45.722 | 46.693 | 49.588 | 52.336 | 58.302 | 29 |
| 43.773 | 46.979 | 47.962 | 50.892 | 53.672 | 59.703 | 30 |
| 55.759 | 59.342 | 60.436 | 63.691 | 66.766 | 73.402 | 40 |
| 67.505 | 71.420 | 72.613 | 76.154 | 79.490 | 86.661 | 50 |
| 79.082 | 83.298 | 84.580 | 88.379 | 91.952 | 99.607 | 60 |
| 90.531 | 95.023 | 96.388 | 100.425 | 104.215 | 112.317 | 70 |
| 101.880 | 106.629 | 108.069 | 112.329 | 116.321 | 124.839 | 80 |
| 113.145 | 118.136 | 119.648 | 124.116 | 128.299 | 137.208 | 90 |
| 124.342 | 129.561 | 131.142 | 135.807 | 140.170 | 149.449 | 100 |

*This table is taken from Table IV of Fisher and Yates: *Statistical Tables for Biological, Agricultural and Medical Research* published by Longman Group Ltd., London (previously published by Oliver Boyd Ltd., Edinburgh) and by permission of the authors and publishers, and from Table 8 of *Biometrika Tables for Statisticians*, Vol. 1, by permission of the Biometrika Trustees.

# The correlation coefficient*

The table gives the values of the correlation coefficient for different levels of significance; $v$ = number of pairs in sample $-2$.

| | | 0.1 | 0.05 | 0.02 | 0.01 | 0.001 |
|---|---|---|---|---|---|---|
| $v =$ | 1 | 0.98769 | 0.99692 | 0.999597 | 0.999877 | 0.9999988 |
| | 2 | 0.90000 | 0.95000 | 0.98000 | 0.990000 | 0.99900 |
| | 3 | 0.8054 | 0.8783 | 0.93433 | 0.95873 | 0.99116 |
| | 4 | 0.7293 | 0.8114 | 0.8822 | 0.91720 | 0.97406 |
| | 5 | 0.6694 | 0.7545 | 0.8329 | 0.8745 | 0.95074 |
| | 6 | 0.6215 | 0.7067 | 0.7887 | 0.8343 | 0.92493 |
| | 7 | 0.5822 | 0.6664 | 0.7498 | 0.7977 | 0.8982 |
| | 8 | 0.5494 | 0.6319 | 0.7155 | 0.7646 | 0.8721 |
| | 9 | 0.5214 | 0.6021 | 0.6851 | 0.7348 | 0.8471 |
| | 10 | 0.4973 | 0.5760 | 0.6581 | 0.7079 | 0.8233 |
| | 11 | 0.4762 | 0.5529 | 0.6339 | 0.6835 | 0.8010 |
| | 12 | 0.4575 | 0.5324 | 0.6120 | 0.6614 | 0.7800 |
| | 13 | 0.4409 | 0.5139 | 0.5923 | 0.6411 | 0.7603 |
| | 14 | 0.4259 | 0.4973 | 0.5742 | 0.6226 | 0.7420 |
| | 15 | 0.4124 | 0.4821 | 0.5577 | 0.6055 | 0.7246 |
| | 16 | 0.4000 | 0.4683 | 0.5425 | 0.5897 | 0.7084 |
| | 17 | 0.3887 | 0.4555 | 0.5285 | 0.5751 | 0.6932 |
| | 18 | 0.3783 | 0.4438 | 0.5155 | 0.5614 | 0.6787 |
| | 19 | 0.3687 | 0.4329 | 0.5034 | 0.5487 | 0.6652 |
| | 20 | 0.3598 | 0.4227 | 0.4921 | 0.5368 | 0.6524 |
| | 25 | 0.3233 | 0.3809 | 0.4451 | 0.4869 | 0.5974 |
| | 30 | 0.2960 | 0.3494 | 0.4093 | 0.4487 | 0.5541 |
| | 35 | 0.2746 | 0.3246 | 0.3810 | 0.4182 | 0.5189 |
| | 40 | 0.2573 | 0.3044 | 0.3578 | 0.3932 | 0.4896 |
| | 45 | 0.2428 | 0.2875 | 0.3384 | 0.3721 | 0.4648 |
| | 50 | 0.2306 | 0.2732 | 0.3218 | 0.3541 | 0.4433 |
| | 60 | 0.2108 | 0.2500 | 0.2948 | 0.3248 | 0.4078 |
| | 70 | 0.1954 | 0.2319 | 0.2737 | 0.3017 | 0.3799 |
| | 80 | 0.1829 | 0.2172 | 0.2565 | 0.2830 | 0.3568 |
| | 90 | 0.1726 | 0.2050 | 0.2422 | 0.2673 | 0.3375 |
| | 100 | 0.1638 | 0.1946 | 0.2301 | 0.2540 | 0.3211 |

* This table is taken from Table VII of Fisher and Yates: *Statistical Tables for Biological, Agricultural and Medical Research* published by Longman Group Ltd., London (previously published by Oliver & Boyd Ltd., Edinburgh) and by permission of the authors and publishers.

# The *t*-distribution

The tabulation is for one tail only, i.e, for positive values of $t$.
For two-tail tests, the column headings must be doubled.

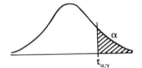

| $\alpha =$ | 0.10 | 0.05 | 0.025 | 0.01 | 0.005 | 0.001 | 0.0005 |
|---|---|---|---|---|---|---|---|
| $v = $ 1 | 3.078 | 6.314 | 12.706 | 31.821 | 63.657 | 318.31 | 636.62 |
| 2 | 1.886 | 2.920 | 4.303 | 6.965 | 9.925 | 22.326 | 31.598 |
| 3 | 1.638 | 2.353 | 3.182 | 4.541 | 5.841 | 10.213 | 12.924 |
| 4 | 1.533 | 2.132 | 2.776 | 3.747 | 4.604 | 7.173 | 8.610 |
| 5 | 1.476 | 2.015 | 2.571 | 3.365 | 4.032 | 5.893 | 6.869 |
| 6 | 1.440 | 1.943 | 2.447 | 3.143 | 3.707 | 5.208 | 5.959 |
| 7 | 1.415 | 1.895 | 2.365 | 2.998 | 3.499 | 4.785 | 5.408 |
| 8 | 1.397 | 1.860 | 2.306 | 2.896 | 3.355 | 4.501 | 5.041 |
| 9 | 1.383 | 1.833 | 2.262 | 2.821 | 3.250 | 4.297 | 4.781 |
| 10 | 1.372 | 1.812 | 2.228 | 2.764 | 3.169 | 4.144 | 4.587 |
| 11 | 1.363 | 1.796 | 2.201 | 2.718 | 3.106 | 4.025 | 4.437 |
| 12 | 1.356 | 1.782 | 2.179 | 2.681 | 3.055 | 3.930 | 4.318 |
| 13 | 1.350 | 1.771 | 2.160 | 2.650 | 3.012 | 3.852 | 4.221 |
| 14 | 1.345 | 1.761 | 2.145 | 2.624 | 2.977 | 3.787 | 4.140 |
| 15 | 1.341 | 1.753 | 2.131 | 2.602 | 2.947 | 3.733 | 4.073 |
| 16 | 1.337 | 1.746 | 2.120 | 2.583 | 2.921 | 3.686 | 4.015 |
| 17 | 1.333 | 1.740 | 2.110 | 2.567 | 2.898 | 3.646 | 3.965 |
| 18 | 1.330 | 1.734 | 2.101 | 2.552 | 2.878 | 3.610 | 3.922 |
| 19 | 1.328 | 1.729 | 2.093 | 2.539 | 2.861 | 3.579 | 3.883 |
| 20 | 1.325 | 1.725 | 2.086 | 2.528 | 2.845 | 3.552 | 3.850 |
| 21 | 1.323 | 1.721 | 2.080 | 2.518 | 2.831 | 3.527 | 3.819 |
| 22 | 1.321 | 1.717 | 2.074 | 2.508 | 2.819 | 3.505 | 3.792 |
| 23 | 1.319 | 1.714 | 2.069 | 2.500 | 2.807 | 3.485 | 3.767 |
| 24 | 1.318 | 1.711 | 2.064 | 2.492 | 2.797 | 3.467 | 3.745 |
| 25 | 1.316 | 1.708 | 2.060 | 2.485 | 2.787 | 3.450 | 3.725 |
| 26 | 1.315 | 1.706 | 2.056 | 2.479 | 2.779 | 3.435 | 3.707 |
| 27 | 1.314 | 1.703 | 2.052 | 2.473 | 2.771 | 3.421 | 3.690 |
| 28 | 1.313 | 1.701 | 2.048 | 2.467 | 2.763 | 3.408 | 3.674 |
| 29 | 1.311 | 1.699 | 2.045 | 2.462 | 2.756 | 3.396 | 3.659 |
| 30 | 1.310 | 1.697 | 2.042 | 2.457 | 2.750 | 3.385 | 3.646 |
| 40 | 1.303 | 1.684 | 2.021 | 2.423 | 2.704 | 3.307 | 3.551 |
| 60 | 1.296 | 1.671 | 2.000 | 2.390 | 2.660 | 3.232 | 3.460 |
| 120 | 1.289 | 1.658 | 1.980 | 2.358 | 2.617 | 3.160 | 3.373 |
| $\infty$ | 1.282 | 1.645 | 1.960 | 2.326 | 2.576 | 3.090 | 3.291 |

This table is taken from Table III of Fisher & Yates: *Statistical Tables for Biological, Agricultural and Medical Research*, published by Oliver & Boyd Ltd., Edinburgh, and by permission of the authors and publishers; and also from Table 12 of *Biometrika Tables for Statisticians*, Vol. 1, by permission of the Biometrika Trustees.

# Index

# Quantitative Approaches in Business Studies